The limits of power

The limits of power

Great fires and the process of city growth in America

CHRISTINE MEISNER ROSEN

University of California, Berkeley

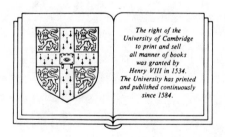

The right of the
University of Cambridge
to print and sell
all manner of books
was granted by
Henry VIII in 1534.
The University has printed
and published continuously
since 1584.

CAMBRIDGE UNIVERSITY PRESS

Cambridge

London   New York   New Rochelle

Melbourne   Sydney

Published by the Press Syndicate of the University of Cambridge
The Pitt Building, Trumpington Street, Cambridge CB2 1RP
32 East 57th Street, New York, NY 10022, USA
10 Stamford Road, Oakleigh, Melbourne 3166, Australia

First published 1986

Printed in the United States of America

Library of Congress Cataloging in Publication Data
Rosen, Christine Meisner, 1951–
The limits of power.
Bibliography: p.
Includes index.
1. Urbanization – United States.   2. Urban renewal –
United States.   3. Fires – Social aspects – Case studies.
I. Title.
HT371.R67   1985   307.7'6'0973   85–7753
ISBN 0 521 30319 2

TO KEN

Contents

Figures and tables

Figures

Tables

Acknowledgments

I would like to acknowledge the many friends, family members, colleagues, and library administrators who in one way or another helped me research, think about, and write this book. Their suggestions and moral support were and still are much appreciated. Special thanks go to Betsy Blackmar, Anne Rassweiller, Adele Hayutin, Michael Corbett, Paul Groth, Don Van Atta, David Hammack, Claudia Goldin, James Banner, Gunter Barth, and Claude Fischer for their advice at critical junctures. I would like to thank Adrienne Morgan, who drew the maps and chart that illustrate the book, for graciously and expertly putting up with the hand-drawn and poorly reproduced maps I gave her to work from. I would also like to acknowledge Steven J. Kovacik for photos used for Figures 7.2 and 7.3.

I am grateful to Melvin Webber for the office space and secretarial support he provided while I was a Visiting Scholar at the Institute of Urban and Regional Development of the University of California, Berkeley. I would also like to thank Chester Rapkin and Michael Munson for the secretarial help and travel assistance they provided through the Fire Research Group at Princeton University. I am also grateful for computer assistance and financial support from the Center for Real Estate and Urban Economics of the University of California, Berkeley.

Thanks are due the staffs of the Boston Public Library, the Boston Historical Society, the Harvard University Map Room, the Maryland Room at the Enoch Pratt Free Library, and the Chicago Historical Society. The staffs of the Inter-Library Loan Departments of Princeton University and the University of California, Berkeley, did me a great service by getting me much of what I needed on loan.

I would like to thank Frank Smith, my editor at Cambridge University Press, as well as Kathleen Neils Conzen of the University of Chicago and Seymour J. Mandelbaum of the University of Pennsylvania, who read the entire manuscript and offered many valuable suggestions for the final revision of the study. I did not take all of their advice, but all of it was extremely helpful. I owe a special debt of gratitude to Stephen Thernstrom, who served as my dissertation adviser. His willingness to let me be as ambitious as I wanted was exactly what I needed to get started with this study, and his encouragement helped to sustain me.

Finally, I want to thank Kenneth T. Rosen, my husband, for his help and encouragement. His emotional support was so important that I hardly know how to begin to thank him, but I do thank him, from the bottom of my heart.

PART I

The conceptual framework

1

Introduction

On October 8, 1871, a terrible conflagration destroyed almost four square miles of densely built up land in the city of Chicago. Because the fire had been fed by tens of thousands of wooden buildings, the disaster stimulated a wave of public demand that the Board of Aldermen pass a law to prohibit the construction of frame structures in the city. The Board never actually passed the ordinance, however. Nor, ironically, did it do anything in response to demands by the Fire Department and others that it appropriate money to improve the water system, notwithstanding the fact that deficiencies in the water system, like the city's wooden buildings, had contributed to the spreading of conflagration.

Nor did Chicago's railroads respond to the demands that they take advantage of the fire's destruction to improve their rail facilities by constructing a union depot to integrate their far-flung terminals and lines, thereby reducing the costs and time-consuming inconvenience of transferring freight and passengers from one line to another. Nor did they satisfy demands that they grade their tracks to reduce the dangers and congestion of their numerous street crossings. The railroad companies built more track and terminal facilities than ever before during reconstruction. They made no major improvements in any of their *existing* facilities, however, again despite an obvious need and an intense public demand for such improvement.

Chicagoans paid an enormous price for their failure to regulate new building strictly, as well as for their failure to secure improvements in their water and rail systems. Not only did the inconveniences and dangers of their railroads continually increase, but Chicago suffered another catastrophic fire fewer than four years later. The second great fire destroyed some sixty acres of densely built up land in the center of the city, including some structures that had only recently been rebuilt after having been demolished by the first great fire.

In 1872, just one year after the first great Chicago fire, a terrible fire took place in Boston. It destroyed sixty-five acres of densely built up land in Boston's central business district. Bostonians also responded to their disaster by calling for improvements in the environment of the burnt district. Like

3

their counterparts in Chicago, they demanded improvements in the building code and the water distribution system in the hope of preventing further conflagrations. In addition, they called on the city to take advantage of the destruction to widen and straighten the area's infamously crooked and narrow streets so as to improve traffic flow and make possible more effective positioning of fire fighting equipment in the future. Again, the need for such environmental redevelopment was clear, the great fire having demonstrated the deficiencies in all of these parts of the environment by burning a large part of the business center to the ground. In this case, Bostonians achieved considerable improvement. But they achieved less than they had originally desired and demanded. Street widenings fell far short of initial expectations and left most of the area's traffic bottlenecks intact. The Fire Department got less improvement in the water system than it had for several years requested. And the revisions of the building code contained loopholes, omissions, and mistakes that appalled insurance underwriters and many other concerned observers.

Great fires took place with alarming frequency in cities in nineteenth and early twentieth century America. Another occurred in Baltimore in 1904 and demolished over one hundred acres of built-up land in the city's business center. Like the great fires of Chicago and Boston, it, too, was followed by a wave of public demand that people take advantage of the destruction to rebuild better than before. Business leaders, public officials, and other concerned observers called for a wide range of environmental improvements in the burnt district, including redevelopment of the district's streets, its harbor, its electrical utility system, its water system, and its buildings. Again there was a long-standing need for these improvements. The area was in a state of environmental crisis that only redevelopment on a massive scale could resolve, a crisis that had helped cause the catastrophic fire. In this case, the people of the city achieved nearly all of their objectives – but not, significantly, without their undertaking far-reaching political reform and not without their having spent many frustrating decades trying unsuccessfully to make the improvements earlier.

What happened in these cities is symptomatic of the conflict, contradiction, action, and inaction that plagued the process of environmental development in nineteenth and early twentieth century America. The events described above took place under the extraordinary circumstances of the aftermaths of disastrous great fires. They were part of a general environmental crisis, however, a crisis caused by the rapid growth of cities in this period. Massive population and economic growth necessitated the redevelopment and adaptation of every aspect of the urban environment to meet the changing needs of city dwellers. This included the reorganization of residential, commercial, and industrial land use patterns, as well as the modernization of housing, factories, warehouses, and office buildings and the improvement of streets, harbor facilities, railroad and streetcar facilities, and water, power, and sewerage systems. Failure to adapt led not only to the numerous fires and conflagrations of this period but also to many serious housing, sanitation, and congestion problems.

The goal of this study is to explain why, at virtually every stage of growth, the achievement of these adaptations lagged significantly behind the need for adaptation. Most people know about the abominable housing and health conditions that existed in the teeming tenements of nineteenth century urban slums. What is often forgotten is that conditions in downtown business districts were often little better. Poor sanitation, crowding, fire, and blight were universal problems in cities in this period. The question is why? Why were conditions so bad? Why did Americans find it so difficult to adapt the urban environment to their needs? With an eye toward present conditions, we may also ask why we continue today to find it so exceedingly difficult to solve our environmental problems.

These are big questions, among the biggest an urban historian can ask. It is the purpose of this book to try to answer them as broadly as possible. To do so, the book will combine traditional narrative history with a theoretical analysis of the problem. The theoretical analysis will draw on the ideas and concepts of several fields of social science, employing the abstract, synchronic style of reasoning used by social science theorists. The narrative history will compare the reconstructions of three cities after great fires in order to analyze the problems of environmental redevelopment in as much detail as possible. The cities studied are Chicago, Boston, and Baltimore; the reconstructions, those that occurred in each place after the great fires of 1871, 1872, and 1904, respectively.

The theoretical style and the narrative style are sufficiently incompatible for the theorists who invent the jargon of the social sciences to have definitionally walled them off into two separate worlds: the world of "diachronic" (historical) analysis and the world of "synchronic" (static, abstract) analysis. As different as they are, however, there is much to be gained from juxtaposing and integrating these two ways of explaining this particular human problem. On the one hand, theory makes it possible to study change in cities in a way that gets beyond the epiphenomena of specific examples of change to a general explanation of the underlying processes at work in all urban development, something no simple narrative of a particular series of events can offer. On the other hand, and just as important, narrative history makes it possible to get beneath the abstractions of theory to an understanding of the kaleidoscopically complex and concrete realities of city growth, realities which are, after all, nothing less than summations of the countless epiphenomena that make up the history of cities, that explain why specific events happened as they did, when and where and how.[1]

Urban redevelopment is a complicated, many-faceted process. The purpose of this study is to analyze the human activity that produced and defined the process in the nineteenth and early twentieth centuries. In recent years urban historians and geographers have invested a great deal of time and energy in delineating and measuring the succession of land use patterns that made up city growth in this period. Identifying sequences of land use patterns and measuring the rates at which these patterns succeeded one another are not the subjects at issue here, however. Instead, human behavior is – human behavior and the conditions and factors that inspired, shaped, and constrained what people did to adapt their environments to economic and population growth.

This concerns power. Most scholars who study power examine the way it is distributed in society. Their interest rests with determining which individuals or groups wield power and which do not. At issue in this book is not the question of who held power in nineteenth and early twentieth century cities, however, but the question of what power was used for and what prevented its use by both the ostensibly "powerful" and the ostensibly "powerless" members of urban society. In short, the focus is on the conditions that limit power.

At the most abstract level, the process of environmental redevelopment can be conceptualized as a three-dimensional relationship between (1) the economic and population growth stimuli provoking land use change, (2) the adaptive environmental change necessitated by the stimuli, and (3) a wide variety of frictions that mediated this stimulus-response relationship. This study concentrates on the third and most subtle dimension, the frictions inherent in the relationship.

It is these frictions that explain the lag between economic and population growth and the achievement of the environmental improvements that city dwellers wanted and required. The frictions were constraints on power, barriers to improvement that people might hurdle, but also might not be able to hurdle, in their attempts to satisfy their environmental needs. These frictions affected the evolution of land use patterns in all cities and towns in Victorian America to one degree or another, in one way or another. This study will concentrate on explaining how they functioned in the places where their impact was most serious: the nation's biggest cities, such as Chicago, Boston, and Baltimore, where massive economic and population growth made the rapid and comprehensive redevelopment of the environment especially imperative and the cost of failure especially severe.

Census figures show that large cities like Chicago, Boston, and Baltimore experienced truly remarkable economic and population growth in the nineteenth and early twentieth centuries. As Table 1.1 demonstrates, large cities not only increased considerably in number in this period, but also attained such big sizes that by 1920 the twelve largest together contained over fifteen percent of the nation's total population. The speed with which Chicago, Boston, and Baltimore, specifically, gathered new residents is indicated in Table 1.2. Baltimore's population grew by an average of 26,670 persons each decade in the forty years preceding the Civil War and by an average of 69,210 people each decade after. Boston's increased by an average of 33,635 per decade before the war and by well over 98,000 each decade after, more than doubling in each of the decades of the 1820s, 1830s, 1840s, 1860s, and 1870s. Chicago, meanwhile, accumulated new residents at the prodigious average rate of more than 350,000 per decade after 1850. A mere town of fewer than 5,000 in 1840, it had acquired almost 50,000 more inhabitants than Boston by 1870 and had passed the million mark by 1890.

These great cities similarly embraced an ever increasing proportion of the nation's total economic productivity. Table 1.3 gives statistics which suggest the great speed with which Chicago, Boston, and Baltimore gathered manufacturing activity. Table 1.4 provides an indication of their increases in commercial activity.

This study is as concerned with the problems of redeveloping the older, built-up core areas of cities as it is with the redevelopment problems associated with the expansion of the areas of dense settlement. Thus it is important to keep in mind that these figures overstate the growth in the core areas by incorporating population and economic activity suddenly added on through the annexation of suburbs. This is not to say, however, that growth did not continue in the central areas. Quite the contrary; growth continued in each central city long after the number of people in the suburbs began to skyrocket. For example, population densities continued to increase in the part of central Chicago that was within two miles of the downtown Loop through 1910 and in some places through 1920 and 1930.[2] Similarly, in central Baltimore, population densities within two miles of the downtown business district continued rising through 1950.[3] Comparable figures are not available for Boston, unfortunately. A data series published by the state of Massachusetts in 1880, however, shows that central Boston experienced sustained growth, at least through 1880. The series shows that in that part of the city located on the original peninsula and excluding all annexations, the number of residents grew, on average, by over twenty thousand persons every ten years through 1860 and by over eight thousand every ten years after that, mushrooming from 56,003 in 1825, to 133,563 in 1860, to 147,075 in 1880.[4]

From the very beginning, these continuous increases in community size

Table 1.1. *Distribution of population in great cities, by size of place*

Size of place	Year					
	1820	1840	1860	1880	1900	1920
1,000,000 or more	—	—	—	1 2.4% 1,206,299	3 8.5% 6,429,474	3 9.6% 10,145,532
500,000 to 1,000,000	—	—	2 4.4% 1,379,198	3 3.8% 1,917,018	3 2.2% 1,645,087	3 5.9% 6,223,769
250,000 to 500,000	—	1 1.8% 312,710	2 0.8% 266,661	4 2.6% 1,300,809	9 3.8% 2,861,296	13 4.3% 4,540,838
100,000 to 250,000	1 1.3% 123,706	2 1.2% 204,508	6 3.2% 992,922	12 3.6% 1,786,783	23 4.3% 3,272,490	43 6.2% 6,519,187

Note: The numerals in each group of three indicate the following: top, number of places; middle, percentage of total U.S. population; bottom, population.

Source: U.S. Bureau of the Census, U.S. Census of Population: 1950, Vol. 1, U.S. Summary, Table 5b.

Table 1.2. *Population of Baltimore, Boston, and Chicago*

Year	Baltimore	Boston	Chicago
1820	62,738	43,298	—
1830	80,620	61,392	—
1840	102,620	93,383	4,470
1850	169,054	136,881	29,963
1860	212,418	177,840	109,260
1870	267,354	250,526	298,977
1880	332,313	362,839	503,185
1890	434,439	448,477	1,099,850
1900	508,957	560,892	1,698,575
1910	558,485	670,585	2,185,283
1920	733,826	748,060	2,701,705

Source: U.S. Bureau of the Census, *Fifteenth Census of the United States: 1930: Population,* Vol. 1, Table 11.

Table 1.3. *Growth of manufacturing employment and value added*

	Baltimore	Boston	Chicago
Employment in *manufacturing*			
1860	17,054	19,283	5,360
1890	83,745	90,805	210,366
Value added in 1879 *prices*			
1860	8,881.7	17,921.1	5,027.2
1890	76,107.9	117,974.1	283,443.9
% of national value *added*			
1860	1.0	2.0	0.6
1890	1.7	2.6	6.4

Source: Allan Pred, *American Metropolitan Growth* (Cambridge, Mass., 1965), p. 20.

necessitated substantial new environmental development and redevelopment. The small walking cities and towns of the early nineteenth century, the nuclei of the emerging metropolises, were not designed to accommodate the crush of people and business settling within them. The areas they covered were simply too small, their one- to three-story buildings too old-fashioned, too poorly drained, too combustible, and too small, their streets too difficult to

Table 1.4. *Growth of foreign and domestic tonnage entered and cleared at ports, total tonnage entered and cleared*

Year	Baltimore[a]	Boston[a]	Year	Chicago
1862	338,179	1,178,444	1862	3,847,246
1877	1,780,695	1,457,115	1883	7,793,336
1910	2,599,147	4,542,269	1910	18,909,646

[a] Excludes coastwise trade.
Source: Baltimore Board of Trade, *Annual Report,* 1858, 1877; Boston Board of Trade, *Annual Report,* 1881; Commonwealth of Mass., *Final Report of the Joint Board on Metropolitan Improvements* (Boston, 1911) , p. 144–45; Chicago Board of Trade, *Annual; Report of Trade and Commerce,* 1875, 1920.

navigate, their sewerage too primitive, and their wells and springs too few and in many cases already too contaminated to provide properly for the new arrivals. Unfortunately, as this study will demonstrate, the cities were also physically and spatially inflexible and thus could not be adapted to the new needs in any prompt and effective way. The result was an ongoing and devastating environmental crisis, a failure to adapt, that made itself felt in serious conflagrations, excessive death rates and frequent epidemics, constant blockages of street traffic, "miasmatic" summer smells, and dozens of other unpleasant and dangerous conditions.

Historians have often examined the housing, public health, congestion, transportation, and pollution problems of Victorian cities. They have not, however, been successful in explaining them completely. Most have followed the lead of Progressive Era social critics and blamed the public health and environmental crises on the corruption of political machines or the greed of slumlords and businessmen. With more sophistication, they have explained the problems in terms of class conflict or the privatistic ideologies of capitalism and American individualism. These arguments certainly help explain the problems. They are, however, simplistic, in and of themselves. They leave one with the impression that the slums were the only areas to suffer from environmental maladaptation. Worse, they imply that had the cities not been run by political machines, or had middle and upper class property owners and businessmen not been so self-seeking, the problems would never have grown to the proportions of a crisis in the first place.

This book will expose the complexities of the development and redevelopment processes. It will examine the market forces, the technological constraints, and the social, geographical, and organizational problems that complicated environmental improvement no matter who was involved in the undertaking and no matter whose interests were to be served or injured by the changes. The bones of the argument will be laid out in the chapters in Part I. The guts of the analysis, however, will be provided in the comparison of the rebuildings of Chicago, Boston, and Baltimore. After the shock of the fires wore off, the people in all three cities welcomed the destruction as an opportunity to "make things better than before." And, in fact, in all three cases they achieved a number of important advances in business and residential location patterns, as well as improvements in building design, street layouts, water systems, and other things, changes that went a considerable distance toward ameliorating long-standing environmental problems. Their accomplishments were limited by the continuing existence of many of the factors that had created the problems in the first place, however. What the comparison shows is that several of the barriers to improvement were so much a result of the economic organization of the urban real estate market, or so inherent in the physical and economic qualities of structures and infrastructures, or so much a function of the unequal distribution of wealth and power in society, or else so much a consequence of the scarcity of urban space and the phenomenon of population concentration that they were fundamental and inescapable components of city growth itself.

2

The barriers to structural improvement

A great many factors obstructed the improvement of structures in all of America's great cities in one way or another, from the beginning to the end of the period under study here. They slowed the process of adapting houses, stores, warehouses, factories, and other buildings to economic and population growth and, when improvements were finally, belatedly achieved, impeded further change. Over the course of the nineteenth and early twentieth centuries, architects, civil engineers, businessmen, and public officials devised ways to make necessary adaptations easier to accomplish. They never, however, managed to overcome all of the barriers to structural improvement, for most defied easy technological or administrative manipulation.

This chapter examines the frictions that impeded this aspect of the process of environmental redevelopment. For the sake of conceptual clarity it focuses entirely on the problems of structural redevelopment, reserving analysis of the problems of infrastructural and spatial change for later chapters. Nevertheless, one important argument will be that none of the processes leading to the physical and spatial redevelopment of cities can be understood in isolation from the others. Building patterns; street patterns; sewerage, water, power, and mass transportation systems; and commercial and residential location patterns all existed in relationship to one another. This interrelationship fostered an equilibrium in the total land use pattern which functioned as an important barrier to environmental change, in and of itself. It will be returned to later.

In 1820, most structures in American cities were small one-, two-, or three-story buildings that clustered densely within a small central area and served a combination of industrial, commercial, residential, and often agricultural functions. The rapid growth of business and industry and population made several fundamental changes absolutely necessary in the century that followed.

First of all, it required the construction of new buildings and continual increases in building size to accommodate the surging demand for more and more space. This involved expanding buildings horizontally to increase the

12

size and number of rooms on every floor, as well as enlarging them vertically to increase the number of floors.

Second, growth necessitated the continual specialization of building design and the repeated renovation of existing buildings to accommodate changing land use patterns. This included adapting homes, churches, barns, and schools in residential neighborhoods to the needs of invading businessmen. It also required remodeling commercial buildings designed for one kind of business for use by businesses in other trades with different physical and spatial requirements. It also included adapting residential structures designed for use by one family for use by many families. In addition, on occasion, it involved modifying nonresidential buildings for use by people invading agricultural areas and business districts in search of dwelling places.

Third, growth compelled the introduction of architectural improvements to protect against fires. As population density increased and the amount of capital invested in the built environment grew, fires became more and more costly in human and financial terms. Crowding also made it easier for fires to spread and develop into ruinous conflagrations. To prevent this, the flammable materials with which buildings were traditionally constructed had to be replaced with fireproof materials. Ways of facilitating escape from burning buildings also had to be developed.

Finally, the intensification of land use made it necessary to introduce various infrastructural conveniences into buildings. These improvements included the installation of indoor water faucets, water closets, sinks, and tubs, as well as the introduction of gas and electric power for heating and light. Traditional quasi-rural methods of providing water, sanitation, light, and heat simply could not adequately accommodate the huge number of people and businesses crowding into great cities during the nineteenth century.

Over time, these adaptations necessitated many fundamental improvements in architectural design and construction techniques, as well as an ongoing process of new construction, demolition, replacement, and renovation. Where such change was slow to occur or happened not at all, the consequence was the development of large stocks of obsolete structures that were incapable of meeting people's needs for space, convenience, economic productivity, safety, and health. The questions asked here are: Why did obsolete structures remain in the urban environment as long as they did? Why were they so difficult to modernize and replace?

Before continuing, we should note that the term "obsolete," as used in this study, does not refer to the nineteenth century's changing definition of the minimum level of space, convenience, health, and safety a residential or commercial building ought to provide. That was a normative concept which evolved as technology advanced and general living standards improved. Instead, as used here, the word refers to any building that was in any way causing overcrowding or public health or fire problems, creating bad business conditions, or otherwise failing to meet the needs of its users and the larger urban community. Thus the term is functionally defined, referring to the objective physical inadequacies of buildings. The word does not carry any implication that the structures so described could necessarily be sufficiently improved to meet all of society's needs at any point in time. Quite the contrary, for reasons to be described shortly, this often was impossible. Thus the term carries the connotation of a failure to achieve some sort of ideal match between facilities and need.

This is the clearest way to conceptualize the problem, since contemporaries rarely agreed on any minimal standard and continually changed their views as to the environmental standards to which urban society ought to aspire. It is also the ideal employed, at least implicitly, by most historians and social critics who have examined and critiqued environmental redevelopment in nineteenth century cities. Whether practical or not, most human beings share the dream that under some set of optimal conditions, all people will be able to enjoy ideal living and working conditions. At the least, most people hope that they themselves will be able to enjoy them. The understanding of what the ideal is has changed over the years. The dream persists, however. The purpose of this study is to explain why Americans fell so terribly short of bringing the dream into reality during the Victorian period. Significantly, by any definition, many buildings constructed in the nineteenth and early twentieth centuries were obsolete from the moment they were built.

The factors that discouraged property owners from renovating and reconstructing unsafe, unsanitary, and otherwise obsolete buildings in this period fall into several general categories. They allowed obsolete buildings to accumulate in rich neighborhoods as well as slums, in business districts as well as residential areas.

Physical durability and
the inelastic demand for obsolete structures

One of the most important frictions in the structural redevelopment process was the physical durability of urban buildings. The steel frame and reinforced concrete structures that people began erecting at the end of the nineteenth century were the most durable ones built in great cities. They had the capacity to remain standing for decades (and may go on standing for centuries), no matter how poorly they were adapted to their users' needs. What is important, however, is that comparatively primitive brick and wood buildings also had life expectancies of many years. These included such poorly designed and typically shoddy structures as New York City's infamous dumbbell tenement houses. Leo Grebler has estimated that the brick old-law tenements on New York's Lower East Side had an average life of more than eighty years. Furthermore, his data show that most old-law tenements were demolished not because of physical deterioration and loss of economic usefulness, but because they had to be torn down to make way for business buildings and street widenings. This suggests that the true life expectancy of these structures was actually much longer.[1]

Even relatively flimsy frame buildings had remarkably long lives in nineteenth and early twentieth century cities. Wooden buildings were vulnerable to fire and dilapidation, of course. Nevertheless, like brick buildings, they offered decades of economic utility, whether or not their owners properly maintained them. In fact, the very lightness of frame construction often discouraged the demolition and replacement of unsafe, unsanitary, and otherwise obsolete and decrepit wooden buildings by allowing their owners to move them from one place to another. This saved them from being wrecked when a new building was constructed on the lot where they had originally been built. Thus in 1935 in Chicago, for example, well over sixty percent of the dwellings in the city's teeming slums were old, ramshackle, tinderbox, wooden workers' houses. According to Edith Abbott, many were more than fifty years old and inadequate to begin with, some dating from Chicago's early prairie days. Significantly, most of the oldest and most obsolete houses were small cottages that had been moved from the front to the rear of their lots to make room for new and larger brick buildings. Some had probably been moved more than once and may have even been transported long distances from the lots on which they had originally been erected.[2]

This sort of physical durability would not have been a friction in the urban redevelopment process if people had simply abandoned their houses, tenements, offices, factories, and stores when they became overcrowded, unsafe, or unsanitary. The fact was, however, that there were many people who demanded to use and were willing to pay to occupy such buildings. In some cases these people did not realize how unsafe and otherwise undesirable their homes or places of business were, at least until disaster struck. In some cases they realized the problems but preferred to stay where they were because of emotional attachments to the structures or their neighborhoods. In most cases, however, they had no choice but to make do with bad accommodations. Technological problems and inefficiencies in the real estate market limited the options that even the wealthiest people had in selecting homes, offices, and work places that satisfied their needs. More on this will be said later. Poverty was the big problem, however. Poverty forced businessmen and residents alike to inhabit strategically located structures, even if the buildings had many obvious physical inadequacies.

Marginal businessmen had no choice but to rent the old, deficient, often wretched stores and warehouses available in business districts, because they could not afford to rent anything better. Like the businessmen who could afford more, they had to locate their firms where they would have maximum access to transportation facilities, financial institutions, and the leading companies in their trades. Only by obtaining the lowest possible transportation costs for the materials they handled, the most accessible trade information available, and other advantages dependent on close association with other businessmen could they hope to survive and prosper. By the same token, impoverished laborers had to accept accommodations in whatever housing was available near the places where they worked, even when this meant living under miserable conditions in the slums. They had no alternative, because they could not afford to pay higher rents and they had neither the time nor the money to commute long distances to work from the cheaper, better housing that might exist in more remote districts.

The people in this position included the vast majority of those who occupied buildings in the great cities of Victorian America.[3] They made the physical durability of obsolete buildings a barrier to structural improvement because they created a large inelastic demand for the use of obsolete buildings. They gave property owners a huge captive market that made ownership of these undesirable, often inefficient structures a profitable use of the land. The owners profited from the persistence of the buildings, despite the relatively low rents they had to charge, because the inelastic demand enabled them to subdivide the buildings and so multiply the number of rents they received, and because it allowed them to neglect maintenance, saving carrying costs. The result was that owners usually enjoyed high rates of return on their investments in the buildings, despite the buildings' failure to satisfy their tenants' and society's needs.[4]

Demolition, replacement, and renovation costs

Another friction in the structural redevelopment process was the high cost of making most improvements. Many property owners simply lacked the financial resources needed to make desirable changes in what they owned.

One problem was the money required to wreck an obsolete structure. Even if property owners sold the recyclable materials remaining after demolition, they might have to pay more than they could afford to tear their buildings down, several hundred dollars to tear down a brick structure, for example, or several thousand dollars to wreck a steel frame building.[5]

An even more serious hurdle was, of course, the cost of reconstruction. It took more money to rebuild a property after demolition than it took to tear it down, usually much more. While it might cost only a few hundred dollars to construct a small frame house, a large commercial edifice could easily run to many thousands, even hundreds of thousands, of dollars during this period. Renovations could also be very costly. By definition, most improvements were capital intensive. Directed toward upgrading the usage of a piece of land and increasing rents, they involved expensive increases in structure size, the installation of more and better fixtures, and improvements in construction. Beginning in the 1860s, municipal building codes and tenement laws also required the use of expensive building materials and capital-intensive building designs to protect against the spread of fire and improve living conditions. This meant that even small improvements could cost a great deal of money, especially those related to the installation of new plumbing. Installing properly ventilated waste pipes in old tenements, for example, could require extensive structural renovations, because many of the new pipes had to be laid on inclines to function correctly, and old structures rarely had room for this. Moving water closets indoors could require the construction of new rooms to make space for the new facilities.[6]

The property tax system added to the heavy price of improving buildings. How much it added naturally depended on the kind of improvement made and the tax rate in the owners' city at the time. In cities where reassessments were infrequent, however, property owners could easily double or even triple their annual property tax bills by tearing down old structures and replacing them with new ones. The scale of increase this often entailed is suggested by demands made in Baltimore, after the great fire of 1904, that the city spread the anticipated tax rise on the new buildings out over several years, holding it to twenty percent in the first year and to one hundred percent per year after that. Property owners feared that a single leap in the tax levy would raise their carrying costs so much as to make their new buildings unrentable.[7] Needless to say, whatever the size of the increase, the additional tax burden permanently increased carrying costs, while creating no offsetting revenue-producing improvement in the property itself, further discouraging the improvement and replacement of obsolete but still economically productive structures.

Finally, the price of improving buildings usually included opportunity costs that further increased the expense of redevelopment. Property holders sometimes had to use funds that could be more profitably invested elsewhere in order to reconstruct their buildings. This forced them to sacrifice income. Another problem was that they could not collect rents while their buildings were being wrecked and replaced. This also forced them to forego income just when they needed cash to help finance the large outlays necessary for an improvement. Leaseholders and property owners owing other forms of ground rent suffered doubly. Unable to collect rents, they themselves had to continue paying rents. Leaseholders also had to face the risk that they might lose their investment if they could not negotiate a new lease at an acceptable rate in the future. Structural improvement also entailed extra, personal sacrifices for those property holders who occupied their own buildings by forcing them to undertake the expensive and inconvenient step of temporarily relocating while the improvement was being made. In addition, owners who had to rebuild before some of their tenants' leases expired had to absorb the cost of removing the tenants from the building. Either they had to wait until the tenants' leases expired, paying the operating expenses and taxes on a partly empty, partly unrented building until they could begin construction of the improvement, or they had to pay lease damages to the displaced tenants, damages which might run into many thousands of dollars. Either way, they, too, were doubly burdened.

All of these costs promoted the persistence of unsafe, unsanitary, too small, and otherwise maladaptive structures. They not only discouraged improvement-minded property owners from making changes by creating psychological impediments to improvement; but they also eliminated large groups of people from the pool of owners who were financially capable of undertaking change. Since there are no studies of the socio-economic stratification of landownership in nineteenth and early twentieth century cities, it is not clear what proportion of owners were so poor that they could not make any improvements at all, although some contemporary studies of the housing problem indicate that this was a severe problem in many slum districts, in at least some cities.[8] In any case, a great many people were incapable of undertaking the many expensive improvements necessary to adapt their properties fully to their tenants' and the larger community's safety, size, and sanitary needs.

On the whole, the credit system reinforced, rather than alleviated, this problem. While there are no studies which document "redlining" in nineteenth century cities, there is no doubt that financial institutions, as a matter of course, made credit more expensive for people wishing to make improvements in blighted and declining neighborhoods, the "high-risk" areas where obsolete buildings were most abundant. In addition, downturns in the business cycle periodically forced banks to pull back on all their lending activities, reducing the amount of credit available for new construction throughout a city. Since most improvements required some form of credit extension, both of these problems simply intensified the cost barriers to improvement, pushing more people completely out of the improvement process.[9]

Property owners with no interest in
structural improvement

Another friction in the process of structural redevelopment was the existence of a large group of wealthy property owners who had no interest in renovating or replacing antiquated buildings, but deliberately pursued a strategy of not making improvements, even though they could afford to make them. Many in this group were income-oriented owners whose only concern was to maintain an uninterrupted flow of rents. Most of these people were widows, heirs, and absentee landowners who were unfamiliar with what they owned and played no direct role in the management of their properties. Relatively well-to-do to begin with, they were often content to leave their estates alone for decades, as long as they continued to provide a steady income. Characteristically risk averse, they had no interest in increasing their rents, except insofar as they could do so passively, as a result of the continual growth in the demand for urban land. As Richard Hurd pointed out in his pioneering study of urban land values, people with valuable business properties often had no idea that their negligence might lead to a substantial depreciation in the value of their estates. They often realized this fact only after it was too late to do anything to reverse a serious decline.[10]

Other property owners in this category were wealthy speculators who entered the real estate market with the sole intention of reaping rents and reselling later at a profit derived from land appreciation. Often they were people who had purchased slum properties in the hope of cashing in on anticipated residential to commercial land use transitions. Since such shifts often failed to occur, these speculators often ended up selling out to other land speculators or becoming income-oriented slumlords.[11] Both sorts of property owners exploited the inelastic demand for relatively cheap, centrally located living and working spaces, either unconsciously or consciously counting on the increasingly intense competition for scarce space by people and business to keep rents and land values high enough to offset the losses resulting from structural depreciation.

How large a proportion of all landowners this group was is not clear, since information on the attitudes held by most individual landowners toward the business of property ownership does not exist. But some impressionistic and quantitative evidence is available which indicates that trust estates and agent-operated properties constituted a very important part of the landholding pattern in most great cities. These are the kinds of land management arrangements associated with income-oriented ownership and land speculation. A study of landownership in San Francisco, for example, shows that in the 1940s and 1950s almost one-fifth of all properties were controlled by trust estates and that these estates accounted for relatively little of the new construction in the city.[12] These patterns developed in the nineteenth century. In 1904 in Baltimore, for instance, a single company, the Safe Deposit and Trust Company, claimed to represent one-tenth of all the properties on Baltimore Street, one of the city's main business thoroughfares, with most of its accounts in the form of trust accounts. Despite the importance of the street, the average value of these estates was only $60,000, for most of the buildings were old, small, three- and four-story brick stores that had not been much improved for decades.[13]

In general, agents and trustees shared their clients' disinterest in structural improvement. Most were charged with the responsibility of protecting their clients' incomes, not with putting their money at risk to make changes in their estates. They received steady commission incomes from the rents they collected, regardless of whether they initiated improvements. In large corporations like the Safe Deposit and Trust Company, they probably suffered from bureaucratic inertia as well.

Agents and trustees were in an excellent position to do nothing, because, like the owners, they could feed on the pent-up demand for relatively cheap structures in the central city. In fact, many apparently deliberately exploited the inelastic demand for cheap space by refusing to make necessary repairs on the buildings under their control, except when they were forced to do so by municipal authorities. This, of course, increased their clients' rates of return, although it also tended to depress or at least hold back increases in the actual levels of return. In addition, agents often leased the buildings to third parties to ensure a steady flow of rents. This placed direct management responsibilities in the hands of individuals who had almost no long-term interests in structural improvement, while further reducing the owners' interest in and control over their property. This made it even more likely that obsolete structures would persist in the urban environment.[14]

It should be kept in mind, of course, that not all speculators and income-oriented landowners were wealthy enough to bear the expense that the renovation or rebuilding of their obsolete buildings required. Many income-oriented landowners, especially widows and orphaned minors who owned only one or two small undesirable lots, depended on their rental incomes for their livelihoods. Even some wealthy rentiers who enjoyed large rental incomes depended on their rents for the maintenance of their upper class life styles, if not quite for their daily bread. Many speculators had all their wealth invested in property and lacked the liquidity and the credit needed to undertake renovations. For these people there was no choice as to whether or not improvements could be made. They were among the owners described earlier who could not afford to make structural improvements.

Market imperfections in the urban real estate market

Other frictions in the environmental redevelopment process which help explain the endurance of obsolete structures in nineteenth and early twentieth century cities were conditions in the urban real estate market. Called "market imperfections" by modern-day economists, they were factors which prevented the real estate market from functioning in an efficient way. In other words, they were circumstances which stopped landowners with both the will and the means to finance improvements from meeting the requirements of business and people in the community who were able to back up their demand for better accommodations with higher rent payments. Given the demand, such improvements should have been profitable for owners; and this profitability, in a perfect market, should have naturally induced the financially able profit maximizers to make the desired changes. The market, however, was not perfect, and the imperfections often made such redevelopment unprofitable, despite the demand. To be more specific, they made supplying high-quality accommodations to relatively wealthy tenants less financially rewarding than supplying substandard accommodations to impoverished workers and marginal businesses, despite the considerably higher rents that wealthy tenants could afford to pay. Thus they helped to make obsolete structures problems which the rich as well as the poor had to suffer. They forced affluent, profit-maximizing landowners to accept relatively low levels of return on property when this was theoretically unnecessary. They also compelled affluent businessmen and residents to crowd into a relatively few desirable, centrally located buildings or accept substandard quarters, even when these people could have afforded better accommodations.

Two different, but often interrelated imperfections served as frictions in the market. Since virtually all new construction in nineteenth and early twentieth century cities took place within the confines of the urban real estate market, both naturally played very important roles in the development of a very large stock of obsolete buildings.[15]

One, the land assembly problem, was caused by landowners' monopoly power in the real estate market. Because land is a spatially fixed good, every owner of land was in a monopoly position vis-à-vis any other person who wished to purchase the owner's property and so in a position to ask an exorbitant price for the parcel. The owner's monopoly power was a problem only to the purchaser who desired to buy a particular piece or pieces of land. Because the improvement of a structure often necessitated the purchase of adjoining lots, however, this was a common obstacle to both the renovation and the replacement of obsolete structures. It particularly impeded tenement reform, since it was literally impossible to construct sanitary multiple-family dwellings on the skinny, "shoestring" lots that characterized the land plats of most great cities. It obstructed other kinds of improvement, however, including the adaptation of stores, warehouses, and middle class apartment buildings. Greedy landowners who refused to sell out to improving property owners could forestall all kinds of structural improvement for long periods of time, no matter how extensive the demand for better buildings.

The second market imperfection, the neighborhood effect, was an "externality" phenomenon, a completely different sort of problem. Externalities are interactions among households, public agencies, or enterprises in which the activities of one economic actor directly affect the utility or production functions of other economic actors through non-market means. In other words, they are spillover effects, in this case the spillover effects that one landowner's investment in a structure had on the quality of services provided by the other structures in the same neighborhood and the spillover effects the government's investment in local infrastructures and community services had on the quality of services provided by the structures in a neighborhood.[16]

The neighborhood effect existed because tenants, residential and commercial alike, derived satisfaction not only from the design and state of repair of the one building they inhabited but also from the externalities resulting from the design, state of repair, and usage of nearby structures, from their association with other tenants in the neighborhood, and from the quality of the streets, the schools, the fire and police protection, and so on, in the area. This meant that the market value of a structure depended as much on the qualities of the surrounding neighborhood as it did on the character of the structure itself. It also meant that a property owner's return on a structural improvement depended as much on general neighborhood conditions and what nearby property owners did with their buildings as it did on the owner's personal investment activity. This naturally limited the extent to which an owner was willing to invest in property improvements.

The neighborhood effect contributed most obviously to the persistence of obsolete structures in poor, run-down, badly polluted, or inaccessible neighborhoods on the periphery of central business districts. In such cases, it slowed the expansion of the business district, leaving overcrowded commercial and industrial firms with unfulfilled demands for better accommodations. Neighborhood effects also played an important part in the persistence of old buildings in blighted areas inside the central business district and within declining residential neighborhoods, where they helped to block the erection of new, more expensive, middle class residential structures and model tenements.

In these situations the spillovers were negative externalities. They prevented change by placing a ceiling on the extent to which the improving property owner could raise rents after the renovation was complete, thus forcing the owner to forego some or all of the benefits resulting from the improvement. Although such an individual created a positive externality by making an improvement, the property owner's slight betterment of neighborhood conditions was necessarily much less than the betterment of the particular building, since any single structure, even one that was fairly large by nineteenth century standards, was almost always just a small, insignificant part of the surrounding neighborhood. As a result, it was difficult for the owner to make a satisfactory return on an investment in improvement and easy to lose a great deal of money. These risks naturally discouraged an owner from attempting a solitary renovation or replacement of an obsolete building. Alone, a property owner simply could not do enough to attract a significantly better class of tenants to a locality to raise the rents sufficiently to make most improvements profitable. Knowing this, all property owners naturally tended to content themselves with the low levels of return that were easily obtained from renting small, poorly designed, unsafe, or unsanitary structures to the overcrowded poor, even if there was an unsatisfied or latent demand for improved buildings in the areas where their buildings were located.

Landowners who ignored the risks involved in making structural improvements in bad neighborhoods often paid a high price for their misdirected ambitions. An example of this was described by Richard Hurd in his 1905 study of the urban real estate market. Hurd discussed the unfortunate fate of a six-story, $340,000 bank and office building erected in an undesirable retail district in Seattle toward the end of the nineteenth century. During the depression of the 1890s, the rents on the building failed to cover operating costs and provided no return on the land at all, even though the small one- and two-story shops next door and across the street paid steady six percent net returns on the value of the buildings and $600 per front foot on the value of the land throughout, and even though similar bank and office buildings in the more desirable areas of the city were also very profitable concerns through the depression period. Often such misplaced improvements had to be foreclosed and sold at a fraction of what they cost to build. The precedents they set undoubtedly discouraged many property owners from making desirable improvements by generating additional psychological barriers to structural redevelopment.[17]

For the property owner who was still determined to take advantage of the unfulfilled demand for improved structures to increase the value of a piece of property, there were only two ways to overcome a serious negative neighborhood effect within the confines of the private market system. One was for the owner to enlist the voluntary cooperation of the other owners in the area in a combined effort to eradicate the negative externalities. The other was for the owner to buy up most of the land in the neighborhood and personally eliminate the externalities. (Often the owner also had to enlist the aid of the municipal government so that street, sewer, and other in-frastructural problems could be reduced, a difficult problem which will be discussed later.) Unfortunately, neither of these solutions was easily accomplished.

On the one hand, the extremely fragmented pattern of landholding in nineteenth and early twentieth century cities made the coordination of vol-untary neighborhood-wide improvement projects almost impossible to achieve. In most of the great cities there were fifteen to fifty narrow building lots lining the two sides of a single block of street, almost all owned by different people or groups of people. And this was often only a small part of a neighborhood, which might cover several blocks containing well over a hundred lots owned by scores and scores of different people. Worse yet, the pattern of landownership was usually most fragmented in the poor, relatively un-developed areas, where negative externality problems were most severe.[18] As noted earlier, some of the property holders were likely to be leaseholders, income-oriented owners, or passive land speculators deliberately pursuing a policy of not improving their buildings and unwilling to go along with any scheme that required that they do so. In addition, many others were likely to be financially incapable of cooperating, especially where the neighborhood redevelopment called for them to demolish and replace their buildings.

To complicate matters, another externality problem undercut the willing-ness of property owners to participate in neighborhood-wide improvement. This second externality problem, the so-called prisoner's dilemma, resulted from the high rate of return an individual property owner received for doing nothing to improve a building while most or all of the owner's neighbors improved theirs. This peculiar situation developed because the improvement activities of several neighboring property owners often created enough positive externalities to allow uncooperative owners to raise their rents with-out any extra expenditure on their part. Because it cost money to make an improvement, they almost always stood to receive a higher *rate* of return if they simply sat back and enjoyed the fruits of the others' labor than if they joined in the improvement process. This naturally encouraged profit-max-imizing individual owners to do nothing to improve their buildings. The problem, of course, was that the very generality of the incentive encouraged all of the property owners in a neighborhood to do nothing, which made it very difficult indeed to achieve enough voluntary agreement and cooperation in a neighborhood to raise its position in the general market.[19]

The land assembly problem, meanwhile, made it virtually impossible for the determinedly improvement-minded individual to buy enough land to eliminate the negative externality without help. As Jerome Rothenberg points out, because of the monopolistic nature of landownership, the process of privately assembling the large number of parcels needed to internalize negative neighborhood externalities inevitably entailed a long, expensive, and difficult "sequence of bilateral monopoly confrontations, with each potential seller eager to squeeze out the full amount of profit to be obtained from the assembler's integrated decision making."[20] Although assemblers usually tried to minimize this problem by making their purchases as surreptitiously as possible, the bargaining process easily broke down, bringing an incipient improvement project to a dead halt. Furthermore, even if successful, the mere assemblage of the land brought the assembler only halfway toward achieving the goal of improving the neighborhood. The tremendous cost of modernizing the properties remained, often serving to delay the improvement process further.

A classic example of a deadlocked monopoly confrontation is provided by the unfortunate situation on a blighted section of Douglas Street (later Lexington Street), a business thoroughfare in Baltimore, at the turn of the century. After a street widening in the late 1880s, some of the lots in this neighborhood were so small and badly shaped that the owners, none of whom could purchase neighboring lots, could do no better than to erect unsightly and almost worthless flatiron buildings only nine feet wide in front and one foot wide in back. As one community leader observed, the problem was that "each of the owners of the adjoining properties, front and back, thinks he holds the key to the situation and holds his property at prohibitive figures and neither can buy." Nor could any outside developer afford to buy. As a result, the entire district was blighted and inefficiently used, despite its desirable location.[21] Clearly, at its worst, monopoly power functioned much like the prisoner's dilemma, discouraging all of the landowners in an area from doing anything to improve the value of the holdings. Naturally, as the number of properties to be assembled increased and the number of monopolists to be dealt with multiplied, the likelihood that a neighborhood could be satisfactorily redeveloped became more and more remote.

As market imperfections, the neighborhood effect and land assembly problems were distinct and important barriers to structural change in their own right. Nevertheless, like the problems described earlier, they cannot be completely abstracted from the more general problems of structural durability and the inelastic demand for cheap, centrally located living and working space. What made people's resistance to improvement economically feasible was that they could very profitably rent their small, unsafe, unsanitary, and otherwise antiquated buildings to impoverished workers and marginal businessmen who had no choice but to accept them. The point to be made here is that their unwillingness to make improvements promoted structural persistence on the neighborhood level, not just the individual level. This limited the availability of decent accommodations for the entire community, rich and poor alike.

Technological barriers to structural improvement

Despite the barriers to new construction and renovation, cities were continually evolving in the nineteenth and early twentieth centuries. For most of the period, however, property owners confronted architectural and engineering problems that severely limited what they could do to redevelop their properties. These technological problems created additional frictions in the process of structural improvement, frictions which prevented even the most ambitious and financially capable improvers from producing homes and other buildings that could physically satisfy the needs of their increasingly congested communities.

These technological problems constrained every aspect of the improvement process, including the most necessary and ostensibly simple changes. Take, for example, the very basic matter of making buildings more spacious. The technological challenge here was to keep tall and horizontally extensive structures from collapsing under their own weight. Traditional wood and stone masonry walls were not strong enough to withstand the immense load and wind stresses created by great heights and lateral extensions unless they were built up from the bottom to thicknesses of several feet and, in many cases, unless they were accompanied by additional interior-bearing walls and columns. Walls three and four feet wide, however, were not only exceedingly expensive but, worse, extremely wasteful of scarce space, consuming large parts of the limited room available on the narrow lots fronting on the streets in most great cities. In fact, on the typical twenty-five-foot-wide building lot, they left the vital lower floors of tall buildings with barely enough room for hallways. In wider buildings requiring interior supports, immovable and often inconveniently placed load-bearing walls and columns also took up valuable interior room and made the reorganization of inside areas difficult or impossible. Thus this solution to the problem was of little use in the city. Heavily trussed vaults provided a possible alternative answer to the problem of carrying roofs across large open spaces. Unfortunately, they could be effectively used only to increase the amount of floor space in one-story buildings. Thus they were economically feasible only in the construction of churches and railway passenger stations and factories in peripheral areas where land was relatively cheap. Domes were also of little use, for they were too heavy for tall buildings and too expensive for private property owners.[22]

The modern solution to this particular technological problem required the emergence of new theories of structural engineering. The most significant breakthrough was the development of ways to construct buildings around steel and reinforced concrete frameworks. The advantage of structural skeletons was that they permitted the transmission of external and internal roof, floor, wall, and utility loads and wind stresses to a building foundation via the steel or reinforced concrete framework. This made possible the elimination of space-consuming exterior and interior load-bearing masonry walls and supports, which not only increased the amount of floor space that could be left open, unobstructed by load-bearing walls and supports on each floor, but also multiplied the number of floors that buildings could carry in both small and large lots. The subsequent development of ways to construct deep pile and concrete pier foundations capable of carrying the heavy loads exerted by tall buildings down to bedrock made further increases in the size of buildings possible.[23]

Unfortunately, these technological advances emerged slowly, severely limiting the possibilities for increasing room size and raising building heights beyond eight or nine stories until the end of the nineteenth century.[24] Many factors retarded their development. These are worth summarizing, for they are indicative of the problems plaguing technological innovation in other areas.

One problem was the prolonged unavailability of most of the new materials required for the development of the new structural architecture. Wrought and cast iron were produced in large quantities early in the period. It was steel that was needed for the efficient mass production of structural members, however. It did not become available for building construction until the mid-1870s, after the Bessemer and open-hearth processes made possible the production of high-grade steel in large volumes at relatively low prices. Reinforced concrete was also developed late in the period. Plain concrete was easy and cheap to manufacture and use in building construction, and it provided excellent resistance to compression, the crushing force exerted by heavy loads on the upper surfaces of structural members. For decades, however, its lack of tensile strength made it serviceable only as an artificial stone in masonry-bearing walls and facade orr mentation. It was not until the late 1860s and 1870s, when means of reinforcing it with steel were developed, that it gained the resistance to bending and stretching flexion and tension stresses necessary for more innovative architectural applications.[25]

But before these new materials could be utilized safely and efficiently, metallurgists, chemists, and engineers had to determine their structural strengths and construction potentials. Engineers and tool and materials manufacturers had to devise new machines and processes so that iron, steel, concrete, and glass sections, blocks, and sheets could be mass-produced, manipulated, and joined with the precision and refinement necessary to erect large, tall buildings quickly and economically. Architects had to experiment with the use of new materials and design concepts.

This process also took years. It was held back by the anomalous findings of much of the basic research, by the absence of reliable and precise methods of quantitatively assessing the requirements for safely and efficiently spreading loads in particular sites and design situations in advance of construction, and by the very nature of the architectural improvement process. As Carl Condit points out, the evolution of structural technology was a "kind of orthogenesis, each structural innovation representing some progressive refinement of the system antecedent to it." The uncertainty of the progression was compounded by primitive iron, steel, and cement materials manufacturing techniques, which introduced a high level of unpredictability into the design process, undercutting the value of the architect's calculation of stress resistance. Mistakes sometimes became visible only when a building began to fail.[26]

Popular and professional attitudes toward the dangers and aesthetics of the new materials and structural designs further retarded the development of the new technology. Most architects and builders found it extremely difficult to detach themselves from traditional architectural techniques. Thus only a few were willing to experiment with the new ideas and materials. In the early part of the nineteenth century, this conservatism stemmed partly from justifiable fears that exposed metal would buckle and collapse during fires and that concrete buildings might topple. After means of fireproofing metal columns and beams emerged and reinforced concrete was developed in the 1870s, however, deep-seated ties to the old ways of doing things generated most of the psychological stumbling blocks. Except in Chicago, where a few innovative architects began experimenting quite extensively with steel frame construction in the 1880s, most big-city architects simply could not let go of familiar materials or architectural styles enough to begin trying to advance the usage of the new ones. Property owners' and the general public's fear of the unknown and distaste for the aesthetics of the new technology reinforced the architects' conservatism, making it even more difficult for them to experiment.[27]

Because of these technical and psychological problems, it was not until the early 1890s, seventy years after the beginning of the period of rapid growth and twenty years after the development of the new materials, that the principles of skeletal construction were well enough developed and the benefits sufficiently clear for architects to begin applying the technology to space-starved commercial districts on any scale, even in cities as congested as New York. There, the first many-storied skyscraper employing skeletal construction was the Tower Building, which was erected in 1889. Only eleven stories tall, it was a hybrid of steel frame construction and traditional mortar-bearing walls. It was not until the later 1890s and early twentieth century that the really space efficient skyscrapers over twenty stories tall were built in any numbers.[28]

Similar difficulties plagued other efforts to solve the technological problems of structural improvement. In the development of fire-resistant construction technologies, for example, the difficulties of obtaining experimental proof of a building material's fire resistance imposed a special burden. It took many decades for architects to appreciate fully the fact that almost no substance was completely impervious to the extreme heats generated by city fires. In the meantime, confusion prevailed as each new major conflagration demonstrated the vulnerability of yet another building material, from wood to brick, stone, terra cotta, iron, steel, and other metals, negating several generations of theories of fireproof construction. Establishing architectural standards for protection against the spread of fire within and between buildings also prolonged the process of making structures safe, since this entailed the development of technically complex formulas for determining such things as the optimal amount of space to leave between timbers in adjoining party walls, formulas which naturally offered much room for disagreement. As a result, the standards themselves, as embodied in building codes and professional debates, often represented something less than the "state of the art" principles of the technology of fire prevention at any given time.[29]

Bettering the provision of water, sanitation, lighting, and heat within city structures was even more complicated. On the one hand, it required the establishment and improvement of public service infrastructures, a subject that will be considered later. On the other, it involved designing new building fixtures and appliances and then enhancing their efficiency, affordability, and safety. This, too, required years of patient experimentation with different building materials, mechanical devices, and design ideas. The first completely sanitary water closets, for example, were not developed until the 1880s. Until then, the "pan closet," an early design which could not be cleaned or flushed properly, was in "almost universal" use, collecting filth and functioning as an indoor cesspool in the homes of rich and (where they could afford them) poor alike. Correcting the deficiencies of the pan closet necessitated experimenting with different metals and porcelains, developing new flushing mechanisms, and changing the physical structure of the appliance. This took several decades. In the process, manufacturers and sanitary engineers patented dozens of different water closet designs, all containing various flaws, before they began to hit upon really sanitary contrivances.[30]

Architects also had to develop satisfactory methods for installing water closets, bathtubs, furnaces, stoves, and other fixtures and connecting them to outside infrastructures, so that they would not leak, start fires, stink, or

contaminate the rooms in which they were placed. This required technological innovation in the construction and placement of various pipes and
drains.[31]

An extreme example of the long time lags often involved in advances of
this sort was the slow development of techniques for safely bringing waste
removal appliances indoors. One problem with Victorian plumbing was that
drains were two-way connections between water closets, sinks and tubs, and
sewers and cesspools. This meant that they not only provided the means by
which wastes could be eliminated from buildings, but also furnished routes
through which the noxious gases given off by the materials putrefying in
sewers could enter people's workrooms, kitchens, and bathrooms. The sewer
gas problem was so intractable, and the struggle to solve it so prolonged,
that it helped give rise to the infamous "plumbing scare" of the 1870s and
1880s, which for a time threatened to reverse the clock and bring the old-
fashioned outdoor privy back into use.[32] The first mechanisms for trapping
drains to block the escape of sewer gas were water traps, like the "bell,"
"round," "D," and "cesspool" traps. These were created by bends and
hollows inside drain pipes, which collected enough water to establish a water
seal against the passage of gas. Designed to prevent the loss of the water
seal through evaporation or siphonage, the early traps were so big that they
functioned as small cesspools, accumulating filth and giving off "more bad
gas than would be found within miles of a well-constructed sewer." Almost
worse than nothing, they were followed by mechanical valves, which were
unreliable and also tended to collect filth. Not until the late 1870s, when
the principles of ventilating traps and drains were fully ascertained, was it
possible to trap drains properly and end the sewer gas scare.[33] Another
problem that had similarly disastrous results was the difficulty of finding a
material to replace the poisonous lead in water pipes which could be welded
as easily and as airtightly as lead. Obviously, the delay in solving problems
like these meant that really safe and sanitary installation was impossible
through much of the period.[34]

Because of their health effects, these kinds of technical problems bore
heavily on the process of adapting city housing to population growth, limiting
what even the most ambitious reformers could do to improve living conditions
in Victorian cities. Housing reform also required that other architectural
problems be solved. In particular, maintaining public health necessitated the
development of housing designs that would simultaneously maximize the
number of rooms per floor and provide an adequate supply of natural light
and fresh air. It was not enough simply to increase the total amount of floor
space available, especially in the era before electric lights and fans became
commonplace. As long as row houses were only two rooms deep and not
blocked in the front or back by other houses crowded together on the same

lot, light and air could easily enter all above-ground rooms through windows. As soon as a lot became more densely built up, however, natural light and ventilation disappeared from the rooms that did not front on the open street. While such a situation might be tenable in warehouses and some other kinds of commercial buildings, it was unacceptable where people had to live and sleep. Dark, stifling rooms and hallways were not only unpleasant breeding grounds for disease; they also led to accidents and fires and facilitated crime.[35] Significantly, the problems arose wherever housing density was great. Thus they confronted builders attempting to provide multi-family apartment housing for middle and upper class people as well as tenements for workers. In fact, in New York City, middle and upper class apartments, or "flats" as they were often called, were officially classified as tenements until the beginning of the twentieth century.[36]

Here, again, progress was slow. By the 1850s the English and French recognized one solution to the problem: the placement of large interior courts in the center of buildings to provide light and air to inner rooms. Unfortunately, American architects and housing reformers failed to realize the efficacy of such arrangements and refused to embrace any workable alternatives for another quarter of a century.

In this case, the prime barrier to technological innovation was not the difficulty of creating new building materials and engineering concepts. Rather, it was the psychological and economic impediments to improvement posed by the American city's narrow building lots, by the land assembly problem, and by landowners' profit-maximizing desires to put as much space as possible to profitable use. Many architects who wanted to build high-density housing for middle class families did attempt to apply the apartment designs popular in France and England to American conditions. In so doing, however, they concentrated on superficial architectural details like facade and staircase design and ignored the crucial inner-court concept, claiming that such empty spaces were undesirable in America.[37]

It was not until 1876, when Alfred White erected America's first European-style model tenement, that a large apartment building with an inner courtyard was finally constructed in the United States. And even then, widespread acceptance of the necessity of such a solution was slow in coming. It took the invention and proliferation of the dumbbell tenement, another "model" tenement design, to demonstrate to the American housing cognoscenti the futility of trying to design satisfactorily high density buildings to fit slender, "shoestring" building lots. In the meantime, people continued to erect buildings with dark inner rooms for both the middle and the lower classes.[38]

In sum, the Victorian era saw the development of architectural and industrial innovations that transformed American building technology. Within the context of city growth, however, the important fact was that these advances lagged behind population and economic growth by many years. They not only emerged later, but evolved gradually, most early inventions representing only partial solutions to the problems of adapting structures to the intensification of land usage. This meant that as new structural designs and appliances were developed and put into use, the progressive innovations that had preceded them became part of the antiquated but durable structural inheritance of the past that needed replacement. By the 1870s, the once revolutionary pan water closet, for example, was as much a part of the city sanitation problem as the old privy vault, the cast-iron facade almost as much a part of the fire problem as wooden siding. The irony was that most of the real technological breakthroughs in architecture emerged close to the end of the nineteenth century, when the rate of growth in the inner city was already leveling off. As a consequence, the process of adapting structures to growth was a continuous process, and the persistence of obsolete structures a cumulative problem.

Other problems affecting
the structural improvement process

Technological problems were not the only factors that caused property owners to erect poorly designed, shoddy, unsafe, or unsanitary buildings. Technology put definite limits on what kinds of improvement could be made at any given time. Nevertheless, within this sometimes severely circumscribed parameter, desirable improvements could still be made. But even when property owners constructed or renovated buildings, they did not always apply all of the technologically feasible advances their increasingly congested communities required. Many factors account for this, including the speculation, market imperfections, and cost constraints discussed earlier. In addition, ignorance, misinformation, and fraud took their toll.

Unscrupulous contractors contributed to the multiplication of unsafe, unsanitary, and otherwise sub-standard buildings by installing such things as inadequate plumbing and thin, flimsy walls of inferior brick, third-rate mortar, and flaky plaster. This cost shaving lined their own pockets, not the owners', and so did not reflect the owners' own speculative strategies. As such, it represented a fraud from the effects of which the owners, as well as the future tenants, would have to suffer.

Another problem was that builders, architects, and property owners were often ignorant about the proper ways to make improvements. Much of the new technology was based not on intuition but on complicated applications of physical laws that had been developed by engineers who had not, in the past, interfered with the activities of ordinary builders and architects. Unfortunately, most builders and architects, and many property owners as well, had their own firmly held ideas about how to design and construct buildings. As a result, they often resisted the "experts' " intrusion and simply refused to listen to their unsolicited advice. "Alas!" complained the *Sanitary Engineer*, for example. "How seldom do architects or owners ask a plumber's advice or permit his suggestions!" The results could be unfortunate, and scattered throughout this journal and others like it were anecdotes about the absurd predicaments that well-intentioned but wrongheaded "improvers" frequently created for themselves.[39]

A third problem was the widespread availability of standard architectural plans for inefficient and unsanitary, but perfectly legal, building designs. Because standardized construction materials were widely available through catalogues, these blueprints often became packaged, stereotypic plans which people used over and over again, whether or not they made economic sense, simply because they were readily available and easily approved by local building authorities. Twenty-five by one-hundred-foot dumbbell tenement plans probably constituted the most pernicious examples of this problem. As housing reformer Ernest Flagg pointed out, developers used these designs without thinking, even to fill large multi-lot parcels of land that suited the construction of much more efficient, sanitary, and profitable block tenements and apartment buildings. In so doing they paid for the construction of unnecessary walls, partitions, corridors, and entrance ways, unwittingly wasting money that was "worse than thrown away," since the vast amount of useless masonry not only took up rentable space, but also made the buildings dark and unhealthy.[40]

What the mix of cost factors, market imperfections, speculation, and ignorance was in the production and proliferation of new, sub-standard buildings is not clear. The point is that these buildings were overdetermined. No one causal factor can be singled out to explain them, either individually or *en masse*. The rich and poor built the structures; and the rich, as well as the poor, had to live and work in them, at least for a time. A related point is that regardless of the factors that led to their creation, once produced, these maladaptive structures became permanent parts of the physically durable built environment, and all of the barriers to change described earlier forestalled their subsequent renovation or removal.

Over time, of course, the geographical mobility of relatively wealthy residents and businesses meant that tenantry of small, flammable, antiquated, and unsanitary buildings became more and more exclusively the province of the poor. As the more affluent classes slowly abandoned their outmoded and wrongheaded improvements, space-starved marginal businesses and impoverished workers speedily moved in. Such downward filtering was one of the most important ways by which additional quarters became available to the poor. As Boston's Committee on the Expediency of Providing Better Tenements for the Poor observed in 1846, it was also the most unfortunate way, since what was really needed was "to build new and *large* structures ... to supplant the present small and inconvenient houses by large, lofty and well-fitted ones: *so that the same number of persons now covering the crowded districts [might] be well, instead of ill, accommodated.*"[41] This downward filtering was both cause and symptom of the structural persistence problem.

The breakdown of the market system and the municipal response

Once rapid economic and population growth began, it did not take long for city dwellers to become dissatisfied with the performance of their free urban real estate market. Public health officials and social reformers reacted in horror to the market's failure to produce housing in sufficient quantity and quality to meet the needs of their cities' mushrooming populations; and as they admitted, their horror did not compare with the anguish of the people who had to live and work in overcrowded, deathly slums. Bad construction also appalled insurance underwriters, businessmen, and property owners, especially when it led to ruinous conflagrations that destroyed whole blocks of buildings. Not only were the physical dangers of poorly constructed, blighted buildings disturbing, but their property-value-reducing "nuisance" qualities were as well.

Those wishing to improve the situation took two routes. One was to seek internal reform of the real estate market by educating capitalists and builders about the great need for new construction and the absolute necessity of safer, more fire resistant buildings with adequate room size, water supplies, and sewerage and ventilation facilities. This involved publicizing the sufferings of the poor and making known the catastrophic effects of fire, as well as disseminating information about new construction techniques and architectural designs. Some housing reformers also became involved in model tenement building as a way to demonstrate physically the practicality of erecting relatively high quality dwellings for the poor.[42]

The other route was to obtain reform from without, through government intervention in the market. Reformers soon learned from hard experience that they could not rely on example and reasoned argument alone to make people change their behavior. As a result, they increasingly concentrated on achieving the power necessary to compel change, attempting to accomplish their goals through governmental legislation.

The case studies in Part II will show that the same economic, psychological, and technological factors that discouraged individuals from undertaking structural improvement within the confines of the free market also undermined efforts to compel change from above. For the most part, reformers were neither willing nor able, physically, economically, or politically, to remedy the supply and demand problems underlying the production and persistence of obsolete structures. They could not overcome the technological impediments to change. Nor could they transcend the other barriers posed by the imperfections in the real estate market and the strong and inelastic demand for relatively cheap, centrally located living and working space created by large numbers of poor people and marginal businessmen. Instead, they tried to adapt buildings to community need almost entirely by regulating new construction through building codes, tenement regulations, and zoning laws, that is, by disciplining the private market. Significantly, even these limited efforts were often frustrated by political conflict and bureaucratic incompetence.

The decision to rely on government regulation of the private market was a deliberate one, based largely on the reformers' belief that the main cause of the city's inability to adapt structures to economic and population growth was speculative profiteering, a problem which they believed could be controlled through legislation and police action. In their view, as Jacob Riis put it, the basic problem was "just a question of whether a man would take 7 percent and save his soul or 25 percent and lose it."[43] As following chapters will show, however, the scarcity of decent, centrally located housing and commercial space was a much more profound problem than this. It was a phenomenon caused by technological backwardness, by the historical accumulation of obsolete but still useful buildings, by the economic organization of the urban real estate market, and ultimately, by the unequal distribution of wealth in urban society.

3

The barriers to infrastructural improvement

The task of adapting the built environment to the needs of rapidly growing urban communities involved much more than the redevelopment of privately owned buildings. In addition, it required that a vast range of improvements be made in street systems, water, sewerage, and power systems, streetcar and railroad systems, government buildings, and parks and other public recreation facilities – in today's language, the infrastructures of cities. Because a large number of frictions also mediated the process by which these infrastructures were redeveloped, they were no easier to improve than buildings.

Adapting infrastructures to the imperatives of economic and physical growth required their technological modernization as well as their physical establishment, physical extension, and spatial reorganization. These improvements can be summarized as follows:

First, in order to supplement or supplant the inadequate supplies of water provided by inefficient private water companies and local wells and springs, it was necessary that high-volume, high-pressure public water systems be established. This was essential for fire fighting and street cleaning, as well as for drinking purposes. It was especially important after industrial waste and seepage from privies and cesspools had polluted the water drawn from local streams, springs, and wells. In addition, once a water system was in place, further growth required that it be continually redeveloped. Not only did additional sources of water have to be tapped, but the old-fashioned wood and iron conduits in use in the 1820s had to be replaced with more durable equipment, distribution pipes extended into unserviced areas, and more and better drinking and fire hydrants provided. Pipe enlargement was also important, for it was a prerequisite for increasing water pressure, which was essential for extending water supplies into peripheral areas, providing water to the upper floors of tall buildings, and fighting fires in tall buildings.

Rapid increases in population density and industrial activity also necessitated the establishment of modern sewerage systems. The growing intensity of land use made street gutters, streams, privies, cesspools, and private

36

drainage pipes increasingly inefficient and unsanitary vehicles for draining rainwater and household and industrial wastes from buildings, streets, and land, notwithstanding efforts by municipal authorities to regulate their construction, maintenance, and use. To replace them, it was necessary to establish public sewerage systems that were capable of carrying the wastes and storm run-offs of entire communities to distant locations where they could be purified or discharged without harm to human populations. In addition, once such systems were in place, further growth made it necessary to upgrade them even more. Collecting pipes had to be enlarged and ventilated, as well as extended into unserviced areas. Deteriorated pipes had to be replaced. As with public water facilities, pipe enlargement was especially important, since the intensification of land usage and the extension of services to outlying districts naturally increased the flow of wastes in centrally located sewers, while the building and paving over of local watersheds swelled the flow of storm run-off in them. Failure to accommodate the increases could lead to the same sanitary and flooding problems the sewers had been constructed to resolve. Worse, where rainwater and sewage flowed through the same conduits, failure meant that a bad storm could send a flood of diluted raw sewage into a city's streets, basements, and waterways (and water supplies), causing a monumental nuisance or, worse, a sudden public health disaster.

Water and sewerage were not the only public services in America's rapidly growing cities that required extensive environmental redevelopment. In addition, steam, gas, and electric power generating plants had to be established and distribution apparatuses built to convey the power. Again, as the demand for mechanical power increased and technology improved, the systems had to be upgraded by the renovation and extension of distribution grids and the construction of new generating plants. Since different companies and government agencies built these facilities over the years, competing systems also had to be integrated and standardized in order to eliminate inefficient, redundant, and incompatible equipment and achieve economies of scale. As sidewalks and rooftops became more and more encumbered with poles, cross-arms, and telephone, telegraph, and electric power wires, these utilities had to be moved underground to make space for pedestrians on overcrowded streets, to keep wires from breaking and crossing during fires and storms, and to protect people from sparks, power outages, and electrocution.

The simple multiplication of underground utilities necessitated massive environmental redevelopment. In some cities, the public rights of way under the streets became so full of conduits that by the 1890s the many sub-surface systems had to be reorganized before the utilities could be renovated or expanded. More generally, these infrastructures had to be integrated and systematized in order to reduce the damage caused by the frequent tearing up of streets for the making of repairs and new construction. In Manhattan, for example, utility companies dug more than 59,000 transverse excavations for utility connections and repairs in the island's 391.5 miles of paved streets in one year, 1891, alone. Together with the many longitudinal excavations made, this averaged out to one excavation for every thirty-five feet of street. As city dwellers, businessmen, and public officials from across the country often complained, this constant digging was making the urban pavement an unsightly and unnavigable "thing of shreds and patches."[1] Solving these problems involved establishing control over the various government agencies and private companies responsible for a city's utilities as well as physically reorganizing the infrastructure.

Above-ground transportation infrastructures also required far-reaching improvements. Narrow and crooked streets had to be widened and straightened, new streets and bridges opened, and dead ends eliminated in order to keep businesses and residents from suffocating in rapidly increasing street traffic. City streets also had to be properly graded, sewered, and paved in order to reduce mud and flooding problems and to eliminate horse-and-carriage-defying hills and potholes.

In addition, railroads and streetcars had to be developed and track networks and terminal facilities constructed to provide for more speedy and efficient mass transport. This was essential for commercial and industrial growth, as well as for relief from inner city traffic congestion and the development of suburbs. This, too, involved repeatedly adding to and upgrading existing infrastructures to accommodate increased usage and the introduction of new methods of locomotion. As with gas and electric utilities, it also involved integrating and systematizing the facilities constructed by competing companies in order to expedite through traffic and the transfer of freight and passengers from one line to another. Where the multiple tracks of many railroad companies crossed one another and hundreds of streets at grade, grade crossings had to be eliminated to reduce street congestion, rail delays, and accidents. In some cities this necessitated relocating or elevating hundreds of miles of track or constructing subways.[2]

Since all of the great cities in this period were heavily dependent on waterborne commerce, the modernization of urban ports was also vital. Docks and wharfs had to be redesigned and enlarged and shipping lanes deepened to accommodate increasingly large vessels and growing volumes of goods. In addition, it was important that generally accessible railway terminals be established in order to reduce the cost and inconvenience of transferring passengers and freight from one mode of transportation to another and to limit street traffic.

Finally, schools, fire houses, police stations, courthouses, and other government buildings had to be constructed and modernized and their locations periodically changed to accommodate the expansion of government services and the growth and redistribution of urban populations. Parks and playgrounds had to be established to take the place of the private lawns and trees swallowed up by new buildings, to give city dwellers some relief from the pollution, congestion, and ugliness of their increasingly built up surroundings.

In short, economic development and the intensification of land use necessitated many improvements in the distribution and technology of a large number of urban infrastructures. It is much more difficult to discuss the frictions that obstructed this kind of environmental development than to discuss the problems of structural development, because of the wide variety of infrastructures involved and the many different kinds of improvement needed. Nevertheless, it is possible to generalize.

Generalizations can be made for three basic reasons. First, redevelopment took place within the framework of America's market and political systems, the distinctive characteristics of which imposed a significant degree of uniformity on the multifaceted process of improvement. Second, redevelopment took place within the context of American cultural and social systems, a situation which also imposed a significant degree of consistency on the improvement process. Finally, and perhaps from an analytical perspective most important, all infrastructures – street, water, sewer, drainage, power, streetcar, railway, harbor, park, and public building systems alike – shared some important physical and economic characteristics. Briefly put, they shared the qualities of capital intensiveness, land extensiveness, and monopolistic production. They also displayed the consumption characteristics of public goods.

Infrastructures were capital intensive in that they required substantial and costly capital inputs in the form of pipes, tracks, pavement, various mechanisms, and so forth. Even parks were carefully engineered public landscapes, promenades, and recreation grounds, rather than virgin fields and woodlands.

By the same token, infrastructures were land extensive in that they formed far-flung land use systems which occupied a great deal of space, either above or below ground. By 1920, each of America's great cities contained thousands of miles of streets, of railroad and streetcar tracks, of water, sewer, and gas pipes, as well as of telephone, telegraph, and electric utility lines. Even small public structures, such as schools and fire stations, were land extensive in the sense that they constituted parts of larger, geographically dispersed land use systems.

Infrastructures were monopolistically produced in that whether produced by private companies or by public agencies, all were typically provided by only one producer at any given site, because of economies of scale, the tremendous costs of production and maintenance, the limited availability of space for infrastructural use, and exclusive franchises and rights of way. Even where city governments attempted to guarantee competition by granting overlapping franchises, monopolies rapidly developed. As the Chicago Street Railway Commission observed in 1900, it was "everywhere found impossible to induce, persuade, require, or compel public service corporations engaged in the same line of business to compete with each other."[3] After a few years of cut-throat competition, they inevitably consolidated or secretly divided the disputed territories among themselves, amicably eliminating rivalry through mutual agreements in order to maximize profits.[4] The only exceptions were the owners of wharf facilities, who were usually numerous, relatively small scale producers, much like the owners of ordinary structures. But even here there was a trend toward the centralization of ownership, with a few large shipping and railway concerns or city authorities taking over more and more of the land in question.[5]

Finally, all infrastructures were consumed in a peculiarly public way that complicated the interaction between the consumers and the producers of public services. All generated positive externalities, like improved health and business conditions, which whole neighborhoods, and often whole communities, passively enjoyed (that is to say, consumed), even if they did not personally use the specific services in question. More important, all were jointly used (again, consumed), directly by many people simultaneously and over time. Unlike the private benefits that private goods like food and clothing provided, infrastructures provided "inexhaustible" collective benefits that individual consumers did not appropriate and use up, but instead shared with other people who were using them at the same time or would use them at a later time.[6]

As it happened, very few nineteenth and early twentieth century infrastructures exactly fit the definition of an economically "pure" public good. (As economists readily point out, few goods do.)[7] Almost all could be overused, so that at some point the addition of one more consumer reduced the benefits enjoyed by other simultaneous users by creating traffic jams, drops in water pressure, sewage backups, and other results of overcrowding. This, of course, was one of the prime reasons that infrastructures needed continual improvement.

What was important, however, was that all infrastructures involved joint consumption, all generated many positive externalities, and all provided "inexhaustible" collective benefits, at least up to a point. Together with their capital intensiveness, their land extensiveness, and their monopolistic character (and together with the political, economic, social, and cultural value systems which provided the institutional context in which their development took place), this public quality of infrastructures led to important frictions in the process of urban environmental improvement, frictions that created the conflict, contradiction, and failure that plagued the process by which public services were adapted to people's needs.

As with structures, it is useful to view a community's delays in achieving needed infrastructural improvements in terms of the persistence of functionally obsolete infrastructures. There is one basic difference, however. Newly established parks and public water, sewerage, power, and mass transportation systems represented novel land uses that were very different from the small-scale, private land uses that traditionally provided recreation space, water, waste disposal, heat, light, and transportation. Back yards, wells, privies, wood piles, and private carriages obviously were not infrastructures, although they provided some of the same services as the infrastructures that would replace them, since they were not land-extensive, monopolistically produced, and jointly consumed public goods. This meant that a city's failure to achieve a needed infrastructural improvement did not, strictly speaking, necessarily result in the persistence of an obsolete infrastructure, especially in the early part of the nineteenth century. Instead, it sometimes involved the perpetuation of an obsolete non-infrastructural (or "proto-infrastructural") land use. Infrastructural improvements that involved replacing a proto-infrastructural land use with an infrastructural one constituted major economic and spatial land use transitions in a way that ordinary structural improvements did not. These transitions embodied very significant changes in the production, consumption, and organization of land usage, changes that made the difficulties of adapting the urban environment to economic and population growth all the more profound.

The problem of physical durability and inelastic demand

Physical durability was as important a cause of the persistence of obsolete infrastructures as it was a cause of the persistence of obsolete structures. Like ordinary privately owned buildings, streets, parks, public buildings, utility conduits, and railroad tracks and depots were capital-intensive land uses with life expectancies of decades. In fact, legal entities like streets and parks had the potential to remain in existence for as long as the laws that set them off as public spaces remained in force. This physical vitality gave infrastructures the capacity to endure long after they had become inadequate, dangerous, or economically impractical.

As with structures, technological progress continually extended the longevity of infrastructures by bringing increasingly stress-resistant materials such as iron, steel, and concrete into use and by improving construction techniques. Even the most primitively constructed infrastructures were remarkably durable, however. The city of New York, for example, established the nucleus of its public water supply in 1800, using mains and pipes constructed out of hollowed logs as the basis of its distribution system. The capacity of these logs was limited, and leakage and blockages were constant problems. Nevertheless, the city stuck with them for nearly thirty years, finally beginning to replace them with iron conduits in 1828. In Boston, the leaky wooden mains laid by the Boston Aqueduct Company in the late 1790s to carry water from Jamaica Pond to the city were not replaced with iron pipes until 1840. By the some token, in Baltimore people made do with sewers constructed in the colonial period into the 1870s and 1880s and, in many cases, into the twentieth century. Many were nothing but brick or stone arches erected over ditches and old stream beds.[8]

Timely repairs helped keep ancient and rudimentary infrastructures like these in use, of course. Even unmaintained infrastructures could be exceedingly long lived, however. One example was Baltimore's McMeachan Street sewer, a wood and stone storm drain the origins of which are lost in antiquity but which probably dated from the late eighteenth or early nineteenth century. As described by the Department of Health in 1887, it was horrendously inadequate and unsanitary. Its wooden floor had rotted away many years before, and the city had not cleaned it, let alone repaired it, in years for fear that it would simply cave in if workers removed any of the dirt that had been accumulating in it. Yet it was still serviceable and very much in use.[9]

The proto-infrastructural land uses that preceded infrastructures tended to display a similar endurance. As horrified city health officials discovered, pumps and wells often remained in use for years after they had become contaminated with seepage from nearby privies and cesspools. Cesspools and privies often continued to be used for decades after they had become health hazards to individuals and the community at large. In fact, many of these proto-infrastructures were so physically durable that they eventually had to be forcibly closed down by municipal authorities.[10]

As was the case with structures, this remarkable longevity and enduring utility functioned as a barrier to change because there was a large, inelastic demand for the use of dangerous, unsanitary, overcrowded, and otherwise obsolete infrastructures and proto-infrastructures. People continued using them, no matter how inadequate they were, because they had no choice but to do so, for they provided essential supplies, like water, and services, like drainage and transportation, that could not be obtained in any other way.

As an editorial in the *Baltimore American* pointed out in 1860 with reference to the problems caused by bad gas lines,

> It is easy to say that no one is compelled to use gas against his will. But this is not strictly true.... When one has gas pipes all over his house, and no other means to substitute for satisfying light, he is compelled to make the best of a bad bargain. Bad as the light is, it is still better than a farthing dip.[11]

By the same token, a person whose home was inaccessible to any gas line had to keep using proto-infrastructural candles (farthing dips) because the meager light that candles provided was still better than no light at all.

This inelastic demand made it economically feasible and physically possible for utility companies and government agencies to ignore a community's need for better public services. When people could not induce or compel producers to make improvements, their only alternative was to move to a different geographical locality with a better infrastructural stock.[12] For many residents and businesses, however, this simply was not possible, either because they could not afford to move to a better area or, for reasons to be explained shortly, because there were no accessible areas which offered anything better.

Economic costs and the problem of site assembly

The capital-intensive, land-extensive character of infrastructures created frictions that slowed or obstructed the process of infrastructural improvement. Utility companies, transportation companies, and government agencies had to pay millions of dollars to buy the labor, the technology, and the materials that went into the construction of the streets, sewers, water works, railroad stations, fire stations, and other infrastructures that city dwellers needed.

They also had to pay large sums of money to acquire the sites on which they placed the new infrastructures and infrastructural improvements. Stores, warehouses, factories, and tenements lined city streets like walls, filling up the land needed for the provision of public services. Cities and utility and transportation companies not only had to buy the land covered by these buildings to make room for new facilities; they also had to move or renovate or demolish the buildings and compensate their owners and tenants for the economic losses they suffered from displacement.

In addition, they often had to pay a high price to take hold of sites that were already filled with other infrastructures. There was usually more than enough open public space available for site assembly in the early stages of a city's development, when street traffic was still sparse and underground conduits and overhead electric utilities were still small and few in number. As streets and sidewalks became more and more crowded, however, and as the number of tracks, pipes, and poles on and underneath them began to multiply, the assembly of this public space became a problem. At this point, for example, the number of streetcar and railroad tracks on a particular street could be increased only if the tracks were laid in the lanes that were already heavily used by carriages and trucks, so forcing the street's regular vehicular traffic onto other thoroughfares. The congestion on pedestrian-jammed business district sidewalks could be reduced only if the electric utility poles that lined them were eliminated or the sidewalks were widened by street narrowing, which further strangulated street traffic. Sewers and gas and water lines could be improved and subways built only if streets were torn up and the many utilities that already crowded underneath them were rearranged.[13]

Finally, in many cases improvers had to pay to make major changes in the land itself. For example, where hard to drain, low-lying ground or difficult to work hardpan and bedrock earth intensified the shortage of readily available underground space for building sewers and other sub-surface infrastructures, the land had to be raised with landfill. By the same token, in places where hills slowed the passage of horse-drawn vehicles or complicated the already complex process of laying sewers, the land had to be excavated and leveled.

Needless to say, all of these preparations were very expensive, not to mention time-consuming.[14] Between the capital costs of constructing infrastructures and the various costs of site assembly, it took cities and utility and transportation companies millions of dollars to build and redevelop most infrastructures. For cities, the cost of site assembly was especially high. Municipal governments did not face serious legal barriers to obtaining the space they needed. Because they had the power of eminent domain, they had only to follow prescribed legal procedures and condemn the property they wanted and the space was theirs. Because public rights of way in the streets provided space for underground and street-way infrastructures, they did not even have to condemn land formally to acquire sites for many kinds of improvements. This was also true of most utility and transportation companies. Because a number of state legislatures and courts granted them the power of eminent domain, they had no problem in taking legal possession of the space they needed to extend and redevelop their infrastructures, at least in many cities.

There were economic problems, however – problems that bore especially heavily on city governments. In addition to the costs of physically preparing a site was the cost of acquiring title to it. The law of eminent domain required that the owners of condemned land be fairly compensated for their property losses. Railroad and utility companies were often able to escape paying fair compensation because they were powerful enough to influence the condemnation juries that assessed damages and determined compensation awards. As several historians have pointed out, this served as an important public subsidy to American business and the private development of infrastructures.[15] Because of their political power, transportation and utility companies in many nineteenth century cities were also able to obtain liberal rights of way to sites in and under public streets simply by asking for franchises and rights of way. This typically required little financial outlay except the payment of influence-procuring bribes.[16]

Cities were not so lucky, however. Because they lacked the political and economic clout of giant railroad, streetcar, and utility companies, they were often forced to pay the full or even more than the full assessed valuation of the property they condemned. Condemnation juries typically awarded damages based on the subjects' exaggerated estimates of what their properties were worth. This meant that in many cases the cost of site assembly for cities completely dwarfed the capital cost of an improvement. The city of Baltimore, for example, spent $6,089,074 to widen and open streets in the fifteen years from 1878 through 1892. It expended less than four percent of this sum, $239,320, for paving, curbing, grading, and demolition materials and work. All the rest it spent on property damages.[17]

To pay for infrastructural improvements, city governments and transportation and utility companies raised money by issuing stocks and bonds, charging fees, and levying and collecting taxes. A friction in this phase of the redevelopment process was the impossibility of raising funds fast enough to provide all the public services businesses and city dwellers needed. The nineteenth and early twentieth centuries were punctuated by frequent depressions and recessions. These periods of retrenchment helped create backlogs of unsatisfied community demand for new and improved infrastructures that later put the companies and the government in even tighter financial binds.[18] In addition, many city governments and utility and transportation companies had to combat the unwillingness of investors to buy their bonds and other securities at anything but devastating discounts. Some newly established companies paid low or irregular dividends that made it difficult for them to sell their stocks and bonds.[19] Others had trouble selling their securities because they had serious political problems or, in an often related impasse, because their franchises were due to run out in a few years and it was not clear under what terms the franchises would be renewed or, indeed, if they would be renewed.[20] Cities often faced similar difficulties in marketing their bonds because of corruption scandals and the problems they encountered in establishing and maintaining sinking funds to pay interest and retire debt.[21]

Other factors also made it difficult for cities to finance infrastructural development. Taxpayer protests often made it politically impossible for them to raise taxes enough to cover the cost of major improvement projects. Worse, the law often made it illegal for them to issue enough bonds. By the 1870s, most cities operated under strict, state-imposed, municipal debt ceilings which limited their debts to fixed sums or to some fraction of their total assessed valuations. Since most cities usually operated at or near the limits, these ceilings often prevented them from undertaking any major infrastructural improvements, even extremely popular ones, for years, even decades, at a time. In addition, some state laws required cities to obtain the approval of a majority of their voters through passage of a bond referendum before issuing any bonds. Some also required them to obtain the approval of their state legislatures. Some, like Maryland's 1867 State Constitution, required them to get both. The purpose of these requirements was to protect taxpayers from spendthrift city governments. They also served, however, to prevent the implementation of desperately needed infrastructural improvement projects. Voters were especially apt to turn down referendums, even ones that promised to provide immense improvements in living conditions from which everyone would benefit. A particularly astonishing example of this was the defeat by the people of New Orleans in 1889 of a bond referendum that would have provided for the construction of a sewerage and drainage system for their marshy, epidemic-ridden, flood-plagued, almost completely undrained and unsewered city. They did not approve funding for the long-overdue system until 1899.[22]

Problems of supply and demand in the private sector

Additional frictions in the infrastructural improvement process resulted from the peculiar, collective way in which infrastructures were consumed and the monopolistic way in which they were produced. The basic problem was that monopoly power and public consumption destroyed the normal *quid pro quo* market exchange by which consumers traditionally transacted with producers to procure the things they wanted. They did this by enmeshing the people who wanted improvements in a web of supply and demand conditions that not only made producers insensitive to their demands, but also made it hard for consumers to express demands.

On the demand side, the market mechanism collapsed because individuals were unwilling to purchase voluntarily infrastructures and infrastructural improvements that many other people would ultimately use, often without paying for them. Few people had enough money to buy an entire infrastructure by themselves, of course. Even if individuals could afford to do so, however, few were willing to pay for anything more than the marginal benefit that they themselves would consume. Collective consumption meant that everyone who would benefit from an infrastructural improvement had somehow to transact with the producer to procure and contribute to its cost. It was difficult for city dwellers to engage in a collective transaction like this, however, because it was hard to achieve enough agreement and cooperation among the large number of people who were generally involved, people who usually had different preferences and abilities to pay. Such transactions were especially hard to bring off when unmarketable, unpurchasable, positive externalities like improvements in community-wide business and living conditions were at stake.

At the same time, the market mechanism collapsed on the supply side because the monopolistic character of infrastructures created the captive markets that producers needed in order to ignore demands for improvements. The market mechanism also broke down because producers were unwilling to provide improvements unless there was sufficient demand to justify production, something the demand constraints frequently prevented consumers from expressing. Finally, collective consumption often made it physically difficult and expensive for producers to charge consumers on a private, market basis for the use of public goods. For example, while it was possible for producers to attach pay boxes to streetcars and meters to the pipes that connected houses to water systems, it was very difficult for them to charge individuals for the proportionate benefit each derived from the collective use of streets, street lighting, sewers, fire hydrants, and many other public services. Worse, it was often nonsensical for them to try to do so, especially by traditional market methods. There simply was no way for them to charge people via the voluntary exchange mechanism of the market system for the positive externalities they unwittingly consumed in the form of better health conditions, better business climates, public safety, and the like.[23]

These conditions served as frictions in the process of infrastructural development because they simultaneously undermined *both* the willingness and ability of consumers to demand improvements *and* the willingness of producers to supply them. People could still use the press, private contacts, and political pressure to try to induce producers to provide the public services they needed. The difficulty was that when companies in the private sector were involved, consumers and producers were nonetheless required to interact within the confines of the market system.

What does this mean? It means that there was a market breakdown that made it very difficult for city dwellers to motivate transportation and utility

companies to provide desperately needed improvements. This was not supposed to happen. In granting corporate charters and franchises to transportation and utility companies, state and local governments usually
commanded the companies to serve the public interest. The fact was, however, that the companies were established to make money for their investors.
As a result, they naturally ignored demands for improvements which could
not generate a satisfactory profit. As a committee of Aldermen noted in a
report on the dismal failure of the Baltimore Water Company to provide the
people of Baltimore with an adequate water supply, "It could not be expected
[that they would] consult the public good when the benefit of the community
could be had only by the sacrifice of corporate interest."[24]

The companies' profit orientation obstructed infrastructural improvement
in several ways. At worst, when ineptly or corruptly managed firms enjoyed
a legal monopoly, it completely stultified development. For example, the
badly mismanaged New Orleans Sewerage Company laid no more than a
few hundred feet of sewers in its nearly twenty years of existence, none of
which ever went into operation. The stockholders and contractors associated
with the company apparently put most of the money raised to finance the
proposed system directly into their own pockets. This unproductive profiteering was a disaster for marshy, epidemic-ridden New Orleans, because
the New Orleans Sewerage Company was the only organization with the
authority to construct a sewer system in the city between 1880 and 1899.
New Orleans remained unsewered and undrained until the end of the nineteenth century, when, as noted earlier, voters finally passed the bond issue
that enabled the city government to take over the project.[25]

Most often, however, utility and transportation companies constructed at
least some of the facilities people needed. The problem was that they balked
at making such unprofitable, but socially desirable improvements as extending their systems into poor or remote neighborhoods, removing pollu-
tion- and congestion-causing facilities, and replacing and upgrading old
equipment to accommodate increased usage, technological change, and
physical deterioration.

Again, the impact on city development and redevelopment was harshest
when a company enjoyed an exclusive franchise to supply an infrastructure
to a municipality, which was usually the case with companies established
before the Civil War. Water monopolies like the Baltimore Water Company,
the Manhattan Company, and the Boston Aqueduct Company, for example,
skimmed only the fattest markets in their respective cities. They tapped their
local springs, streams, and ponds, laid some pipes in the most remunerative
downtown areas, and then did next to nothing to improve their systems
unless forced by government authorities or extreme public pressure. In the
process, they left huge middle class districts as well as most poor areas

completely unsupplied, while refusing to provide free or cheap water and hydrants for such public purposes as fighting fires. They also failed to maintain their pipes and pumping facilities properly, periodically forcing their customers to bear long disruptions in service. And they refused to develop new sources to replace local supplies of increasingly brackish and contaminated water.[26]

Competition made the companies more sensitive to people's needs. In fact, competitive streetcar, railroad, gas, and electric utility companies sometimes raced to gain footholds in very marginal areas in order to forestall the subsequent entry of other firms and to lay the groundwork for territorial monopolies which could be of considerable value later. In so doing, they sometimes went so far as to cut prices, accepting short-term losses in the hope of future gain.[27]

This sort of cut-throat competition rarely lasted very long, however, for the companies soon tired of losing money and, as a result, reestablished and consolidated their monopoly power by merging or by peacefully dividing disputed territories among themselves. What is important is that while they might compete to build new infrastructures and thus extend their territorial hegemony, as profit-maximizing institutions they were extremely reluctant to redevelop existing infrastructures, since the people who used them had no choice but to use them no matter how inadequate they were. With no internal motivations to make such changes, most telephone, telegraph, and electric companies, for example, refused to voluntarily take down their dangerous and encumbering poles and rooftop fixtures and move their hazardous overhead wires underground. Gas companies refused to replace their old, small, leaky pipes. Railroad and streetcar companies declined to voluntarily interconnect and systematize their lines and terminals so that interruptions in travel and traffic could be reduced and the transfer of freight and passengers facilitated. Needless to say, this bias against infrastructural redevelopment was an especially serious problem in the inner city, where most antiquated infrastructures in a city usually were located.[28]

It would be easy to blame these failures on simple greed and abuse of monopoly power. There was more involved, however. The fundamental cause was the fact that infrastructures were public goods, while the companies were profit-making institutions that had to make their investment decisions within the context of the private market. As all economic actors do, the managers of these companies based their decisions on their evaluations of the utility to be derived. Because of the way the market system worked, however, their assessments of utility inevitably encompassed only the private benefits accruing to the companies themselves. They did not include unmarketable positive externalities and unprofitable, "inexhaustible" collective goods, for these things could not be traded on the market and monetized and distributed internally as profit. This meant that by their very nature as market institutions, the companies chronically underproduced many kinds of infrastructural improvements.

Problems of supply and demand in the public sector: institutional barriers to government involvement

Theoretically, government intervention in the infrastructural improvement process offered the perfect solution to this market breakdown. As political institutions operating outside the private market, rather than profit-maximizing institutions operating inside it, governments not only were much freer to produce unremunerative public goods and unmarketable positive externalities to meet consumer demands, but they were also far more responsive to non-market forms of demand articulation, such as voting, petitioning, and other kinds of public pressure, than were private companies. In addition, their taxing powers gave them an important, non-market means to finance improvements. This gave them extraordinary power to make improvements in areas where the inhabitants could not afford to pay for them. It also gave them the means to finance improvements that could not be paid for through ordinary market transactions between consumers and producers.

Government officials accordingly attempted to counteract the private sector's insensitivity to public needs through regulation, subsidization, and, on occasion, municipal production. Unfortunately, however, they operated under certain constraints, one of the most serious of which was the nature of government decision making in nineteenth century cities.

Government intervention in the infrastructural improvement process replaced the narrowly focused, "bottom line," market-based decision making practices of the private sector with a process of political decision making that was based on the democratic idea of consensual agreement. Unlike utility and transportation company executives, who operated in a corporate arena on behalf of stockholders, government officials operated in a political arena on behalf of voters and taxpayers, who were the very people who used and paid for infrastructures. In essence, the officials took the separate consumption and production activities that the market normally arbitrated and proceeded to fuse them into a single decision making process: the politically arbitrated process of government decision making.

The problem was that because thousands, even millions, of people consumed and paid for infrastructures, all the difficulties and dilemmas of large-group decision making were incorporated into the production process.[29] Disagreements could and often did stifle the improvement process, even where there was an obvious and objective community need for improvement.

People disagreed about the desirability of undertaking specific improvement projects on many grounds, not all of which were relevant to the exigencies of particular community needs. For example, some people inevitably opposed improvements simply because they did not want to pay for them with their hard-earned tax dollars, regardless of the benefits. Others fought improvement projects because they did not see themselves as the obvious beneficiaries. As Sam Bass Warner, Jr. has pointed out, people's interest in their neighbors' welfare was undermined by privatism, the American cultural tradition that values individualism and the quest for personal happiness and wealth above all else. The demographic growth and geographical expansion of cities also made it increasingly difficult for many city dwellers to perceive their interdependence and understand the need to share their tax dollars to improve their own and their increasingly multitudinous neighbors' lives.[30]

Another source of dissension was the displacement and inconvenience that infrastructural improvements caused. Site assembly was not only a serious economic barrier to change; it was also an important social and political problem. Space was scarce in nineteenth and early twentieth century cities. As a result, a proposal to take any bit of space out of private hands for public use inevitably set off waves of outrage and protest among the users, residents, and owners of the site in question. People fought to save their real estate investments and their homes from condemnation and the wrecker's ball when street widenings and other infrastructural improvements involving the demolition of buildings were proposed. They also strove to save their neighborhoods from the congestion, noise, smoke, and danger of the railroads, from the smells and miasmas of municipal abbatoirs and garbage dumps, and from the dangers and disease of hospitals and prisons.[31]

In extreme cases, when all else failed, people threatened with displacement vowed to stop change with violence, or else they simply refused to move. When the streets in Boston's slum-ridden Fort Hill District were leveled and widened in the 1860s, for example, the area's impoverished denizens clung to their houses "until the roofs were taken off and their rooms laid open to the sky." The police finally had to evict them forcibly.[32] More frequently, however, the individuals and corporations so affected turned to the political process to stop unwanted change. Their ability to pressure judges, state legislators, and city council members to compromise, delay, or block improvements created powerful political site assembly barriers to infrastructural improvement.[33]

Here again, privatism reinforced the friction. People typically opposed improvement projects that threatened them with harm, regardless of whether the benefits to the community as a whole outweighed the injury done to them as individuals.

The problem transcended selfishness, however, for in some cases it resulted from land use trade-offs that played one kind of public interest against another, that played people's need for parks against their need for efficient street and mass transportation networks, for example, or the need of pedestrians for space to walk against the need of other people for space to drive vehicles. The lawyer Samuel W. Bates summed up the problem well in 1872 when he spoke on behalf of a group of Bostonians who were protesting the creation of another passenger railway line in congested downtown Boston:

> There is a limit to space. The old doctrine that two bodies cannot occupy the same space is as true today as it ever was . . . and the question is, in certain cases, which shall give way? Shall the people in the cars be crowded, or shall the cars and the other travel in the streets be crowded? There is inconvenience, injury, evil in both cases, but which shall give way?[34]

The fact was that none of the parties ever wanted to give way, and in some cases there was no objective answer to the question of which represented the greater public good. This caused large-group decision making problems that complicated collective decision making in truly profound ways.

Finally, people disputed the desirability of instituting particular improvements for more mundane reasons, arguing with each other on grounds that were more or less extraneous to any specific improvement plan. For example, they often failed to see eye to eye on general government expenditures and so quarreled over such things as what the overall size of the municipal budget should be and how much the city should spend on one public service vis-à-vis the rest. They were also divided along political lines, disputing the merits of improvement plans because of political rivalries and fights over spoils, like the patronage that construction would provide.[35]

Because the government decision making process was a democratic consensus building process, these large-group decision making difficulties seriously constrained the public sector's capacity to respond to city dwellers' needs for more and better public services. It was not that government was deaf to many expressions of demand in the way that the private sector was, however. Instead, the problem was that the super-sensitive political dynamic of government decision making opened up the infrastructural improvement process to endless disputation and stalemate.

It took public officials in Boston over twenty years to approve a plan to construct a desperately needed public water works system, for example. They began debating the advisability of constructing the system after a disastrous fire occurred in 1825. They continued debating it for more than ten years, until an informal citizens' referendum finally forced them to begin drawing up plans for the actual construction of the system. They then debated the relative merits of several competing plans for another ten years, after which they agreed to build the Cochituate System. Even worse, public officials in Baltimore temporized over plans to construct a public water system for more than thirty years from start to finish. They debated the issue for more than five years, until fires, a cholera epidemic, and the brackish and insufficient waters of the local water company finally produced a consensus on the desirability of construction. They then wrangled over what plan to institute for another twenty years, when they finally agreed to build a system that drew water from the Gunpowder River.[36]

State and municipal laws compounded the public sector's vulnerability to this kind of inaction. They did so by fragmenting municipal decision making authority to such an extent that infrastructural improvement became a question of reaching not one but many political agreements, a difficult process in each case that put the improvement plans at the mercy of the vagaries of large-group decision making.

Most city councils were made up of two houses, both of which had to approve an improvement plan before it could be implemented. In addition, at least one city council committee had to approve each plan, as did the mayor and, in some cities, various executive branch committees. Most Victorian era city governments labored under narrowly framed and antiquated city charters that did not specifically grant them the authority they needed to undertake some kinds of improvement. As a result, in these cases, city officials had to engage in another complicated step in the consensus building process, this time one that involved securing approval from the two independent houses of state government. As noted earlier, most cities also operated under state-imposed bond referendum requirements. This meant that city officials also had to secure the formal approval of a majority of the voters in order to finance some improvement plans. Finally, in those instances in which improvements were especially controversial, city officials often had to obtain judicial endorsement of their plans from justices at various levels of the state and federal court system before they could implement them.[37]

Needless to say, each of these institutionalized steps in the government decision making process gave the opponents of an improvement plan an opportunity to kill it. The Boston City Council repeatedly petitioned the Massachusetts legislature for authority to assess betterment taxes to help finance street improvements between 1845 and 1865, for example. Each time the legislators ignored or defeated the Council's request. The legislators' stubborn independence forced the city to defer making some much desired street improvements for more than twenty years.[38]

By the same token, in the 1880s, 1890s, and early 1900s, the Illinois Supreme Court almost singlehandedly prevented public officials in Chicago from carrying out plans to force the city's streetcar companies to systematize and modernize their infamously antiquated and inconveniently arranged tracks, routes, and terminal facilities. In this particularly dramatic example of municipal impotence, the Court stopped improvement by repeatedly upholding the "vested rights" conveyed to the streetcar companies in 1865 by the state legislature when the legislature passed the controversial "99 Year Act," which extended the companies' franchises to ninety-nine years. The State Supreme Court's position enabled the street car companies to retain complete control of Chicago's streets until 1906, when the Supreme Court finally declared the "99 Year Act" unconstitutional. Because of the nature of the franchises, the city of Chicago had no power to force the companies to make improvements and no power to make the improvements on its own until after the beginning of the twentieth century. And even then, the State Supreme Court played the role of spoiler, preventing the city from acting to improve the situation. Despite the passage of a series of referendums in which Chicagoans authorized the city to municipalize the streetcar lines, the Court prevented the city from carrying out this plan of action by disallowing a state law that would have permitted the city to finance municipalization by issuing special debt certificates that would have skirted its restrictive municipal debt ceiling.[39]

In sum, like private companies, city governments operated under a great many institutional constraints that prevented them from moving quickly to provide the public services that city dwellers needed. The important thing about these supply-side problems was that they had a cumulative effect. The delays involved in building a consensus at one level of government added to the delays involved in reaching a consensus at every other level. Together these delays could stall the infrastructural improvement process for decades.

Problems of supply and demand in the public sector: problems of collective demand articulation

The interjection of the government into the infrastructural improvement process did not completely solve the demand articulation problems that obstructed the provision of public services in nineteenth and early twentieth century cities. The demand-side frictions were far more subtle and insidious than the supply-side frictions. They obstructed the adaptation of the environment by making it difficult for city dwellers to induce suppliers to provide the public services they wanted through the political process.

As explained earlier, it was almost impossible for people to express effective, collective demands for public goods through the individualistic *quid pro quo* exchange process of the market system because of the problems of joint consumption, externalities, and monopolistic production. Yet the only formal mechanisms for articulating demand through the political process were the election vote and the petition. Unfortunately, the vote, the more readily available of the two, was an extremely unwieldy and indirect mechanism. It merely gave voters the right to participate in the selection of public officials, which was not, of course, the same as the power to endorse or reject a political candidate's stand on any particular issue. As a result, people could not use the vote to communicate clearly a collective desire for a specific infrastructural improvement, unless that improvement was the paramount issue in an election, which was rarely the case. Most political campaigns in nineteenth and early twentieth century cities turned on issues such as ethnicity and party identification and organization that were usually unrelated or only indirectly related to the improvement of specific public services.[40]

To complicate matters, the vote served merely as an indicator of demand. Unlike the *quid pro quo* of the private market, it did not function as a mechanism for articulating effective demand, for it did not enable voters to acquire desired improvements immediately. Instead, even at best, it simply enabled successful voters to get their demands placed on a legislative agenda for further governmental consideration. It was up to legislators and administrators to transact with producers to produce an actual improvement. This, in turn, required the successful resolution of a problematic and often very convoluted legislative or bureaucratic consensus building process.

The right to petition legislators and administrators for specific improvements provided citizens with a less oblique way of making their collective needs known. Like the vote, however, petitions merely functioned as demand indicators, as instruments for influencing government agenda setting. They were not a means by which city dwellers could directly acquire public goods and services.

Because of these inherent weaknesses in the formal mechanisms of collective demand articulation, people who were determined to obtain public improvements as quickly as possible turned to less formal, more direct methods of influencing decision makers. Not surprisingly, given many legislators' and bureaucrats' interests in personal aggrandizement, they found political proxies for the *quid pro quo* transactions of the private market to be the most expedient instruments for obtaining their desires. The most obvious proxy was, of course, a monetary bribe, but non-pecuniary exchanges also offered effective surrogates for the market mechanism. Unlike the vote, such *quid pro quo* transactions gave private citizens a way to secure an official's commitment on a specific measure. As a result, as innumerable political reformers, muckrakers, and urban historians have pointed out, the "big payoff" became one of the principal bases of government decision making in nineteenth century cities.

Urban historians have often interpreted these pay-offs as benefits with which machine politicians rewarded their supporters. In an influential book,

Seymour J. Mandelbaum has gone so far as to link this reward system to a political communications failure that resulted from the lack of effective intra-city postal, telegraph, and telephone service and the absence of an unbiased, unsegmented urban press, a situation which, he argues, forced government officials to pay bribes in order to mobilize support for government expend-itures in the socially and geographically fragmented cities of the nineteenth century. In Mandelbaum's words, "The lines of communication were too narrow, the patterns of deference too weak to support freely acknowledged and stable leadership. Only a universal payment of benefits – a giant pay-off – could pull the city together in a common effort."[41]

There was, as Mandelbaum asserts, a serious communications gap that pay-offs were designed to bridge. The gap resulted from problems that were much more fundamental than the technological conditions to which he refers, however, namely, the very nature of the public goods that government pro-vided and the intrinsic weakness of the vote as an instrument of collective demand articulation. These factors forced the *users* of urban public services to turn to political equivalents of the market's *quid pro quo*, as well as power-hungry politicians.[42]

Lobbying gave city dwellers a more ethical way to manipulate decision makers, but it was a less potent demand articulation mechanism. Proponents of a particular improvement simply used their own influence or the influence of colleagues and agents to try to convince officials that their improvement would produce an important public benefit, rather than promising them that it would yield an important private benefit.

The problem with these two relatively effective demand mechanisms was that only rich and powerful people had ready access to them. Unlike the vote and the petition, they were not formally institutionalized as universal and equally available rights of all enfranchised citizens. Instead, their use depended on people's wealth and influence and access to individual legislators and administrators, properties which were very unevenly distributed in urban populations. Precisely because they functioned as superior communications mechanisms, however, government decision makers relied on them to gather the information they needed to decide how to allocate their limited funds. Their receptiveness to lobbied and pay-off-backed constituent demands prejudiced the whole process of government decision making against the needs of poor and politically weak groups in favor of the relatively narrow interests of a few, comparatively privileged individuals and groups.

Unfortunately, the widespread use of betterment assessments to finance some infrastructural improvements reinforced this discriminatory tendency in the dynamic of government decision making by establishing financial incentives that actively discouraged poor citizens from demanding desirable improvements. Betterment assessments were mandatory, one-time taxes levied at the time an improvement was constructed on the landowners whose properties abutted on the improvement. They had two big advantages as instruments of municipal finance. Designed to force landowners to pay a part of the cost of improvements that directly benefited their properties, they enabled city officials to undertake more improvements than would have been possible if the officials had had to rely exclusively on regular tax revenues and debt financing for the purpose. They also legitimized, to some extent, the construction of improvements at the behest of land speculators, since they forced these people to contribute directly to the cost of making speculative improvements.[43]

The problem was that because they were special taxes levied on abutters, betterment assessments served as another friction in the infrastructural improvement process that made it difficult for poor people to get improvements constructed in their neighborhoods. On the one hand, impoverished property owners could not afford to pay betterment taxes. On the other, ambitious, income-oriented, absentee slumlords had no desire to pay them. People who could not or would not contribute to the cost of an improvement rarely petitioned, lobbied, or bribed officials to get one instituted. Quite the contrary, they often strenuously resisted being forced to pay for something they had not requested in the first place.[44]

These class biases in the process of demand articulation contributed to the persistence of obsolete infrastructures both by giving certain groups special powers to block improvement plans and by giving some groups special powers to obtain them. Because their funds were limited, cities were always in a position of having to choose among competing claims on their budgets. What the biased articulation of demand did was constantly encourage them to make trade-offs that exacerbated environmental problems. First, it encouraged officials to construct improvements in upper and middle class areas, rather than in poor districts, since middle and upper class people generally had the upper hand in the demand articulation process. Second, it encouraged officials to extend infrastructures into outlying areas at the behest of land developers, rather than redevelop existing ones in settled areas, because land developers who hoped to make a large sum of money developing real estate were generally far more aggressive demanders of improvements than people who merely wished to better public health, safety, and convenience. Finally, it encouraged officials to take a piecemeal approach to infrastructural improvement, rather than a coordinated, planned approach, because petitions, bribes, and special interest lobbying entrapped decision makers in an inherently particularistic and *ad hoc* process of information gathering and project development.[45]

All of these effects discouraged infrastructural redevelopment in poor neighborhoods. Significantly, they also resulted in a general prejudice against inner city improvements that disadvantaged commercial as well as residential neighborhoods, hurting their poor and comparatively well-to-do inhabitants alike.[46]

Municipalities were almost always busy paving and repaving the heavily traveled streets of inner city business districts. Beyond this, however, business districts were in much the same position as inner city slums, for city governments concentrated on extending basic public services into rapidly developing outlying areas at the expense of redeveloping them in densely settled, aging inner city areas. It is true that like suburban real estate developers, powerful corporations and business district property owners enjoyed privileged positions on the demand articulation continuum that generally gave them an advantage in demanding that improvements be made. The fact was, however, that it was in built-up business districts that powerful corporations and property owners were most severely threatened by the site assembly problem and were in especially strong positions to block improvement.

Apathy further discouraged infrastructural redevelopment in the inner city, in business districts as well as residential areas. As noted earlier, once basic public services were established, people tended to make do with what they had, no matter how unsafe, inadequate, or inconvenient it was. Since merely complaining about a problem was usually not enough to produce a change, this sort of acceptance amounted to a failure of demand articulation.

Ignorance also took its toll. Many infrastructures were literally invisible because they were underground. Others were figuratively invisible because they were so taken for granted that people paid little attention to them or so technically complex that few people wanted to think about them. It was easy for inner city residents to put up with an obsolete infrastructure that they could not see or only dimly understood, at least until it completely broke down and caused a terrible accident, epidemic, or fire. As the *New York Evening Post* observed in 1900 in regard to the problems of renovating New York City's subterranean maze of antiquated water, sewer, gas, and other utility conduits, "The proverb, 'out of sight, out of mind,' applies with peculiar force to everything underground, especially when the very magnitude of the problem discourages its discussion."[47] Indeed, as this study will later show, because of the transitory nature of most disasters, even complete breakdowns often failed to generate enough public interest to force a government to undertake a desperately needed improvement. This meant that one of the most important demand barriers to infrastructural improvement was the lack of any expression of public demand for some improvements, either ineffective or effective demand, until long after the infrastructures became seriously dysfunctional.[48]

The growth of machine politics in the second half of the nineteenth century appears to have reinforced the class and geographical biases in the demand articulation process, strengthening the public sector's tendency to ignore the inner city in favor of extending public services to the suburbs. The work of keeping up these machines both discouraged machine "bosses" from making infrastructural improvements in inner city areas and made it politically feasible for them to neglect making such improvements. Machine politicians found it efficient to finance their machines with the lucrative bribes and graft they could obtain from provision of the public improvements demanded by residents and real estate developers in outlying middle class areas. Indeed, they sometimes found this an effective way to broaden their power bases to include segments of the new suburban middle class. At the same time, the jobs, legal aid, and other social services generated by these machines made their impoverished constituents devoted followers who loyally supported them in every election, whether or not the politicians provided them with infrastructural improvements.[49]

The development of public interest lobbies ultimately helped offset some of these demand articulation problems. Civic groups like the Citizens' Associations formed in Chicago and other cities were established on a permanent basis to investigate city problems and promote general community improvements. The public interest label was, of course, self-assumed. Members, however, clearly viewed themselves as countervailing forces against special interests, like land developers and transportation corporations, which lobbied for only those local improvements that would benefit themselves. As a result, these groups pressed for the kinds of improvements that special interests typically ignored or opposed and that grafting politicians generally eschewed. Since the leaders of most public interest organizations were business and industrial elites, the groups tended to focus their lobbying efforts on the redevelopment of obsolete infrastructures in commercial and industrial districts. Significantly, however, some, like the Citizens' Association of Chicago,[50] pursued a concept of the public interest that was broad enough to embrace environmental problems in working class districts, in both peripheral and central areas. Thus some groups also helped create a more powerful public demand for neglected improvements outside the business area as well. Similar organizations, like tenement house reform associations and settlement house associations, also lobbied for parks, sewers, and other infrastructural improvements in working class districts on behalf of the relatively inarticulate or apathetic laborers who lived there.

As much as they helped redress imbalances in the demand articulation process, however, these organizations generally had a relatively limited impact on the process of infrastructural improvement itself, at least until progressive reformers gained control of city government at the end of the period under study here. Few existed until the last few decades of the nineteenth century. In fact, most were not founded until inner city infrastructures had already begun breaking down. One of the first, the Chicago Citizens' Association, was not established until 1874, after Chicago had suffered two disastrous great fires. Once the organizations were established, members spent decades struggling against the vested interests protected by political machines, unable to exert much influence on public policy except during inevitably short-lived reform administrations. As noted earlier, the problem was that the mere expression of a demand in the political arena did not automatically guarantee that the demand would be satisfied. As a result, even after progressive reformers gained sustained power in America's great cities, the public interest organizations' activities were usually little more than critical first steps in what was still a long and complicated process of infrastructural improvement.

Thus it was that for a wide variety of reasons government intervention failed to eliminate many of the barriers to environmental redevelopment created by the failure of the private market to provide the public services that city dwellers needed. Like the institutional constraints, the biases in the demand articulation process never completely stopped officials from paving streets, extending or redeveloping sewers and water mains, or building parks, schools, and fire stations in working class districts and inner city areas. They did, however, lead to an emphasis on improvements in outlying middle and upper class areas that slowed the improvement process elsewhere. The crux of the problem was that city budgets were limited, while the need for more and better public services was virtually unlimited. This made trade-offs between competing demands on city treasuries inevitable, trade-offs that, because of the nature of the demand articulation process, benefited the suburbs and the middle class at the expense of aging, overcrowded central business districts and unsanitary, overcrowded inner city slums.

Technological and informational constraints

Despite the many barriers to infrastructural improvements, city governments and utility and transportation companies did, over time, manage to develop and redevelop the public services under their control. As was the case with structural improvement, however, a lack of requisite technology created frictions that impeded the process of improvement. Technological innovation was critical to almost every kind of improvement in this period, from the mundane to the complex, from, for example, the pavement of streets to the construction of electric power networks and generating plants. Almost every change required the development of new materials, new machinery, new design theories, and new construction techniques. Because these technological innovations emerged slowly, civil engineers were nearly always limited in their efforts to design infrastructures that would meet their communities' changing needs.

No analysis of the evolution of modern civil engineering will be attempted here. The important point is that the general material and experimental problems that retarded the emergence of modern architecture, problems discussed in some detail in the last chapter, also held up progress here. Like architects, civil engineers had to develop and improve their construction techniques and designs in a gradual and experimental way. Much of the pioneering work in the use of structural iron and steel and reinforced concrete was, in fact, done by them. As one engineer pointed out in an 1878 article on the prospects of substituting steel for iron in bridge construction, innovation was continual. It was also, however, slow, painstaking, and risky. "Only those who have engaged in the building of iron bridges from the beginning to the present day," the engineer wrote, "could give a full and correct account of all thought, anxiety, and patient experimentation gone through with to develop the present forms" of wrought-iron construction currently in use.[51]

As the contention and confusion evident in professional debates over emerging and competing infrastructural technologies make clear, the need to experiment had many costs. Not only did technological progress lag behind environmental necessity, but even when innovations were achieved, engineers frequently failed to recognize them immediately as such and adopt them on a universal scale. Their ignorance made design mistakes and the rapid obsolescence of new infrastructures inevitable.

To complicate matters, civil engineers had difficulty correctly anticipating future economic and population growth, especially in the first half of the nineteenth century, when city growth rates defied all attempts to base predictions on past experience. The rapidity with which migrants and immigrants poured into cities amazed even those people who studied population statistics professionally. In Boston, for example, in 1845, the leading expert on the city's population growth surveyed the teeming slums in the city's North End and argued that the area could not hold any more inhabitants than it already did. "Where is there room for more?" he asked. Yet the massive influx of immigrants from Ireland was just beginning. Needless to say, this inability to plan for future needs further doomed conscientious and well-meaning engineers to the making of mistakes.[52]

As Chicago's trouble with its sewerage system makes clear, these two technical problems interacted synergically, sometimes permanently deforming infrastructures that had been painstakingly designed by presumably well-intentioned engineers. Devised in the mid-1850s, Chicago's sewerage system was a unified storm and sanitary drainage system that was composed of a network of brick feeder pipes and larger brick collecting pipes that emptied into the Chicago River. Because sanitary engineering was still in its infancy, and because it was difficult to predict the course of Chicago's growth, the designers of the system made serious mistakes in developing their plans. Significantly, their misguided decisions produced a legacy of problems that continue to plague the city today.

One mistake was their decision to have the sewage drain directly into the Chicago River. At the time, this appeared to be the most advantageous means of disposal available. The engineers believed that the river would dilute the sewage enough to render it harmless before it entered Lake Michigan, the city's source of drinking water. They also believed that storms and freshets would flush out any sediment that might settle to the bottom. If necessary, lake water could be pumped into the river. The plan appeared to be much safer and cheaper than the only other politically and economically feasible method of disposal, which was to drain the sewage into artificial reservoirs and make it available for use as manure. Since the engineers expected little demand for the manure, they feared that the reservoirs would quickly fill up and become dangerous to public health.[53]

Because the Chicago River was still relatively clean and the technology for safely turning sewage into fertilizer had barely begun to be developed, this assessment of the alternatives was undoubtedly completely reasonable. But it overestimated the strength of the current in the river and did not take into account the future growth of slaughterhouses, rendering establishments, and other industries of this type upstream. The last oversight turned out to be particularly disastrous, for within a few years the rapidly increasing quantity of wastes and other foul material being dumped into the slow-moving river destroyed any possibility of the waterway's acting as a natural purifier of the city's sewage. This excessive influx of sewage not only contaminated the lake; it also created a major sanitary hazard in the heart of the community. The city repeatedly attempted to eliminate or reduce the problem in the next decades. It did not even begin to meet with success until the twentieth century, however, when the Chicago Sanitary and Ship Canal project, the biggest, most expensive public works project in the world up to that time, was finally completed, the current in the river reversed, and the sewage made to flow into the Mississippi River rather than the lake. Thus serious problems had been designed into the plan of the system from the beginning.[54]

The engineers' decision to construct a unified storm and sanitary sewerage system turned out to be a similar mistake. Unified systems create substantial pollution dangers if the collecting pipes ever back up and flood, since they mix sewage with storm run-off. They are especially hazardous in places like Chicago where low, flat land makes it extremely difficult to achieve enough of an incline in the collecting pipes and sufficiently high outfalls to prevent flooding during storms. Unfortunately, engineers did not generally recognize this fact until the late 1890s and, until then, hotly debated the relative merits of the combined and separate plans. The matter was especially unsettled back in the 1850s. Chicago's municipal engineers evidently considered constructing two systems, for they stated in their 1855 report and plan that some "very respected" authorities were recommending the separate systems idea as the only means of achieving "perfect drainage." They concluded, however, that separate systems were "unnecessary," since other, equally respected experts advocated the combined plan.[55]

Regrettably, they then compounded the resulting flooding danger by deciding to use narrow three- to six-foot drain pipes for the sewer mains, even though they freely admitted that the pipes lacked the capacity to handle all of the run-off from bad storms and would become more and more inadequate as the city expanded. They took this decision on economic and practical grounds, arguing that they could not design a drainage system that would be completely safe from floods "without enormous expense" and that, furthermore, the pipes could easily be replaced later with more technically advanced conduits, to the benefit of the entire system.[56] Unfortunately, this last assumption was, of course, completely wrong. Redevelopment was not easy and, rather than upgrade existing pipes, the Department of Public Works simply extended them across the city. Except for a few local renovations necessitated by breakdowns and other emergencies, it did not begin the replacement process until the 1920s. Indeed, almost a hundred years after the first sewers were laid, engineers were complaining that many of the original mains were still in use, despite their by then very primitive construction.[57]

Had the engineers foreseen how difficult it would be to tear up the streets and redevelop the system, they might well have opted for a dual system, or at least used larger pipes in the beginning. Unfortunately, they did not. Thus they unintentionally condemned the city to a history of severe flooding and, because the system mixed sewage with storm water and emptied it all into the Chicago River and thence into Lake Michigan, to serious pollution and health troubles as well. The opening of the Chicago Ship and Sanitary Canal and the construction of sewage treatment and water purification plants considerably reduced the threat to the water supply in the twentieth century. Nevertheless, flooding and pollution problems remained and have continued to plague property owners and beach goers into the 1980s. Today Chicago's streets and basements are still regularly flooded with a mixture of sewage and rainwater during storms, and the local rivers become receptacles for raw sewage roughly one hundred times per year, despite the construction of sewage treatment plants. The lake itself receives raw sewage at least once per year, on average, whenever the rivers become so gorged that officials are forced to open the gates closing them off from the lake to keep them from overflowing.[58]

Again, these flaws were unwittingly designed into the system at the beginning and, as a result, can be solved only by a complete redevelopment of the entire system, something that has been held up by all the physical, economic, political, and institutional barriers to infrastructural improvement discussed earlier.[59] This kind of problem was a pervasive friction in the infrastructural improvement process in the nineteenth century. Like architects of that era, civil engineers made impressive strides toward developing the technology that would enable them to solve the environmental problems of rapidly growing Victorian cities. Unfortunately, however, they progressed too slowly. As a result, they often had to design and build infrastructures before they had obtained the knowledge to build them properly. Worse, they sometimes misread their communities' emerging needs and so made poor use of existing technology, such as it was.

Other constraints

Mistakes made by well-meaning but misguided engineers were not the cause of all the flaws incorporated into the infrastructures of Victorian cities, however. Even within the sometimes narrow parameters imposed by inadequate technology and faulty forecasts of future need, engineers usually had the capacity to build infrastructures that represented significant progress over the infrastructures and proto-infrastructures they replaced, if the private companies and government agencies that employed the engineers let them do what they thought best and had the wherewithal to pay for all the land, labor, and material the engineers needed to implement their plans. The problem was, of course, that corporate and government decision makers often chose to do less than was technically feasible and sometimes could not afford to undertake all that was required, for the same physical, economic, political, and institutional reasons that they tended to postpone making improvements in the first place. These problems have already been discussed in detail. The only difference is that instead of forestalling improvements, in this case they served to undermine the effectiveness of improvements that were made.[60]

The picture should not be overdrawn. No matter how inconvenient they were to use, how costly they were to maintain properly, or how dangerous they were to public health or safety, most infrastructural improvements were definite advances over what they supplanted. Moreover, as technological and informational constraints were overcome, more and more improvements did, indeed, come to represent remarkably effective adaptations of the built environment.

Nevertheless, the large-scale, land-extensive, capital-intensive, collective, externality-ridden character of infrastructures did create barriers to infrastructural redevelopment that prevented city dwellers from obtaining infrastructures that were fully adapted to their needs. Some misbegotten infrastructures were so dysfunctional that they simply self-destructed. They quickly wore out, as did the primitive wood and stone pavements in use in most cities through much of the nineteenth century, or burned up, as did Chicago's wood-roofed water works and wooden sidewalks, or collapsed under their own weight, as did the western arched approach to Philadelphia's South Street Bridge and badly designed sewers in many cities. Most were not so bad as this. Almost all were indeed flawed, but they were also serviceable parts of their environments that endured for decades, no matter how inadequate they were. This, of course, was what made the persistence of obsolete infrastructures such a serious problem in nineteenth and early twentieth century American cities.

Infrastructural improvement and municipal reform

Given the severity of the public health problems and the other dangers and inconveniences that resulted from the widespread failure to adapt infrastructures in prompt and effective ways, it is not surprising that city dwellers tried to increase their power to obtain the public services they needed. Not all people could or would act on their unhappiness with the environment, and many escaped the problems by moving to comparatively bucolic suburbs. A large number of people, however, worked hard to achieve reform.

They approached the task of making business and government more sensitive to their needs from several directions. At first they usually attempted to work through established channels, through the market and the political process and the press, to articulate their demands and bring pressure to bear on the public and private organizations responsible for making improvements. When this failed, however, as it often did for the reasons described earlier, they turned to more extreme means to achieve their ends.

These more drastic efforts took two forms. The first involved restructuring the corporate decision making process to force utility and transportation companies to take unremunerative social benefits into account and meet community as well as private needs. This reformers attempted to do by eliminating or at least curtailing the companies' monopoly power and their slavish adherence to the principles of profit maximization. Their strategies included granting additional franchises to companies to foster competition and, when this failed, passing regulatory ordinances, making franchises more prescriptive and restrictive, establishing regulatory agencies, and, most radical of all, municipalizing the companies.[61]

The other approach was to reshape the institutions of public decision making in order to lessen government decision makers' vulnerability to divisive outside pressures from private interests and political bosses, so as to make them more responsive to the general community need. This reformers attempted to accomplish by making public administration more bureaucratic and businesslike. In general, their methods included introducing civil service reforms to eliminate political patronage, in order to bring more highly trained and presumably less corruptible and less partisan people into public administration and insulate government from spoils and politics. Their reforms also involved reorganizing the administrative arm of the city government and shifting some of the council's traditional prerogatives to the executive branch to give non-elected, presumably highly trained and professional administrators more control over budget setting and decision making in general. Their innovations entailed, as well, introducing more modern and "objective" bureaucratic systems of information gathering and policy formulation, systems based on scientific research and the expertise of professional planners, engineers, and non-partisan public interest groups and citizens' commissions in order to replace the old, inherently biased and *ad hoc* methods based on hearings, petitions, and the *quid pro quo*. In addition to these administrative changes, the reformers attempted to restructure the elective branch of government by introducing at-large elections and recall and referendum laws and, in so doing, to reduce the power of political machines and establish an institutional basis for a legislative concern for the general public needs of cities.[62]

Because these reforms were attempts to change the institutional basis of corporate and governmental decision making power, they inevitably propelled reformers into power struggles with the adherents of the existing order. As a result, the effort to obtain infrastructural improvements helped precipitate and shape the great municipal progressive reform movement of the late nineteenth and early twentieth centuries, particularly that part of the movement that historians have labeled "structural" or administrative reform, which was directed specifically at securing changes in the institutions of municipal government.

Historians have written a great deal about the middle and upper class roots and goals of the progressive administrative reform movement, often arguing that it was little more than a blatant attempt by middle and upper class businessmen and professional people to expel the working class and their political machines from city governments and remake municipal administration in their own bourgeois image.[63] In point of fact, however, the movement was far more than a simple effort to impose a business ethos on government and assert the social and political power and prestige of a particular class. To the contrary, the reforms were directed at utility and transportation companies as well as governments. And they were intended to make business operations more governmental, as well as governmental operations more businesslike. Social reformers as well as businessmen and professionals participated in the administrative reform movement. They pursued the reforms as a means of achieving a wide variety of goals, liberal as well as conservative, one of which was the aim of modernizing infrastructures to provide better, cheaper, and more abundant public services.[64]

As this study will later show, the reformers met with considerable success, at least in the first decades of the twentieth century. The Progressive Era was a time of great improvement in urban infrastructures in a number of cities, not only because many of the technological obstacles to improvement had finally been overcome but also because administrative reforms had finally reduced some of the institutional barriers to change. As a result, progressive reform not only changed the shape of city government; it helped give birth to modern city planning.

At the same time, as this study will also show, profound obstacles to infrastructural redevelopment remained. The reforms did nothing to affect the underlying physical and economic causes of the infrastructural persistence problem, for these resulted from the political, economic, social, and cultural context in which they operated, as well as from the extremely durable, capital-intensive, land-extensive, public, and essentially monopolistic characteristics of the infrastructures themselves. The effort to achieve the adaptation of infrastructures in nineteenth century cities culminated in a movement to pass regulatory laws, civil service laws, and other administrative reforms largely because reformers viewed corporate profiteering, corrupt machine politics, and administrative incompetence as the prime villains behind their cities' environmental problems and, indeed, most of their other social and economic ills as well. By no means were their efforts completely misdirected. As later chapters will demonstrate, however, some barriers to infrastructural redevelopment ran much more deeply than this, going far beyond the reach of simple institutional manipulation and regulatory reform.

4

The barriers to spatial change

In addition to compelling the modernization of structures and infrastructures, the multiplication of people and business activity in nineteenth and early twentieth century cities necessitated the reorganization of commercial, industrial, and residential land use patterns. In the early nineteenth century, American cities were little more than small towns, most of their land being given over to compact mixtures of middle class homes, workers' cottages, boardinghouses, stores, artisans' and blacksmiths' shops, saloons and coffee shops, stables, lumber yards, ropewalks, distilleries, and small factories, all within walking distance of one another. Economic and population growth necessitated a reorganization of this mixed pattern of land usage that was as fundamental as the transformation it required of the built environment. The cities were initially so small and geographically undifferentiated that they simply could not physically accommodate the great influx of people flowing into them without undergoing far-reaching spatial redevelopment.

The changes can be summarized as follows. First, population and economic growth required the territorial expansion of the densely built up sections of the cities, together with an overall intensification of land use in these areas. Physically enlarging the areas of dense usage was especially necessary, for without such expansion, growth could be accommodated only through crowding and, in the absence of adequate structures and infrastructures, overcrowding, to the detriment of public health, local business conditions, and the general quality of urban life. Both vertical and horizontal expansion provided relief from the pressures on the land. Because of the physical, economic, and technological barriers to structural change, however, the latter was particularly vital.

Second, growth made a transformation of the internal organization of commercial, residential, and industrial activity patterns necessary, compelling the emergence of separate commercial, residential, and industrial districts to take the place of the unspecialized, mixed land use patterns of old. Territorial localization created positive externalities by slashing firms' intra-city transportation costs and facilitating face-to-face business dealings and speeding the circulation of information about market conditions, three particularly important benefits in an era lacking cheap and ubiquitous telephone and radio communication. Clustering also led to scale economies by enlarging local markets, in that groups of firms in the same and related lines of trade together attracted many more customers than individual firms could alone. It also fostered the development of industries which processed inputs and outputs at a cost savings, in that a cluster of firms in the same and related industries gave specialized manufacturers a large enough market for their products to warrant their going into business.

By giving firms an edge in their increasingly competitive and volatile local, regional, and national markets, these agglomeration economies stimulated the development of a central business district in the heart of all large Victorian cities. They did so by compelling merchants, bankers, manufacturers, and commerce-dependent professionals to bid land away from residential users in the desired central areas by paying higher rents than residents could afford to pay.

Agglomeration factors also stimulated change in industrial land use patterns. In the beginning, most manufacturing, craft, and artisan businesses congregated in central cities, mixing in with commercial and financial businesses in order to take advantage of general economies of agglomeration. The development of large-scale, mechanized industrial production techniques made this spatial mingling of commercial and industrial land use increasingly untenable, however, because it required the construction of large factories that were almost impossible to build in crowded central business districts. Large factories gave manufacturers a competitive edge in the industrial marketplace by enabling them to take advantage of important internal economies of scale. In order to build them, however, manufacturers had to sacrifice direct access to centrally located wholesale and retail firms and financial institutions for locations in comparatively remote areas near waterways, railroad lines, and other transportation facilities, where land was relatively cheap. The external economies provided by territorial agglomeration still made it uneconomical for them to scatter the factories randomly across the countryside, however. Instead, they forced manufacturers to bid land away from other land users so that they could group together as much as possible in these outlying areas. The result was that over time specialized industrial districts developed outside the emerging central business districts of all large nineteenth century cities.

Third, population and economic growth required the internal specialization of residential, commercial, and industrial districts. It compelled the emergence of financial, warehousing, transportation, and retailing zones within business and industrial areas, as well as the development of working class, middle class, and upper class zones in residential districts. Growth also necessitated the physical enlargement of these sub-districts and, as economic and population heterogeneity increased, their further internal specialization as well. In business and industrial areas this expansion and spatial reorganization process was made necessary by firms' needs for space and maximum accessibility to one another as they grew in size, multiplied in number, diversified into new activities, and specialized in particular lines of trade. In residential areas, it was necessitated by the skyrocketing number of poor people who lacked the time and money to commute long distances to central business and industrial districts and so had to cluster as close to them as possible. It also resulted from wealthier people's desires to escape the inner city and its congestion, pollution, and appalling poverty and the social disorganization that characterized neighborhoods inhabited by the very poor.[1]

Finally, the growth of population and economic activity in cities necessitated the geographical isolation of noxious and unsafe land uses, like slaughterhouses, rendering establishments, tanneries, garbage dumps, and lumber yards.

Most cities were not, of course, mere jumbles of residential, industrial, and commercial land uses at the start of the nineteenth century. Even in the seventeenth and eighteenth centuries, central wharfs had provided a focus for the activities of bankers, merchants, government and religious institutions, and some manufacturers. More peripheral harbor, river, and lakeside areas had similarly provided foci for more land-intensive and noxious industrial concerns like tanneries and breweries. Things had progressed so that by the early nineteenth century, a number of the major Eastern port cities already contained small working class or immigrant districts and small upper class enclaves alongside these incipient central business districts. Many also contained scattered working class shanty towns on their peripheries.[2] What was important about these early examples of land use specialization, however, was that they were completely dwarfed by the comparatively large regions of unspecialized land use surrounding them. They were also exceedingly small in relation to future needs, rarely encompassing more than a few blocks. And they were very mixed in character, even on the level of individual buildings, many structures serving a combination of residential, commercial, and industrial functions.

These conditions meant that as business firms multiplied and grew, they had to displace existing residents and other firms engaged in unrelated activities in order to take advantage of the economies of agglomeration. As the population grew, impoverished workers who could not afford to commute to work had to displace more well-to-do residents who could afford to do so. Displaced firms and people, of course, had to relocate somewhere. The resulting supplantation and filling-in processes were ongoing and simultaneous movements that ultimately enveloped entire walking cities as well as their rural environs. The consequence was a multi-faceted transformation of urban land use patterns.

Taken together, these spatial adaptations of urban land use reflected the modernization of the national economy and the evolution of urban social structure in the nineteenth and early twentieth centuries. Not only did they mirror the breakdown of the household economy, the rise of the modern corporation, and the intensification of economic stratification in society. But, in addition, the increasing geographical distances separating neighborhoods paralleled the increasing social distances dividing classes, ethnic groups, and different sectors of the economy. As a result, the spatial adaptation process was not an unmitigated blessing for many city dwellers or, for that matter, for the urban community as a whole. To uncompetitive businessmen and tradesmen, for example, high rents and spatial displacement often meant giving up desirable locations, shops, and dwellings (or the hope of ever having them) and lowering career and life expectations. For a community, meanwhile, the expansion of the built city and its division into separate and increasingly remote commercial, industrial, and working class, middle class, and upper class residential districts brought increased community fragmentation and political parochialism, conditions which made it all the more difficult to mobilize the support needed to improve urban infrastructures and living conditions, especially in poor areas.[3]

These negative effects aside, however, the reorganization of urban land use patterns was a natural adaptation process that provided significant benefits to society, and not only to the individual firms that could afford to localize in desired centers of agglomeration and the middle and upper class families that could afford to move to well-to-do suburbs. The territorial agglomeration of firms in business and industrial centers benefited society in general because it provided positive externalities and external economies of scale which reduced the per-unit cost of producing and marketing manufactured goods and professional services. The development of separate manufacturing districts, meanwhile, made possible the proliferation of large factories, the internal economies of scale of which further cut the real per-unit cost of producing goods by facilitating the specialization of labor and the use of high-power machinery. In each case, this promoted the economic expansion needed to support the nation's growing population. It also produced savings in the cost of production, savings that were, at least in part, passed on to consumers in the form of lower prices or reinvested in the production process to pay for further growth.

Even suburbanization benefited the larger community, since the outward migration of central city residents provided the population turnover needed to relieve congestion in the inner city. Geographically speaking, suburbs were the physical manifestation of the success with which city dwellers managed to accommodate themselves to population growth through the expansion of settlement rather than through the pure intensification of land use. Although individual suburban neighborhoods tended to replicate the class divisions in society, as a group they were not the exclusive preserves of the middle and upper classes but were also refuges for working class people. Most important, the growth of suburbs benefited even those people who were forced to remain within the inner city, for it furnished an outlet for population pressure in the city center.

This study demonstrates that like structural and infrastructural improvement, these spatial adaptations were subject to constraints and frictions that retarded and obstructed the desirable and economically "rational" accommodation of economic and population growth. To be sure, both businesses and people seem to have been quite mobile both within and out of nineteenth and early twentieth century cities, marginal firms and laborers especially so because of the pervasiveness of renting, the widespread use of short one- and two-year leases, and the rapid rise of urban land values.[4] As this study will demonstrate, however, this flux took place largely within the confines of established land use patterns. Because of certain barriers, the overall organization of commercial, industrial, and residential activity in nineteenth and early twentieth century cities changed very slowly. Land use patterns were not, of course, completely inflexible. Indeed, as the conversion of old mansions into tenements and office buildings shows, the spatial reorganization process was often considerably easier than the structural improvement process. Still, the territorial displacement of one pattern by another, even the displacement of a slum by business or industry, was generally a time-consuming and difficult operation that often lagged substantially behind the need for change.

The result of the frictions in the process of spatial redevelopment was the intensification of land usage within established spatial patterns. Economic and population growth had to be accommodated in some way. Because of the obstacles to displacement, most new households and businesses either filled in existing specialized residential, commercial, and industrial districts and sub-districts or scattered into any available space in less congested or mixed sections of the inner city, becoming interspersed among the existing inhabitants of the area. In the latter case, they mingled with people of other classes and businesses engaged in other lines of trade, rather than supplanting them *en masse*, perpetuating the traditional heterogeneity of urban land use. Impoverished immigrants, for example, usually crowded into the few transitional or slum neighborhoods in a city already abandoned by first class businesses and well-to-do residents, while also becoming thinly scattered in various other parts of the inner city and squatting on vacant land outside it, giving up proximity to the job market in the central city. The difficulty they had extending their territorial hegemony in the crowded central area was expressed by the way in which they dispersed and even more so by the intensity with which they used every inch of the scarce space available to them in inner city districts. As Oscar Handlin pointed out in regard to the development of Irish slums in Boston, not only were existing houses, warehouses, and factories in places like the North End divided and subdivided, but "every vacant spot" – every previously uninhabited yard, court, cellar, and closet "behind, beside, or within an old structure" – was built upon or converted into dwellings to make room for more people.[5]

Despite their need for agglomeration economies and despite their power in the urban real estate market, businesses followed suit. New trades found it impossible to monopolize a compact space in order to take maximum advantage of the economies of agglomeration but, instead, became scattered over many blocks, sharing territory with other firms in other lines of business. Other trades managed to establish cohesive centers of agglomeration, but then found it impossible to spread out in any territorially cohesive way to accommodate the trades' growth. Boston's boot and shoe wholesalers, for example, successfully localized in two compact trade centers in the late 1850s and 1860s. Unable to expand the centers, however, they had to cope with a threefold increase in the number of firms in the trade, much as the city's Irish immigrants had to accommodate population growth by doubling, tripling, or quadrupling the number of occupants of the small four- and five-story buildings inside the centers. By 1872, six or more firms were crowding into many single addresses, and in one case an amazing thirty-one firms occupied the same building. Meanwhile, roughly fifteen percent of the trade had to disperse into other areas. Squeezed out of the centers of agglomeration and unable to displace the occupants of adjacent buildings, they became thinly scattered along nine other streets across the central business district.[6]

Given the constraints to be described, these patterns were all perfectly natural responses to the imperatives of population and economic growth. The problem was that they did not provide the benefits that would have resulted from a more rapid expansion and specialization of land use patterns. Instead, in the absence of effective structural and infrastructural improvement, they simply increased the problems of overcrowding.

Demand constraints

Two of the most significant barriers to change in land use patterns were wage earners' need for easy access to their places of work and businesses' need for easy access to transportation facilities, financial and professional services, and other firms. These accessibility requirements slowed the development and expansion of specialized districts and sub-districts because they undermined people's willingness and ability to displace unlike land uses on a scale large enough to cause a rearrangement of overall land use patterns. They especially impeded the flow of business and residential activity out of the center toward the peripheries of cities. Significantly, they were constraints that were technologically as well as economically based, resulting as much from the primitive condition of intra-urban transportation and communications as from the economic needs of land users themselves. Transportation and communication within cities during the nineteenth century largely depended on the slow passage of people and animals through crowded streets. As a result, the time and money that people spent moving goods, information, and themselves across distances, even very short distances, substantially increased the economic and psychological costs of living, working, and conducting business in cities. The need to minimize these costs made accessibility a matter of direct geographical proximity.

The restraining effect of these demand conditions was most obvious in the evolution of working class districts. Most unskilled and semi-skilled laborers and industrial workers toiled ten to twelve hours per day at least six days per week for wages that barely covered rent and food and that left nothing for daily omnibus or streetcar fares. Because of their hours and exhausting work, few could spend more than thirty minutes commuting to their jobs one way, which was about what it took to walk one and a half miles. And the vast majority evidently felt that they could not spend even this much time and effort at such a tiring and unremunerative chore. In Philadelphia, for instance, even as late as 1880, more than half of all industrial workers still lived within a five-minute (three-tenths of a mile) walk of their place of work, and more than eighty-five percent resided within a fifteen-to twenty-minute (one mile) walk.[7] Quick and easy access to a job was especially important for wage earners with families in which several members worked and for irregularly employed workers who had to seek new jobs frequently. This need restricted the bulk of the blue collar laborers in a given community to homesites in the immediate vicinity of the business and industrial centers that employed them. They also made any substantial or discontinuous change in workers' patterns of land usage largely dependent on a territorial reorganization of those industrial and commercial centers, at least until the end of the century, when the development of cheaper and more rapid electric street railways permitted many more workers to ride to work, opening up large new areas of settlement.

Commercial and industrial land use patterns also exhibited considerable spatial inertia, an inertia that was, at least in part, the result of the centripetal forces created by the high cost of traversing a city. Transportation costs especially affected the development of central business districts. With the exception of groceries, saloons, and other small shops serving scattered neighborhood markets, most commercial, financial, and professional concerns required quick, easy, and frequent communications and face-to-face interactions with customers, clients, lawyers, brokers, and bankers, as well as other firms in the same and related lines of trade. This interdependency not only funneled firms into central business districts but also encouraged them to stay within several blocks of one another (the maximum distance a businessman or messenger could easily travel on foot in just a few minutes in congested downtown streets). Thus, it also slowed the expansion of the districts.[8]

Industrial land use patterns were generally more malleable than this, since as long as manufacturers retained business offices in the central business district, they could trade off accessibility to the business center for internal economies of scale in deciding where to place their factories. The high cost of land in central business districts and well-established industrial districts, in fact, frequently forced industrialists to locate large new factories in relatively remote areas or forego building them at all. Nevertheless, here, too, the difficulty of transporting goods and people within cities circumscribed location decision making, discouraging the spatial reorganization of existing land use patterns. Manufacturers not only had to minimize the distance between their factories and the harbor and rail facilities from which they obtained their raw materials and through which they shipped their goods to market. They also had to minimize the distance between their factories and the factories of the firms to which they sold output and from which they purchased processed inputs. In addition, those dependent on water power had to minimize the distance between the factories and the source of power. As in central business districts, these distances were usually measured in terms of blocks or even adjacence, not miles, at least as long as the intracity transport of heavy and voluminous materials continued to depend on slow, inefficient, costly, and often unreliable horse-drawn wagons and carts. Thus here again, once districts of specialized land use were established, transportation costs tended to funnel business into existing centers of agglomeration. The economies that manufacturers enjoyed by maintaining close proximity to the large, skilled labor markets that grew up around industrial districts further stabilized existing land use patterns.

Manufacturers could spread out by constructing private railway sidings to link outlying factories to the depots and switching yards that served the firms in the heart of an established industrial district. This enabled firms to extend the borders of a district peripherally. The important thing about railway lines and terminals, however, was that once established, they became physically durable urban infrastructures that would be subject to only very limited spatial rearrangement. Thus they also concentrated industrial activity within geographically contained areas.[9]

The groups least affected by high transportation and communication costs were, naturally, those middle and upper class residents who had enough money to ride trains or streetcars to work on a regular basis and enough free time to spend an hour or two on a daily commute. These people also faced accessibility constraints of a sort, however. As journey to work studies and other more impressionistic materials indicate, many professional, managerial, and clerical workers valued convenience, preferring to live within a quick walk or streetcar ride of their offices, even when it was not an economic necessity that they do so.[10] Such preferences (as opposed to needs) for accessibility fostered inertia in land use patterns by promoting the persistence of upper and middle class neighborhoods in inner city areas that had become, environmentally speaking, more appropriate for commercial, industrial, or working class use because of the noise, street congestion, pollution, disease, and crime resulting from nearby businesses, factories, or slums.

The development of city telephone networks and electric streetcar and subway systems revolutionized intra-urban communication and transportation in the last years of the nineteenth century, drastically reducing these accessibility constraints. This introduced an unprecedented amount of flexibility into urban land use patterns at the close of the period under study here.[11] The high cost of traversing city space was never, however, the only demand factor holding up the displacements necessary for the adaptation of residential, commercial, and industrial activity patterns to economic and population growth.

Another barrier was people's emotional attachment to particular localities. As a number of humanistic geographers have pointed out, urban space has always had a subjectively perceived value for land users, in addition to its objective economic value.[12] As Walter Firey showed in his 1947 study of land use in central Boston, the two values have often diverged considerably, land users sometimes attributing a utility to a particular locality that is completely unwarranted economically. What was important about these non-economic ties to neighborhoods in the spatial evolution of the nineteenth century city was that they sometimes prompted land users to buck the imperatives of economic rationality and remain in ostensibly undesirable areas in large enough numbers to prevent "natural," economically logical land use transitions from occurring.[13]

This sort of impediment to change had a particularly visible effect on residential land use patterns. Boston's Beacon Hill, for example, remained an upper class district despite its proximity to slums and business, its high land costs, and the development of more magnificent Back Bay and suburban areas, at least in part because the city's leading families treasured its historical association with the great statesmen, business leaders, and literary heroes who had once resided there and because they derived great satisfaction from keeping old, family homes. Certain ethnic neighborhoods, such as Irish South Boston, exhibited a similar spatial continuity, at least in part because the achievement of a high degree of ethnic homogeneity and the proliferation of ethnic associations gave residents a heightened sense of cultural identity and of belonging that far outweighed their desire to raise their families in more pleasant areas.[14]

Significantly, however, sentimentality also influenced commercial and industrial land use patterns. Businessmen as well as ordinary people tended to identify themselves increasingly with particular neighborhoods the longer they remained associated with them, investing them with symbolic meaning that met basic human needs for security and a sense of place. In a still very localized and personalized business world in which most dealings were conducted on the basis of face-to-face interactions, this identification process had a practical side, since it tended to affect the public as well as firms, giving specialized districts and individual establishments a spatial prominence and imageability that helped attract customers and clients and accustom them to regular dealings with the concerns. It also, however, had a purely emotional dimension, which sometimes verged on the irrational. As sociologists and other investigators discovered, businessmen and manufacturers often refused to leave their current locations and move even a few blocks to obtain better accommodations and greater economies, simply because they had "always been there" and were afraid to move or had never even considered moving. This sort of conservatism especially affected poorly managed and aging companies. Where a high degree of territorial agglomeration was achieved and the spatial identification process accordingly reinforced, however, it could influence entire trades, helping to root them to particular neighborhoods and making it all the more difficult for them to adapt to growth through relocation.[15]

As Walter Firey has pointed out, under certain conditions this collective emotional attachment to neighborhood continuity could become stronger over time until it approached the intensity of a spatial "fetish" that might block "natural" shifts in land usage for generations, even centuries.[16] In its more mundane form, however, it simply tended to retard change, postponing or prolonging transitions for a few years or a decade or two or three, rather than completely obstructing them.

What gave these psychological constraints, and the economic ones as well, such power to shape the spatial adaptation process was the dichotomous way in which they affected the demand for urban space. Not only did they tend to tie groups of potentially mobile land users to their present locations, but they also tended to tie the firms and residents that the potentially mobile land users considered displacing to their locations, encouraging them to remain rather than make way for a shift in land use patterns, even when this meant absorbing higher rents, taking in boarders, making do with smaller quarters, or, for property owner-occupiers, foregoing the profits resulting from property conversion.

Land users' resistance to displacement created a friction in the process of spatial redevelopment that was as powerful a barrier to change as the unwillingness to move that tied potential displacers to their old locations. This barrier was primarily expressed in economic ways, especially through high rents that made it financially unattractive or impossible for land users to displace others. In addition, however, it made itself felt in such political ways as exclusionary property covenants and neighborhood associations, zoning regulations, violent popular outbursts against change (such as the race riots that accompanied and largely blocked the expansion of the black ghetto in Chicago during World War I), and other strategies by which threatened land users attempted to stave off change by making displacement illegal, too frightening, or too dangerous for potential displacers to seriously consider intruding into their neighborhoods. Where effective, these impediments complicated the land use succession process by forcing businesses and residents to leapfrog undisplaceable land users and either disperse into or reconcentrate in some comparatively remote area.[17]

The need to leapfrog made most contemplated moves all the more drastic. This in turn made people and businesses even more reluctant to locate outside established districts. On the one hand, leapfrogging compounded the economic barriers to change created by the costliness of intra-urban transport and communication, for it compelled land users to move farther beyond the work places, transportation facilities, or agglomeration centers they depended on than was financially feasible for them. On the other hand, and perhaps almost as important, leapfrogging seems to have intensified the psychological barriers to change by sometimes forcing people and businesses to move farther than was psychologically feasible for them.

Psychological factors are, of course, always difficult for the historian to document, so it is necessary to be somewhat speculative here. As various humanistic geographers have demonstrated, however, people make sense of the space around them in limited, subjective ways by building up mental images of a city's topography that highlight the relatively few places and pathways they frequent or that have some cultural significance for them, while collapsing the rest of the city's geography into relatively unstructured, unknown, and unmeaningful background areas.[18] Because of this natural bifurcation, people in large, heterogeneous, and geographically balkanized nineteenth century cities were unlikely to have had much information about suitable accommodations in unfamiliar localities even a few blocks beyond their own neighborhoods, work places, cultural centers, or well-trod streets. Moreover, their lack of familiarity with other areas and consequent inability to identify themselves with them was likely to have increased their anxiety about leapfrogging to them, encouraging them to view the areas as being out of bounds or somehow inappropriate for them, regardless of the economic or environmental amenities they might offer. This was even more likely when land users faced the prospect of leapfrogging into a substantially different area – a drygoods firm, for example, facing the prospect of a move into a grocery and provisioning district or a nearby slum. Psychological barriers like this may not have been as overwhelming as the economic ones, especially to impoverished workers and marginal firms looking desperately for a place, any place, to settle, at least temporarily. As events in Chicago, Boston, and Baltimore after the great fires of 1871, 1872, and 1904 suggest, however, they played an important role in at least some aspects of the process of adapting land use patterns to economic and population growth.[19]

Finally, the need to leapfrog made it more difficult for groups of businesses that derived economic benefits from clustering together to adapt to growth through relocation by complicating location decision making. The problem was that agglomerated firms had to move in tandem in order to maintain the economies of agglomeration. Not only were such large-scale, multiple moves difficult to accomplish from the standpoint of obtaining enough space in a desirable locality for the firms to reconcentrate, a constraint which will be taken up in more detail shortly, but they were also hard to undertake from a demand standpoint, since in large groups the interested parties were likely to disagree over such basic issues as the location of the new center and even the need for a move. Small companies that depended on the market externalities resulting from physical proximity to large trade leaders often had little choice but to try to follow if these leaders decided to relocate. As a result, a decision by one or more of the most important companies in a specialist business or industrial center to leapfrog to a new area could precipitate a mass migration. Significantly, however, it was those leading firms that often had the least reason to be dissatisfied with their present location and that usually had the most money or identity invested in their present stores or factories. Thus they were frequently the least likely to be interested in moving. Because of the co-location interdependencies between them and the others, their inertia translated into a general inertia that affected all the firms.[20]

Supply constraints

In sum, a wide variety of highly interrelated factors undercut land users' willingness to supplant unlike land users. As important as they were, however, these demand constraints were only a part of the land use succession problem. People and businesses in nineteenth and early twentieth century cities did not make their location decisions on flat, "featureless plains," as is often assumed by urban theorists, nor, in deciding where to settle, did they take only place, land cost, and accessibility to other land users into account. Instead, both geographical terrain and the distribution and quality of structures and infrastructures crucially affected their decision making. This meant that property owners, transportation and utility company managers, and public officials played vital roles in the process by which specialized commercial, industrial, and residential districts evolved out of the mixed land use patterns of the walking city. It also meant that the physical, economic, technological, and institutional factors that discouraged the improvement of structures and infrastructures also obstructed spatial change.

There were two kinds of conditions that mediated the process of spatial redevelopment on the supply side. They were the natural geographies of cities and the improvement activities of property owners, utility and transportation companies, and government officials.

Property owners and company and government officials helped slow and shape the reorganization of land use patterns in Victorian cities because they controlled the built environment and because all land users had basic structural and infrastructural needs which they had to meet (or at least nearly always did their best to meet) in any relocation. Manufacturers, for example, needed shops and factories that were close to transportation facilities, as well as adequate water, sewerage, and power service. Businessmen needed stores, warehouses, counting rooms, and offices, preferably ones that were located on or near the streets that would give them maximum access to financial institutions, other businesses, and customers. Residents required water and housing and, as their incomes permitted, environmental amenities beyond these basic needs. In addition, most urban land users had certain neighborhood requirements. Most city dwellers, indeed all but the most marginal businessmen and shanty-building squatters, criminals, and extremely poor workers, had neighborhood needs because of the so-called neighborhood effect, that is, because they derived satisfaction not only from the characteristics of the individual buildings they personally inhabited and the particular infrastructures they used but also from the design and state of repair of all the other buildings and public services in the vicinity and from their association with the other people who lived or worked in the surrounding area.

These needs created frictions in the process of spatial change, because they meant that people's ability to move depended as much on the physical availability of suitable structures and public services in the areas to which they were willing and ready to relocate as on their willingness to move there.

The neighborhood effect made it necessary that environmental redevelopment occur on a fairly massive scale before commercial, industrial, or residential land users would collectively invade an area. Unfortunately, the barriers to structural and infrastructural improvement discouraged this kind of redevelopment. The result was that property owners, transportation and utility company officials, and government officials took part in the spatial evolution of their cities whether they actively improved their properties or not, their inactivity playing into land users' decision making by encouraging inertia.

The lay of the land also created supply-side frictions in the process of spatial change. It did so because certain territorially extensive, spatially disruptive infrastructures and topographical conditions physically blocked the reorganization of some land use patterns. For example, steep hills, very narrow and dead-end streets, and poorly connected street grids obstructed the expansion of commercial and industrial districts in most cities, because they interfered with the flow of street traffic and impeded the delivery of goods and customers by horse-drawn vehicles.[21] Rivers and large railroad depots and switching yards that cut off business streets did the same thing.[22] So did wide thoroughfares where traffic impeded communication between people on the opposite sides.[23] By the same token, large, undrained, disease- and mosquito-breeding marshes and swamps tended to discourage all kinds of urban land use, remaining virtually vacant although they were otherwise desirable locations, at least until some government agency or private real estate developer finally assembled the land and mobilized the capital to fill them.[24]

Land users were often able to leapfrog these obstructions. In antebellum Boston, for instance, overcrowded wholesalers in the North End made more room for themselves by leapfrogging the residential Fort Hill District, which had traditionally shut the business district into the North End, and reconcentrating farther south. The very need to leapfrog tended to retard adaptations such as this, however. And in any case, as long as the obstructions remained, they usually continued to create serious environmental problems. After Boston's wholesale merchants leapfrogged the Fort Hill District, for example, the hill remained a steep, slum-ridden, disease-plagued hump in the middle of the central business district that interfered with the flow of traffic from one side of the business center to the other until the city razed it in the late 1860s and early 1870s.[25]

More to the point, however, in some cases the obstructions were simply too immense for land users to leapfrog. The extensive railroad depots and yards on the edge of Chicago's central business district, for example, originally built as close to the business center as possible for convenience, hemmed in the district so thoroughly that they ultimately helped stimulate the development of some of the first steel frame, high-rise architecture in America.[26] In situations like this, the only way land users could overcome the barriers to lateral expansion was to remove or redevelop the obstructing infrastructure, grade the constricting hill, drain and fill the offending swamp, or bridge the obstructing waterway. This, of course, inevitably required government action, which again interjected all the barriers to infrastructural redevelopment into the process of spatial change.

The barriers to structural and infrastructural improvement need not be rehashed here. The important point is that they both reinforced and were reinforced by the demand constraints that impeded the reorganization of land use patterns. The negative externalities generated by a neighborhood of old, unimproved buildings, for example, not only made it more difficult for property owners to redevelop their estates for new, more valuable uses by simultaneously compelling and obstructing coordinated improvements on the part of all the owners in the area. But at the same time, the bad conditions repelled potential new users by causing a reduction in articulated (as opposed to latent) demand for space in the area. This, in turn, made the property owners all the more unwilling to risk their money in upgrading their estates. By the same token, land users who could not move long distances or did not want to be displaced not only helped create political barriers to environmental change by petitioning city governments and seeking court injunctions against proposed improvements. In addition, by their very immobility, they gave income-oriented property owners and utility companies the captive markets they needed to pursue their unimprovement strategies.

The only time the barriers to environmental improvement actually facilitated land use succession was when the increasing inadequacy of unimproved buildings and infrastructures finally forced relatively high class businesses and residents to leave a deteriorated area in search of better accommodations. This opened up such localities to more marginal businesses or residents, making the downward filtering of structures and neighborhoods possible. This was one of the most important dynamics in the spatial development process in nineteenth and early twentieth century cities. It must be kept in mind, however, that the demand constraints encouraged even high class land users to remain in inadequate quarters and avoid making ostensibly rational moves. Furthermore, their mobility depended on their ability to obtain better quarters elsewhere. Thus, even here, there were powerful frictions present in the process of spatial redevelopment.

The government response

As in any situation as fraught with potential conflict and frustration as this, people inevitably turned to government for help. The role that public officials played in spatial redevelopment was somewhat paradoxical, however. On the one hand, at the behest of real estate developers, social reformers, and crowded land users, public officials attempted to facilitate change by manipulating the supply and demand constraints that naturally impeded it. On the other hand, at the behest of threatened property owners and land users, they also manipulated supply and demand factors to prevent change.

The most important tool with which government officials could influence the demand for space was their power to make infrastructural improvements. As noted earlier, the quality of the streets, public utilities, and other infrastructures in a particular area crucially affected the desirability of that area for any given group of land users. This meant that infrastructural redevelopment was often a prerequisite for spatial redevelopment. As a result, public officials had a great deal of leverage with regard to the direction of change, for their power to make infrastructural improvements gave them a means to determine when and where an infrastructurally dependent spatial shift, such as the development of a new industrial district, would take place. The power to open and widen streets was an especially powerful tool for manipulating land use change. It not only gave officials a way to make certain areas more attractive to new users and out-of-the-way areas more accessible to them, relaxing the demand barriers to spatial change. It also gave officials a means of encouraging the construction of bigger and better structures, because street improvements entailed the demolition of the buildings standing in the way. Thus it also relaxed the structural barriers to spatial change.

City governments undertook infrastructural improvements for many reasons, and the goal of shifting the pattern of land usage was not, of course, always one of them. It was often one of them, however, and often explicitly so. For example, in the 1850s, the city of Boston undertook the extension and widening of Devonshire Street, which was then an upper class residential street, specifically at the request of improvement-minded property owners in order to help them redevelop it for business.[27] Similarly, the city of Baltimore widened slum-ridden Douglas Street, demolishing all the buildings on both sides, in order to clear it of its slums and make it available for more valuable commercial use. In Mayor Robert Davidson's words, the city "owe[d] it to itself to do away with the miserable slums which now exist there," on aesthetic and moral as well as economic grounds.[28] The fact that slum clearance and business growth usually raised property values and thereby enlarged a city's tax base reinforced the link between infrastructural and spatial redevelopment in the public mind. Indeed, in most cases, cities could make street improvements in the inner city if and only if they could justify them in terms of their beneficial effect on taxes.

Municipal authorities also used their police powers to influence the reorganization of land use patterns. They began passing laws against the establishment of polluting and hazardous "public nuisances," like slaughterhouses, lumber yards, and soap factories, very early on. These laws usually gave them the power to control only the location of new concerns, however. They did not enable authorities to eliminate undesirable land uses from the central city completely. As the Baltimore Board of Health noted in 1878 in a discussion of the difficulties of expelling slaughtering and butchering evils from downtown Baltimore and nearby slums, once established these concerns "naturally opposed the abandonment of their costly improvements" and naturally refused to move against their will without fair compensation. In the face of such opposition, city governments were rarely able to compel the migration of offending land users by any means other than the exercise of the city's power of eminent domain, a practice that was much too costly to use except under extraordinary circumstances.[29]

By the end of the nineteenth century, however, officials had begun to develop a legal answer to this difficulty. Their solution took the form of elaborate building codes and, ultimately, zoning laws. Both building codes and zoning laws (which were really only glorified building codes) directly attacked the supply side of the spatial change process by specifically prohibiting the construction (and sometimes providing for the removal) of structures associated with unwanted land use. Because city governments had a well-defined right to protect the citizenry from hazardous and undesirable structures in the built environment through regulation by means of the exercise of their police powers, this kind of control sidestepped the problem of compensating displaced property owners and land users altogether. Thus it gave officials an effective, almost cost-free means to regulate the locations of dangerous and polluting land use, as well as the locations of such "nuisance" uses as laundries, saloons, dance halls, and pool halls. Significantly, in a number of cities, this approach to the public control of land use patterns culminated in comprehensive zoning and master planning regulations by which public authorities attempted to predetermine all aspects of land use in their cities.[30]

What was interesting about this power of regulation was that governments used it both to prevent and to promote spatial change. What was especially important was that no matter how governments exercised the power, they simultaneously served the interests of some property owners and land users and violated the interests of others. That governments were able to manipulate spatial change through the improvement of infrastructures and the regulation of structures demonstrates the interconnectedness of structural, infrastructural, and spatial change. That they played both sides of the spatial change dilemma was a paradox that dramatizes the conflictive nature of a process of environmental redevelopment that involved troublesome trade-offs between competing interests.

As this chapter and the two that precede it have demonstrated, all three kinds of environmental redevelopment made it necessary for trade-offs to be made between land uses and land users competing for the same scarce space in cities. This is the key that interrelates the separate processes of structural, infrastructural, and spatial redevelopment in nineteenth and early twentieth century cities. As the following chapters will show, as inertia built up in all three parts of the environment individually, the interactions between them created a land use equilibrium that fostered continuity and circumscribed decision making power in every dimension. At the same time, however, this interconnectedness also held out the possibility of comprehensive change, a chain reaction of urban redevelopment, when even one of the barriers to change was suddenly removed. Yet in the midst of change, frictions in the redevelopment process remained that prevented people from achieving all the environmental improvements they needed and desired.

PART II

Three case studies

5

Theory and narrative history

Transitions can be difficult, the analytical transition from theory to historical case study no less so than the physical transition from the land use patterns of the pre-industrial walking city to the land use patterns of the industrial metropolis. They are often necessary, however. The conceptual framework developed in Part I draws heavily on the analytical constructs of the social sciences in order to explain the problems of urban redevelopment in a comprehensive, theoretical way. Part II does something very different. It examines the frictions that shaped and obstructed the urban redevelopment process historically, in order to show how they made themselves manifest and to demonstrate, as vividly as possible, how important and how deeply entrenched in urban life they were. The frictions were often hidden from the people who participated in the redevelopment process. They were always there, however, sometimes operating beneath the surface of events, sometimes perfectly apparent, embedded in the human interactions and environmental conditions that over time composed the histories of America's great cities. To make them less abstract, to show how they expressed themselves in daily life, this part of the book will examine them in the context of the massive redevelopment projects provoked by the great fires that demolished huge sections of Chicago, Boston, and Baltimore in the late nineteenth and early twentieth centuries.

As the accumulation of serious environmental problems in America's Victorian cities indicates, it is possible to study the factors that limited people's power to adapt the urban environment to their needs at any point in the growth of a great city. The following chapters will analyze the problems that arose in the aftermath of great fires, because these disasters give us a unique opportunity to see what happened in rapidly growing cities when one of the barriers to environmental redevelopment, the physical durability of structures, was suddenly removed. In all three places, the sudden, temporary elimination of this single friction set off a rapid and far-reaching chain reaction of planned and unplanned structural and infrastructural improvement and spatial change. This activity not only reveals the powerful role that physical durability played as a barrier to change. More important, it makes it possible to trace, in very concrete, dense, and human ways, how the remaining frictions continued to undercut people's ability to adapt their environments to their needs, obstructing improvement and, once a land use equilibrium was upset, shaping change.

Like urban theorists, urban historians are by temperament and training interested in understanding the nature of change. Unlike theorists, however, historians also know how important it is to reach an understanding of the *course* of change. For this, theory, as helpful as it is, goes only so far. As Oscar Handlin has written, "However useful a general theory of the city may be, only the detailed tracing of an immense range of variables in context," only the painstaking examination of "*a* city specifically in all its uniqueness" can reveal the ways that the processes described by theory played themselves out in life.[1] One might add that only by such examination can we begin to understand the interrelationship which exists between the underlying conditions that structure and constrain urban development and the role that individual initiative plays in city growth and the solution of urban problems.

As described in the preceding chapters, the frictions in the process of environmental development are little more than heuristic devices for organizing and summarizing insights into urban problems gleaned from engineering, architecture, and several social sciences so as to make certain concepts available to historians who may not have considered them before. As such, they cannot even begin to convey the kaleidoscopic complexity and material reality of the city building process. The frictions were not abstractions, however. Nor were they aberrations or mere "kinks" in an otherwise smooth and automatic process of environmental development that were somehow separate from the stimulus-response dynamic of development. Quite the contrary, they were at the heart of the city building process, organic determinants of both the course of city growth and the spread of many urban problems.

The case studies will illuminate this. They will also give us a means to compare and contrast the dynamics of environmental improvement in three different places. Thus they will enable us to consider the ways that different topographical conditions, different environmental problems, different political conditions, and different people influenced the process of city growth. By enabling us to compare and contrast redevelopment in the 1870s with redevelopment in the early 1900s, the case studies will provide insight into the origins of the urban progressive reform movement and the rise of modern city planning.

Each of the rebuildings to be discussed here was totally unique, of course. It could hardly have been otherwise. Significantly, however, the rebuildings also showed considerable similarity. Some degree of repetition is inevitable in a comparative study. But in this instance, it is analytically significant, in and of itself, for it is an expression of the inescapable presence of the frictions in the urban redevelopment process, frictions that in an infinite number of ways and configurations constantly mediated people's responses to their changing environmental needs, limiting their power to make necessary adaptations in their surroundings. The narratives that follow tell how the residents of three demolished cities tried to obtain the power they needed to make their environments better than before. They met with both success and failure. Ironically, in some instances the very success of their efforts to take power proves the depth of their inability to solve their problems. If the differences among the rebuildings dramatize the importance of historical circumstance in urban redevelopment, this underlying commonality highlights the profundity of the barriers to change. It is a profundity that only such a comparison can demonstrate, a common bond that even the differences among the rebuildings help to explain.

6

The rebuilding of Chicago

The great Chicago fire was one of the worst urban conflagrations in history. It began shortly after nine o'clock, Sunday evening, October 8, 1871, in a small, wooden barn on DeKoven Street owned by the O'Leary family. Contemporaries generally believed that it was started by an angry, unmilked cow that kicked over a kerosene lamp and set a barn ablaze, but no one knows how it really began. All that is certain is that once begun, it quickly overwhelmed the Fire Department and swept across the city like a storm. Fed by wooden buildings dried out by months of drought, and propelled by strong winds and tornadolike convection currents, it roared across the city's wooden streets and down its wooden sidewalks, demolishing an average of sixty-five acres of buildings every hour, approximately $125,000 worth of property every minute, for twenty-seven hours.

It shut down the water works early Monday morning and burned out of control until a rainstorm finally put it out about midnight Monday night. In the process it reduced close to four square miles of the city (see Figure 6.1) to smoking rubble, including the city's entire central commercial district, many of its finest middle and upper class neighborhoods, and acres upon acres of working class cottages and shanties. It ruined approximately $200 million worth of property, including 8 bridges, 15,000 water service pipes, 121 miles of sidewalks, 80 business blocks, several hundred warehouses, a number of hotels, theaters, churches, and railway depots, and roughly 16,000 other buildings. It partially destroyed the water works and damaged almost half of all the city's wooden pavements. It also made close to 100,000 people homeless, nearly a third of the city's total population, and killed several hundred more.[1]

Not surprisingly, the immensity of this destruction shaped the reconstruction effort from the very start. Most Chicagoans were hard put just to find food, water, and shelter for their families and so could not give much immediate thought to rebuilding. As Elias Colbert and Everett Chamberlin, chroniclers of the disaster, explained, the destruction was so far-reaching and so complete that "even those who had not been burnt out of home, as well as office, know not whither they might drift in the general 'sea of

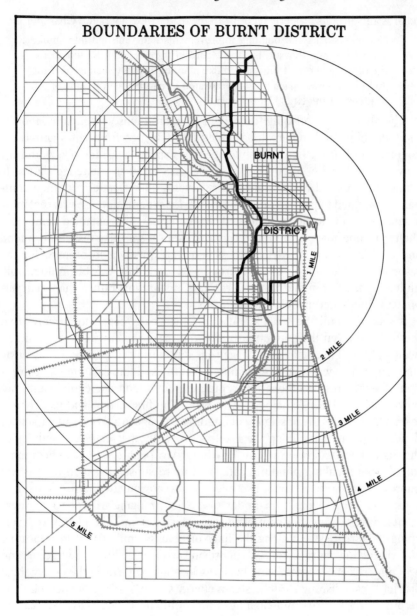

Figure 6.1.

troubles.' " Although everyone was determined to get the city back on its feet, no one knew how, or if, this could be accomplished. The fire had burnt away not only much of the city but also most of the written records on which the city depended for its existence, including most of its bank and mercantile records and all of its property records. In the words of Colbert and Chamberlin:

> Not only stocks and building improvements had vanished into smoke
> and thence into thin air, but the record of the one, and the title to the
> site of the other, had vanished in like manner. It really seemed as if the
> wail of *La Somnambula* must be repeated in chorus by every one of the
> residents of the city, "All is lost now."[2]

The shock wore off quite quickly. The expressions of sympathy and the
food, clothing, and money that flooded into Chicago from cities across the
country and Europe helped to buoy people's spirits considerably, as did the
Governor's decision to convene a special session of the state legislature to
render the city aid and the news that several out-of-state insurance companies intended to pay their policies in full. By Wednesday, life was regaining
a semblance of normality. Most of the homeless had obtained temporary
shelter in one form or another; relief workers were busy distributing food
and clothing to the needy; businessmen were meeting to prepare for the
resumption of business; and the process of rebuilding was beginning. Still,
understandably, for the first several days restoration rather than redevelopment dominated people's thoughts.[3]

It was not until the week's end that Chicagoans began to perceive that
the fire had given them an opportunity to remake the city better than it had
been before. Then, however, began an outpouring of proposals for environmental change which demonstrated that the sudden, calamitous destruction of structures had indeed disrupted the city's land use equilibrium, not
only physically but psychologically as well. The first major land use change
to be taken up was the possibility of building a great central railroad passenger
depot on public land along the lakefront to unify the scattered facilities of
the many lines entering the city.[4] By Saturday, people were also beginning
to talk about making buildings safer and more substantial than before and
improving the water system, two needs made obvious by the fire.[5] Soon all
sorts of improvements were under discussion, ranging in scope from permanently relocating the central business district[6] and completely redeveloping the street system along the lines of Haussmann's Paris[7] to relocating
and viaducting railroad tracks,[8] improving harbor facilities,[9] regrading and
widening streets,[10] centralizing business location patterns in the commercial
district,[11] establishing a public steam energy supply system,[12] expelling dangerous lumber yards and planing mills from the central city,[13] replacing
wooden sidewalks with ones more impervious to flame,[14] and generally building on a grander scale.

These plans were embodied in the slogan "New Chicago." The words
epitomized the attitude Chicagoans developed toward their city after the first
shock of the destruction had worn off and quickly became the code word
for the whole reconstruction effort. Significantly, however, the new city that

was created only imperfectly reflected the proposed improvement goals. The fire had created more interest in environmental change than had previously existed. By its destructiveness, it had also made the environment more amenable to change. It had not, however, affected the other economic, political, geographical, and technological barriers to redevelopment. To the frustration of many Chicagoans (and the relief of many others) these remained and shaped the course of reconstruction.

Making buildings fireproof

Chicagoans aspired to many kinds of structural improvement in the aftermath of the fire. They wanted more buildings and buildings that were bigger, more substantial, and better adapted to their users' needs than those the fire had destroyed. Needless to say, they especially wanted buildings that would not succumb to another conflagration.

On Saturday, October 15, six days after the great fire had begun, the *Chicago Tribune* sounded the first cry in the battle to secure the city against future holocausts. Declaring that Chicago "must rise again, and not only must she rise, but *rise to stand*, as long as the world revolves," the paper called on the City Council to enact and strictly enforce a new fire ordinance that would outlaw the construction of any frame buildings in any sections of the city "which are now or are likely to become central."

The need for more public control over construction practices was, of course, as obvious as the heaps of rubble and piles of ash that covered the burnt district. As the *Tribune* and other papers pointed out in attacks on the city's traditional construction practices, Chicagoans had brought the disaster on themselves by building "fire traps everywhere and anywhere, on every fifty feet of ground in 30 square miles of populated area." Like most eastern cities, Chicago had had a limited fire ordinance which prohibited wooden construction in part of the city. The ban applied only to a very small section of the central business area, however. Even there it had not provided for the actual removal of any existing wooden structures, nor prohibited wooden roofs and other flammable exterior work from being constructed on new buildings. To make matters worse, the city government had shown little regard for fire safety even in its own building practices. As the *Tribune* observed, not only had the Board of Public Works built the city a system of wooden sidewalks "which served as fuses to convey flames from house to house," but it had foolishly crowned the water works with a wooden mansard roof, "so that whoever would burn down the city speedily had surely had only to wait for a fresh wind to throw some brand against the Water Works engine house to disable the Fire Department at once." The inevitable result was that the threat of conflagration had been present everywhere, even in the best commercial areas and residential neighborhoods, where property owners had spent money lavishly to put up massive "first class" edifices.[15]

The Board of Aldermen quickly went to work on the problem, making an important but small first step in reducing the fire threat. Two weeks after the *Tribune*'s editorial, it passed an ordinance to extend the existing fire limits (which basically covered the part of the central business district lying in the East Division) to incorporate a small, adjoining section in the West Division.[16] The timidity of this action showed that Chicagoans were already caught in a tangled web of barriers to optimal redevelopment that undercut this seemingly perfect opportunity to replace wooden buildings with brick and stone ones on a comprehensive scale.

One problem was the upcoming municipal election. Half the seats in the city's unicameral City Council (the Board of Aldermen) were being contested, a tense political situation that distracted advocates of environmental improvement until the election was over in mid-November. Proponents of a strict fire ordinance tried without success to keep Chicagoans from getting caught up in a divisive election during this critical first stage of the rebuilding process. They formed a fusion party, called the "Fire Proof Party," and attempted to run only one slate of candidates for office. Their goal was to sidestep a contentious political race, while simultaneously breaking the power of the regular party machines, so as to demonstrate to the world that Chicagoans were "united and harmonious" in their desire to rebuild the city properly and determined to see that the reconstruction process would be administered only by the "very best, ablest, and purest men of both parties." This, the fusionists believed, was necessary if Chicagoans were to obtain the aid and investment credit they so badly needed to rebuild the city. Unfortunately, the plan failed. The Democratic and Republican politicians the reformers had not deemed virtuous enough to qualify for nomination on the fusion ticket formed their own opposition party, so the bitter partisan clashes the reformers hoped to avoid happened anyway.[17]

As the name of the fusion party suggests, making buildings fireproof was one of the most important issues in the election. The whole election campaign, however, was an example of the demand articulation problems that plagued attempts to obtain a public good, whether it was a physical public work or a government regulation to control private activity. For the Fire Proof fusionists, the key to obtaining a fireproof city was electing candidates nominated by the Fire Proof Party. In their view, as a speaker at one of their meetings stated, prospects of the city's being properly rebuilt "depended entirely upon the men who might be elected."[18] In fact, however, it depended on getting a majority of Aldermen who represented many conflicting interests (regardless of their positions on political reform) to agree to pass a liberal fire ordinance, and on moving fast enough to prevent the city from being rebuilt in wood.

As it turned out, nearly every Fire Proof ticket candidate won election. By then, however, thousands of frame buildings were already being erected, many inside the existing fire limits, re-creating the physical barrier to change the fire had just destroyed. Some of the wooden buildings inside the limits were temporary structures constructed with the permission of the Board of Public Works on the condition that they be torn down within a year. Most, however, were apparently being built without the formal permission of the Board, and thousands of others were going up outside the limits altogether and so were beyond any regulation at all. As a horrified *Tribune* reported after the excitement of the election had begun to pass and its editors had had time to take a look around and see how the rebuilding was actually progressing, Chicago was being filled with buildings that were "worthless, except as fuel to feed the next great fire."[19]

The real political contest to secure a fireproof city did not begin until after the election, when the lame duck Board of Aldermen began formally considering a new fire ordinance. Despite the victory of the Fire Proof candidates at the polls, the Aldermen took up a piece of legislation that would continue to divide the city into two sectors, an inner district in which all wood construction would be prohibited and a large outer district in which only wood buildings with more than two stories would be outlawed. Outraged advocates of a total ban immediately responded by passing a competing resolution to outlaw frame buildings everywhere in the city. In addition to a prohibition on wooden construction, they called for the exclusion of all planing mills, oil refineries, varnish manufactories, and other hazardous industries from the city limits. They called for the confinement of all lumber yards to a small area along the lakefront at the mouth of the Chicago River and to two narrow districts along the north and south branches of the river some distance outside the central business district. In order to encourage people to replace the flammable wooden buildings with brick and stone edifices, they also demanded that Chicagoans be prohibited from renovating, enlarging, and moving existing wooden buildings.[20]

What followed was a prolonged political battle as the proponents of the competing ordinances fought to achieve the legislative consensus needed to enact one law or the other. Although eliminating vulnerable wooden buildings from the environment seemed to be a universally desirable goal, in fact both proposals entailed complex trade-offs between different groups of property owners, trade-offs that prevented any simple resolution of the issue by pitting different Chicagoans against each other in a contentious struggle to protect the city's homes and commercial and industrial buildings.

On one side, most middle and upper class people saw the comprehensive ban on wood construction as an essential environmental reform and the partial ban as an unmitigated evil. They believed that winds blowing across the prairie could easily sweep embers and firebrands from buildings burning in the areas in which frame construction was permitted to structures in the protected inner zone. This not only deprived even the most well built edifices of full security from fire, but it also threatened to drive fire insurance rates sky high, depriving well-to-do Chicagoans of the full value of their standing buildings.[21]

Supporters of the comprehensive ban also objected to the limited fire ordinance because it allowed people to move wooden buildings from one place to another. As a result, as the *Tribune* noted, under the rules of the limited proposal, not only could an owner of a "first class" structure in the outer zone suddenly find the building blighted by a newly constructed "fire trap or tinder box next door," but worse, an owner of a structure in the protected inner zone could wake up one day to find the building blighted by "some old rotten tenement" that had been trundled in from somewhere else and that might be "rented out at extortionate rates for prostitution, gambling, or another equally disreputable business." House moving was common in Chicago and had, in fact, happened in the past. Indeed, some unscrupulous real estate speculators had apparently used their mobile buildings to blackmail the owners of substantial buildings, forcing them to pay to keep ramshackle shanties away. Respectable middle class property owners naturally regarded such activity as abhorrent.[22]

Many people also opposed the limited ordinance because they believed that it would lead to the construction of substandard buildings all over the city. They believed that reconstructing the city on a comprehensively safe and substantial scale was the key to attracting new business and foreign credit into the city, something that was necessary if Chicago was to reassert its position as the Midwest's leading business center. Failure to regain primacy would further reduce their property values.[23]

In sum, in the eyes of its supporters, the comprehensive fire ordinance was superior in every way to the limited ban on frame construction. Not only would it make the city safer and more prosperous, but some hoped it would slow down the chaotic and unaesthetic physical expansion of the city. It might also serve a valuable social reform function by bringing about the construction of better housing for the poor. According to the *Chicago Tribune*, brick houses would reduce workers' fuel bills by one-quarter in addition to saving four or five thousand people from being burnt out of their homes in winter. Brick construction would also, of course, hold down their fire insurance costs.[24]

On the other side, however, most working class people and many of the owners of peripherally located land saw the partial ban on wood construction as a fair and flexible solution to the fire problem and viewed the comprehensive ban as evil. Both the city's working class residents and its so-called cheap-lot speculators wanted to preserve their right to build structures out of wood. The owners of peripherally located land liked frame construction because it facilitated real estate speculation, wooden buildings being comparatively easy to tear down or move away to make space for more valuable buildings. Workers, meanwhile, literally depended on frame construction for building and owning their own homes.

Chicago's workers owned a large share of the city's working class housing stocks. They had been able to build and own their own houses, despite their poverty, because land outside the central business district had been relatively cheap, because many landowners had been willing to lease land to them, when they could not afford to buy it, and because the Board of Aldermen had never before done anything to stop them from building wooden shanties and cottages, the only kind of housing they could afford to build. They liked being able to move their houses, because this enabled them to keep the capital they had invested in the structures when their landlords pushed them off the land by raising rents or refusing to renew ground leases. Needless to say, it was much cheaper to transport wooden shanties than it was to move brick buildings. This meant that the comprehensive ban on wooden construction threatened not only the investment strategies of the city's land speculators but also the investment strategies of the workers. Worse, it threatened many workers' way of life.[25]

The trade-offs necessitated by the two competing fire ordinances mirrored the larger economic divisions in Chicago society, pitting the poor against the relatively well-to-do. This social cleavage, in turn, reflected back upon the conflict over the ordinances, further polarizing the opponents.

One consequence was that the advocates of the comprehensive ordinance, socially and economically distanced as they were from the working class proponents of the limited ordinance, were able to convince themselves that brick construction was, in the final analysis, as cheap as frame construction and that, therefore, workers who wanted to build their own homes should, if they had any sense at all, be in favor of the more far reaching law. This conviction rested on the mistaken belief that brick houses cost only about ten to fifteen percent more than wooden ones, a small increment that reformers believed would easily be offset by lower fuel costs and insurance rates.[26]

In fact, however, brick housing cost more than twice as much to build as frame housing. The huge price differential was a result of the grade of the streets in the outlying districts having been raised by seven to eight feet to accommodate sewers and improve surface drainage. Since only the streets had been lifted, home builders had to raise their houses to bring them up to street level. Brick houses required massive seven- to eight-foot-high brick foundation walls that had to extend several feet underground to support the weight of the structures, while frame houses could be raised on wooden stilts. According to the spokesmen for the workers, these brick foundations alone cost more than the whole of a wooden house. This put brick houses completely out of reach of most poor people, even though they were indeed safer and cheaper to heat and maintain than wooden homes. Unfortunately, because they had had no experience with it, the advocates of the comprehensive ordinance evidently did not even know that this difficulty existed.[27]

Another consequence of the social split was that it was easy for the middle class proponents of the comprehensive law to deny the fact that the prohibition against house moving would be a source of considerable suffering for the poor. As far as they were concerned, Chicago's "house-moving business" was primarily a cheap-lot speculators' enterprise, the means by which slumlords got rid of the ugly and dangerous shanties with which they filled their lots after property values rose. They gave short shrift to arguments that the prohibition would cause many workers to lose their homes. They did not even believe that working class people were an important source of home ownership in the city. "Nineteen-twentieths of Chicago's cottages are built by speculators rather than the poor," the *Times* asserted, for example. "Fortynine-Fiftieths," it declared later. These misconceptions led advocates of the comprehensive ordinance to deny stubbornly that the additional cost of building with brick and the prohibition on house moving were in any way legitimate reasons for opposing their law.[28]

As these socially based mistaken assumptions demonstrated, the middle class supporters of a total ban on wood construction had no understanding of how costly their improvement would be in human terms. Consequently, it was easy for them to see any softness on the fire limits issue as a sign of stupidity or, worse, as evidence of cynical manipulation of popular sympathy for the sufferings of the working poor. It was also easy for them to dismiss categorically the opponents of the comprehensive ordinance as "speculators and their hired clacques" and "bummers [corrupt machine politicians] and their notorious dupes."[29] This obdurate wrongheadedness made it impossible for the middle class to participate in any meaningful debate on the issue. And this, in turn, enraged the working class. The upshot was that after two months of inconclusive debate among the Board of Aldermen, the conflict came to a head with a working class march on City Hall that represented a self-conscious confrontation between Chicago's upper and lower classes.

The march on City Hall was a manifestation of the most fundamental obstacle to structural improvement of all: poor peoples' inelastic demand for substandard structures, in this case, a demand complicated by the desire of many poor people to own their own homes. It was born in Chicago's North Division, a district filled with impoverished German, Swedish, and Irish immigrants. The great fire had destroyed over ninety-five percent of all the buildings in existence there, most of which had been small wooden houses owned by immigrant residents.[30] The leaders of the local German community, the largest and best organized immigrant group in the area, planned the demonstration at a meeting that a local Alderman had called to determine how his constituents wanted him to vote on the fire limits issue. The meeting was apparently the first opportunity that area residents had had to voice their opinions of the fire limits publicly, and it quickly turned into a mass protest against the comprehensive ordinance.[31]

The rhetoric of the speakers at this and another mass meeting the next day makes clear that the protestors fully recognized that it was their own poverty that made the improvement of structures impossible. It also makes clear that, as a result, they saw the ordinance in class terms as an attack by the upper classes on their material well-being and their economic independence. The preamble to a petition opposing the ordinance put it his way: "There are evil counsellors who persistently urge upon our public authorities the assumed necessity of *crushing out* the poorer lot owners by preventing them from rebuilding in such a manner as their limited means enable them to do" (emphasis added). One resolution stated, "Instead of enjoying the blessings of independent homes, our laboring people would be crowded into those terrible tenement houses which are the curse of eastern cities. The effect of the great fire would then have been to make the rich richer and the poor poorer." One speaker went so far as to say that making the rich richer and the poor poorer was the real goal of the ordinance all along. "The face of it was," he declared, "that foreign speculators and capitalists wanted to make 20%" by loaning money on brick buildings. The petition emphasized the plight of impoverished cheap-lot owners who would have to sell their lots at terrible losses if not allowed to build wooden houses and pointed out the unfairness of a law permitting wooden sheds, cornices, bay windows, and sidewalks while prohibiting workers from building wooden homes.[32]

The bitter resistance this inspired is evident in the rhetoric of some of the speakers at the meetings. As one of the leaders of the march, Anton Caspar Hesing, publisher of the German-language newspaper, the *Staats Zeitung*, said, "I will support the law to the fullest extent so long as it is a reasonable law, and if it is not calculated to crush out our lives. But if they insist on carrying out its demands, we will apply force to resist it. . . . If they send a force against us," Hesing added in perhaps his most extreme statement, "we can bring 5,000 citizens against their 300 policemen. I need not tell you who would prove victorious in such an emergency."[33]

The march began about seven o'clock, Monday night, January 15, when a crowd of about a hundred people assembled at the corner of Market and Illinois Streets. They were soon joined by men carrying torches and banners. They then moved on to Alderman Thomas Carney's nearby grocery store, where they listened to speakers who instructed them to go to the City Council and express their wishes in an orderly, respectable, gentlemanly way. After this meeting broke up, they began their walk to the City Hall. As they proceeded, other groups of demonstrators joined them, carrying banners and playing music, until the crowd finally swelled to several thousand people. As the procession went on, it became, as planned, more and more a parade, accompanied by a band and drummers, men on horseback, banner carriers, torch bearers, and thousands of people singing and yelling. Some of the marchers were marginal youths, drifters, and other riffraff looking for excitement. Most of the participants, however, were respectable German, Irish, Swedish, Norwegian, and native homeowners and would-be homeowners, many of whom even the most conservative newspapers had to admit appeared to be "good citizens." Like the rhetoric of some of the speechmakers, however, the slogans on some of the banners displayed the deep fears and class-based tensions that helped to motivate the protest. Among these slogans were the phrases "Leave a Home for the Laborer," "Don't Vote Any More for the Poor Man's Oppressor," "The Voice of the People," "No Barracks," "No Tenements," and "The Relief, Temperance, and Fire Limits Swindle Must Be Cut Down." Most radical of all was a banner that on one side displayed a square and compass and other carpenter tools arranged to resemble a skull and crossbones and on the other side showed a man hanging from a scaffold and bore the words "This is the Lot of those Who Vote for the Fire Limits."

The protestors' plan was to march to the temporary City Hall established after the fire and present the Aldermen with their petitions. As it happened, however, the leaders lost control of the by then very large and increasingly unruly crowd once the demonstrators reached City Hall. Hesing was at City Hall when the marchers arrived. He asked fifteen of the banner bearers to take their banners and accompany the leaders into the council chamber to present the group's petitions. At this point, however, another man began addressing the assemblage on, of all things, temperance, and people began hooting him down. At about the same time, some police and Aldermen came out and attempted to prevent the demonstrators from carrying any banners into the hall. Soon hundreds of people began surging into the building. Several policemen and a sergeant-at-arms attempted to stop them but succeeded only in infuriating them, and scores of people pushed their way up the stairs and into the council chamber. Inside, the demonstrators tried to discuss their grievances with the few Aldermen who had not already fled, and, in the confusion, ex-Alderman Conlan, another leader of the march, and Hesing attempted to make short speeches to explain why the North Siders opposed the comprehensive fire ordinance. In the middle of Hesing's speech, some people out on the street began throwing bricks through the windows. The crowd in the chamber panicked momentarily, but then the janitor turned off the lights, and everyone began to leave. The demonstration was over.

The confrontation between the classes over the fire limits continued, however. The middle and upper class residents of Chicago responded to this "uprising" of homeowners and would-be homeowners with roars of outrage and horror. The tenor of their reaction is aptly conveyed by this screaming headline in the *Times*: "Mongrel Firebugs Break Up Session of the City Fathers!" Liberal Republican papers such as the *Times* and the *Tribune* naturally were especially aghast. Even the *Evening Post*, which normally sided with the "regular" Republican Party – that is, with the Republican machine and its working-class constituency – was appalled by the breakdown of law and order and headlined its description of the demonstration, "A Thousand Lunatics Storm City Hall and Drive Out the Aldermen."[34]

Like the rhetoric of the demonstration itself, the initial overreaction to the march by the editors and writers of the middle class press makes clear why the social and political division in the city made calm, rational debate on the fire limits issue so difficult. Both the *Times* and the *Tribune* saw the demonstrators as a mob manipulated by "un-American" and "unreasoning" foreigners, a corrupt, political-machine mob composed "in great part," in the overwrought words of the *Times*, "by the law defying creatures who have heretofore composed the constituency of the Aldermanic thieves . . . and deadbeats" defeated in the last election by the reformers running on the Fire Proof ticket. Most significantly, from a class perspective, both newspapers saw the protest as a communist uprising, as "one of those rare cases of communism that has thus far been vouchsafed to the American people," which reminded a writer in the *Tribune* of the "bloody periods" of the French Revolution and the editor of the *Times* of the riots in Paris during the Revolution of 1848. What particularly upset them was the "invasion" of the council chamber by the demonstrators, with their banners bearing "red hot" slogans. Both saw the machine behind this communistic excess, which indicates how blurred the class and party tensions in the city were. Thus the *Times*, for example, concluded, "The assault of this mob of riotous bummers raises an issue which precludes compromise. A war is declared by the bummer element which must be fought out along this line."[35]

Despite the inflammatory rhetoric of some of the demonstrators and the near riot in the council chamber, however, there is no evidence that any of the organizers of the march intended it to be the first shot in a war against the middle and upper classes or the advocates of political reform. To the contrary, they plainly intended to use it simply to articulate their demands on the fire limits issue alone. The leaders of the demonstration believed that it was the best and indeed the only way that the North Siders could make their interests on this matter known to the reform Aldermen elected on the Fire Proof ticket, over whom they had no formal or informal control. Along with the other participants, they also believed that this extraordinary method of demand articulation was perfectly legitimate. German workingmen meeting under the auspices of the Arbeiter Society, for example, formally endorsed it, affirming the right of the citizens of the city to protest oppressive laws that threatened the well-being of the working class.[36] Hesing compared it to the abolitionist agitation that occurred before the Civil War.[37] According to Hesing, even the banners that had so upset the middle class were meant to serve legitimate and essential demand articulation functions. One of the leaders of the protest, Alderman Schaffner, had told the people at the mass meeting held before the march that the other Aldermen "would only be influenced by such visible signs." Well aware that any loss of discipline would only stiffen the opposition, the leaders of the demonstration had repeatedly called upon the demonstrators to restrain their passions and make their wishes known with as much gentlemanly dignity as possible. In fact, they had made the people at the earlier mass meeting take an oath to behave themselves during the entire demonstration. But in the end, the leaders had lost control of the protest, which had allowed the intense class feelings underlying the workers' rejection of the comprehensive ordinance to come to the fore.[38]

Significantly, the demonstration might have been avoided if the government had been willing to negotiate with the North Siders. Hesing had offered to discuss an alternative to both the comprehensive and limited ordinances. He had developed a plan for the people of Cincinnati. It involved turning over control of construction practices to property owners on a block by block basis and allowing a majority to determine by vote whether wooden buildings would be permitted on their blocks. The plan had been a great success in Cincinnati, and Hesing believed it offered a way out of the conflict between the two plans here. Unfortunately, however, the Mayor and the Board of Aldermen had refused even to talk with him about it. This had forced him to turn to the mass protest to make his plan and the widespread opposition to the comprehensive ordinance known.[39]

Despite the initially hostile reaction of the middle class, the demonstration served its purpose well, making the rest of the city aware of the North Siders' position and the intensity of their feelings on the fire limits matter. Hesing followed up the march with speeches, interviews, and letters that were carried in most of the city's English-language newspapers. These also helped to instruct people on the matter.

An impressive shift in general opinion followed. Two days after the demonstration, the *Evening Post*, which had been calling the protestors "lunatics,"
retreated from that stance, declaring that public sentiment had calmed considerably now that everyone could see that the demonstration had been
undertaken by "respectable people."[40] A few days later, a group of "first
class" North Side property owners meeting on the issue generally displayed
a similarly subdued mood, with several speakers declaring their willingness
to settle for an ordinance that would protect their rights "without being too
oppressive on the poor." They appointed a committee that included Hesing
himself to draw up a compromise ordinance.[41]

Even the *Times* ultimately moderated its opposition to a two-zone ordinance. Having always insisted that any rational person would wholeheartedly
embrace the comprehensive plan, it at first refused to accept the validity of
Hesing's arguments against it, dismissing any compromise as a "truculent,
servile, and ignominious surrender to the bummer Ku Klux mob." The
editors of the paper even called Hesing a "liar" for asserting that brick
houses would require expensive brick foundation walls extending four to
five feet underground.[42] After a respectable architect wrote to the paper and
corroborated Hesing's claim,[43] however, the editors abruptly stopped their
hysterical barrage of criticism against the bummer mob and ceased calling
for a comprehensive law. Although they basically dropped their editorial
coverage of the issue, at one point they even defended a proposal to permit
the relocation of wooden buildings on behalf of landless homeowners.[44] Only
the editors of the *Tribune* kept up the attack, refusing to admit that workers
had a legitimate grievance against the comprehensive ordinance and stubbornly maintaining to the end that the "defense of the poor" argument was
"pure hypocrisy."[45]

Because of its effectiveness as a demand articulation mechanism, the
demonstration quickly inspired legislative action. The Board of Aldermen
met two days after the march to consider petitions for and against the
comprehensive ordinance. The Aldermen read several substitute bills providing for a more limited ban on wood construction and passed an amendment to the existing ordinance based on Hesing's Cincinnati plan. Establishing
a consensus on where to put the fire limit boundaries and whether to allow
the repair, improvement, and relocation of existing wood structures remained
a problem. As a result, the debate continued for several weeks and the
Chairman of the Board of Aldermen quickly accumulated a "stupendous
pile" of amendments.[46]

What is important, however, is that the Aldermen ultimately passed an
ordinance that gave the North Siders just about all they wanted (see Figure
6.2). The new law not only sanctioned the construction of wooden frame
structures in all but a small section of the North Division along the Chicago

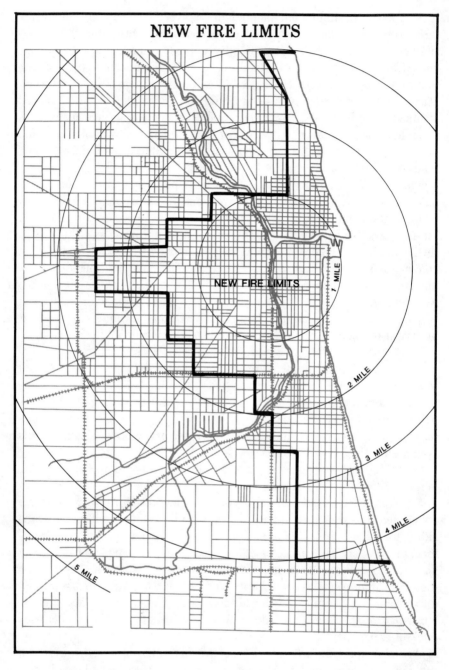

Figure 6.2.

River (and most of the West and South Divisions as well), but also permitted, with a few exceptions, the relocation, repair, and improvement of existing frame structures within the protected inner zone. The ordinance went considerably farther than the ban it replaced, since it enlarged the inner zone, prohibited the establishment of new, fire-hazardous manufactories like planing mills and blind factories in the inner zone, completely banned the manufacture of explosive materials in the inner zone, and included Hesing's Cincinnati amendment. However, it contained no provisions for effective enforcement of its prohibitions. Thus it did little to stop people from building wooden houses even in the inner zone.[47]

One of the ironies of the struggle over the fire limits was that the proposed ban on wood construction was never, in any of its formulations, a particularly effective instrument for fireproofing the city. Although all of the proposals outlawed frame construction in at least some part of the city, even the strictest ones permitted flammable felt and tar roofs, wooden sheds and outhouses, wooden sidewalks, wooden cornices and window frames and other wooden exterior work, and various unsafe construction practices in the protected zones. This was a reflection of the technological and conceptual constraints people operated under in attempting to improve environmental conditions during this period.

An even bigger irony was that by the time the issue was finally resolved, four months after the conflagration, the city had already been largely rebuilt in wood. Cities were not able to use their police powers to condemn or compel the renovation of structures that violated building laws in any sweeping way until the twentieth century. Thus even if a strict, enforceable comprehensive ordinance had been passed it would not have had much of an impact on Chicago's building stock for many years, at least in the built-up sections of the city. The advocates of a comprehensive law fully realized this. Soon after the November election, the editors of the *Tribune* urged the old Board of Aldermen to hurry and pass a comprehensive law before the new Board took office, since, they argued, "every" owner of a vacant lot who "is mean enough to put his neighbor's property at risk and has capital enough to pay for a post and clapboard is making all haste to begin before the [new] ordinance takes effect."[48] Because no one was about to prohibit desperately needed new construction in the half-demolished city until a strict new ordinance could be passed, however, especially in winter, there was nothing that could be done to prevent the reconstruction of a wooden city.

Because of the failure to pass a comprehensive fire limits law in the immediate aftermath of the disaster, an important legacy of the great fire was the construction of a city of homes that were owned by workers as well as middle and upper class people. The high wages and good hours workers received to rebuild the city fueled a working class housing boom that encompassed the South and the West Divisions as well as the North Division and that even spread into the cheap land beyond the city limits in some places.[49]

Because of the physical durability of these wooden structures, however, another legacy was the slum housing that social reformers decried during the rest of the nineteenth century and the first four decades of the twentieth. Owing to the success of this and later attempts to prevent the extension of the fire limits, the landscape of working class Chicago was dominated until the time of urban renewal by small, dark, difficult to heat, tinderbox cottages that were often crowded two or three deep on a single lot.[50] Like the editors of the *Times* and the *Tribune*, social critics and historians have often been quick to blame slum conditions like these on profiteering land speculators, builders, and slumlords. As the battle over the fire ordinance shows, however, the real source of the problem was the inelastic demand for inadequate housing caused by the poverty that gave so many people no choice but to live in unsafe, unsanitary, and overcrowded homes.

The post-fire housing relief effort of the Citizens' Relief and Aid Society mirrored these conundrums. In an entirely commendable attempt to reduce people's sufferings, the Society's Shelter Committee spent a large part of the $4.2 million in aid sent to Chicago immediately after the fire on shelter for the homeless. The Committee first provided those in need with tents. It quickly found these insufficient, however, and so embarked upon a program of giving the needy much more substantial structures. These included 7,983 houses for families who had owned and lost homes on owned or leased lots, as well as 10 barracks for people who had not previously owned their own houses but had simply rented rooms in tenement houses. The Committee spent about $125 on each of the houses it gave away, a sum which covered a cook stove, cooking utensils, several chairs, a table, a bed, and bedding, as well as all the construction materials necessary for building the house itself. Most of the recipients were laborers who put the houses together themselves. In addition, the Committee paid the construction costs for the houses it gave to widows and other people who were incapable of supplying their own labor.[51]

All this made the housing relief effort a remarkable example of nineteenth century subsidized working class housing construction. The problem was that the houses embodied all of the inadequacies of the houses constructed by speculators and the poor themselves. Simple twelve- by sixteen-foot and twenty- by sixteen-foot balloon-frame boxes lined with felt paper and topped with wooden roofs and iron chimneys, they were hardly more than wooden shanties. The recipients constructed them in exactly the same places as they would have had they paid for them on their own. In many cases, this meant that two or three houses were crowded on a lot on some of the cheapest and, according to the City Physician, most insalubrious land in the city.[52]

Like the rest of the housing being built by and for the poor, most of the relief structures became permanent components of Chicago's physical landscape.[53] The editors of the *Tribune*, ever concerned about the quality of the city's building stock, noted the profound irony of the situation. Although silent on the question of whether the Association's money might have been better spent on better accommodations for the poor, they warned that the "relief shanties" should never be allowed to become permanent. They urged that the occupants be encouraged to leave the "shanties" for more fireproof houses "provided with all the sanitary comforts and conveniences . . . as soon as their wages will authorize them to do so."[54]

Here again, what observers like the editors of the *Tribune* never seem to have fully realized was that there would always be people who were too poor to obtain something better. This was a reality that not only made the construction of such structures inevitable in the absence of any laws prohibiting their construction, but also made the voluntary abandonment of the buildings virtually impossible once they had been built.[55]

Other improvements in Chicago's building stocks

In addition to stimulating this abortive effort to outlaw all frame construction in Chicago, the great fire led to attempts by property holders and land speculators to increase the number of buildings available for business use and to build commercial structures that were more beautiful as well as better adapted to the needs of business than those the fire had destroyed. In contrast to the attempt to end all frame construction, many of these efforts were actually successful. Here, too, however, the way in which Chicagoans set out to obtain change reveals the continuing significance of a wide variety of frictions in the process of environmental redevelopment.

Chicagoans especially wanted to expand the stock of commercial buildings in the central city. Despite the rapid growth of business activity in the city, most of Chicago's centrally located commercial edifices had for years been confined to the few blocks below Wells Street on the south side of the Chicago River lying on the four east-west streets closest to the river. As crowding, ever increasing land costs, and the enthusiastic way in which businessmen had snapped up space in new stores and warehouses as soon as it became available indicate, this tiny corner of the city (shown in Figure 6.3) had simply been too small to accommodate the ever growing needs of businessmen for more and more space. Stores and warehouses had begun

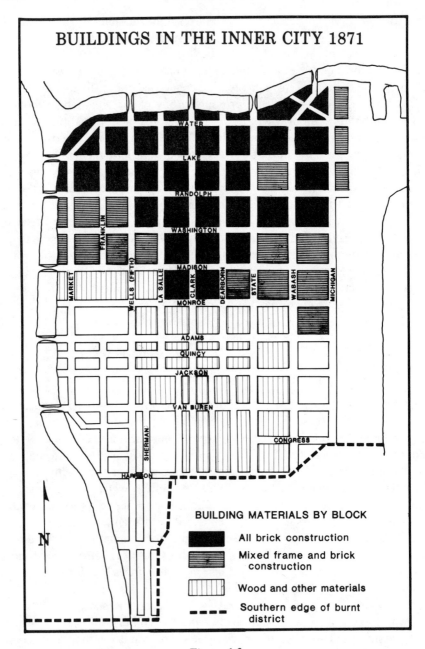

Figure 6.3.

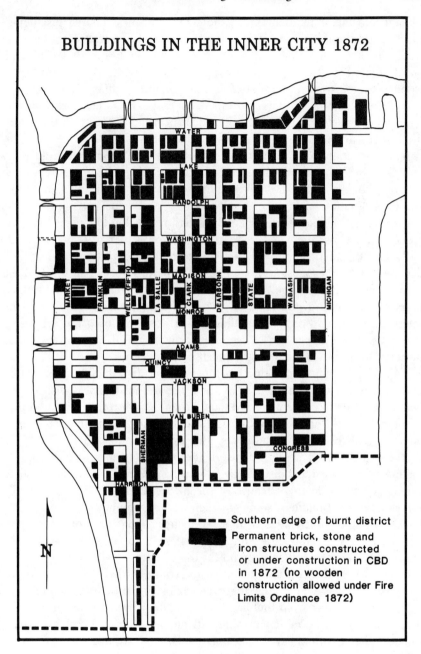

Figure 6.4.

to spill into the slums that ringed the central business district just before the fire, largely in response to the construction of a new streetcar line on Madison Street, the Board of Trade's move to the corner of Washington and LaSalle Streets, and Potter Palmer's mighty efforts to turn run-down, wooden State Street into a first class business thoroughfare. This new development had not amounted to much, however, as a sustained boom in land prices makes clear. In fact, there had been only a scattering of commercial construction, even along Madison and State.[56]

Reconstruction more than solved this problem, as the map in Figure 6.4 indicates. Indeed, it resulted in such a large increase in the number and size of stores, banks, and warehouses in the center of the city that an actual surplus of commercial space developed and land values on some streets began to fall. The newspapers began discussing the development of surplus space and a consequent fall in rents before the winter was out. By mid-1873, the President of the Chicago Board of Trade, thoroughly alarmed, declared that the expansion of commercial building stocks had reached the point where it had become "certainly all that could be expected in a full ten years of such improvement as was likely to have been made without the intervention of the fire." Concluding that it was therefore "not surprising that many of the upper stories are only partly occupied," he warned landowners to refrain from any further such construction.[57]

This far-reaching turnaround was the direct result of the fire's destruction of structures in the central city. Because the central business district was hemmed in by Lake Michigan and the Chicago River on the east and north, property holders could expand Chicago's centrally located commercial building stock only by constructing new buildings in the uncommercialized area on the southern and western edges of the business center or by enlarging buildings in the business district itself. They had been unwilling and to some extent unable to do this because of the physical durability and economic value of existing buildings, some of which were substantial stores and warehouses, some of which were fashionable mansions, but most of which were nothing more than wooden shanties.

Considering the pent-up demand for more commercial space in the area and the ease with which antiquated structures might have been torn down or moved, it may seem strange that a collection of old buildings could have stopped landowners from building new stores and warehouses in a highly desirable section of a rapidly growing city like this. That a number of small wooden shanties could have done so may seem even stranger. The obstacles to redevelopment that these buildings posed resulted less from the cost of moving or demolishing them, however, than from the kinds of use to which their owners and tenants put them.

The buildings' physical and social characteristics generated neighborhood effects that, at best, slowed the course of commercial redevelopment and, at worst, made redevelopment nearly impossible. The houses in the slums on Market, Franklin, and Wells and on the streets in the notorious "Conley's Patch" vice district, for example, were so old and dilapidated that most resembled shacks. They sheltered a criminal and working class population that, in the opinion of observers, made the area "a good place to keep away from." Prostitutes, thieves, gamblers, transients, and the area's other disreputable or merely impoverished inhabitants discouraged redevelopment by creating a lucrative captive market for property owners, many of whom evidently made small fortunes by simply holding their properties and letting them deteriorate. Together with the ramshackle buildings, the inhabitants of this area discouraged redevelopment by distorting the demand for change, since their presence repelled other kinds of users and so turned businesses' demand for conveniently located new commercial space into an unsatisfied want. As one observer wrote, the district was potentially a very valuable one for commerce, "being eligibly situated in respect to some of the most important thoroughfares in the business portion of the South Division." But because the area "had for 50 years [sic] been possessed by such tenements and such tenants . . . the redemption of its character and its use for business purposes for a great while to come were matters of much uncertainty."[58]

The positive neighborhood effects generated by more substantial buildings functioned in a different way, of course, but with much the same result. Along Michigan Avenue, for example, "dwelling houses of the most magnificent description" were the barriers to change. Impressive mansions lined the west side of the street. Their prestige, their tree-filled yards, their proximity to Lake Park, and their open, panoramic views of Lake Michigan discouraged commercial redevelopment, not by repelling business but by encouraging the residents, most of whom owned the land on which the homes stood, to keep their mansions. The area suffered the negative neighborhood effects caused by proximity to business and the noisy Illinois Central freight trains that constantly rumbled along the tracks running above the lake just beyond Lake Park, not far from their front doors. The positive effects far outweighed these problems, however. As a result, homeowners clung to their lovely and prestigious old structures, despite the profit they could have made from redevelopment, defying the businessmen and railroad owners who desperately wanted to take over their land and who thought it "perfectly absurd" of them to "resist the march of progress."[59]

The great speed with which property holders rebuilt these non-commercial areas for business use after the buildings were destroyed makes clear just how powerful a barrier to change the buildings and their attendant neighborhood effects had been. The redevelopment of the western slums was especially remarkable. The fire completely cleared the area, not only dispersing the inhabitants, but reducing the district's wooden structures to ashes and so leaving barely any rubble. Marshall Field, John V. Farwell, William Coolbaugh, and other men involved in the drygoods and banking trades rushed to take advantage of the opportunity for commercial construction this mass destruction suddenly presented, buying and leasing land and arranging for the construction of new stores and warehouses and banks in the area along Market, Franklin, and Wells, between Madison and Monroe. Perhaps hoping to beat other businessmen and developers to the punch, or perhaps simply fearing a return of the old conditions, they moved as rapidly as possible, with some, like Field, beginning construction less than two weeks after the disaster. Other businessmen and landowners quickly followed their example, completing the commercial transformation of the area. The first stores and warehouses were ready for business less than four months after the conflagration.[60]

Not surprisingly, this redevelopment both involved and stimulated a great deal of real estate speculation. In the four blocks south of Madison between Franklin and the South Branch of the Chicago River, for example, at least eighteen sales involving twenty-one of the forty-seven lots and sublots on the blocks took place in the first six months after the fire, and a booming market in options, leaseholds, and mortgages developed.[61] What is significant, however, is that most of the people taking part were businessmen who were contracting for or building larger quarters for themselves, in addition to positioning themselves to take advantage of a rise in land values, at least in the initial stages of reconstruction. This emphasizes the extent to which this new construction represented a solution to the extreme congestion in the old central business area. Similar, almost overnight transformations of other residential areas occurred on Michigan Avenue as far south as Harrison, the edge of the burnt district, and in other areas on the periphery of the old business center.

The course of reconstruction inside the old business district was comparatively slow, especially in the most established streets east of Washington and south of State. In fact, the pace was so much slower that it became a matter of considerable alarm among capitalists and other observers who began to fear that the area would never be properly redeveloped. In mid-February, for example, the *Tribune* warned that the area north of Washington and east of State was running the risk of being given over to saloons and sailors' boardinghouses and becoming what Franklin and Wells had been before the fire.[62]

This delay in reconstruction was partly a result of the fact that there were far more lucrative speculative opportunities available outside the old business center. For example, William Coolbaugh, the owner of the Union National Bank, seemed to forget temporarily about reconstructing the Union National at its original site at the corner of LaSalle and Washington. Instead, he rushed to buy land in the peripheral slums and to build a new bank at the corner of Madison and Market, which contained enough space for four other banks. He hoped to make a killing by renting the space in the new building to other banks for $80,000 per year and then profiting from the tremendous increase in land values that would result from the movement of financial concerns into this former slum area. Coolbaugh did not finally announce plans to rebuild at the Union National Bank's original site until early February, five months after the fire, and he seems to have done so then mainly because other bankers had expressed a stubborn unwillingness to follow him to the former slum.[63]

There were much more profound reasons for the comparatively slow rebuilding of the area than this, however, factors that help illuminate the general problems of structural improvement in central business districts. They were the anti-improvement, income orientation of the majority of property holders there, the prevalence of small lots held by different owners, the long prosperity of the area in the years before the fire, and the difficulty of getting structural redevelopment going under such constraints, despite the conflagration's obliteration of the existing buildings.

Inertia was a long-standing and especially serious problem on Lake Street, where it became a topic of much commentary. In the early 1850s, property holders had constructed "costly and elegant" stores and warehouses on the street, thereby making the critically located thoroughfare Chicago's most prestigious business street. For almost twenty years, the landowners had enjoyed the rewards that went with the street's excellent reputation and its consequently high land values, notwithstanding the narrowness of the lots and buildings. Having invested so heavily in making Lake Street this important, however, the owners had done next to nothing to maintain its position, neither reconstructing the buildings nor renovating them to prevent deterioration, let alone adapting them to their tenants' changing needs and tastes. Instead, as property records show, they had simply leased or entrusted the properties to second parties, who, it appears, had had even less interest in investing in capital improvement than they. In the mid-1860s, people like Potter Palmer had begun to exploit their inaction, luring some of their best tenants away by building far larger, far more magnificent stores and warehouses on thoroughfares like State Street. Even then, however, Lake Street owners had not tried to restore Lake Street's declining reputation by improving their buildings.[64]

The fire did not change their position. In fact, it was not until late February, nearly half a year after the conflagration, that their attitude toward reconstruction began to change. The reasons for the change help illuminate the collective dynamic of the barriers to redevelopment.

The street's property owners were demoralized in the aftermath of the disaster. As the *Evening Post* put it, "For a time property owners were paralyzed and uncertain whether to rebuild or dispose of their property, even at the sacrifice demanded." Unlike property holders in the peripheral slums, many of whom sold out in the first few weeks after the fire to ambitious developers, they were unwilling to divest themselves of their land. They simply did not know what to do.[65]

General redevelopment finally began when one property holder, Isaac Burch, leased five adjoining lots on the east side of Lake, which had been entrusted to two other men, to John W. Doane, an ambitious risk taker. Doane immediately announced plans to construct a huge warehouse for the grocery wholesale trade to cover the entire five-lot site. At the time many people considered Doane's act to be "both bold and hazardous," given the low morale of the other owners. Nevertheless, together with the newspapers' increasingly alarming predictions of the impending loss of all business to the street, it galvanized the other property holders into taking action. What happened was that they finally began to work together to achieve an ambitious redevelopment of the street. In the words of an observer, they "clubbed together and rebuilt much broader stores, with higher rooms such as are adapted in every particular to the wants of the wholesale trade," and thus successfully rebuilt the street for central business district use.[66]

The catalytic effect of Doane's announcement illuminates the follow-the-leader aspect of structural redevelopment. In the process, it highlights the barrier to change caused by the unwillingness of most property owners to initiate improvements which depended for their success on simultaneous improvement by many other owners to overcome negative neighborhood effects. The cooperative aspect of the redevelopment of the street also illustrates a related barrier to change, the land assembly problem. The Lake Street property owners could not have covered the street with so many large new warehouses and stores without some form of land assembly, because the lots were very narrow and landownership highly fragmented. Significant assembly by land purchase was out of the question because very few owners were willing to put their valuable property on the market. Development, therefore, depended on cooperation or on the creative leasing of large plots, like Isaac Burch's leasing of several adjoining lots to John W. Doane. Contemporary reports indicate that cooperation and follow-the-leader imitation were what transformed the street into an important wholesale center. Needless to say, the transformation would not have taken place without the total destruction of the owners' collective income sources, which suddenly put them all in the same position, giving them the motivation they needed to improve their individual properties collectively.[67]

Significantly, the "clubbing together" phenomenon that occurred on Lake

Street took place elsewhere in the business district. Though certainly not the only way that reconstruction took place, cooperation was important even in the peripheral slums where many lots of land changed hands, both because of the difficulty of assembling the large contiguous parcels and the huge amounts of capital required to undertake large redevelopment schemes and because of the desirability of building on a large scale to maximize future tenants' agglomeration economies. Interestingly, the *Tribune* and the *Times*, in their paranoid way, sometimes referred to these cooperative redevelopment efforts as "rings" and "combinations," pejorative terms that they usually reserved for political machines and corrupt business monopolies, apparently because certain politicians were involved in some of the cooperative schemes. These conspiratorial labels gave the redevelopments a patina of connivance and venality that, on the political level at least, was probably undeserved, since in all likelihood most participants took their cues from the bolder, more ambitious "ring" leaders in a fairly spontaneous, follow-the-leader manner. Such talk reflected the significance of this kind of redevelopment, however. It further testified to the way that the need to rebuild quickly, on a massive scale, loosened the barriers to structural improvement on a collective level.[68]

The extension of the fire limits also contributed to the expansion of the city's supply of centrally located commercial buildings. The passage of the first revision of the existing law in late October stretched the prohibition against wooden construction into the Western Division and to the southern edge of the burnt district at Harrison Street. This change in the law was especially important because it came so early in the reconstruction process, before the area had been rebuilt in wood. Just how far the expansion of the number of commercial buildings in the central city would have gone if this prohibition had not been passed is, of course, unclear. Given the rapidity with which wooden buildings were thrown up outside the limits and the powerful barrier to commercial construction that such structures and their attendant neighborhood effects usually created, however, it is certainly unlikely that property owners would have gone so far as to produce the surplus of commercial space that they did, in fact, bring on the market. As it happened, the fire limits ordinance cleared much more land for commerce than central business district concerns had any need for. As a result, a great deal of space west of Monroe Street was simply not built upon at all for some years after the great fire.[69]

All of these changes were, of course, closely tied up with the larger question of spatial redevelopment. So were the changes in the supply of industrial and residential buildings in the city. This interrelatedness is one of the present study's most important analytical points and will be discussed in more detail later.

What is important to emphasize here is that the structural redevelopment of the central business district represented a significant improvement in the quality of Chicago's building stocks, and not just a reorganization of the central city's patterns of land usage. First of all, there was the dramatic increase in the number of buildings suitable for commercial use. Second, there were measurable advances in the buildings' spatial and architectural amenities.

The qualitative improvement that brick and stone stores and warehouses made over wooden shanties is so obvious as to need no further comment here. In addition, however, the new buildings represented far-reaching advances over most of their supposedly first class predecessors. Although they still contained dangerous amounts of wood and other combustible materials, many of the new buildings benefited from more substantial foundations, thicker walls, and a comparatively careful mixing of mortar and laying of brick, improvements that made them more structurally sound than the often hastily and carelessly constructed stores and warehouses they replaced. Furthermore, many contained more passenger and freight elevators, advances that made their upper stories much more accessible than before. According to observers, they also contained more and better-designed fire escapes than the buildings they replaced. With a few exceptions, the new buildings were considered much more attractive as well.[70]

Most important, however, a large proportion of the new buildings were much more spacious than those the fire had destroyed. They not only tended to consist of one or two more stories than their four- and five-story predecessors, but because of land assembly or the cooperative way in which they had been built, they also tended to occupy more ground. On Lake Street, for example, most of the new business blocks contained stores that occupied one and a half lots and averaged thirty-seven feet in width. This was an important advance over the single-lot, twenty-five-foot width that had been standard before the fire. More impressive, there were stores and warehouses on other streets that were forty to more than one hundred feet wide and one hundred and sixty or more feet deep. John V. Farwell's "monster" new store on Monroe Street, for example, was ninety-six by one hundred and ninety feet. Field & Leiter Company's new structures on Madison were forty by one hundred and ninety and one hundred and sixty-one by one hundred and ninety. The extra space was a boon to wholesalers, retailers, and hoteleries and other concerns, for it not only gave them much more display and storage room than they had ever had before; more important, it gave them flexibility to arrange their quarters for a better transaction of business and admission of light.[71]

Business also benefited from a fall in rents, since the unprecedented surplus of commercial space the rebuilding brought to market reduced land values on Lake and other streets in the old business center. This was not particularly advantageous for landowners in the old business center, but it was a big gain for tenants.[72]

What must be kept in mind is that both the achievement of these improvements and the manner by which they were obtained make clear the extent to which supply-side frictions ordinarily discouraged property holders from delivering the improved accommodations that businessmen needed, wanted, and in many cases had the economic wherewithal to pay for. By loosening these barriers to change with its massive destruction of buildings, the great fire made the large-scale improvement of the built environment possible.

The conflagration could not loosen all of the obstacles to structural improvement on the supply side, however, just as it could not eliminate the demand constraints that resulted from the poverty of the working class. To be specific, it could not bring progress to construction technology. Like the working class's poverty, this fact took a heavy toll on building safety, as well as other improvement goals.

Chicagoans failed to achieve a fireproof new city because, in large part, they did not have the economic and political ability to do so, as has already been shown. Technology also figured in their failure, however. The reason was that architects and engineers did not yet know how to make buildings fireproof, or even safely fire resistant.

Efforts to build high-rise structures to meet the needs of Chicago's growing population ran up against the same blank wall. The great fire led to talk about the desirability of erecting tall buildings, evidently as much because of the solution they seemed to promise to the twin problems of congestion and urban sprawl as because of the pecuniary rewards they held out to investors. In one particularly enthusiastic article on the subject, for example, a writer discussed the possibility of erecting many-storied elevator apartment buildings with aerial gardens and roof arbors to provide Chicago's middle class with roomy and pleasant homes conveniently located in the space-starved inner city. He concluded that the "burning of our city cut a good many Gordian knots in a very summary fashion. Chicago, like New York, has been built without regard to purpose or law of the ultimate best. But" he added, "with the removal of so many obstructions, there can be no valid reason why a vast improvement in the system and compactness of building might not be inaugurated."[73]

In fact, however, the great fire had not cut the Gordian knot of the slow, step-by-step technological innovation process on which the development of such high-rise architecture depended, any more than it had severed the Gordian knot of poverty, which perpetuated the existence of unsafe, unsanitary slum housing in the city. As it happened, the conflagration drew a number of new architects into Chicago, including some who would ultimately play important roles in the development of high-rise steel frame architecture. Unfortunately, however, it could not change the evolutionary nature of technological innovation, which prevented such people from creating this architecture overnight. As a result, "sky dwelling places," like fireproof buildings, remained dreams in the minds of visionaries for many years to come. The fire could neither transform the social organization of the city nor modernize construction technology. As a result, ignorance and poverty continued to prevent the achievement of many desirable improvements in the city's building stocks, despite the complete rebuilding of a nearly four-square-mile section of the city. Such failures were as much a part of the legacy of reconstruction as the admirable successes.

Improving infrastructures

The Chicago fire caused people to demand improvements in nearly all of Chicago's infrastructures. These included improvements in streets, sidewalks, and the water system, as well as rail and port facilities. The demands stimulated a burst of environmental redevelopment that, like structural redevelopment, simultaneously demonstrated that the fire was a powerful stimulus for change and that strong and deep-seated barriers to change remained.

With no water in the city, the demand for more and better water service was especially frenetic. The most immediate need was to get the burnt-out water works back in operation, a task that took two weeks. As the newspapers, the Fire Department, and other concerned Chicagoans were soon pointing out, however, simply repairing the water works would not solve the city's water problems.

The *Tribune* raised the public cry for a system-wide redevelopment of water service when it called for a comprehensive fire limits ordinance. The paper demanded that a special system of reservoirs and mains be established to provide water for fire fighting purposes independently of the regular (and presently burnt-out) water works.[74] The Fire Department and other commentators voiced support for this idea, while renewing old demands for the installation of modern fire hydrants at every street corner in the central city and the purchase of floating fire engines for the Chicago River. Soon other critics were enlarging upon these plans with proposals that the entire system be redeveloped to increase the supply of water for ordinary household and industrial purposes.

A thorough revamping of the system was necessary because the existing water works and network of distribution pipes could provide neither the quantity of water nor the pressure that users required. Mechanical pumps forced water from Lake Michigan into a standing pipe that was one hundred and thirty-six feet high. This was high enough to create sufficient gravitational power to push the water through the city's nearly two hundred and fifty miles of mains and distribution pipes. Unfortunately, however, it was not high enough to create the pressure needed to fight large fires or, indeed, to supply the second stories of buildings located outside the center of the city. Old, extremely narrow mains and distribution pipes further reduced the already inadequate pressure created by the standing pipe.[75]

Critics suggested a number of ways to overcome these systemic problems. Most proposed variations on the *Tribune*'s original idea of creating some sort of supplemental water system to ensure the availability of additional sources of supply when the regular system was overtaxed or put out of commission by heavy use or a large fire. In most plans, this involved increasing the number of hydrants and establishing a network of reservoirs and artesian wells in every street intersection, or even "every" yard, workshop, warehouse, and livery stable in the central city, to make sure that additional supplies would be handy in times of need.[76] The more ambitious proposals went a step farther with plans for upgrading the technology of the water works in order to solve the water pressure problem at its source. The Fire Department and other commentators proposed that several sets of relatively small Holly pumping works be built across the city to drive water through the mains and distribution pipes mechanically. The Holly pumps would give the Board of Public Works the mechanical power they needed to increase and otherwise adjust the water pressure in different parts of the city at will. This, proponents argued, would benefit the city in two ways. It would allow the Fire Department to get rid of its expensive steam pump fire engines, since the Holly pumps would make extremely high, system-generated pressures possible. Perhaps even more important, it would give the Board of Public Works the flexibility to deal with the many demands of different residential and industrial users in a cost-effective way.[77]

The ultimate value of these suggestions was inevitably limited by the level of technology of the day. Nonetheless, proposals showed that some people were attempting to deal with Chicago's water problem in a positive, dynamic manner, with plans that reflected state of the art engineering ideas.

Unfortunately, neither the Board of Aldermen nor the Board of Public Works attempted to implement any of the recommendations during reconstruction. They did not even *try* to carry out the relatively modest proposals to upgrade and significantly increase the number of fire hydrants in the densely settled portions of the city. The Board of Public Works did improve the water works building by replacing the wooden roof the fire had destroyed with something more impervious to flame and by otherwise attempting to fireproof the structure. It also added a few up-to-date fire hydrants to those it had already installed in the most valuable sections of the central business district. Other than this, however, government officials did not come close to partially – let alone systematically – redeveloping the water system. Instead, they concentrated on "restoring" the pipes and hydrants the fire had destroyed and on extending water service into newly developing areas on the periphery of the city.[78]

The government's inaction reflects the redevelopment advocates' inability to articulate their demands for change in an effective way. Thus, like the defeat of the comprehensive fire limits ordinance, this failure to act illuminates some profound barriers to environmental change. In this case, the people calling for environmental redevelopment did not even manage to get a public decision making body to consider and debate their plans officially, let alone defeat them officially. The Board of Aldermen turned a deaf ear to their ideas, while the Board of Public Works ignored all but the cries for hydrants in the business center, only to dismiss summarily the possibility of significantly increasing the number of hydrants there for "want of funds."[79]

According to the Fire Commissioners, who described the communications gap in a report on the causes of the great fire, the problem was that the city government simply was not interested in this kind of infrastructural improvement. Neither the members of the Board of Aldermen nor those of the Board of Public Works were in the habit of listening to demands involving the redevelopment of the water system, nor had they been for years. The Fire Commissioners had been "advising and entreating" city officials to increase the number of fire hydrants in the city, to build fire reservoirs, to buy floating fire engines, and to build a set of Holly pumping works to increase water pressure since the mid-1860s, but they had had absolutely no success. The reason? "NOBODY NOTICED 'US,' " they explained with justifiable frustration. "None of these things were noticed by the mayor, the common council [Board of Aldermen], or the newspapers," they said. "The only thing we could do was ask for an increase of the engine companies, so that we might be prepared as well as possible to contend with the great fires which were and still are likely."[80]

A widespread lack of public interest in the water system partly accounts for this state of affairs. Apparently, at this point at least, the vast majority of people in Chicago simply did not care very much about such things as building new fire hydrants and introducing Holly pumping works, notwithstanding the catastrophe they had just experienced, perhaps because these improvements could not immediately and visibly benefit them personally. As a result, improvement proponents were unable to put the kind of public pressure on government decision makers that would have compelled them to take action.[81]

There was more at work here than this, however. As an extremely intense and widely supported effort to improve the system would show just a few years later, the demand articulation problem also resulted from the distribution of power in the city government and from the organizational biases and institutional autonomy of the Board of Public Works, the agency entrusted with the responsibility of constructing all of the city's public works. City law prevented members of the Fire Department and its parent agency, The Board of Police, the natural, intra-governmental spokesmen for water system improvements, from implementing any changes. The law even prevented the Fire Department from undertaking small-scale projects of purely departmental interest, like the construction of new fire hydrants. It turned these powers over to the Board of Public Works, which, unfortunately, was interested only in extending water infrastructures into previously unserviced areas. The Board's fixation on service extension at the expense of system redevelopment evidently resulted from the comparatively intense and compelling nature of the demand for service extensions by suburban real estate developers and from the pecuniary and political benefits that extension accordingly provided members of the Board and their political machines. Unfortunately, the Board was as possessive of its relatively unrewarding power to install fire hydrants, fire reservoirs, and Holly pumps as it was unwilling to make use of it, and being the municipal bureaucracy it was, zealously guarded its right to exercise its institutional prerogatives as it saw fit. Its hostility to redevelopment, coupled with its autonomy and monopoly on power, made it virtually impossible for the Fire Department and concerned people to express their demands for improvements in fire service in an effective way, without first mounting a political reform movement to make the Board receptive to their interests. Political reform was, of course, a complicated matter. As it turned out, it would take a second catastrophic fire (in 1874) to stimulate a reform movement strong enough to force the Board to begin instituting the redevelopment proposals.[82]

What is striking about this demand articulation problem is that the great Chicago fire, horrible as it was, did not galvanize people into cutting across the communications gap to secure improvements in the water system. The fact was, however, that the immensity of the destruction in Chicago itself also contributed to the demand problem and the government's inaction.

First of all, everybody in the city, from the members of the Board of Aldermen and the municipal bureaucracy on down, was so preoccupied with the work of restoration that there was little time or energy to spend on other matters.[83] Second, it cost so much to repair and replace the government property the fire had destroyed that there was almost no money left for ambitious improvement projects. The city had already reached its newly state-imposed debt ceiling, so it could not finance improvements by issuing municipal bonds. Moreover, it had relatively little cash on hand, notwith-

standing the timely receipt of $2,955,340 in state aid, because of careless
tax collection procedures, unsound budget setting practices, and recent State
Supreme Court decisions which retroactively prohibited the city from collecting betterment assessments. The lame duck Board of Aldermen had
rescinded nearly $1.5 million of the city's next taxes. To make matters even
worse, the state assembly had ordered municipal tax rebates on destroyed
property to help the propertied victims of the fire rebuild.[84] These problems
forced officials to set priorities and make trade-offs among competing demands on the public purse. More important, they put a limit on the number
of improvements for which ordinary citizens were willing to fight.

The failure to redevelop the street system makes this aspect of the reconstruction process especially clear. A number of New York newspapers
caused quite a stir in the immediate aftermath of the great fire by calling
upon Chicagoans to remake their streets. They urged that the people of the
city exploit the "grandest opportunity ever yet offered to a community to
build the model city of the world," suggesting among other things that
Chicagoans macadamize their fire-damaged wooden pavements, replace their
wooden sidewalks with ones more impervious to flames, superimpose a network of broad diagonal avenues and boulevards over their inconvenient and
"prosaic" gridiron street pattern, and develop a system of open plazas where
the new thoroughfares intersected with the regular streets. They argued that
the fire had created a golden opportunity to carry out such improvements
relatively easily and inexpensively, since it had cleared the land, eliminating
one of the biggest obstacles to opening up new streets.[85]

The suggestions evidently struck a responsive chord in the hearts of many
Chicagoans. As H. W. S. Cleveland pointed out, people were tired of the
monotony of the endless grid and wanted quick and direct ways to cross the
city diagonally.[86]

Nevertheless, the ideas never caught on politically. As the *Times*'s and the
Tribune's reactions to them suggest, even people who were committed to
improving the environment lacked the time and energy to consider seriously
trying to get the city to implement them. The editors of both papers thought
the proposals had too much merit to ignore completely. Both, however,
dismissed them in terms indicating that they considered them to be more
than a little ridiculous in light of the city's dire physical and financial straits.
The *Times*, for example, wondered whether the city's "well meaning eastern
friends" had proposed the "oppressively grand" plans under the delusion
that Chicago had been "reduced ... with the exception of sundry heaps of
rubble" to the open, unbuilt prairie condition "in which the enterprising
aborigines left it." The *Tribune* was even more sarcastic. "Supposing the
wheel-spoke system of streets to be the best one," its editorial went, "and
that our citizens would have the opportunity and grace, amid all their other

cares of the next five years, to learn how to 'radiate' successfully according to the proposed system, they have not the money wherewithal to put into operation." The project would cost millions of dollars, the *Times* pointed out, "millions that are just at present wanted for other purposes." It was not that the ideas were bad, but that, in point of fact, the streets were in reasonably good shape, the fire having destroyed only the wooden paving blocks, and those in only a few places, mostly in the North Division. Fireproofing of sidewalks was necessary, but the "Haussmannizing of Chicago" would have to be "postponed . . . or passed along for the benefit of the new cities to the westward."[87]

As efforts to redevelop streets in Boston and Baltimore would show, street improvements of this type were, indeed, extremely difficult and expensive to achieve, even after a fire had cleared the land. These statements suggest, however, that Chicagoans, unlike the people in the other cities, "amid all their other cares of the next five years," could not even give the proposals a second thought. As a result, none of the plans was acted on.

Despite these failures, the great fire had a profound impact on both the water system and the street system. A vast suburbanization of Chicago's population accompanied the reconstruction process, as will shortly be explained. This suburbanization, in turn, stimulated a chain reaction of infrastructural extensions to serve the newly populated districts. Between April 1, 1872, and April 1, 1874, the Board of Public Works added sixty-four miles of new mains and distribution pipes to the water system. It also added thirty-four miles of new collecting pipes to the sewerage system, nine miles of paved streets to the street system, and close to a hundred miles to the city's network of wooden sidewalks, all in response to the outward expansion of Chicago's population. So even though reconstruction did not lead to any significant redevelopment of these public services, it did lead to substantial additions to them.[88]

What is interesting about the extensions is that the Board undertook them completely independently of any planning impulse generated by the fire, carrying them out in its customary business-as-usual, *ad hoc*, piecemeal manner in response to petitions from homeowners and real estate developers. The Board seems to have had little choice but to follow this standard, from-the-bottom-up operating procedure. In fact, it did not even consider any planned alternative.

Legal, political, and economic conditions account for this. The law compelled property owners to pay for street improvements themselves, originally through betterment assessments and, after the state outlawed betterment assessments in late 1871, through private contracts arranged directly through the Board. This meant that the Board could undertake street extensions only at the request of property owners.[89]

The city paid for water, sewer, and sidewalk improvements with general tax revenues, so the Board of Public Works did not have to play the role of private contractor to extend these infrastructures by law. Nevertheless, for political and practical reasons, it was still in the inflexible position of having to do as property holders bid. The reason was that it customarily made these extensions on the basis of petitions from the people who would benefit from them. Budgetary and practical constraints prevented it from acting on all requests at once, of course. Nevertheless, property holders often decided what improvements would be made, either by lobbying Board members directly or by having their Aldermen and ward bosses pressure them. As John Rauch, the City Physician, noted in a report on Chicago's sewerage problems, even if the Board of Public Works tried to rebuff their demands, property owners and real estate developers could always get the infrastructural extensions they wanted if they had sufficient economic clout. They simply pressed the Board of Aldermen for street paving orders, favors the duly elected Aldermen were happy to supply since the city did not pay for street improvements. This compelled the Board to lay down water and sewer pipes before the streets were paved as a matter of economy, forcing it to commit its limited budget to the extensions, whether it wanted to or not.[90]

This from-the-bottom-up decision making procedure had the same sort of preferential impact on the distribution of infrastructural extensions as it did on infrastructural redevelopment in the inner city, ensuring that certain improvements simply would not be made. As Rauch explained in his sewerage report, prevailing budgetary constraints made demand articulation a devastatingly competitive contest on all counts. As a result, rich and powerful property owners and real estate developers got services. But the people and departments that were too weak or too poor or too apathetic to manipulate the Board effectively did not (see Figure 6.15). There were "many" instances both before and during reconstruction, Rauch wrote, when

> ...interested parties...secured sewerage, even to a deviation from the system, when other streets, not far remote and strictly in accord with the system, were neglected, although sewerage in them was much more needed, owing to their density of population, low ground, and nature of soil. Little did these parties think or care that the enhanced value of their property incident to drainage was at the expense of the lives of some of their fellow beings, to whom life was as near and dear as to themselves.[91]

The manner in which these trade-offs took place makes clear that the same general problem was behind *both* the city's failure to redevelop infrastructures in the inner city and its reluctance to extend sewers, streets, and water services into poor, outlying neighborhoods in a planned, coordinated, prompt way. In attempting to excuse its preferential treatment of middle and upper class suburban developments, the Board of Public Works often cited the budgetary constraints that prevented it from making everybody happy. As its handling of extensions shows, however, the root problem was the Board of Aldermen's and the Board of Public Works' whole approach to planning infrastructural improvements. Both Boards depended on "the people" to tell them, through votes, petitions, political pressure, and political *quid pro quos*, what improvements the city should make. Because of the unequal distribution of wealth and influence in society, this made them inordinately receptive to the demands of articulate real estate developers and middle and upper class homeowners and, by distorting governmental information gathering, made them deaf to other definitions of the public interest. Because of Aldermanic pressure, the Board of Public Works may have attempted to be more evenhanded in its treatment of water service extensions, or so the comparatively large number of miles of water mains and distribution pipes it laid suggests. Inevitably, however, the Board favored extending infrastructures into outlying middle and upper class residential neighborhoods at the expense of everything else, for there was nothing to countervail the socio-economic bias in the demand articulation process on which the Board's from-the-bottom-up approach to planning infrastructural improvements was based. Even in the case of water improvements, more extensions did not eliminate its bias. There were many poor families in outlying districts who had to go without convenient municipal water service, even for daily drinking purposes, while water was extended down practically uninhabited streets picked out as the future sites of middle and upper class homes.[92]

The railroads and reconstruction

Plans to improve the city's railroads fared no better. Like its water and sewerage infrastructures, Chicago's railroad infrastructures were not meeting people's needs at the time the great fire took place. Over two hundred heavily laden trains chugged in and out of the city every day along tracks operated by twenty-five different lines.[93] They made the city the economic wonder of the Midwest. They also, however, generated monumental negative externalities that damaged the economy, property, and people in many ways.

There were many problems. Scattered, unconnected passenger stations and freight depots created frustrating and costly inconveniences and inefficiencies that plagued the transfer of freight and passengers from one line to another. Worse, as extensive as they were, the tracks, depots, and other facilities were already inadequate for the increasing amount of business they had to carry. Unfortunately, in most cases they were about as fully developed as possible, given the dimensions of existing rights of way. This created on-

line congestion that further inconvenienced users and that exacerbated management and scheduling problems. Worst of all, the system's thousands of
miles of track and switching facilities crossed thousands of public streets at
grade in some of the most densely settled sections of the city. As a result,
the steady stream of trains caused incessant street traffic blockages and killed
and injured hundreds of people every year. The steam-locomotive-drawn
trains also created a tremendous amount of noise and smoke, which in
combination with the street problems, blighted entire neighborhoods and
helped turn them into slums.

Because conditions were so bad, the great fire and the reconstruction
process caused a groundswell of demands for all sorts of improvements. The
railroad companies and the city's business interests demanded that a union
depot be constructed to unify and centralize the terminal facilities of the
different lines in order to make the transfer of passengers and freight more
efficient and convenient. They also called upon the Board of Aldermen to
allow more lines into Chicago in order to bring the city more business. In
addition, companies that had been sharing roadbeds with other railways
demanded their own rights of way. By January, this resulted in fifteen applications for new routes of entry into the city. At the same time, property
owners, residents, and other critics of the industry insisted that the companies
take measures to relieve the dirt, noise, and street and safety hazards the
lines caused. They demanded, for example, that the companies viaduct street
crossings and that the government take action to prevent the trains and track
from completely usurping streets.[94]

In this case officials at all levels of government were more than willing to
heed the calls for change. The problem was that it was often physically or
legally impossible for them to take action on them.

None of the demands fell victim to the communications barriers that
stymied the other calls for infrastructural improvement. One reason was that
many people called for the improvements with an enthusiasm that resulted
from a widespread sense that, in this case at least, the fire had indeed created
an unprecedented opportunity to achieve long-needed changes.[95] An even
more important reason, however, was a widespread realization that if the
city did not begin to organize the railroads for the exigencies of the present
and the future, the problems would only continue to worsen. The editors
of the *Times* summed the fear up very well:

> Our railway connections are enormous, and every year will see them
> becoming greater and more unmanageable, if they shall not be regulated
> by some system other than that of permitting every railway to enter at
> any point along which it shall choose to purchase its right of way from
> our municipal legislators. ... If the thing is now a nuisance, words will

fail to express what the results will be when we shall have doubled our
lines of railways and our population. WHAT SHALL BE DONE?[96]

Bowing to the power of the press, the pressure of lobbying business
interests, and the force of public opinion, the Board of Aldermen quickly
appointed a committee to consider the goal of establishing a union depot.
The Aldermen began debating the possibility of consolidating dispersed
rights of way and viaducting grade crossings. They also moved to admit the
new lines and began developing a comprehensive plan for laying out the
new rights of way to minimize the railroads' negative effects on property
and the quality of life.[97]

For all this, however, the improvement effort was not a great success.
The Board of Aldermen established four new railroad rights of way in 1872
and a fifth in 1873, providing new trackage for fifteen lines. It also developed
a plan of railway organization, while the railroads ultimately constructed five
large new depots near the center of the city. No union depot was constructed,
however. Nor did the city government manage to reduce the number, dangers, and annoyances of grade crossings or reduce the problem of railway
blight. Instead, the hazards, inconveniences, and pollution associated with
the trains and tracks relentlessly increased because of site assembly difficulties that made essential spatial and physical redevelopment of the system
impossible to achieve.[98]

The failure to build a union depot was especially serious. The managers
of the Illinois Central Railroad proposed the plan. The Illinois Central (and
its associated roads, the Michigan Central and the Chicago, Burlington &
Quincy railroads) had a right of way that ran along the Lake Michigan
lakefront, just a few feet beyond the beaches of Lake Park. As a result, the
plan the company proposed involved filling in the submerged lands east of
Lake Park and covering the area with tracks and switching yards and the
union depot, an elaborate edifice that would be built in the three northern-
most blocks of Lake Park. This was an enlarged version of an earlier Illinois
Central plan to build a smaller depot on Lake Park and develop the submerged lands beyond for its own use. The Illinois Central, the Michigan
Central, and the Chicago, Burlington & Quincy desperately wanted the new
facilities because of the inadequacies of the Illinois Central's old station and
two-track approach. But they had been prevented from making the improvements by a court injunction. Now they turned this initial plan into a
grandiose union depot plan in the hope that it would generate the public
support they needed to overturn the court injunction. The scheme worked,
at least up to a point. Government officials, businessmen, and the managers
of the other railroads immediately embraced their lakefront union depot idea
as the answer to all of Chicago's railway problems.[99]

The plan had many natural attractions. The site, Lake Park, was a long strip of open shoreline that stretched well over a mile along the eastern side of Michigan Avenue from Park Row on the south all the way up to Randolph Street and the Chicago River on the north. The plan to cover it with railroad facilities received enthusiastic support from so many quarters because many people thought that it was, as the *Evening Post* put it, the "spot marked out by nature," the "easiest, cheapest, and the most expedient" place to bring railroads together. The reason was that the park and the virtually limitless submerged land beyond it not only could provide the railroads with the large amount of space they needed to construct their much wanted "mammoth" union depot and switching yards but would also give them direct access to the port facilities at the mouth of the Chicago River. In addition, the site would give them room to build new docks and wharves. By virtue of its length and openness, the lakefront would also give the companies a long straightaway to the union depot and the port along which they could run their trains at top speed without crossing any public streets. As the *Tribune* pointed out in an enthusiastic editorial on the subject, a union depot at any other central site would require that a "perfect wilderness of track" be constructed over the existing gridiron of the street system, which would exacerbate the city's already horrendous street congestion and be a "constant and increasing jeopardy to life and limb." Thus the lakefront was the only site on which a union depot could be constructed which would not intensify, and might actually relieve, the city's street traffic and safety problems.[100]

What made the lakefront union depot plan especially attractive, however, was that Lake Park seemed to be the only area in the central city that could be turned over to the railroads without the need to undertake the costly and time-consuming process of assembling private property. In other words it was a site that seemed to offer a detour around the site assembly problem. It was, of course, a public park. The state legislature, however, had consigned it to railway usage in 1869 when it passed the Lake Front Act. The Lake Front Act confirmed the city's earlier grant of lakefront development rights to the Illinois Central, the Michigan Central, and the Chicago, Burlington & Quincy railroads, the legality of which had been in question. In addition, it empowered the city to sell to the companies the park's three northern blocks for the construction of a passenger station. The plan had fallen through, for at the time, outraged Michigan Avenue homeowners had managed to obtain a court injunction to stop the implementation of the Act in the hope of saving their magnificent lake vistas. The Board of Aldermen, equally outraged by the paltry $600,000 sum specified for the sale of the land, had furthermore refused to sell the three blocks to the railroads. Now, however, the site appeared to be readily obtainable, both because the union depot plan was so much more popular than the Illinois Central's more narrowly conceived original plan and because the fire had destroyed the Michigan Avenue homes, presumably eliminating the need to protect the lakefront vistas that the court injunction had been intended to preserve.[101]

Railroad men hoped the idea would go over well, and to an impressive extent it did. Several newspapers and business leaders heralded it as the answer to Chicago's railway problems. The Board of Aldermen appointed a committee to reconsider the sale of the park's three northern blocks. Even Michigan Avenue homeowners rallied behind it, with nearly all of the parties to the injunction withdrawing from the suit less than ten days after the conflagration.[102]

Nevertheless, the project soon fizzled out. The major reason was that some people wanted Lake Park to remain a park. The way in which they obstructed the plan sheds light on the way in which the site assembly barrier to infrastructural redevelopment historically worked.

Ordinarily, of course, the opposition of a handful of public parks advocates would not have been enough to stop the implementation of an improvement project that had the strong support of the railroads and many of the city's most influential business and government leaders, as well as authorization from the state. What the opponents did, however, was overpower the companies with the court injunction.

J. Y. Scammon led the attack on the union depot plan. A lawyer, banker, civic leader, and wealthy Michigan Avenue mansion owner, Scammon and his neighbors had gotten the U.S. District Attorney to file the original injunction suit against the Illinois Central after the state had passed the Lake Front Act in 1869. They had persuaded the federal government to take their part and act as their trustee, apparently by promising to pay the court costs. The state courts had granted the injunction on several grounds, including complicated title questions and the claim that when the land west of Michigan Avenue had been platted and sold in the 1830s, the land to the east in Lake Park had been reserved as public grounds to remain forever free and unmolested for the benefit of the purchasers of the platted Michigan Avenue lots.[103]

As noted earlier, most of the burnt-out Michigan Avenue homeowners liked the union depot idea, so Illinois Central officials quickly obtained releases from most of the parties to the injunction suit. Scammon and two or three other men, however, stubbornly refused to withdraw, and the courts refused to lift the injunction. As a result, the Illinois Central still could not begin the redevelopment of the park. To compound the company's troubles, the District Attorney also filed suit to stop it from filling in any more of the submerged land in Lake Michigan and erecting any more freight houses, elevators, and railroad tracks beyond its legal right of way, activities it had been pursuing to the extent possible since the passage of the Lake Front

Act. This threatened to prevent the company from expanding its two-track approach to the city, a necessity if its business were to continue to grow, let alone if the other railroads were to join it at the lakefront.[104]

To get around these obstructions, the railroads petitioned the state legislature to give them the authority to take by eminent domain the land they needed for a union depot. A law granting them this power was passed on April 10 and went into effect on July 1. By then, however, it was already too late for the lakefront union depot or, indeed, for any sort of union depot plan.[105]

The problem was that the city's railway companies needed to rebuild their burnt-out facilities as quickly as possible. Thus they began abandoning the idea of the lakefront union depot as soon as it became clear that Scammon was going to fight the project. The idea was too good to die an immediate death, but die it did. By October 19, some companies were putting forth the suggestion of an alternative union depot in the West Division. By December 16, plans were "daily growing in favor" of bringing the roads together at two West Division union depots on either side of the Chicago River, with a tunnel beneath the river to connect them. In early January, with fifteen new lines clamoring for admittance to Chicago, city Aldermen, who were taking an increasingly active role in the affair, proposed a plan to build three union depots: one for the East Division near the mouth of the Chicago River, one for the West Division on three or four blocks of land north of 12th Street and west of the river, and one for the North Division on land near the old Chicago & Northwestern depot on Kinzie Street. Getting the companies to agree on such a large-scale scheme remained a problem, however, as did land assembly, with the railroads complaining that they could not afford to purchase all the necessary land even if they got the power of condemnation. Thus the union depot idea finally disintegrated completely. The result was that not one depot but five separate depots were soon being constructed in various places within a half mile of the central business district, most on the old sites of the depots the great fire had destroyed.[106]

As it turned out, even the right of eminent domain did not enable the Illinois Central to appropriate the lakefront. This shows just how serious this site assembly problem was. The Illinois Central continued trying to develop filled areas on the north and south ends of the park and other sections of the lakefront outside the park, but its opponents continued fighting its activities in the Illinois legislature and the courts. In 1873, the General Assembly repealed the Lake Front Act, in effect repealing the Illinois Central's development rights. The company kept trying to expand its inadequate facilities, however, so the conflict continued in the courts. The case became one of the state of Illinois's most celebrated and long-lasting litigations. It pitted the city, the state, the federal government, and the company against one another in a series of bitter struggles over land and water titles, riparian rights, and harbor jurisdictions that went on for thirty years, until 1902, when the U.S. Supreme Court permanently barred the company from making any more encroachments into either the harbor or the lakeshore.[107]

Throughout the debate over the union depot plan, the Park Board steadfastly adhered to the goal of preserving Lake Park and even used the filling of the lake with fire debris to further park enlargement and beautification goals. This activity helped give shape to some of the lawns, gardens, and walks of today's Grant Park.[108]

The park advocates' success makes the lakefront confrontation a rather unusual event in the annals of nineteenth century urban history. Nonetheless, it not only dramatizes the power of court injunctions as a general barrier to infrastructure change but also illuminates some larger complexities of the site assembly problem in general. As with all above-ground infrastructures, the construction of a union depot would have required the substitution of one kind of land use for another and, as a consequence, a fundamental trade-off between the interests of certain land users and those of others. Trade-offs like these inevitably generated strife.

In this case, the substitution would have been especially difficult to make, since it would have entailed sacrificing either the community's *bona fide* need for an integrated railway system or its equally *bona fide* need for an inner city lakefront park. Both the depot and the park were significant public goods. Chicago already had a fairly extensive park system. At the time, however, Lake Park was the only park within walking distance of both the poor and the rich residents of the densely settled South Division urban core. Perhaps even more important, it was the only park that was immediately accessible to the central business district. Thus it was the only one that could provide the thousands of people working in Chicago's business center relief from the pollution, congestion, and general hustle and bustle of the commercial district.

Not surprisingly, the advocates of the lakefront depot did not admit that Lake Park represented a significant public interest. This is also very revealing of the complexities of the site assembly problem. The railroads and their supporters lambasted Scammon and his friends for their "selfish" attempt to block the public good. They argued that even if there had once been a valid reason to keep the site a park, it no longer existed now that business was taking over the mansions on Michigan Avenue. As an editorial in the *Tribune* put it, the "privilege" of overlooking Lake Michigan was of "no advantage to business property. . . . On the contrary, it is highly advantageous that both sides of [Michigan Avenue] be occupied." In the words of a wealthy business and civic leader, William E. Ogden, the commercial invasion "disposes of the former desire and ambition to preserve it for elegant residences, and raises the question of what most enhances or detracts from the value of the property for commercial uses." The editors of the *Times* made the same point with sarcasm. The lake view that the "theopolistic brother Scammon" and his fellow Michigan Avenue homeowners "so much delighted in will henceforth waste its aesthetic influence upon grocers, clerks, and blackguard draymen."[109]

These arguments followed the prevailing tendency to view parks as benefits for wealthy homeowners and boons to residential property values, in fact if not in theory. They also reflected an argument of the injunction which held that Michigan Avenue homeowners had an easement on an unobstructed view of the lake by virtue of various city ordinances and the promises made when the land on Michigan Avenue originally was sold. What was significant was that in consigning the public interest to the railroads, the depot's defenders made no allowance for the possibility that Lake Park could also provide important benefits to the community at large, including business district merchants and lawyers and grocers, clerks, and draymen. Needless to say, some regretted that Lake Park would be lost. They argued, however, that it would be a sacrifice that the city would have to make, since the lakefront's "only" value now was as a "business site." Thus the editors of the *Evening Post*, for example, called the park a beautiful "diamond" but concluded that the city could no longer "wear" it. "She cannot even polish it. ... Let her sell her solitaire. Let her put her jewelry upon the market."[110]

In all likelihood, Scammon and his friends similarly failed to acknowledge the merit of the union depot's claim upon the public good. Unfortunately, the papers did not print what they had to say about the issue. Whatever they said, the underlying problem was, of course, the finitude of urban space. There simply was not enough room for both an open park and an extensive set of union depot facilities in the same place.

This limiting fact of life plagued all the efforts to expand and redevelop the city's railway system during reconstruction. The railroads demanding entrance to the city constantly confronted it, as did the residents living in the neighborhoods through which the proposed lines were to pass and the city officials attempting to organize the massive entry. In this case, the problem did not prevent change. It did, however, create a bitter battle over where the routes would lie.

The members of the City Council's Committee on Railroads had responsibility for drawing up the final ordinances authorizing the companies' rights of way. They ran into troubles as soon as they began trying to locate the new roads. The first ordinance they formally considered concerned the LaSalle and Chicago Railroad Company. It epitomized their problems. As originally drafted by the City Council, the bill was apparently no more than a restatement of the LaSalle's own sweeping request for admittance into the city. It called for the city government to give the company a diagonal route across the West and South Divisions that sliced through upper class and working class residential areas and crossed a number of important business streets, antagonizing rich and poor property holders and businessmen alike. The people that it and the other ordinances threatened responded immediately. As the *Times* put it, "mad" with fear that "Puffing Billy" would ruin their neighborhoods and destroy their property values, they "pestered" the committee with petitions and "asphyxiated" it with arguments to eliminate or relocate the new roads.[111]

The wave of protest forced the committee members to work out a master plan of trackage organization in order to minimize the injury to private property. The plan they developed had five general points. The first was a commitment to locate new rights of way on routes adjacent or as near as practicable to the route of some other railway company already having tracks within the city. The second was a commitment to limit each right of way to a single route of double track. The third was a requirement that each company granted a right of way share its roadbed with two other railroads, meaning that the companies would have to triple up on each right of way. The fourth was a requirement that each railroad build at least two viaducts per year to reduce the number of grade crossings in the city. And the fifth was a requirement that the companies permit connections with other railroads, that they allow sidetracks to warehouses, factories, and coal and lumber yards, and that they keep all the streets they crossed or occupied in good repair.[112]

These principles compelled the Committee on Railroads to redraw several of the requested rights of way. They also officially ended the old practice of granting virtually unrestricted privileges and an entirely new route to each new line admitted to the city. Committee members conceded that no new track could be laid without causing "more or less" damage to private property. They were confident, however, that the plan nevertheless would both satisfy the railroads and "give more general satisfaction, and result (as a rule) in much less injury to private property than the former practice of giving entirely new routes to each railroad admitted."[113]

The Committee's handling of new lines was, indeed, a significant advance over the old method, from a planning perspective at least. For all its merits, however, it did not bring Chicagoans much closer to a real solution of the basically unsolvable site assembly problem. The city was now committed to limiting the size and number of new rights of way. But the necessity of replacing one land use with another remained, and, if anything, the blitz of petitions and remonstrances increased.

The plans threatened railroad interests, at least to some extent, so the railroads continued to oppose the new entries. Many established companies did not want the new lines to come into Chicago at all. They protested that locating the new rights of way next to their tracks would be damaging to their business. The managers of the Chicago and Northwestern, for example, complained that the Committee's plan to put the LaSalle and Chicago right of way next to its roadbed would make its tracks inaccessible from one side and prevent it from using its property as it wished. To complicate matters, the incoming companies also felt imposed upon. They protested the Committee's requirement that they triple up. As one railway man told a *Times* reporter, the railroads already had more business than they could handle on a single double track; they had no space on any right of way to share.[114]

More important, the Committee's plan, if implemented, would injure residents and property holders; so they also continued to send a steady stream of remonstrances to the Committee. Even shifting the proposed routes did not eliminate this source of opposition. The Committee on Railroads moved the route of the LaSalle and Chicago to Rebecca Street in response to petitions from homeowners on York Street, for example, placing it between existing Chicago, Burlington & Quincy and Chicago and Northwestern rights of way. They expected Chicago, Burlington & Quincy and Chicago and Northwestern officials to object to the new route, as, in fact, they did. They were sure, however, that "property owners will be best satisfied with it and that is the main point."[115]

They could not have been more wrong. The change must have been a relief to homeowners on York Street. The people on Rebecca Street, however, were furious. They met to protest the new ordinance and find some way to "beat" it. To them the proposed route was not a compromise among many competing interests, but an "injustice" that would "deprive them of their homes and subject their children to be killed." They had worked "for years to buy their little homes," which were "as dear to them as the marble palaces" of the rich were to the rich. To protect them, they prepared a resolution for the City Council requesting the removal of the right of way to some other street, some vowing to "take the law into our own hands" if the demand were not met. Their displacement and their anger represented the human side of the site assembly problem.[116]

Like the Rebecca Street homeowners, most of the people hurt by the new rights of way were working class families living in small cottages in the South and West Divisions. The Committee on Railroads directed the new lines into their neighborhoods, partly because they were at a disadvantage in the political battle over where the roads would go, partly because the decision to lay the new tracks along existing rights of way concentrated the lines in their neighborhoods, which were often theirs because the districts had already been depreciated by trains and hence left alone by other classes, and partly because the Committee members evidently believed that railways caused less damage where they injured cheaper land and homes. Thus many working class neighborhoods suffered doubly from the city government's pattern of constructing infrastructures: once from its reluctance to extend them crucial public services and once again from its willingness to route railroads through their neighborhoods.

Poor people were not the only ones hurt by the lines, however. Inevitably some of the new routes adversely affected middle and upper class property owners as well. These people were just as dismayed at the prospect of displacement and just as unwilling to turn their neighborhoods over to the railroads as the poor, with some, like the men on Rebecca Street, also pledging to "take the law into their own hands and have the tracks torn up."[117]

Rich or poor, the injured parties protested that the money the railroads were supposed to pay them would be hopelessly inadequate recompense for the property losses, displacements, and other suffering the railroads caused. The ordinances left it up to them to sue the aggressing companies individually. This put them at a serious disadvantage in the compensation procedure. In the words of a remonstrance against the Columbus, Chicago, and Indiana Central Railway, the travesty was that ordinary citizens, most of them extremely poor, would either have to "litigate with a mammoth corporation of capitalists, backed by the best legal talent in the country" or have to accept whatever "pittance" the companies might offer. To the remonstrants either option would mean that they were "robbed."[118]

Concerned observers recommended that the railroads viaduct their tracks or depress them and viaduct the streets in order to reduce the nuisances, annoyances, and safety hazards they inflicted on the people living in (and passing through) the neighborhoods through which they ran.[119] The Committee on Railroads incorporated the suggestion into its plan by requiring the companies to viaduct at least two street crossings per year. Unfortunately, these safeguards also ran up against serious site assembly problems. The city's sewers prevented the sinking of tracks more than five to ten feet below street grade. This meant that even if the companies depressed their tracks, street viaducts at least ten feet tall were necessary. Such infrastructures injured abutters by cutting off first-story windows, destroying views, and generally lowering property values. To complicate matters, they also penalized the railroads, since both viaducting and depressing tracks created grades that complicated switching and since, in any case, constructing the improvements forced the companies to pay property damages and construction and upkeep costs that added nothing to their revenues.[120]

All sides articulated their unhappiness with the Committee on Railroads' plans forcefully enough to catch the Committee members' attention. As in all such conflicts, however, the outcome depended on the participants' influence over the decision makers, and, as in all such struggles, certain groups had more influence than others. As a result, the confrontation had losers as well as winners.

The winners included the property holders who managed to keep the railways out of their neighborhoods. They also included the railroads. Despite the Committee's restrictive master plan, the railroads achieved most of what they wanted, for as it turned out, the Committee's restrictions, as unprecedented as they were, were not as exceptional as they seemed. On the one hand, the viaducting requirement was unenforceable because of the weak language of the ordinance. On the other, the spatial limitations were basically cosmetic. Most of the railroads with established rights of way already shared their privileges with two or more companies on their own initiative. The sharing companies leased partial interests in their rights as an expedient to circumvent the difficult and time-consuming process of obtaining private rights directly from the city. Furthermore, many of the "new" lines were not really new at all. Some of the companies had only a technical existence, their franchises being held by corporations like the Pennsylvania Central that already owned or leased rights of way within the city. Others already leased rights of way from other lines and were merely seeking their own rights. This meant that the restrictions were hardly unique burdens for the truly new lines. It also meant that for fictive companies even the acquisition of one-third interests in new rights of way was a major gain for the mother companies. The requests for entry were, of course, ploys established companies used to expand their inadequate facilities beyond the narrow limits of the double-track rights granted in the past. As such, they testify to the difficulties the lines faced in attempting to adapt themselves to growth. Needless to say, however, property holders were outraged to discover that some of the intruding "new" lines were not legitimate new lines at all.[121]

The most visible losers were, of course, the residents and property holders, mostly poor, whose neighborhoods and homes were blighted by the new roads. Significantly, however, the community as a whole also lost. To be sure, the people of Chicago benefited from the increased railroad business the new roadbeds helped to funnel into the city. Because of the multiplier effect, this increased business brought economic gains to all segments of society. At the same time, however, the people of the city suffered the unrestrained increases in traffic congestion and the safety hazards and transfer inconveniences the new tracks and trains caused.

As in the case of the lakefront depot, the most ardent champions of the railroads lambasted the companies' adversaries for their selfish opposition to the public good. Thus the *Evening Post*, for example, told its readers that "all" the railroads were doing was asking for "*simple permission* to come into the city, to pay damages for the property they damage," in order to bring prosperity to Chicago. The question was, it flatly stated, "whether or not the whole people of Chicago shall be made to suffer untold loss by the stumbling blocks put in the way of these new roads, or whether the handful of property owners affected by them shall yield their opposition and simply receive payment for the damage done." The paper called on every Alderman to "act as if he himself were the Mayor and represented the whole city and not a mere fragmentary part of it," arguing that "only as the whole city is prosperous can any section hope to be."[122]

In fact, however, the situation was infinitely more problematical than this, involving many complex trade-offs between individuals and groups and between public and private interests. Even the *Evening Post* admitted this as the displacing effects of the new rights of way became apparent. Only a few weeks after it had published the above statements, it began calling on the city to "plan ahead" and force the railroads to depress or viaduct their tracks. The paper compared conditions in Chicago to those in New York City, and the analogy made plain that the editors were beginning to see the full dimension of the problem the city faced. The railroads in both cities, it said, were causing "enormous" loss of life and necessitating either "the total abandonment of square after square for purposes of local business, or the removal of the locomotives from the streets."[123]

The friction of site assembly did not always cause such problems. For example, it affected, but did not seriously undercut, the federal government's plan to improve burnt-out government buildings in the central city. The great fire destroyed a Post Office and a Customs House, both of which had been located on a fifth of a block of land at the northwest corner of Dearborn and Monroe. Both had been considered "much too small . . . even for present purposes." Because of technological restrictions on vertical expansion, federal officials had proposed to enlarge them through horizontal expansion involving the appropriation of the entire block of land on which they had been built. The government had the right to take the land by eminent domain. There was still a site assembly problem, however, in this case caused by the extravagant land prices property owners demanded the government pay them. They insisted that the land was worth at least $2,179,000, almost a million dollars more than its 1870 assessed value. The upshot was that the government took bids on other blocks and finally purchased a block two blocks south of the old site for $1,250,000. The extra space permitted the government to construct much larger buildings, including the biggest Post Office in the country. Many people complained bitterly about having to walk the two extra blocks to pick up and post their mail. Nevertheless, the huge buildings enabled officials to consolidate functions which they had previously had to carry out in scattered locations for lack of space. Thus they made the government's execution of its business more convenient and, presumably, more efficient, without seriously damaging larger community interests.[124]

Significantly, however, the railroads posed problems that were much more fundamental. As a result, reconstruction had much the same impact on the railroads as it had on the city's water, sewerage, and street systems. Reconstruction caused a considerable expansion of all four infrastructures, to the benefit of many people and corporations and, in important ways, the community in general. At the same time, though, in all four cases, critical redevelopments were not achieved. The failure of the union depot plan was especially detrimental. The number of railway tracks in Chicago dramatically increased without any solution of the system's many systemic physical and spatial problems. As a result, the dire predictions made by the advocates of the lakefront union depot plan literally came true. Large parts of the South and West Sides became a "perfect wilderness of track," exacerbating traffic congestion and constantly and increasingly jeopardizing life and limb. Like the problems with the sewerage and water systems, these hazards primarily affected the older business and working class sections of the central city. They were, however, problems that would have harsh consequences for the whole community later. They were the product of rapid infrastructural expansion without essential redevelopment.[125]

The dynamics of spatial change in the business and industrial districts

The Chicago fire did much more than stimulate the redevelopment of structures and infrastructures. In addition, it caused a permanent reorganization of residential, commercial, and industrial land use patterns that turned an old-fashioned walking city into a comparatively modern nineteenth century industrial metropolis in less than two years' time.

Chicago was a young city when the fire took place. Its land use patterns were essentially pre-modern and pre-industrial. Its central business district was still a tiny area of less than twenty blocks that was filled with a dense mixture of commercial and industrial activity. In addition, this very heterogeneous central place was still hemmed in by larger and even more heterogeneous districts in which the homes of rich, middle class, and working class families intermingled with stores, bars, brothels, lumber yards, warehouses, and various kinds of factories. With the exception of a number of packing houses located in the relatively remote stockyards and some other land-intensive industrial activities such as the brickyards situated along the south branch of the Chicago River a good distance out on the prairie, these densely settled, mixed residential, commercial, and industrial neighborhoods were largely confined to the relatively limited area within a one- to two-mile radius of the central business district. Large property holders still held most of the land south of 16th Street and west of Reuben Street (Ashland Avenue) in the form of large, undivided estates that were uninhabited except by squatters.

The fire changed this permanently and dramatically. By the time reconstruction was complete, the central business district had doubled in size and experienced significant internal spatial differentiation among firms in different lines of trade. It had moreover become a more commercially homogeneous place, having lost most of its remaining heavy manufacturing. In addition, more commerce and industry had spread into the West Division. A new industrial district had emerged along the west fork of the south branch of the Chicago River between Ashland and Western Avenues on what had been open prairie. Residential land use patterns had also undergone significant reorganization and expansion. Many people had resettled on the edges of the newly expanded central business district. Many more had moved to peripheral sections of the South, West, and North Divisions. And more still had left the city altogether to make their homes in new and now booming suburbs.[126]

As contemporaries noted, it would have taken many years for such a radical transformation of land use patterns to have taken place under normal circumstances. As the rest of this chapter will show, the shifts were not smooth and autonomous spatial adjustments to normal growth stimuli. Instead they were catch-up responses to pent-up spatial needs, parts of a complicated chain reaction of physical and spatial redevelopment in which a few land users were prime movers, others passive followers, and others reluctant, even angry and resistant victims, forced to accommodate themselves to unwanted neighborhood transformation or to move against their will.

One of the most dynamic areas of spatial activity was the center of the city. The maps in Figures 6.5 and 6.6 delineate the kinds of spatial changes that occurred in the core of this area, the central business district. These maps display the locations of firms in the wholesale grocery, wholesale fancy goods, wholesale drygoods, and banking trades in 1871 and 1874. They show the spatial patterns of several important trades that were representative of what happened to firms in the financial and light wholesaling businesses throughout the district.[127]

A comparison of the maps makes clear that commercial land use patterns underwent two major shifts during reconstruction. The most obvious change was the westward and southward expansion of the district as a whole. The district more than doubled in size, from fewer than twenty-two blocks to more than forty-five, pushing south beyond Madison toward Jackson and

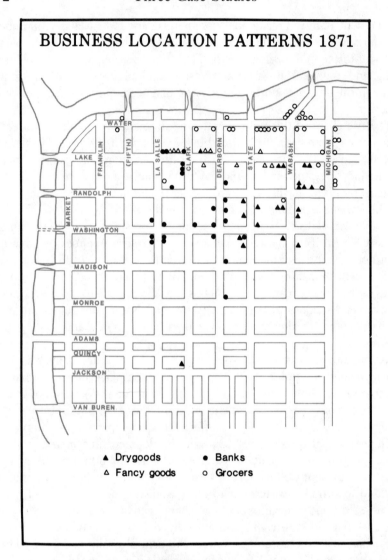

Figure 6.5.

Van Buren Streets and west past LaSalle toward Market Street and the south branch of the Chicago River. Concomitantly, the district's center of gravity jumped south from Lake to Washington, moving west in the direction of the river.

The other general shift was a profound internal reorganization of land use patterns within the district. Firms moved from one place to another, sometimes scattering their trades over large territories, sometimes breaking them up into small sub-centers. In a few trades, some firms even moved out

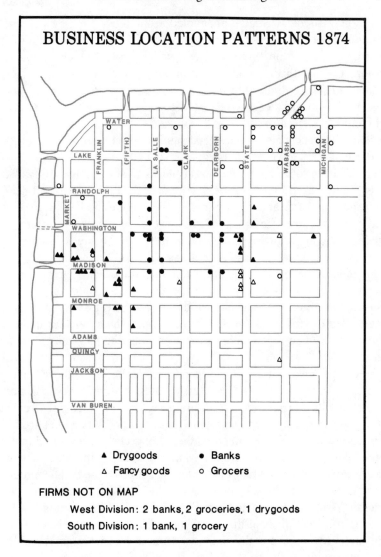

Figure 6.6.

of the central business district altogether to locations in the North, West, or South Divisions.

There was no standard pattern of reorganization on the individual trade level. The city's banks, for example, spread out from locations on eleven street blocks (a street block being the piece of a street stretching from one intersection to the next) to locations on eighteen street blocks. In the process, their spatial center of gravity shifted west, with the proportion of banks east of Washington Street plummeting from seventy to forty percent, while the proportion west of Washington doubled from thirty to sixty percent. In addition, three banks moved completely beyond the central business district, taking up addresses on three different, widely spaced blocks in the West Division. Despite this general expansion and migration, however, banking remained a fairly centralized business geographically, since all the banks that stayed in the business center relocated to sites that were no farther apart than contiguous street blocks.

Wholesale grocers also experienced significant territorial expansion. Unlike the banks, however, they became a spatially fragmented trade. They spread out from locations on ten street blocks to sites on twenty-two street blocks. Many stayed in the northeast corner of the business district near the intersection of Water and River Streets, where the trade had been concentrated before the fire. Close to a fourth, however, scattered over a large area, some leapfrogging to the opposite side of the central business district as far west as Market Street and as far south as Madison Street.

The much smaller fancy goods wholesale trade also became spatially fragmented, even though it spread out from four street blocks to only five. Completely abandoning their old stand on Lake Street, five companies reconcentrated on one block on State Street, while the other four companies became scattered on isolated blocks between Franklin, Jackson, and Wabash Streets.

The comparatively numerous drygoods wholesalers also moved out over a large section of the expanded central business district. They split up into two territorially separate, geographically cohesive, functionally discrete subcenters, one a retail-oriented sub-center situated on State Street around its intersection with Washington Street, the other a commission- and jobbing-oriented sub-center situated around Madison and Monroe Streets between Market and Wells. As the maps indicate, the shift to State had begun before the fire, four of the seven firms classified by the City Directory as "fancy wholesale" and "wholesale and retail" having had addresses there in 1871. By 1874, however, all six of the stores then classified as such had addresses in this area, five on State, the sixth just around the corner on Washington, on the other side of the bank at the intersection of Washington and State. Meanwhile, all but three of the remaining twenty-six firms in the trade had leapfrogged all the way from what had then been the southeast corner of the central business district, around the intersections of Lake and Randolph Streets with Wabash Street, to the new southwest corner of the district between Market and Wells and Madison and Monroe Streets.

It is, of course, difficult to find in-depth information on the individual location decisions that produced these changes. Nineteenth century businessmen usually located their firms without leaving a public record of the thinking that led them to choose one location over another. Several of

Chicago's newspapers and magazines followed the redevelopment of the central business district closely, however, describing much of what was going on in considerable detail. Therefore, it is possible to explain in general terms the basic process by which these remarkable spatial shifts took place.

The great fire prompted, but did not determine, the changes. In order to resume trade as quickly as possible, the burnt-out firms rushed to find quarters wherever they could in the unburnt areas on the South and West Sides. As a commentator recalled a year later, they "greedily seized upon" rooms wherever they found them, taking "thousands of places" that they would have previously "refused disdainfully...with an almost incomprehensible avidity." Most ended up in temporary shanties thrown up in Lake Park, or in hastily converted barns, churches, and middle and upper class homes, crowded together with several companies in completely different lines of trade. The result, as an observer noted, was frequently "whimsical in the last degree." A shoe store, for example, might end up in the same house as a button factory and several lawyers', doctors', and insurance offices. Few businessmen considered such situations to be satisfactory permanent arrangements.[128]

It was in the midst of this mad scramble that a small group of businessmen, John V. Farwell, Marshall Field and his partner Levi Lieter, and two or three other men in the drygoods and banking trades, began the process of establishing a new spatial order. They did so by inaugurating the large-scale construction of warehouses and stores in the burnt-out slums on the southwest border of the old commercial center that was described earlier in this chapter in the section on structural redevelopment in the central business district. By taking advantage of the opportunity the fire provided to redevelop this area, these men set off a chain reaction of spatial change in the central business district as a whole.

Field, Lieter, Farwell, and the others began the structural redevelopment of the old burnt-out slum so surreptitiously that the newspapers did not begin to take notice until the rise of new warehouses in the area compelled them to pay attention. The men moved so quietly, in fact, that they left the press with no clear idea as to how the transfer had taken place or who had started it – Farwell or Field and Lieter or the principals of another leading drygoods firm, Hamlin, Hale & Co.[129] Their secrecy was motivated, of course, by their desire to purchase the land while it was still slum-cheap, which was no small matter since they intended to do nothing less than turn the former slum into an expensive, first class business area.

These developments had a dramatic impact on the location decision making of the smaller drygoods firms. While Field, Farwell, Hamlin, and Hale were busy planning their new buildings, the smaller drygoods firms were temporizing over where to establish their new permanent quarters. As soon as the transfer of the big companies became known, however, the smaller firms began making arrangements to follow. According to observers, it was as if the smaller drygoods merchants had just been "waiting to see the hand of their great leaders." Some of the smaller dealers apparently were "shocked" that J. V. Farwell & Co. and Field, Lieter & Co. had decided to make such a drastic move. With the exception of three firms, however, all of them followed, in order to take advantage of the agglomeration economies that close proximity to the large firms would give them. In the words of the *Landowner*, the large companies' transfer destroyed the "old landmarks" of the drygoods trade. Thus they "compelled" the other houses to move in tandem "in order to keep their customers."[130]

Like Field's and Farwell's sudden moves, the other firms' abrupt collective transfer emphasizes the extent to which the slums had made the congested central business district a prison for the companies crowded within it. It also underscores the extent to which the fire's destruction of the slums represented the physical destruction of the district's prison walls. As noted earlier, Chicagoans had for years been well aware that the slums around Madison and Monroe were "eligibly situated" for "business purposes."[131] It took the destruction of the locality's ramshackle buildings and the displacement of their disreputable inhabitants for real estate developers to begin the structural redevelopment that would permit the area's incorporation into the business center. Once it became clear that wholesale drygoods dealers were going to relocate there in mass, the area became attractive for other central business district uses, so other property owners began arranging to rebuild on an ambitious scale.

The commercial redevelopment of the southwest slums in turn stimulated a second, far more chaotic stage in the process of spatial change. This new phase began when further commercial construction in the slums set off the belated wave of reconstruction that ultimately filled the old business center with first class stores and warehouses, a process described earlier in this chapter. Most observers expected the old central business district to be redeveloped for commercial use. As noted earlier, however, the property owners in the north and east sections of the old district were psychologically paralyzed in the immediate aftermath of the disaster and were not reconstructing their properties at all. Since businesses could not establish permanent quarters without buildings, this paralysis led to fears that the portion of the city south of the Chicago River, north of Washington, and east of State would simply cease to be an integral part of the central business district. In late February, the property holders in the area finally started to rebuild. Their long-overdue awakening did not result in an orderly return to the spatial arrangements of the past, however. Instead, it set in motion additional forces of spatial uncertainty and change.

What happened was that some of the formerly immobilized property holders began strenuously competing with the more active landowners to get their tenants back. Faced with drastic losses if their commercial tenants did not return, they started cooperating with each other to build bigger and better buildings that were specifically adapted to the needs of particular lines of trade. In so doing, they increased the amount of floor space under construction to such an extent that they forced all of the property owners in the central business area to compete for tenants. This put the final organization of the district up for grabs, for it made the ultimate spatial distribution of Chicago's commercial firms the spoils of successful real estate development.[132]

Observers repeatedly remarked on the "extraordinary" efforts property holders were making to capture tenants. These included making sweeping rent reductions, constructing luxurious and specially designed facilities for future occupants, and even naming buildings after potential tenants. The intensity of the competition is conveyed by an anecdote in the *Tribune* that compared the people who were scrambling to regain good commercial tenants to "the boy who was digging for a woodchuck. A man came along and said: 'Do you think you'll git him, boy?' 'Git him! I've got to have him! We're out of meat!' "[133]

This competition helps explain why most central business district land users dispersed over a relatively large area. Desperate property owners were pulling companies in all directions, splitting trades into small sub-centers and scattering them about. This spatial fragmentation may have served functional purposes. At the time, however, it surprised and alarmed observers, who feared that it would pit companies in the same field against one another on the basis of location, forcing them to "sacrifice their profits" simply to attract customers to their particular locations.[134]

The competition in the real estate market tapered off during the spring of 1872 as more and more businesses successfully arranged to purchase, build, or lease permanent quarters. Even then, however, many property owners continued trying to entice businesses from one area to another. This remained a source of both real and potential spatial instability for at least a year, until the panic of 1873 put an end to almost all commercial real estate development. In the summer of 1873, in fact, the district's last great redevelopment scheme emerged with a vengeance, which suggested that, had the crash not intervened, real estate developers would still have had a great deal of competitive energy to expend. In July, a group of wealthy landowners announced a grandiose plan to construct cooperatively Chicago's first great central market, an idea that involved covering the four blocks between Jackson and Adams Streets and Clark and the South Branch of the Chicago River with huge crystal palaces. The plan was never implemented. Had the promoters been able to go ahead with it, however, it would have fulfilled a widely felt community need for a central market. It would have given whole-sale grocers and meat and produce dealers a truly first class place of business, undoubtedly pulling many of them out of their scattered locations elsewhere in the business center. Thus it would have probably stimulated another wave of spatial change in the already protracted rearrangement of central business district land use patterns.[135]

In short, property owners played leading roles in the process of spatial change in the central business district throughout the reconstruction period. In some cases, especially in the first phases of the redevelopment process, they stimulated spatial redevelopment by building large structures for their own use. In many other cases, they stimulated it by erecting large stores and warehouses for others, with their tenants, the actual users of the land, playing relatively passive, dependent roles as the beneficiaries of their construction of the buildings. As the inertia that preceded the frenzy of developer-induced spatial change indicates, the great fire unleashed this change by temporarily eliminating a powerful barrier to structural redevelopment: the physical durability of structures in both the existing central business district and the surrounding slums.

The fire did not eliminate all of the frictions in the process of spatial change, however. Although many supply-side barriers to change were lifted, powerful demand-side barriers remained. They compounded the confusion created by the cut-throat real estate market.

Businessmen expressed their various hopes and frustrations about the future of their trades in Chicago's newspapers. Their articles and letters to the editor revealed that drygoods merchants were not the only businessmen searching for places to expand and centralize their businesses. Real estate brokers, for example, wanted to concentrate in and around a great central real estate exchange in order to facilitate procurement of mortgages and the sharing of market information. Lawyers wanted an exchange to localize their profession and facilitate information flow. So did the city's bankers.[136]

At least one trade actually achieved this goal. As the map in Figure 6.7 shows, the fire insurance trade managed to increase its already high degree of concentration, the firms' power in the real estate market no doubt having been enhanced by the money they received from frightened property owners.

This was exceptional, however. Most trades had neither the organizing ability nor the market power needed to achieve the desired locus and degree of spatial concentration among the dozens, even hundreds, of firms in their lines of business. Large office trades such as real estate and law, with some eight hundred to more than one thousand firms each, were simply too large and economically diverse to consolidate so closely. But even Chicago's much less numerous, far more economically powerful banks could not coordinate such a spatial reorganization.

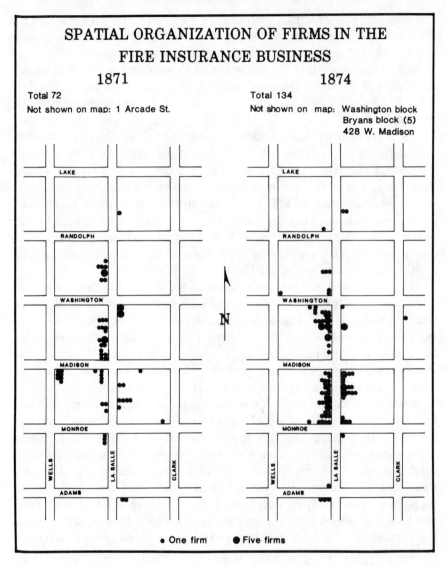

SPATIAL ORGANIZATION OF FIRMS IN THE
FIRE INSURANCE BUSINESS

1871   1874

Total 72   Total 134
Not shown on map: 1 Arcade St.   Not shown on map: Washington block
                                                              Bryans block (5)
                                                              428 W. Madison

• One firm   ● Five firms

Figure 6.7.

Like the drygoods trade, the banking community had ambitious members who were willing to initiate the reorganization of the trade. In fact, they had promoters for two completely different relocation plans.

The first was advocated by William Coolbaugh, the owner of the Union National Bank. Coolbaugh was a member of the so-called Farwell Ring of businessmen-speculators who were trying to integrate the slums around the junction of Market and Madison Streets into the central business district.

His plan was to start a mass migration of the city's banks into this area by constructing a magnificent new bank building that would be large enough to accommodate at least five separate banks. The problem was that none of his colleagues were willing to follow him. Although most acknowledged the advantages of having all the banks centralized in one place, they refused to make Coolbaugh a rich man by leapfrogging to his still remote corner of the former slum.[137]

The other plan was advocated by a group of bankers who liked the idea of centralizing the trade but did not like Coolbaugh's plan for accomplishing this change. They proposed concentrating the banks in and around a large bank block, a central banking exchange, to be built somewhere on Washington Street between LaSalle and State Streets, a much more central and prestigious location. They suggested that the building be financed by the banking community itself, through the issuance of stock, so that it could be owned and operated entirely for the benefit of the banks, rather than an individual real estate speculator like Coolbaugh.[138]

This plan was extremely popular, so much so, in fact, that the newspapers discussed it as if it were a *fait accompli*. As the papers pointed out, all banks wanted good offices in a good location, especially if they could have "the extra facilities and safety" that a central exchange would give them. The banks also liked the joint-stock aspect of the project, since it promised to make the building a secure and profitable investment for them, as well as an advantageous place in which to carry on their business.[139]

Nonetheless, this plan failed, too. As popular as it was, it was never more than talk, even though some bankers apparently went so far as to begin the search for the exchange site. The reason was that while the plan's promoters were looking for a place to construct the exchange, the other bankers were continuing to search for their own buildings and building lots. Even the owners of the Commercial National Bank, among the most enthusiastic supporters of the plan, kept on hunting for a place to build or lease their own bank building. A *Times* reporter regretfully reported that as time passed, the dynamic of this uncoordinated and increasingly competitive decision making process was rendering "the consolidation of these institutions so much the more unlikely and unsuccessful." Week by week, it was not only removing more and more suitable exchange sites from the real estate market but, in combination with property owners' competitive bidding for commercial tenants, also scattering the banks down LaSalle, Madison, Clark, and a variety of other streets. The result was that both reorganization plans failed. Coolbaugh was left completely in the cold. He not only failed to lease his new bank building out to other banks, but also finally had to move his own bank back to the center of the central business district. More to the point, the banks did not even manage to individually reconcentrate on Washington Street between LaSalle and State, the area they had agreed was the most desirable place for them to agglomerate. Instead, as noted earlier, they spread out from locations on eleven street blocks to locations on eighteen.[140]

The bankers' behavior illuminates the ties to place, the personal conflicts, and the decision making problems that served as demand frictions in the process of spatial change. Some trades also suffered from leadership problems that prevented them from achieving certain kinds of desirable change. As a *Times* reporter discovered when he talked to the city's wholesale meat dealers, not all lines of business had ambitious Fields and Farwells to direct or even try to direct an advantageous spatial reorganization. The meatmen wanted to relocate and centralize into an advantageously situated, first class market building. When the reporter asked why they were not taking steps to obtain land and build the market, however, the typical reply was, "Hanged if I know, what does the rest of 'em say about it?" No one was willing to take the initiative. So the dealers were being spatially redistributed around the central business district on the basis of their own inertia, the rent gradient, and property owner initiative.[141]

The great fire did not affect these demand-side barriers to spatial change. It did, however, temporarily eliminate powerful supply-side barriers. What was significant about the land use pattern that finally emerged was that it was generally an adaptive improvement from the land users' perspective. Despite the fragmentation of trades, business generally benefited, both because the enlargement of the business district enabled firms to obtain larger and better equipped quarters and because it enabled them to spread out enough to enjoy lower rents.[142]

The advantages of these changes were clear to all, except perhaps the property owners whose holdings consequently fell in value. The real estate editor of the *Evening Post*, for example, called the reorganization a boon for business, concluding that "what Chicago was before the fire, in one particular, it is hoped she will never be again – and that is the indiscriminate huddling together of all businesses in one little corner, making rents an intolerable tax on the business energies of her merchants." The real estate editor of the *Times* was even more exuberant. In a column on the enlargement and beautification of the business district, he concluded, "In many respects the fire has been an advantage, and the time may not be far distant when it may be seen to have been A GOOD THING in all respects that Chicago went up as it did."[143]

For many companies the benefits ranged from lower rents and superior facilities to improvements in the way in which they conducted their businesses. J. V. Farwell's "monster" new warehouse, for example, gave him the space he needed to move into the retail trade. Marshall Field and Levi Lieter's new warehouses gave them room to expand their lines of goods and open new departments. They ultimately decided that their new location was not the ideal place for their retail trade and opened a separate retail store at the corner of Washington and State Streets. In addition to giving them still more storage and display space, this allowed them to split their retailing and wholesaling businesses, a step toward specialization that improved the efficiency of their operations.[144]

Like the suddenness of all this spatial change, the benefits that it provided business highlight the extent to which a land use equilibrium had prevailed before the fire, holding spatial as well as structural redevelopment in check. It also underlines the shattering of that equilibrium. As public reaction to the shifts suggests, the old equilibrium had not only stiffened land use patterns, but had also constricted people's perceptions of the possibilities for change. But now, that psychological equilibrium was gone. Writers often discussed the reorganization of land use patterns in a tone of amazement and pleasure which revealed that they had an exciting fresh perspective on land use in the business center. The real estate editor of the *Evening Post*, for example, commented on the expansion of the commercial district, pointing out that "as a rule merchants do not own their own stores" and asking, "Why then should they all congregate into the smallest possible space and thus enable the landlord to demand an exorbitant rent, by putting into a dozen blocks the business that should be extended over fifty blocks at least?" He was clearly pleased by this discovery. Why indeed! No doubt most businessmen shared his delight.[145]

The spatial reorganization of industry

The great fire's impact on the spatial organization of Chicago's industrial activity was considerably less far reaching than this. Nevertheless, it, too, produced a reorganization of business location patterns that helped modernize land use while revealing a great deal about the frictions in the process of spatial change in nineteenth century cities.

The maps in Figures 6.8 and 6.9 display a rather contradictory picture of land use reorganization.[146] They show the rise of a new industrial district in the West Division between Ashland Avenue, Western Avenue, 22nd Street, and the west fork of the South Branch of the Chicago River. While the new industrial area was still quite small at the close of reconstruction, containing only thirteen factories and some thirty brickyards as of the end of 1873, several of the factories were among the largest and most important in the city. Built to take advantage of unprecedented economies of scale, many covered several acres of land and were engaged in the heaviest of heavy iron and steel manufacturing. They included the McCormick Reaper

Works; Wells, French & Co. railroad bridge and car works; F. E. Canada & Co. bridge and car works; Columbian Iron Works; Union Rolling Mill Co.; Joliet Rolling Mill Co.; and other large concerns. The factories collectively employed over 3,000 men.[147]

The rise of this new district was a significant change. Other than this development, however, the overall pattern of industrial activity was very stable. The maps show that Chicago's manufacturers had agglomerated before the fire into large, specialized industrial districts the outlines of which reconstruction left basically unchanged. Of course, the bulk of this manufacturing activity lay in the West and South Divisions, completely out of the fire's reach. Even in the North Division, however, where the fire had demolished most factories, the pattern of industrial land usage stayed basically the same, the vast majority of manufacturers rebuilding their establishments on the ashes of their old ones.[148]

Needless to say, the unscathed firms in the Western and Southern Divisions had every reason to stay in place and continue manufacturing their products without the disruptions of a move, given the costs of moving and the strong internal and national demands for manufactured goods. By the same token, burnt-out firms had every reason to reconstruct without making time-consuming and expensive searches for new locations. Search and rebuilding costs had been and still were some of the most practical barriers to spatial change.

What makes the continuity especially noteworthy, however, is the doubling of manufacturing activity in the city. According to Everett Chamberlin, manufacturing in Chicago grew by one hundred and thirty-seven percent from 1871 through 1873. The value of iron manufacturers alone grew by seventy-five percent. In addition, the number of firms skyrocketed, according to S. S. Schoff, by well over twenty-seven percent in just three years.[149]

Most of this expansion and multiplication of factories occurred within the confines of prevailing land use patterns, taking place not through the reorganization of land use, but through the intensification of industrial activity in established manufacturing centers. Thirteen manufacturers built large factories out in the new district on the prairie. The rest, however, stayed in the old centers, both new and expanding old firms building their new facilities on vacant land or, more often, on land that had previously contained cheap shanties and stores, displacing or squeezing together the people who had been living there. This intensification of industrial land use took place despite the development of the new manufacturing center and frequent newspaper reports about its advantages and the large number of manufacturers supposedly planning to relocate there. Thus it documents the way in which existing rail and river routes, existing residential labor markets, and the agglomeration economies generated by existing factories channeled indus-

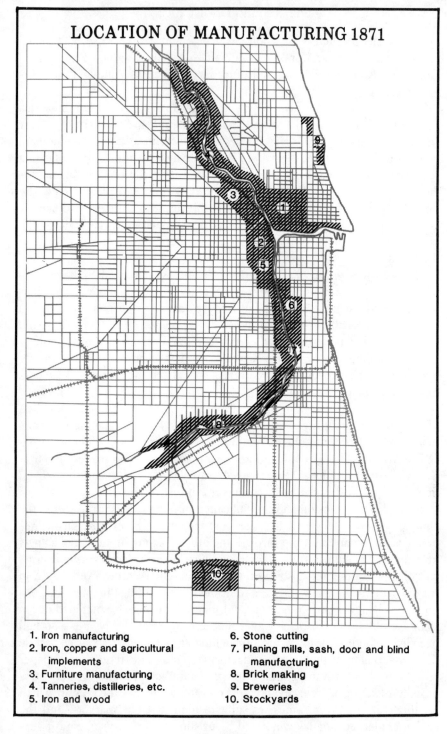

LOCATION OF MANUFACTURING 1871

1. Iron manufacturing
2. Iron, copper and agricultural implements
3. Furniture manufacturing
4. Tanneries, distilleries, etc.
5. Iron and wood
6. Stone cutting
7. Planing mills, sash, door and blind manufacturing
8. Brick making
9. Breweries
10. Stockyards

Figure 6.8.

LOCATION OF MANUFACTURING 1874

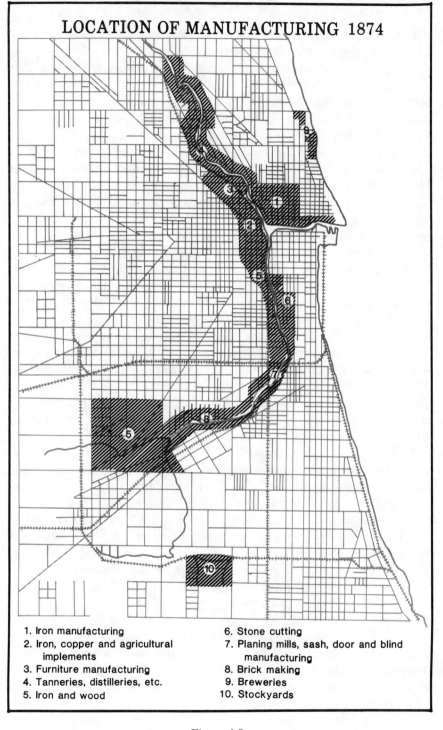

1. Iron manufacturing
2. Iron, copper and agricultural implements
3. Furniture manufacturing
4. Tanneries, distilleries, etc.
5. Iron and wood
6. Stone cutting
7. Planing mills, sash, door and blind manufacturing
8. Brick making
9. Breweries
10. Stockyards

Figure 6.9.

trial activity into established manufacturing districts, thus serving as passive sources of inertia in the process of spatial change.

Significantly, the old patterns persisted in spite of efforts by civic leaders and public authorities to banish hazardous and polluting manufacturing activity from the densely settled inner sections of the city. Reformers tried to use the comprehensive fire limits ordinance to push wood and flammable oil manufacturing from the city limits entirely. Although they failed in this respect, they succeeded in banning the establishment of new planing mills, sash, door, and blind factories, ammunition and fireworks factories, and the like from the area protected by the fire limits ordinance passed in February. The city's industrial interests managed to minimize the impact of this ban, however. They succeeded not only in confining it to new factories but also in keeping any effective enforcement mechanism out of the law.[150]

Manufacturers also staved off an ordinance proposed by the Board of Health which would have effectively eliminated most distilleries, slaughterhouses, rendering establishments, soap factories, and similar concerns from the city. The law would have prohibited both the construction of new concerns and the operation of existing ones between May 1 and October 1 in the part of the city bounded by Fullerton Avenue on the north, Western Avenue on the west, and 31st Street on the south, which was most of the city. The Board of Health proposed the ordinance to solve sanitation problems resulting from the failure of an earlier project to reduce industrial pollution in the Chicago River and Lake Michigan by reversing the flow of the river. In this case the manufacturers managed to defeat the proposed bans in their entirety.[151]

Both victories testify to the force of will it sometimes took manufacturers to stay in place in the midst of rapid economic and population growth. Thus they highlight the importance of demand-induced inertia in the spatial development of nineteenth century cities.

The manufacturers' success also testifies to more subtle demand factors that discouraged change. Chicagoans both disliked and could not live without dangerous and polluting manufacturing activity. The towns surrounding the city had already outlawed slaughterhouses, rendering factories, and similar concerns to protect their residents from unsanitary conditions and miasmatic smells. Chicago's manufacturers warned that if the Board of Aldermen followed suit they "would have no remedy" but to leave the region "altogether." This presented government officials with a difficult policy dilemma regarding jobs and economic growth. They wanted to get rid of dangerous and polluting industry, but their unwillingness to sacrifice the prosperity the companies provided made it very difficult indeed for them to restrict the firms' right to locate and do business in the city.[152]

The remarkable endurance of the old patterns of land use easily overshadows the change that occurred in the spatial organization of industry in the city. It does not, however, completely mask the change or negate its importance. The new industrial district that grew up on previously undeveloped prairie was dwarfed by the older manufacturing districts in the inner city. Nevertheless, it represented an important step in the development of capital- and land-intensive manufacturing in Chicago and the emergence of a zonal pattern of land use characterized by a discrete inner commercial core and a widening industrial periphery.

The significance of this development is dramatized by the size of the factories that were built. The new McCormick Reaper Works was the largest farm machinery works in the world. It contained several factories spread out over twenty-three acres of land, the largest alone containing six acres of floor space. It employed eight hundred men and $150,000 worth of machinery, including two furnaces capable of smelting thirty tons of pig iron per day and a huge three-hundred-horsepower, sixteen-ton, low-pressure fly-wheel steam engine that powered all of the other machinery in the factories.[153] Several other firms constructed factories that were almost as large. The Wells, French & Co. factory, for example, was capable of producing twelve hundred freight cars and ten thousand feet of railway bridging per year. The F. E. Canada car works was capable of turning out one hundred and seventy-five freight cars and six passenger cars per month. The new Joliet Rolling Mill could smelt sixty tons of iron ore per day. The even larger Union Rolling Mill could turn out one hundred and fifty tons of steel and iron rails per day. Each of these factories employed hundreds of workers.[154]

Newspaper reports show that the McCormick brothers' decision to transfer their reaper works and rebuild on such a mammoth scale triggered the take-off of the area. It did so by stimulating interest in the region on the part of other manufacturers (and the press) and by spurring the expansion of the area's transportation facilities, which itself stimulated further interest.[155]

What makes the district's rise especially interesting, however, is, paradoxically, the light it sheds on the factors that ordinarily discouraged the rise of new industrial districts. The fact was that the owner and developer of the land in the district, Samuel J. Walker, had been trying to turn the area into a manufacturing center ever since he had bought the land in 1854. What is more, a number of manufacturers had been negotiating with him to buy the land to build large new factories since at least the early 1860s.[156]

The McCormick brothers were among the manufacturers who had been considering a move for several years. Their experience epitomized the demand-side problems that held back this kind of spatial change. The McCormicks built their first reaper works in 1856 on the border of the central business district on Rush Street at the mouth of the Chicago River. It soon became much too small for their needs, so small, in fact, that by the mid-1860s, they were losing significant market share in a market that they had virtually created. They could not buy enough land on Rush Street to enlarge the factory adequately. So in 1864, they began dickering with Walker over the price of his land in preparation for a move to what was then cheap real estate on the periphery of the city. Significantly, however, they would not build their large new factory on Walker's site until the summer of 1872, after the great fire, despite what one brother was already in the early 1860s calling the "miserable, cramped arrangement of things" on Rush Street.[157] The McCormicks were stopped by a wide variety of family troubles: the death of one brother (William), squabbles over his estate, and disagreements between the remaining brothers, Cyrus and Leander, over a wide variety of issues, including the question of whether a new factory should be built at all. They were also restrained by caution, by a lack of faith in Walker's "visionary ideas" about the future of his still remote piece of prairie, as well as by a lack of trust in Walker's ability to fulfill contractual promises that had been made regarding the preparation of the site.[158]

It was not until the great fire demolished their Rush Street factory that the McCormicks finally agreed to make the change. Even then, however, they found their relocation decision difficult to make. Remarks made by Cyrus's wife, Nettie Fowler McCormick, in the June 30, 1872, entry of her journal reveal the great stress the prospect of the move still caused the brothers more than seven months after the fire. "I constantly urged Mr. McCormick to go forward with the new factory *this year*," she wrote. "Not wait for *next year* to make the decision whether to build or not – make it now – decide now. . . . Thus have I urged my husband for months. I believe he will do it. . . . He has told me lately that I have been urging him on with whip and spur."[159] In the end, of course, the brothers built their large new factory. They also, however, rebuilt their old works on Rush Street.

The McCormicks' decision making travails reflect the practical and psychological problems that affected all businessmen considering long-distance moves, especially leapfrogs outside established manufacturing centers to undeveloped areas. The McCormicks' indecision may have been intensified by the fact that they lived right down the street from their old factory. They were hardly passive, unambitious business managers, however. Hence they were hardly men who would have found it unusually difficult to relocate.

What is important from the standpoint of understanding the general process of spatial change is the fact that the McCormicks' problems were also Walker's problems and, in an abstract sense, the problems of all real estate developers. In other words they were *both* supply-side and demand-side frictions in the process of spatial change. Walker had to attract at least one major manufacturer in order for his district to take off as an industrial center.

Thus the practical and psychological factors that discouraged individual businessmen from migrating to undeveloped areas also discouraged the collective land use change that was the basis of successful real estate development.

Significantly, the great fire liberated many other manufacturers from their inadequate factories and locations. It is impossible here to provide a complete survey of the manufacturers that moved from the central business district and the oldest, most densely settled inner sections of the West and North Side industrial districts to better quarters in more peripheral areas. Several notable transferees should be mentioned, however. One was the Peter Schuttler Company wagon works, one of the oldest and most respected manufacturing concerns in the city. The factory had been located since 1843 at the corner of Randolph and Franklin Streets. After the fire, it was moved across the Chicago River to the corner of Clinton and Monroe Streets. Another important transferee was the Chicago White Lead and Oil Company, which lost two factories to the fire – one at 173 Randolph Street and another at 313 West Lake Street. This firm regrouped at the corner of North Green and Fulton in what Schoff called the "most extensive" paint and white lead factory in the city.[160]

There was also a peripheral movement among many of the light manufacturing firms that remained inside the central business district, an expansion that paralleled that of the central business district itself. The maps in Figures 6.10 and 6.11 show how the city's clothing manufacturers and boot and shoe manufacturers spread out across the area.[161] This internal spatial change occurred in association with the rearrangement of the district's wholesale trades. It allowed large firms (like the C. M. Henderson boot and shoe company), some of which employed well over several hundred workers each, to continue carrying on their manufacturing, warehousing, and sales operations in one place while enjoying the benefits of physical expansion.[162]

In short, the great fire stimulated the abrupt departure of a number of firms to more peripheral, more economically "rational" locations. Thus it helped cause a reorganization of land use patterns that might not have occurred for years but that, like the McCormicks' transfer, may well have been contemplated for many years. The changes hardly split manufacturing completely off from the commercial center. They did, however, contribute to the rise of the new industrial district. They also increased the commercial specialization of land use in the central business district, while contributing to the intensification of industrial land use in the established manufacturing districts. Thus they gave impetus to three modernizing trends. As in commercial reconstruction, the fire's stimulus was a twofold one which galvanized structural as well as spatial change. Significantly, the fire also stimulated

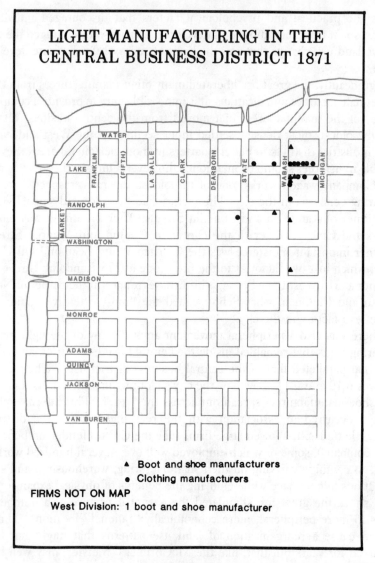

Figure 6.10.

structural improvement independent of the relocation of business, causing many burnt-out firms to enlarge their factories even though they did not move.[163] All of these improvements testify to the importance of the durability of structures as a barrier to environmental redevelopment in the period before the fire, as well as to the environmental improvement and industrial growth stimulated by the destruction of this barrier to change.

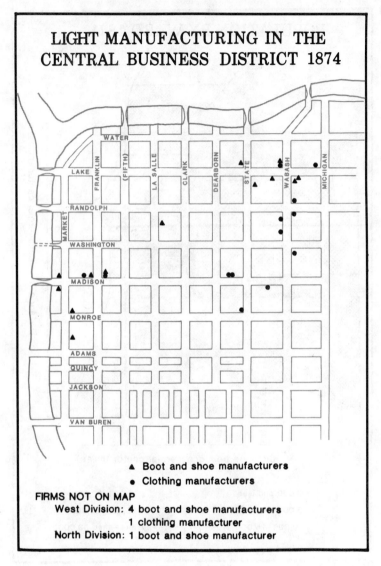

Figure 6.11.

The spatial reorganization of people

Reconstruction was also a time of residential land use change. As the maps in Figures 6.12 and 6.13 show, several significant shifts took place. The territory of residential settlement greatly expanded. Most people left the center of the city, moving out of the inner sections of the North Division

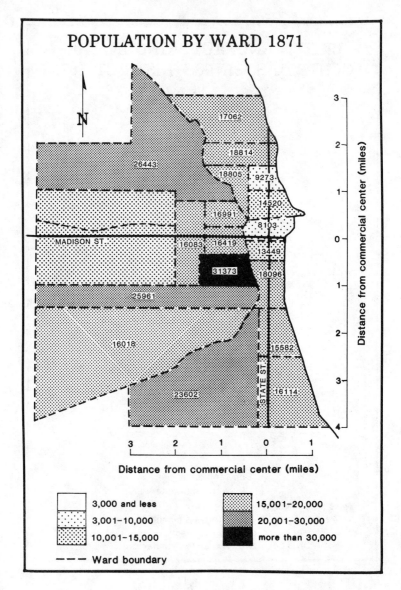

Figure 6.12.

as well as out of the expanding central business district. At the same time, population densities in the rest of the city generally increased.

Some important changes that do not show up on the maps also took place. Rich families left the burnt-out lakefront upper class enclaves of the North Division, the Near South Side, and the Union Park area of the West Division in large numbers. At the same time, large new upper class neighborhoods

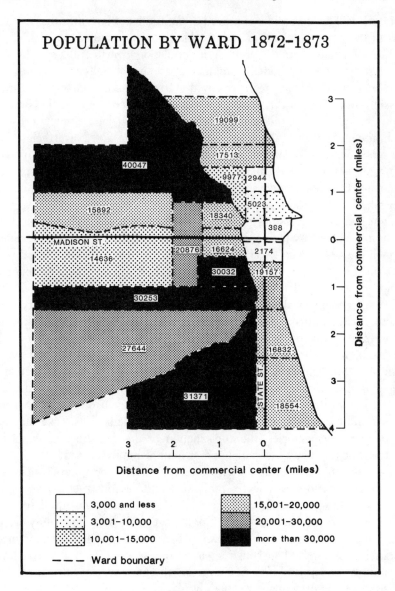

Figure 6.13.

emerged farther south along the lakefront in the South Division. There was also a rapid multiplication of people in Chicago's suburbs. These shifts coincided with movement among the city's working class population that increased the spatial segregation of upper and working class land use patterns. In general, Chicago's poor people spread westward onto the prairie, while its well-to-do residents moved along the lakeshore into the southern part of the city and lakefront suburbs like Evanston and Hyde Park.[164]

These changes were the product of population growth and a set of sometimes competing, sometimes complementary spatial pulls and pushes that were generated by the great fire, by the attractions of the relatively inexpensive land lying on the periphery of the central city, and by the simultaneous reorganization of commercial and industrial land use patterns. As such, the shifts were only partly the outcome of the fire. Nevertheless, like the other changes in land use patterns, they vividly show how the interrelationship between physical and spatial redevelopment stimulated chain reactions of land use change in the aftermath of the fire's destruction of four and a half square miles of buildings.

Four factors pulled working class residents into more peripheral sections of the city. One was the southward expansion of industry along the South Branch of the Chicago River and the rise of the new manufacturing district developed by Samuel Walker. This industrial growth stimulated a reorganization of working class residential land use patterns because laborers had to live within short walks of their work places. Interestingly, migratory manufacturers had to make their remote factories more accessible to prospective employees by buying land and building houses and other lodgings. The McCormicks, for example, purchased land to resell to their employees for home-building purposes so that they could attract job seekers to their new reaper works, three miles away from the central business district and difficult to reach from the established residential area. They also erected boarding houses and cottages to create a labor market for themselves. Like the construction of the factories, the construction of this housing highlights the interrelationship between spatial and structural redevelopment.[165]

The other three factors pulling workers toward the periphery of Chicago were the high and steady wages they received to reconstruct the city, their desire for homeownership, and the convenient installment purchase plans that were then available to them. Good wages and installment buying put cheap lots within the reach of many people, making it possible for many working class families to construct or purchase homes for the first time. Most of the cheap land was, of course, on the periphery of the settled area. This inexorably drew many people toward the city limits.[166]

Far more important than these demand pulls, however, were the spatial pushes that set Chicago's working class in motion. The great fire provided one obvious push. It sent people fleeing in terror from their burning neighborhoods. It was only one of many propelling forces, however, and a relatively insignificant one at that. Many working class families returned to their old neighborhoods almost as soon as the fire's flames were out to begin rebuilding their demolished houses – at least wherever they were able.[167]

The expanding central business district exerted a much more powerful and permanent push on workers' land use patterns. The commercial redevelopment of the burnt-out slums on the southwest boundaries of the old business center forced the impoverished former residents to leave the area by replacing their demolished houses and businesses with first class business buildings that rented at prices no worker could afford. In fact, as noted earlier, it was the residents' displacement that made the area attractive, as well as readily available, for commercial redevelopment. Their forced departure was what stimulated the general drop in commercial rents as well as the far-reaching physical improvement of the central business district as a whole.

Many observers applauded business's clean sweep of the area. As a writer in the *Tribune* wrote in regard to the redevelopment of Madison Street, "The rickety, frame shanties on the south side, inhabited no one knows by whom, the unpleasant butcher's store on the northeast corner of Fifth Avenue [Wells] . . . the two-story frame buildings on the southeast corner decorated with many colored socks and woolen shirts . . . these and the other objectionable features of Madison Street have all been swept away."[168] Another writer celebrated the elimination of "brothels . . . pawn brokers, jew clothiers, junk dealers, second hand furniture dealers, cheap boarding houses, etc.," from Wells Street. He wrote, "In fact, Wells contained a class of buildings and population that Chicago could not feel sorry at the loss of. . . . The fire, with all its train of misfortunes, did not do badly solving this difficulty for Chicago. It swept away all the obnoxious features of the street, and forever."[169]

The displaced people did not simply disappear, of course. Many moved across the river to the boarding houses in the West Division. Others transferred to the still-standing slums south of the burnt district, where, as a consequence, a new vice district rapidly took shape.[170]

The new fire limits ordinance generated a similar pushing force on working class land use patterns by prohibiting workers from reconstructing their wooden houses in certain areas in the center of the city. The proposed total ban on wood construction, had it passed, of course, would have exerted an even stronger push. As William Ogden, a big North Side landowner pointed out, an effective comprehensive fire law might have "depopulated" the burnt-over sections of the residential city by completely preventing workers from rebuilding their own homes. This was because he and his fellow landowners had no intention of constructing durable brick tenements that were difficult to demolish or move, since their personal long-range plans for the land were to profit from future commercial development.[171]

The introduction of the new railroad rights of way put another push on Chicago's workers. The Board of Aldermen attempted to avoid this by spatially consolidating the different lines. As noted earlier, however, this did not solve the displacement problem. Instead, the tripling up of railroads on the rights of way and the grouping together of three or more rights of way turned some areas into uninhabitable railroad highways, for it involved covering adjacent streets with the tracks of ten to twelve different railroads. As the *Tribune* pointed out, this meant that the streets could have "ten or more railroads in constant motion" at the same time. The noise, traffic, and safety hazards this created compelled residents to leave the vicinities of the tracks. The lines, of course, all led to the depots and switching yards constructed on the edge of the central business district. The development and expansion of these facilities also pushed working class families toward the city limits.[172]

Intensifying these outwardly propelling forces were the multiplication and physical expansion of factories in the central city. Unlike commerce, industry did not sweep any territory completely bare of residential life. It did, however, put a spatial squeeze on workers in a given area.[173]

Further intensifying the pushes was population growth. The fire increased the already prodigious rate at which Chicago was acquiring new inhabitants by drawing people who hoped to take the jobs created by the work of reconstruction. According to the *Evening Post*, between thirty thousand and forty thousand people entered the city in the first six months of reconstruction. In combination with the fire's destruction of roughly fifteen thousand dwellings, this massive inflow of new residents completely overwhelmed the existing housing stock. The resulting "housing famine" drove up workers' rents by seventy-five to one hundred percent in the central city. This encouraged the sub-division of existing structures, the doubling and tripling up of housing on individual lots, and other changes that increased population densities in established neighborhoods. And all of these things together increased the pressure on workers to set out for the periphery of the city in search of cheaper rents.[174]

Significantly, working class residents resisted many of these displacing forces. Their resistance attests to the importance of the barriers to spatial change in residential land use. Workers' opposition to the new railroad rights of way has already been chronicled. Their revolt against the comprehensive fire ordinance has also been described. In addition, they resisted the limited ordinance after its approval by the Board of Aldermen by repeatedly violating the new law.[175]

Their attempts to avoid displacement resulted from ties to place that were caused by property ownership and their emotional and practical attachments to their neighborhoods and homes, which they repeatedly pointed out were as "near and dear" to them as their wealthier neighbors' mansions were to them. Other, more practical problems also made them resist the idea of moving. These included the trouble of searching for a new place to live and the limited availability of accessible places to which poor people could relocate, given their poverty, their need for quick access to their jobs, the housing famine, and the railroads' increasing ubiquity. Their only choice was often to stay in established working class districts and put up with increasingly serious overcrowding, pollution, congestion, and danger. One man described the situation succinctly and effectively at a protest meeting against a right of way in these words: "If fifteen railroads are coming, then where the h—— are we going to?"[176] The harsh fact was that there was often little they could do but stay.

Not surprisingly, these barriers to change were no less painful for Chicago's working class than were the centrifugal forces of displacement. By May, with the housing shortage reaching crisis proportions and their frustration mounting, the union men in the city's building trades were beginning to discuss the possibility of a general strike for higher wages to help them pay for more and better housing. Nothing came of this except for fearful reassurances from the Mayor and some newspaper editors that the crisis was a result not of some conspiracy but of the "irresistible laws of supply and demand"[177] – an observation that was, needless to say, an accurate assessment of the situation the city's workers faced. While these conditions did not produce any overt class conflict at the time, however, they were laying the groundwork for the strikes and riots that would shake the city a few years later.

In short, a wide variety of factors influenced the process by which working class land use patterns changed in the aftermath of the great fire. Ties to place mediated the response of poor people to the centrifugal pushes and pulls that drove them toward the outskirts of Chicago. As a result, there was increased crowding in working class neighborhoods, as well as a territorial redistribution of these neighborhoods, as poor people moved from the commercial city center and spread out onto the prairie.

Members of Chicago's upper class also found themselves buffeted by the dislocating impact of the fire and the expansion of business and the railroads. Like the poor, they found themselves pushed out of their old neighborhoods. Far more than their impoverished neighbors, however, well-to-do people found themselves pulled by the attractions of the lands beyond the boundaries of their old neighborhoods.

The great fire hurt the rich in a way that it did not hurt the poor, because it not only destroyed their homes but also consumed the beloved and irreplaceable old trees that had shaded their homes and made their neighborhoods pleasant and prestigious living environments. The destruction of the trees resulted in a desolation and, perhaps more important, a loss of homelike familiarity which residents found excruciating. One well-to-do memoir writer described the ruins of his family's and his mother's homes, expressing his sense of bereavement in this way: "The lots were swept clear by the fire fiend. Ulmenheim! Where were originally those ten native elms who gave the home a name, endeared by ten years of loving association? All dead; 'burned to death.' " As one despondent woman, grieving for the loss of her home with all its "years of accumulated treasures and associations of every kind," wrote soon after the conflagration, "I shall never have a home again, a house sometime, undoubtedly. I shall have – I must live out my appointed time – but a house which simply bears the mark of the builder and upholsterer could never be home to me if it were ever so elegant." Such losses cut the emotional ties to home and hearth that had formerly bound many of Chicago's upper class residents to their old North Side neighborhoods. Thus they made it much easier for these people to consider relocating. In some cases, the losses may have even driven the rich to move.[178]

The hasty scattering of business and light industry into the South and West Sides exerted a similar spatial push on upper class neighborhoods outside of the North Division. Burnt-out businesses temporarily took over Lake Park under permits issued by the Board of Public Works. For over a year their shanties ruined the lake view from the Michigan Avenue mansions still standing south of Harrison Street. Even more disrupting, throughout the South Side other businesses moved right into the mansions, forcing residents to occupy upstairs rooms and make extended visits to the country. Businesses also moved up West Madison Street into the West Side, disrupting life in the upper class neighborhoods around Union Park. Commerce's intrusion into these heretofore "sacred" aristocratic enclaves lasted only a year or two in some places. By thoroughly unsettling the character of life during that time, however, it helped send residents in search of quieter places in which to make their homes.[179]

The expansion of the steam railroads on the Near South Side added to the commercial push on upper class land use in this area. In the words of one angry South Side resident, the railroads were turning the neighborhood streets into "a prolonged and perpetual switchyard," creating a "perpetual terror and alarm" for all the people who had to use them. This further undermined the quality of residential life.[180]

Wealthy people often responded with as much anger to these dislocating intrusions as poor people did. The agitation that many felt is evident in the words that one man used to describe the encroachment of business on the Near South Side in an otherwise temperate article on reconstruction. He compared the commercial takeover of the mansions in the area to the "descent of the barbarians," lashing out at the "carelessness even recklessness" of the "invasion." "Down Wabash and Michigan Avenues, hitherto sacred to the finest families," he wrote, "rushed the Visigoths of trade in a wild irresistible horde, with speculation in their eyes."[181]

Well-to-do people also tried to protect their homes from the incursion of the railroads. For example, after successfully preventing the construction of a union depot on Lake Park, Michigan Avenue resident J. Y. Scammon organized a petition movement to get all steam locomotives outlawed from the Near South Side. Other people prepared suits against the railroad companies. Others attended protest meetings and vowed to take the law into their own hands and have the tracks torn out.[182] Such resistance was often no more successful than the workers'. Nevertheless, it testifies to people's attachment to their neighborhoods and their unwillingness to be displaced and, hence, to the existence and importance of the barriers to spatial change.

What set the response of the upper class to the pushes on their land use patterns apart from that of the working class was the greater ease with which the rich could move away from their old population centers. Superior economic positions and much less rigid commuting requirements not only made it easier for them to move from the inner city than workers but also enabled them to spend much more money on land. As a result, the displacements caused by the fire and the intrusion of business and the railroads did not put the same kind of spatial squeeze on them as they put on workers. Instead, they generated a powerful stimulus for geographical dispersion that was practically unsullied by the curse of overcrowding that plagued the working class.

The strong pulls generated by the attractions of the boulevards south of 16th Street and of suburbs such as Hyde Park, Lake View, and Evanston augmented these centrifugal forces. The appeal of these areas stemmed from relatively low land prices – which made the construction of houses on large, even park-like, grounds possible – and from the semi-rural amenities available to the wealthy outside the central city.[183]

The fire played a crucial role in making these attractions effective pulls on the upper class. It did so not only by destroying well-established trees and gardens on the North Side, which made the pastoral amenities of the suburbs more appealing to Chicagoans than they had been before, but also by forcing those it left homeless to find temporary quarters outside their old neighborhoods. This encouraged many families to try living in the suburbs temporarily, when ordinarily they would not have even considered doing so. As the real estate editor of the *Evening Post* pointed out, because of high rents in the central city, "thousands of our citizens who have never thought of going to the country to live have made up their minds that in the present situation they can do no better." Evidently, this forced migration caused many wealthy families to recognize the advantages of suburban life for the first time. With suburban real estate developers and newspapers touting the suburbs' trees, birds, pure air, and freedom from "temptations such as theaters and saloons," moving to the suburbs and to prestigious Far South Side streets like Prairie Avenue and Drexel and South Park Boulevards became the popular thing to do.[184]

Needless to say, these pulls and pushes did not overpower every member of Chicago's upper class. Quite the contrary, a small but important contingent of wealthy families even returned to the desolated North Side, becoming the nucleus of what would later be called the city's "Gold Coast." The partial restoration of the area took place slowly, however. Despite an early announcement by wealthy property owners that the destruction of the North Side gave them a much appreciated opportunity to rid the area of working class shanties and make a fashionable "West End" of it by covering the district with "neat cottages and handsome villas," almost no first class residential reconstruction in the area east of North Dearborn Street and south of Lincoln Park was undertaken for several years. This stood in sharp contrast to the rapid construction of mansions on the Far South Side, causing much concern.[185]

The slow pace of redevelopment was a result of the area's environmental problems. On the one hand, the North Side was one of the best sections of the city for residential use because of its proximity to the central business district, the lake, and Lincoln Park, its good drainage, and its excellent water supply and sewerage and gas service. On the other hand, it was plagued by the pollution and miasmatic smells generated by the tanneries, slaughterhouses, and distilleries on the North and South Branches of the Chicago River, which the river and the prevailing winds delivered directly to the mansion district. Residents also suffered from the close proximity of hundreds of wooden shanties and scores of factories, which brought fire hazards as well as unavoidable social contact with the working class. Families like the McCormicks, for example, had shared prestigious Pine Street (which was only eight blocks long) with warehouses and a soap factory and had had to put up with a view of the shanties on the "Sands" on Sand Street and the lakefront. Families on prestigious Cass Street had had to live with a local alley filled with "frame shanties, poor people, and a great deal of sand." And now, to make matters even less pleasant, as noted earlier, the fire had stripped the territory of its priceless trees.[186]

In light of these conditions, the partial rebirth of the upper class enclave, slow as it was, is quite surprising. It clearly dramatizes the basic stability of land use patterns in the midst of change. The elite families were in no hurry to return, but return many of them did, because of the area's accessibility to the central business district and because of their long association with the neighborhood.

Such persistence notwithstanding, there was an important spatial reorganization of upper class residential patterns. Many of Chicago's wealthy families retreated from the North Side, the Union Park area, and the Near South Side, transferring their "allegiances" to the avenues of the Far South Side and a host of suburban towns. This caused a burst of suburban growth that was never checked, especially in the towns that lay just north and south of Chicago along Lake Michigan. As a consequence, the North Side permanently lost its image as Chicago's "garden spot," and the main developer of the elite but relatively new Union Park district went bankrupt.[187]

The comparatively thinly populated, distinctly north-south suburban shape of the new upper class land use pattern stood in sharp contrast to the new working class pattern, with its dense concentration of population near the center of the city that spread westward out into the prairie. The greater distances and different population densities that now separated the two groups reduced the traditional intermixing of Chicago's classes, helping imprint the cultural and economic class divisions of society onto the social geography of the city.

Because the emergence of separate working and upper class residential land use patterns was a physical as well as spatial development, the differences between them were expressed in terms of housing patterns, as well as population distribution. Figure 6.14 shows the different material compositions and amounts of ground covered by the houses in a block of land in the working class district and a block in the prestigious Prairie Avenue upper class district in 1884. The diagrams make clear just how far apart both the spatial organizations and the living conditions of the two classes could be. The blocks were at the opposite ends of the social scale, the poor block containing the homes of impoverished workers residing in the particularly congested inner city, the rich block containing the homes of captain of commerce Marshall Field and other, only slightly lesser luminaries. The physical contrast between the two was accordingly extreme.[188]

The chain-reaction dynamic of physical and spatial land use change is evident in these contrasting housing patterns. The ultimate step of the chain reaction was not housing, however, but the extension of water, sewer, street, and horse railway systems to the newly developed residential districts. As noted earlier, the Board of Public Works extended infrastructures into outlying areas at a furious pace in the aftermath of the great fire. It did not keep up with the demand for service extension in the rapidly expanding city, however.[189] Nor did it extend infrastructures readily to the poor as it did to wealthy homeowners and influential real estate developers.[190]

The map in Figure 6.15 makes clear how much longer poor people generally had to wait than rich ones to receive infrastructures in their neighborhoods. It shows the sewer system in 1873, revealing the superiority of the public services the city had provided the residents of upper class districts. Even in older parts of the city the poor often had sewers (and pavements)

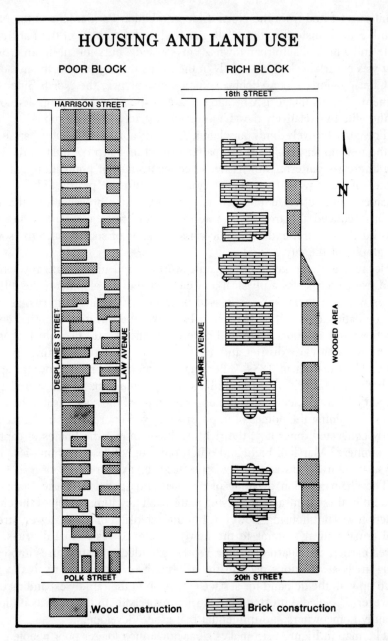

Figure 6.14.

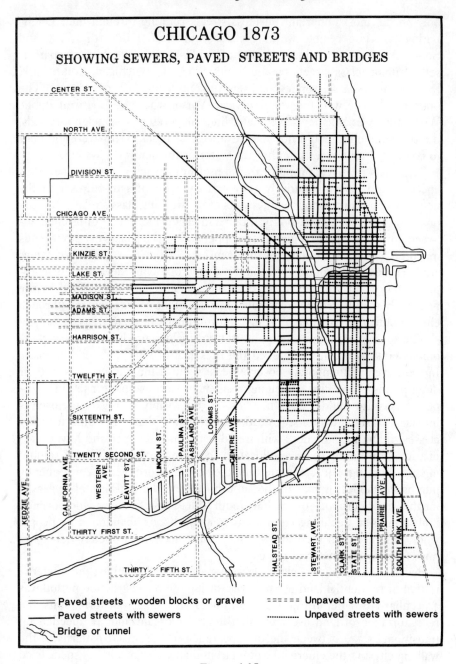

Figure 6.15.

only on the most important business streets running through their neighborhoods. More remote working class sections of the North, West, and South Divisions were almost devoid of public services, while even sparsely settled upper class streets on the South Side, like Michigan, South Park, Prairie, and Indiana Avenues, had sewers as far south as 35th Street.[191] The poor also had to wait for water service. Worse, when the Board of Public Works finally established sewer water lines in working class neighborhoods, the residents often could not take advantage of them. Many were too poor to connect their houses to either the water or the sewerage system.

The city's relatively prompt extension of infrastructures into upper class enclaves and its comparatively slow extension of infrastructures into the neighborhoods of the poor were results of the working class's relatively weak position in the process of political demand articulation. The difference between infrastructural development in upper and working class neighborhoods mirrored the contrast between the mansions of the rich and the cottages and shanties of the poor. Both kinds of environmental development completed the chain reaction of physical and spatial change stimulated by the fire, and both reflected the comparative inability of the poor to demand (through either political or economic means) improvements in their areas.

The spatial, economic, and political trends which produced these dichotomous land use patterns masked the presence of Chicago's middle class. Indeed, even contemporary observers lost sight of the middle class in their descriptions of the city's changing residential land use patterns. This happened because middle class families did not visibly segregate themselves into large, distinct districts. Instead, they evidently blended in with the other classes, filling in interstices within and between the upper and lower class districts, consuming space and location according to the quality and amount of land, housing, and commute time they could afford. Many consequently purchased modest homes in the suburbs and on the outskirts of the fashionable neighborhoods of the Far South Side. Most, however, took over or built houses in declining central city neighborhoods abandoned by people who, wealthier than themselves, could afford to move to better neighborhoods on the perimeter of the city.[192]

Because of the middle class's lack of geographical visibility, the modernization of residential land use patterns during the reconstruction period was a peculiarly two-tiered trend. For all the far-reaching transformations, the reorganization of land use was still a limited reorganization, a speeded-up transitional stage between the disappearance of the mixed patterns of the walking city and the emergence of metropolitan Chicago with its specialized central business district, its extensive separate upper and middle class suburbs, and its congested, slum-ridden, industrialized, working class core.

Conclusion

In sum, the great fire's temporary destruction of a single barrier to environmental change, the physical durability of structures, precipitated a wide range of changes in Chicago's physical and spatial land use patterns. It led not only to the expansion and internal reorganization of the central business district, the emergence of a new industrial district, the reorganization and expansion of residential districts, and the growth of Chicago's suburbs but also to the creation of a large brick district in the center of the city, the erection of new railroad depots, and the construction of miles of water service pipes, sewers, steam railroad tracks, horse railway tracks, and roads.

Chicagoans paid for nearly all of this construction through ordinary governmental and private channels. The money sent to the Relief and Aid Society for the construction of temporary shelters for the homeless was the only exception. The state government provided $2,955,340 in emergency aid shortly after the disaster, two-thirds of which had to be devoted to the payment of interest on the municipal debt. Even this money, however, was provided under an existing contract between the city and the state, as payment for the state's assumption of the debt the city had incurred when it deepened the Illinois and Michigan Canal. Attempts to obtain more state assistance failed, as did efforts to get the federal government to provide low-interest building loans. As a result, the rest of the funds for the work of reconstruction came entirely from regular municipal revenue appropriations, insurance payments, private mortgages, and people's savings.

Chicagoans generally expressed pleasure with the fruits of their massive expenditures. As one writer said in a guide to the city published in 1873, reconstruction enabled them to feel that they finally had something solid to substantiate their boasts about the greatness of the city. "Chicagoans," he wrote, "had always indulged a trifle in brag, and people in other cities would have it that there was nothing behind all this talk. But here was an opportunity, if there ever was one, . . . to make good their boasts. That they have done so, an applauding world will bear testimony."[193]

Most observers were especially pleased by the extension of the fire limits and the "palpable superiority" of the new structures in the business center. Although most decried the proliferation of wooden shanties outside the limits, and a few criticized the "questionable taste" of some of the buildings in the commercial district, they lauded the architectural style of the vast majority of new warehouses, banks, and stores, as well as the new buildings' greater size, their five-, six-, and seven-story heights, and their physical solidity and fire resistance. Workers, meanwhile, appreciated having the right to continue constructing their wooden homes legally.[194]

The rationalization of land use patterns stimulated by the fire also impressed people. "Chicago property now stands better classified and its future more distinctly marked than could have been possible before the fire," one writer enthusiastically declared. "The different departments and grades of business are assigned," he added, "and although in some localities an artificial development may vary the result, nothing can change the general rule. Within the city, homes for the poor, quarters for the humble trades, districts for the chief manufacturing enterprises, retail streets of the various trades, boulevard regions and the meaner purlieus, are distinctly marked and foreshadowed." He and others acclaimed this development because it made it possible for capitalists and small land purchasers with even "a modest shrewdness and foresight" to know the character and future values of "each section and quarter of the city."[195]

What really impressed most people, however, was the rapid spatial expansion of Chicago. They marveled at the growth of suburbs, at the spread of substantial houses into the previously empty streets south of 22nd Street, and at the proliferation of workers' cottages and shanties in the far reaches of the West Division. They applauded the expansion of the central business district and the clearance of the slums that had bordered on it prior to the fire. They cheered the rise of the new industrial district west of Reuben Street. Even the "more sanguine" had not expected the city to expand anything but "slowly, very slowly, a block in one or two years" before this sudden burst of growth.[196]

These self-congratulations were well deserved on many counts. The people of Chicago had, indeed, witnessed a spatial transformation of the city. In addition, they had managed to extend the fire limits. They had also improved the quality of structures in the central business district. And they had extended water pipes, sewers, and other infrastructures to a remarkable degree.

They had not, however, eliminated their overcrowded slums or solved their pollution, water, street congestion, fire, and railroad problems. These persisted, a painful testimony to the strength of the physical, economic, political, social, and technological obstacles still impeding the environmental adaptation of Chicago to the imperatives of growth.

7

The rebuilding of Boston

On the evening of Saturday, November 9, 1872, a fire broke out at the corner of Summer and Kingston Streets in Boston. It was first noticed as a reddish glow in the basement windows of the building shortly after 7:00 p.m. and was soon seen "roaring up the elevator" to the upper stories. By 7:20 the flames had attracted a crowd of onlookers, but the first alarm was, inexplicably, not sounded until 7:24. By the time fire companies finally began to arrive, the building was "one vast furnace," the heat so intense that no one could get within fifty feet of it and so powerful that the building's granite walls began to explode, sending stony fragments flying in every direction in pieces up to thirty pounds in weight.[1]

From the start, the Fire Department found itself no match for the heat and the flames. The delay in sounding the first alarm was only one of its problems. For a variety of reasons, the Department had no fire houses in the central district where the fire broke out. Ordinarily, it had gotten around this difficulty by dispatching several fire steamers to a blaze whenever a first alarm in the business area came in. On November 9, however, most of the horses in Boston were suffering from a plaguelike disease called epizootic. Half the Department's horses were too sick to stand without support, and almost all the rest were too weak to be put into service. The Department had hired men to haul the equipment through the streets and had had to change its running card to reduce the number of engines slated to respond to a first alarm from six to one. On the night of the fire the men pulling equipment proved to be as swift as horses, but because of the change in the running card, several of the engines normally scheduled to move immediately to a fire arrived at the scene five to ten minutes late. Thus the original delay was compounded, and the opportunity to stop the fire while it was still small, lost. The flames were soon completely out of control. They leaped across Boston's narrow streets with ease and grabbed entire blocks of buildings at once. Less than half an hour after the first alarm was sounded Chief Engineer John C. Damrell found it necessary to order a general alarm to bring in fire engines and men from throughout the city. Only minutes later he had to call for help from Cambridge and Charlestown as well.

Even with outside help the fire fighters could not cope with the conflagration. The streets were too narrow for effective positioning and use of equipment. Even worse, the water supply was insufficient. Most of the water pipes and hydrants in the fire area had been laid decades earlier for residential use. They were too small and old-fashioned to carry the huge amount of water needed to put the fire out. As a result, steamers robbed each other of water and often had to stop pumping so that others in seemingly more critical locations could have more of the desperately needed fluid. In places, the intense heat caused hoses to explode or kept firemen at such a distance from burning buildings that good hoses became useless. The great demand for water also so reduced the water pressure that the streams of water that did go through rarely reached beyond the second or third story of tall buildings, leaving the fire free to ravage rooftops and upper stories unimpeded. "It was not that there were not enough engines," a fireman recalled later. "There were none capable of throwing a stream within a dozen feet of the kindling wood cornices. It was terrible to watch the puny streams that never reached the eaves but were wasted on the granite of the lower story while the flames ran gayly along the dry pine window casings . . . unhindered by a single drop of water."[2]

By 10:00 the fire had engulfed almost ten acres, burning out most of Boston's drygoods and woolen dealers. By midnight it had moved as far as Congress Street, destroying nearly fifteen additional acres, including a large part of the leather wholesaling district and a number of wharves in the harbor. By 1:00 a.m. it had crossed Pearl Street and begun to wreak havoc in the boot and shoe district. It not only continued to defy the efforts of the Fire Department, now considerably augmented by men and equipment from around the state; it also burned against the wind.[3] It spread quickly and dramatically. An observer recalled: "A whole block of houses on one side would be burning furiously when not a spark of flame could be seen on the other side. All at once the fire would burst out almost simultaneously along the whole line, and in less time than it takes to write it the roofs would be falling in and the walls tumbling with a loud crash."[4] In desperation the Chief Engineer authorized the use of explosives to stop the flames, but to little avail. Carelessly used, often in buildings that had already begun to burn, the gunpowder in many cases only spread the flames, prolonging the struggle.

The fire burned out of control until late afternoon Sunday, fed by leaking gas, poorly used gunpowder, and the ubiquitous wooden mansard roof. It was rekindled on Sunday night by gases exploding in sewers and not brought under complete control until dawn on Monday.

On Monday morning Boston began to assess the destruction. Spectators found the area completely unrecognizable, "a mass of ruins from one end to the other." Businessmen wandered among "dreary piles of calcined granite and smoking heaps of dull red brick," searching for the sites of their stores and warehouses, bewildered, constantly forced to ask each other where they were in the once familiar place. Stone, brick, twisted iron columns, and other debris lay everywhere, in piles up to twelve feet high, obliterating everything, even the lines of the streets.[5]

For all the waste, the fire had wreaked only a fraction of the havoc the great Chicago fire had caused just a year earlier. In fact, in thirty-six hours it had demolished only about sixty-five acres, about what the Chicago fire had consumed each hour, on average, for twenty-six hours.

Still, all who viewed or heard of the disaster gawked in amazement at the immensity of the destruction. The burnt area was the heart of the wholesale business district of a city whose economy was based on commerce (see Figure 7.1). The conflagration had burnt out close to a thousand businesses, including every large wholesale clothing dealer in the city except one, every wool house, and almost all of Boston's drygoods, boot and shoe, and leather dealers. It had also damaged many of the city's publishing concerns and had wiped out a host of other businesses that ranged from banks and bagging concerns, iron and steel warehouses, carpenter shops, and dye and chemical firms to hardware stores, restaurants, and paper suppliers. It had laid waste to 776 buildings assessed at $13.5 million, in addition to mercantile and personal property estimated at more than $60 million. Unlike the Chicago fire, the Boston fire had not swept across the residential city. It had, however, consumed a number of lodging houses and killed at least fourteen people. It had also thrown thousands of men and women out of work.[6]

The people of Boston responded to the catastrophe with a zeal for rebuilding better than before and with a burst of environmental planning that far surpassed that of their counterparts in the Windy City. On Monday, November 11, the Board of Aldermen appointed a Citizens' Relief Committee to provide aid to the people who had lost jobs or homes to the conflagration. The Aldermen also began organizing the work of cleaning up and reconstructing the burnt district.[7] Simultaneously, newspaper editors, businessmen, burnt-out property owners, ministers, and city and state government officials began calling for far-reaching environmental improvements in the area, changes that had previously been virtually unthinkable because of the inflexibility of the built environment. They pressed for wider and straighter streets, for the laying out of new thoroughfares, and for the discontinuance of certain old ones. They urged the regrading of the burnt district and the establishment of a conveniently located railroad terminal. They called for the provision of a new system of water mains and fire hydrants and for the establishment of more accessible fire houses. They demanded building codes which would mandate more fireproof building structures,

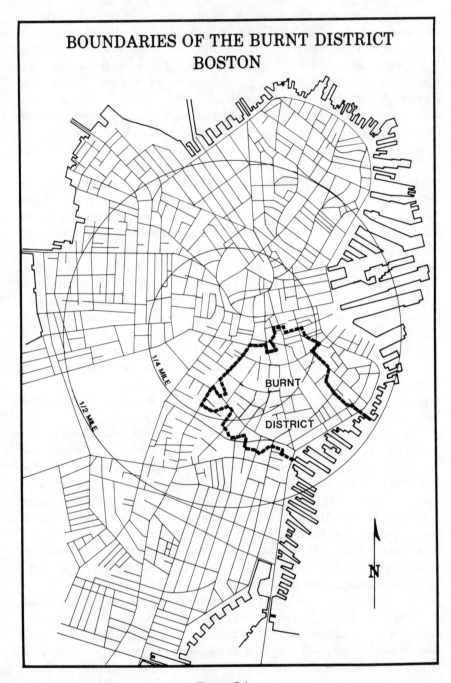

Figure 7.1.

and they called for more beautiful and capacious buildings as well. Certain groups urged the creation of large plazas near the new Post Office on the western edge of the burnt district. Some went so far as to urge an integrated program of street betterment for the entire central city, and the Massachusetts legislature proposed a plan for improving the grades and drainage of the ten-mile-square metropolitan area.[8]

The speed with which Bostonians recognized the opportunity for environmental improvement and city planning probably resulted from the comparatively small extent of the destruction. Unlike the people of Chicago, they were not burnt out of "home as well as office." Every influential individual and interest group in Boston with any concern for the condition of the business district seems to have shared the realization that the fire had given the city an extraordinary chance to make a wide range of long-needed improvements in the burnt district. Even outsiders expressed this opinion, joining in the call upon the city to redesign its street and water systems and abolish all its wooden roofs.[9] Unlike in Chicago, there were no naysayers in Boston dismissing the improvement demands as ridiculous and unmanageable, at least at this early date.

This remarkable unanimity doubtless resulted at least in part from the shock of the disaster and the necessity of finding some trace of good in it. Ministers thundered about the need to make a benefit of the catastrophe so that the will of God might be fulfilled. Newspapers often headlined their editorials on improvement "The Bright Side."[10]

The response was more than a simple psychological release, however. Bostonians were eager to resolve environmental problems that had been plaguing them for years. A part of the "old" residential South End, the burnt district was actually a relatively new section of the commercial district. Cows had grazed on pastureland on Summer Street as late as 1815, and expensive homes and townhouses had dominated parts of the landscape into the 1850s and 1860s.[11] It was still, however, the focus of severe fire hazard, traffic, cellar flooding, and other environmental problems.

Most of the burnt district's problems were, in fact, the direct result of its rapid transition from semi-rural to residential to intense commercial land use. New as many of the area's stores and warehouses were, for example, they could not meet the immense and still increasing demand for commercial space placed on them by rapid economic growth. Thus, like similarly outmoded buildings in pre-fire Chicago, the buildings were contributing to a skyrocketing rise in rents. As in Chicago, this was increasing businesses' dissatisfaction with the prevailing land use equilibrium.[12] Worse, most of the buildings were terrible firetraps, notwithstanding their recent construction and their substantial brick and granite facades. Wooden beams and columns typically supported facades and exterior walls, as well as wood-lathed and sometimes wood-veneered interior walls, wood floors, wooden elevator shafts and stairwells, and wooden mansard roofs. The timbers in the floors were placed six to twelve inches apart, and walls were furred and lathed in such a way that like the elevators and stairwells, they created air passages which could turn a building into "a perfect system of flues" at the touch of a flame, drawing fire from room to room and from wooden floor to wooden floor to wooden roof.[13]

Most of the area's infrastructures were in equally bad shape. Its water pipes and fire hydrants had been laid decades before the conflagration, when the territory was still residential. Now they exacerbated the fire hazards created by the wooden buildings, because they were incapable of providing the water pressure needed to fight ordinary fires in tall, four- and five-story, highly flammable warehouses and stores, let alone put out a major conflagration.[14] To make matters worse, there were no fire houses in the area, not even one reasonably close by, despite repeated calls by the Fire Department for their establishment.[15]

Sinuous narrow streets created additional problems. Their twelve- to forty-five-foot widths, many dead ends, and badly located junctions slowed the passage of fire steamers and made the proper positioning of fire equipment difficult. They also caused constant traffic "snarls, blockades, and collisions." Barely adequate for residential use, they made the area a nightmare for businessmen and coach and delivery truck drivers, especially those trying to cut across the district to get from the North End or the State Street financial center to the railway terminals at the South End. The only direct route between Milk and upper Summer Streets was Hawley Street, which in one place was a mere twelve feet wide. The only routes joining Washington and upper Summer with Congress, Pearl, and the streets beyond were just as narrow and much less direct unconnected lanes and passageways. Worst of all, many of the district's streets were so tightly packed with parked delivery carts during the active wholesale business seasons that they could scarcely be used for normal travel at all.[16]

Parts of the district also suffered from serious drainage problems. Much of the area was land that had been reclaimed from the sea or streams and swamps by real estate developers when the district was being developed for residential use. As a result of poor planning or work, heavy rains flooded many cellars on many streets, damaging stored goods and forcing businessmen to spend much time and money shifting and drying goods or finding places to store them elsewhere. Indeed, on the man-made land near Dock Square, many basements were so low that they flooded at high tide.[17]

It was these long-standing, frustrating problems and dangers, as much as anything else, which led to the explosion of interest in instituting street improvements, in enacting new building codes, in constructing new fire houses, and in laying better water mains and hydrants. Comprehensive planning, at least on a limited scale, was nothing new in Boston. In fact, in the past decade government officials had spent millions of dollars leveling Fort Hill and replatting the streets there. They had also spent millions filling in land, laying water pipes, and grading and constructing streets in South Boston and the Back Bay. This broad planning had largely been confined to improvement of undeveloped areas owned by the city. Nevertheless, the experience had begun to turn people's minds toward the possibilities of comprehensive planning in older districts requiring redevelopment.

Now, buoyed by the nineteenth century's faith in the inevitability of progress, and not deterred by an upcoming municipal election as Chicagoans had been, Bostonians moved to take advantage of what many believed to be a God-given chance to turn ideals into reality, entering into the reconstruction process with the greatest confidence that they could indeed achieve the environmental improvements they so desired. "The opportunity for reconstructing the streets of the devastated district will never offer again," the editors of the *Post* declared a few days after the fire. "What was an irregular assemblage of narrow and sinuous streets may thus become the finest portion of the city, with broad highways and solid and fire-defying structures."[18] "These much needed improvements in the business center might not have been practicable for a generation to come had it not been for the devastative fire which has suddenly stripped the territory almost bare," echoed the editors of the *Boston Globe*. "But now that the disaster has taken place, they are perfectly feasible."[19]

The expressions of confidence and solidarity which flowed from cities across the nation cheered and encouraged those advocating the improvements. Supporters of redevelopment exulted in the belief that the "same alacrity, courage, and zeal which have distinguished the gallant firemen in their prolonged and desperate struggle with the flames, now . . . animate every heart in the community and assure a signal triumph over misfortune." They reveled in the expectation that "nothing" made the city's "great future so secure as this admirable determination of its public citizens" to turn the disaster to their advantage. The fire, they affirmed, had "burned out whatever constitutional obstacles tended insensibly to obstruct" Boston's "natural growth."[20]

These hopes were not entirely misplaced. The rebuilding did, in fact, enable Bostonians to make significant, planned improvements in their built environment. The process by which the improvements came into being was difficult and convoluted, however. To the frustration of those involved, it illustrated not only the ways in which a disaster could stimulate change, but also the limits to change. The great fire had, indeed, temporarily eliminated the obstacles to environmental redevelopment posed by the physical durability of structures. Like the people of Chicago, though, the people of Boston quickly discovered that it had not altered the many powerful political, technological, and economic factors that had always stood in the way of optimal redevelopment. As a result, the community consensus concerning the desirability of improvement disintegrated, and the opportunity to achieve many greatly needed individual improvements soon slipped beyond the city's grasp.

Improving Boston's crooked and narrow streets

The effort to achieve the hoped for street improvements dramatized, with special force, the possibilities and contradictions inherent in the opportunity for change provided by the great Boston fire. Driven by the demand for change, the City Council nearly enacted a radical plan to redesign the street system completely. The plan itself, however, helped set the economic and political forces of retrenchment in action.

The big demand for extensive changes in the street system was the community's response to the area's long-standing traffic problems. Accidents, street blockages, and slow, inefficient traffic flow were the most visible and universally frustrating manifestations of environmental maladaptation that Bostonians had confronted in the business district in the years before the conflagration. The problems were extremely old, extending back to the city fathers' failure to lay out a comprehensive street plan. The only major thoroughfare serving the whole area during the colonial period had been the road to the neck of the Boston peninsula, called Washington Street at the time of the great fire. Much of the land had been empty pasture and had not contained any streets at all.[21] In the late eighteenth and early nineteenth centuries, property owners had created new roads in order to open the undeveloped land for residential construction. Having only a limited amount of land at their disposal and only their own immediate interests in mind, however, they had not planned the streets for future intense commercial use. Instead, with the exception of Franklin Street, which the great Federalist architect Charles Bullfinch had laid out in a relatively wide curve, they had created nothing but short, narrow, badly graded, and mostly unconnected residential lanes, like Otis and Arch Streets and Winthrop Place, which went virtually nowhere and had to be connected to the more important streets by even narrower alleys and passageways.[22]

The city government had not been able to do much to improve these conditions over the years. One problem had been that it had had no power over the construction and maintenance of private streets, but could only set standards for accepting them as public streets.[23] Another, far more serious problem had been that, despite decades of trying, the city had not been able to obtain the authority it needed to levy betterment assessments on abutters to offset the high costs of condemning land and paying property damages, until the late 1860s. Abutters had sometimes been among the most vociferous of those demanding improvements. They had never, however, voluntarily offered to move or tear down their buildings and rebuild on smaller lots without insisting on the payment of heavy damages. Since commercialization and rising property values went hand in hand, this land assembly problem had made street improvements increasingly difficult for the city to undertake until 1868, when a new state law finally gave it the power to force abutters to bear some of the land assembly costs.

To get around this problem, the city of Boston, like the city of Chicago, had resorted to the practice of working on an individual basis with property owners to get improvements made. The Boston Board of Street Commissioners had informed property owners giving notice of their intention to redevelop their buildings what street grade and width the city planned to establish as the standard on their streets, in the hope that the property holders would then build in compliance with the standard of their own accord. At times, the Commissioners had also negotiated for the actual widening of the section of the street abutting a proprietor's land, taking advantage of the owner's own intention to demolish the buildings to pay lower damage costs. Occasionally, they had also made a partial widening simply because the termination of a lease or leasers enabled them to widen without paying lease damages.[24]

This haphazard and piecemeal procedure had frequently served only to intensify problems, however. In many places, it had resulted in streets of uneven widths, which created traffic bottlenecks and added to the difficulties facing pedestrians trying to make their way through the congested thoroughfares. It had also antagonized those property owners who had compliantly built stores and warehouses to conform to contemplated street grades and widths, who had then had to wait years before their buildings could be properly used. In any case, the method had not been one that could bring about much far-reaching change.

The city finally extended Devonshire Street to Summer Street in the late 1850s, creating the long-hoped-for direct route between Summer and State Streets. It had done little more than this, however. Immersed in the work of grading and laying out streets in the Fort Hill area and the recently filled lands of the Back Bay, South Boston, and the South End, the Street Commissioners had generally ignored this well-established commercial and wholesale center. As a result, almost every street in the area was still about as crooked and narrow as it had been in 1820.[25]

The great fire, however, changed everything. Now, with the memory of the flames easily jumping the streets still fresh, public officials, newspaper spokesmen, and businessmen alike suddenly and loudly embraced the idea of improvement, creating an almost irresistible demand for change. For example, the day after the fire, William Gray, the Chairman of the Citizens Relief Committee, publicly pledged the Relief Committee's and his own support for street improvements, even going so far as to acknowledge and endorse the huge expense the project would involve. Businessmen and property holders meeting with the Relief Committee at the Tremont Temple to discuss the problems of reconstruction demanded the widening, straightening, and regrading of the streets on the basis of a "comprehensive and liberal plan," also "earnestly" pledging their support for the City Council's exercise of its powers in the execution of the task. Other, smaller groups of burnt-out businessmen and landowners also called for the improvements.[26] George K. Richardson, President of the National Union Bank and an important community leader, spoke for them all, declaring that "now" was the time "for such radical changes to be made in the streets of the burnt district as will avoid the inconveniences of old, and at the same time render... structures less liable to fall prey to another fire."[27]

This sudden explosion of demand for comprehensive redevelopment temporarily overwhelmed the old barriers to improvement, forcing city officials to pay attention and take measures to solve the district's street problems. Accordingly, on Monday, November 12, the day after the fire was put out, the City Council appointed a Joint Standing Committee on Streets, ordering it to prepare a new plan for laying out the streets. The next day the Council moved to stop property owners from re-creating the old physical barriers to improvement by commanding the Department of Survey to stop issuing all permits for the erection of permanent buildings in the burnt district and by ordering that all permits for temporary structures be subject to the express stipulation that the buildings be "removed, in whole or in part... without expense to the city, whenever directed by the Building Department or the Joint Committee on Streets." Two days later, fearing that this was not a strong enough safeguard, the Council ordered the Department to stop issuing permits completely until the new lines of the streets were fixed.[28]

Bostonians were generally in agreement on the basic goals of street improvement. They shared four basic aspirations. The first was to guard against the spread of fire by widening streets and eliminating very narrow streets and lanes. The second was to improve traffic flow by widening and straightening crooked and narrow streets, by removing the jogs left by piecemeal widenings in the past, and by altering street lines to connect adjoining streets more directly and eliminate dead ends. The third goal was to alleviate drainage problems by raising the grades of the lowest streets. The fourth was to lay out new streets and rearrange others in such a way that new crosstown thoroughfares could be created within and between the burnt district and surrounding parts of the business district. This was the most ambitious of the objectives. One hope was to create one or more thoroughfares which would extend across the burnt district to connect Oliver, Pearl, Congress, and Federal Streets with Washington or the upper part of Summer Street, creating a new avenue from the South End to the North End. Another was to realign Federal or Congress so that it would connect with Eastern Avenue, a street planned for the newly filled South Boston flats.[29]

Pushing this last objective farther was a smaller group led by William L. Burt, the Postmaster of Boston. Burt was a Harvard-educated lawyer who had served as Brigadier General for the Union during the Civil War. A man with a strong personality and a habit of taking charge and getting things done, he had been an active participant in city politics since his appointment as Postmaster in 1867. Having spearheaded the relocation and rebuilding of the Post Office to Devonshire Street in the late 1860s, Burt had become very concerned about the traffic congestion in the surrounding warehouse and financial districts, as well as about the fire hazards posed by the narrow streets.[30] He now suggested that the city begin a series of improvements, to be completed over a lengthy period of time, which would create extensive fire barriers in the business area as well as make the burnt district the hub of a new city-wide traffic system. The map reproduced in Figure 7.2 shows the broad changes Burt proposed for the central city as a whole.[31]

There was such a wide consensus on these general improvement goals that even the most radical proponents of change had a powerful voice in the development of the burnt district street plans. Indeed, the first plan that the City Council considered proposed nothing less than a fundamental redesign of the entire burnt district street system. The Board of Street Commissioners and the Joint Committee on Streets recommended taking the whole territory of the burnt district by eminent domain and laying out the "streets and building lots anew, without reference to existing lines." The plan required that the city secure from the Massachusetts legislature the power necessary to take possession of the district, to issue bonds to pay for the estates thus taken and the improvements made, and to appoint appraisers and commissioners to value each estate and lay out the streets in the new pattern. The bonds would be sold at public auction and secured and paid out by the proceeds from the later resale of the land.[32]

Several engineers drew maps showing possible innovations in the street system, some of which included radical changes of the type the Council was considering. Most of these maps have been lost to history. One, however, prepared by an engineer named Walling, was reprinted in the *Daily Advertiser*, and it appears in Figure 7.3. It shows the City Council to have been considering a straighter, more grid-like system with wide streets, which would have done away with all narrow and crooked lanes while maximizing the number of cross-town thoroughfares. (The *Daily Advertiser* printed this map

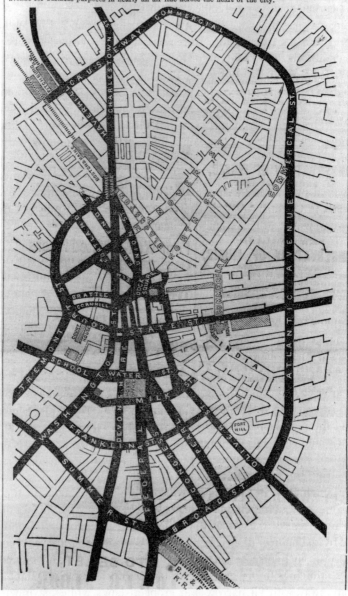

STREET WIDENINGS AND EXTENSIONS—GENERAL BURT'S PLAN.

To the Editors of the Boston Daily Advertiser:—

The following plan represents the extension of Washington and Devonshire streets through Haymarket square to Charlestown street, as now ordered, and the proposed widening and extension of Federal, Congress and Pearl to State street, showing a continuous street from the Boston, Hartford and Erie station to Charlestown bridge, parallel to Atlantic avenue, and affording a wide avenue for business purposes in nearly an air line across the heart of the city.

Figure 7.2.

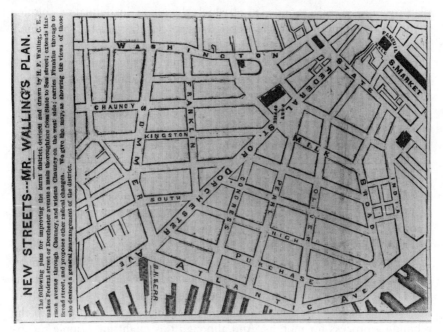

Figure 7.3.

upside down and sideways, probably to make it look more radical than it was. Here it has been reoriented for purposes of comparison.) Some reports suggest that the Council was considering avenues of eighty- and one-hundred-foot widths. The Walling plan proposed the elimination of one important thoroughfare, apparently Devonshire Street, so that the size of building lots would be normal despite these greatly widened streets.[33]

The plan was ambitious, intended to eliminate the defects in the street system once and for all. With its eminent domain provisions, it was also designed to do away with the site assembly problem and the concomitant conflict between private and public interests which had obstructed attempts to institute street improvements in the past. The Street Commissioners and the members of the Joint Committee on Streets fully appreciated these advantages. As a result, they moved as quickly and smoothly as possible, promptly appointing several "eminent legal gentlemen" to begin preparation of the bill the city would have to submit to the state legislature in order to obtain the authorization it needed to implement the plan.

But the Street Commissioners and Joint Committee members immediately ran into trouble. Opposition from businessmen and City Council members developed, attacks on the legality of the plan were launched, and the opportunity for improvement began to be constricted.[34] The challenges to the plan rose on several grounds, all of which show how inadequate a solution to the site assembly problem the proposal to take the entire district by eminent domain was.

People objected that the costs of condemning all the land would be unbearable. Ignoring the provision which earmarked the monies from the resale of the land for the funding of the bonds (and the city's past success in reselling lands taken under the assessment law for a profit), foes argued that Boston would be crippled by the increase in the city debt. The *Daily Advertiser*, for example, graphically deriding the plan, raised the "spectacle of the honest old town staggering half crushed beneath the overwhelming burden," unable to continue functioning as an effective city government.[35]

Others argued that the project would lead to an unacceptable postponement of the reconstruction of the district. The plan threatened an "almost wanton sacrifice of precious time," they argued. With every day's delay they feared the "permanent establishment of Boston's business in New York." It had taken years to get the state to authorize the Fort Hill redevelopment project. A similar struggle was likely to occur, critics charged, in getting this legislation passed. But even if the act were approved quickly, a rush of litigation to block the takings would be inevitable and might hold up the rebuilding process for months. And although this might not cripple reconstruction, the technical problems in laying out new streets and lots would unnecessarily retard the rebuilding of stores and warehouses and damage business. Preaching haste, critics argued that needs of commerce made the plan impossible to implement. "Whatever is to be done, must be done quickly," they insistently declared.[36]

Lawyers working on the preparation of the bill added legal objections. They argued that the plan might be unconstitutional. They feared that the General Court would not be able to give the city disposition and control of the land under the discontinued streets when its easement in them for street purposes terminated. "Under the law of the land," they claimed, "the land would revert to its previous owners whose rights rested in the abutter," not to the city. How this would have stopped the city from taking the district by eminent domain is not clear, but in the opinion of the City Solicitor, it was not enough to block the city's use of eminent domain "in such a case."[37]

The biggest problem with the plan, however, was not time, nor money, nor constitutionality. It was the eminent domain solution to the site assembly problem itself and the fact that the taking of the burnt district by eminent domain threatened a complete redistribution of landholding patterns in the business area. This fear, hinted at but never fully articulated publicly, lay behind all the arguments against the proposal, most of which boiled down to attacks on eminent domain. The city had not settled on a method for disposing of the land taken. Presumably it would have auctioned it off as it did land taken under the assessment act. In any case, the street improvements and the opportunity for purchasers to put together large lots would have tended naturally to raise land values. Former landholders might then have been unable to repurchase their old estates or, worse, unable to buy any land at all. In any case, a truly radical change in the street system of the kind proposed by Mr. Walling would have cut up the old plots so thoroughly that even a semblance of a return to the old pattern would have been impossible. Although some property holders would have been sure to benefit, the possibility of such a fundamental change was apparently unsettling to them all. To the Joint Committee on Streets, for example, the plan was too "arbitrary." To the *Daily Advertiser*, which reflected the opinion of businessmen on this subject, it was a "quixotic scheme" which smacked of an encroachment on the institution of private property. The paper accused the city of trying to become the "absolute owner" of the territory, as it had become the absolute owner of Fort Hill, South Boston, and Back Bay lands. "Ask for no further powers which are needless," the paper cried, "be conservative . . . alter as little as possible."[38]

In reply, supporters argued that the changes were necessary, regardless of the problems, and that "extraordinary emergencies suggest extraordinary expedients." Mr. Walling responded to charges that his plan for the radical rearrangement of the streets would cause unacceptable delays in the rebuilding process by pointing out that during the Civil War, army engineers had built in only four or five days long bridges which would have taken months to construct by ordinary methods. He also noted that the city of Brooklyn had been able to lay out the streets in the annexed section of Long Island quickly and accurately with the use of elevated wires. He was sure that "here, too, adequate expedients would suggest themselves by which new streets could be located with precision and dispatch, and the lots defined as fast as they might be desired." There could be no satisfactory answer to the problem of land redistribution, however.[39]

Foes of the plan far outnumbered supporters. On November 15, at a Committee of Conference called by the City Council, burnt-out property holders and businessmen quickly rejected the proposal. Even Postmaster Burt, the most enthusiastic advocate of extensive improvements, declaimed against it in favor of his own, more conservative plan. The attending Councilmen sent the rejection on to the Board of Street Commissioners and the Joint Committee on Streets. The Commissioners and Committee members deliberated over this rebuff and the legalistic arguments concerning the possible unconstitutionality of the plan. They then backtracked and reported negatively on it. On November 18 the City Council disapproved it.[40] Thus the city eliminated the only alternative it had to the old system of negotiation with individual abutters for the achievement of street improvements, giving up its opportunity to remove a legal and economic straitjacket that had greatly restricted its ability to institute improvements in the past.

Instead of the radical rearrangement of the streets, the City Council adopted a resolution calling for a plan which would improve travel through the streets "without seriously interfering with the interests of individual owners of estates."[41] The plan it approved had been drawn up by the City Surveyor the day after the fire, and property holders had already indicated general satisfaction with it. It preserved most of the old lines of the streets. It did not preclude significant improvements, however. As the map in Figure 7.4 shows, even within the constraints imposed, the City Council intended to fulfill its major goals at least partially.

The main changes projected for the district included the extension of Chauncy Street to the corner of Devonshire Street so as to relieve the congestion on Devonshire and Washington Streets and create a new diagonal route from State Street to the South End; the enlargement of Winthrop Square; the widening of Otis Street; and the widening and straightening of Devonshire Street and Winthrop Square to make a better connection to Lincoln Street and improve the flow of traffic from Devonshire to the South End. Elsewhere, the plan proposed that Franklin Street be extended to Oliver Street (over Sturgis), creating the first thoroughfare across the district, and that Pearl Street be extended to Congress to eliminate the crooked lane of Bath Street. It also called for the widening of the streets surrounding the new Post Office and the joining of Congress and Federal Streets at Milk Street in front of the Post Office. These last two proposals were based on Postmaster Burt's plan to improve traffic flow and simultaneously create in the heart of the business district a grand plaza that would function as a fire barrier and provide an appropriate setting for the Post Office. The merging of Congress and Federal would improve transportation by eliminating the frequently jammed turn onto Milk Street (required under the old system) leading from the upper end of Congress onto Federal (which had no outlet onto State Street). Federal was also to be widened and straightened so that it could be connected to the Eastern Avenue bridge which was tentatively planned for the channel separating Boston from South Boston. This would create the hoped for thoroughfare to South Boston. Atlantic Avenue would be widened to one hundred feet to provide a broad beltway on the periphery of the burnt district for cross-town traffic. Several other less important streets were also to be widened and a number of alleys extended so that they would be more streetlike.[42]

A comparison of this plan with the Walling and Burt maps reveals the basic conservatism of these proposals. Yet it embodied significant improvements that would help relieve the congestion of the streets and increase the efficiency of traffic flow.

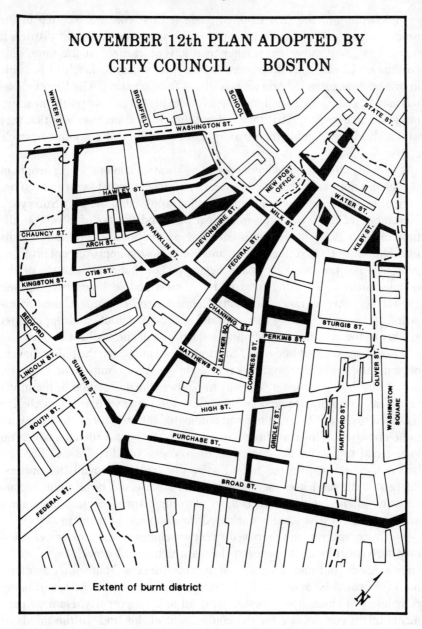

Figure 7.4.

In accepting it, the City Council made its first constructive step in the process of reconstructing and reforming the streets of the burnt district. It was a small step, however, smaller than anyone realized at the time. The November 12 plan was little more than a hastily drawn sketch of possible improvements, intended primarily as a basis for discussion. The Street Commissioners and City Council members fully expected to hold public hearings on it and change it.[43] What they did not then fully appreciate was that they would also have to guide the plan through a political and economic obstacle course.

The most obvious obstructions were, as always, economic. The people of Boston did not want to pay for an extensive restructuring of the street system, even one as comparatively moderate as that proposed in the City Surveyor's November 12 map. Both the municipal debt and the tax rate were at all-time highs because of the city's energetic public building program and its Fort Hill, Back Bay, Suffolk Street, and South Boston improvement projects. Although the tax rate had finally begun to fall that year because of the establishment of a sinking fund in 1871, most people vigorously opposed any further increase now. Most City Council members, in fact, doubly opposed an increase, fearing that it would speed the middle and upper class exodus to the suburbs, accelerating a shrinkage of the tax base.[44]

These fears created budgetary constraints beyond which the policy makers planning the street improvements refused to go. What is important, however, is that this financial barrier was only the outward manifestation of the much larger site assembly problem and the more fundamental barriers to change it caused to exist. The great fire had eliminated the structures upon the land to be improved. This constituted an important saving for the city, which no longer had to pay for demolition or the owners' building losses. The fire had not, however, affected most leases, nor had it changed the owners' interest in the land itself or the return the land would bring upon reconstruction of the buildings. In fact, by allowing owners to build anew on a grander scale, it had actually enhanced their interest in many instances.[45]

For many abutters the proposed street widenings and extensions entailed only very small losses of property, losses which would quickly be offset by large gains in land values because of improved access. Many other abutters, however, would be assessed for betterment taxes for the privilege of being completely or close to completely deprived of their property. Damage payments might compensate for the confiscation of the land. In the minds of many people, however, money alone would not be sufficient recompense for the loss of established places of business, the loss of accustomed and rewarding sources of steady income, or, for those with very little property in the area, the possibly permanent loss of their only stake in the central business district. As one angry man protested, the improvements threatened to leave him a strip of land with room for no more than an apple cart, and selling apples was "a business he did not want to go into." Even the highly condensed extracts of the improvement hearings published in the newspapers reveal the bitterness this caused.[46]

These conditions translated the site assembly problem into a host of political as well as economic barriers to improvement. They encouraged abutters to insist on lease and property damages based on the most inflated property values they could possibly expect to get after reconstruction. They also drove abutters to participate actively in the decision making process, to pressure City Council members and the Street Commissioners directly to change or drop the plans.

Both activities were significant obstacles to the implementation of improvements. Threats of budget-busting damage suits were nearly as potent a weapon against street improvements now as they had been in the past, despite the 1868 betterment assessment law, because landowners had had great success in getting the assessments reduced in the courts, and the men planning the street changes knew it.[47] Political pressure was just as potent because City Council members and Street Commissioners, having lost their bid to take the burnt district by eminent domain, continued to adhere to their traditional from-the-bottom-up approach to decision making, basing their deliberations on input derived from public hearings and, of course, abutters' private dealings with Board and Council members. Many abutters were among Boston's most important business and community leaders. They frequently engaged former Governors, Mayors, and City Council members to plead their cases, which naturally enhanced their influence. The public apparently did not participate in the hearings. Indeed, according to some critics, the Street Commissioners intentionally cut the public out of many of their deliberations, heeding only the abutters' objections. All this put the planning process at the mercy of people with a vested interest in compromising and restricting the improvements.[48]

Significantly, most of the opponents of the burnt district street improvement plan did not want to defeat the whole improvement project. As the Street Commissioners pointed out in a report, "everyone was pleased at the idea of a good wide street." The problem was that "nearly all wanted to have the land taken from the opposite side."[49] Needless to say, the Board could not satisfy all the demands to take the land from the opposite side, any more than Chicago's Committee on Railroads could satisfy all the demands to keep the railroads out of people's neighborhoods and still create new rights of way. This generated monumental planning dilemmas which put officials under immense pressure to abandon their original improvement plans and goals.

Exacerbating these land-assembly–generated decision making problems were institutionally based decision making problems caused by a complex division of authority over the planning of the improvements. The state legislature had no role in this part of the improvement process, but three independently elected bodies of the city government did. They were the Board of Street Commissioners (created by the state in 1870), the Board of Aldermen, and the Common Council. The members of the Board of Street Commissioners held the powers formerly exercised by the Board of Aldermen to determine and implement street widenings and extensions. The members of the two houses of the City Council had to approve or veto all improvements costing more than $25,000, however, which meant that the Board of Aldermen and the Common Council still had to pass on almost all of the burnt district projects.[50] Thus the Street Commissioners not only had to work within the general budget set by the City Council but also had to coordinate their individual decisions with all the members of both the Board of Aldermen and the Common Council. The existence of a Joint Committee on Streets helped reduce the chance for serious conflict between them, but consensus sometimes could not be reached. On several occasions the two houses held their own hearings and debates on particular proposals and shaped policies quite independently of the Street Commissioners.[51]

Like the pressures from property holders threatened by proposed improvements, these institutional problems bore heavily on the deliberations of the Street Commissioners. One result was a considerable delay in the commencement of the improvements, an irony in light of the fact that the need for haste had been given as a major justification for the adoption of the conservative plan. Hearings and Council debates on the burnt district street improvements dragged on into April, pushing the granting of building permits and the commencement of most store and warehouse reconstruction into the middle of the year.

A more serious consequence was the further compromising of the original goals of street reform. Because they were wedded to a from-the-bottom-up decision making process, it was impossible for the Street Commissioners to escape the cross-pressures generated by City Council members worrying about reelection and property holders attempting to get the improvements shifted to the "opposite side." As a result, they had to adjust their aims. As they indicated in a report, they had to pursue a "conservative course," trying to do what they could to improve the facilities for business and travel "with the least injury or inconvenience to the abutters possible."[52] They abandoned the dream of eighty- to one-hundred-foot thoroughfare widths in favor of much more modest widths, sanctioned uneven street widths, and did not touch many troublesome bottlenecks. By January they had retreated to such an extent that even the editors of the *Daily Advertiser*, who were among the most strident opponents of radical change, began to warn that they had gone too far. The editors declared that the many objections raised against the improvements had "blinded" officials to the advantages of broader streets and avenues. Thus, they warned, the desirable moderate plan seemed to be in danger of dying as had the aborted radical improvement plan.[53]

A few examples of the city's handling of individual widenings and extensions suffice to show these barriers to change in action (see Figure 7.5 and compare it with Figure 7.4). One is the extension of Chauncy Street from the South End three blocks into the burnt district to the corner of Milk and Devonshire Streets in front of the new Post Office. Proponents touted this plan as a way to relieve congestion on Washington and Devonshire Streets, while providing a remarkably straight and continuous avenue all the way from the Dorchester Highlands to the Charleston Street Bridge. The controversy it caused shows how the contention which accompanied almost every improvement distorted the planning process.

In a series of hearings, the plan stimulated an outpouring of objections and conflicting demands from property holders from all over the southwest corner of the burnt district. It naturally drew protests from owners of estates on Milk, Summer, and Franklin Streets, whose properties would be directly injured by the opening of the street. It also, however, drew vigorous objections from advocates of the nearby Hawley Street widening, who apparently believed that the Chauncy Street extension would make their properties less valuable by diverting business from their newly improved street to Chauncy. In addition, it attracted criticism from the proponents of the plans to widen nearby Otis and Arch Streets. They joined the other opponents in arguing that the Chauncy Street extension would be too expensive, suggesting that their Otis and Arch widening would be a cheap, adequate alternative. (In reply, the backers of the Chauncy improvement argued that the Otis and Arch Street plans were based on "false economies," as they opened up no new thoroughfare across the city.)[54]

The discord forced the Street Commissioners to seek a compromise improvement which would satisfy the demand for better transportation with a minimum of injury to competing remonstrants. They found one: the extension of Arch Street over Franklin through Morton Place to Milk Street. This was considerably more advantageous than the plan simply to widen Otis and Arch, which would have left the southwest corner of the street system basically as it had been before the fire. It fell far short of the Chauncy proposal, however, for it created a crooked street that went only two blocks and dead-ended at Milk Street and Summer Street at inconvenient distances from the nearest connections to the financial district and the South End. Thus it produced the same sort of sharp, traffic-jam–generating corners that had caused so many difficulties at the Federal, Congress, and Milk Street junction.[55]

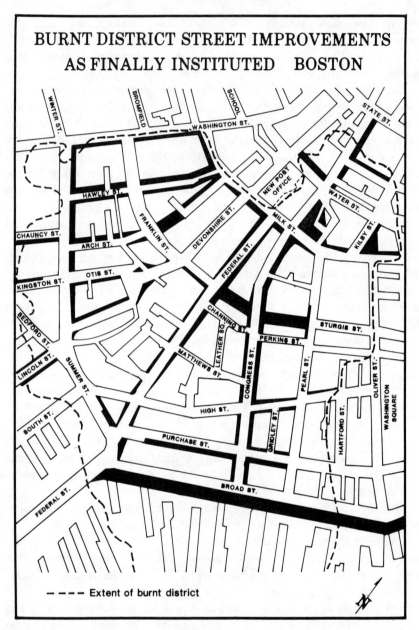

Figure 7.5.

As the handling of the plan to merge Federal and Congress Streets shows, this halfway measure was representative of the sort of compromises the Commissioners made all over the burnt district. The Federal Street improvement was a two-part change. It called for widening Federal along all of its length inside the burnt district and then merging it with Congress Street at Milk Street. The widening was meant to improve traffic flow. The joining of the two streets was meant to improve the movement of traffic between State Street and the South End by eliminating the difficult dead-end turn onto and off Milk Street. Since Federal Street was one of the few streets to run all the way to Dorchester, the merger would also open up a direct and efficient route from the financial district to that suburb.[56]

The problem was that the merger required that all the land at the head of Federal between Federal and Congress Streets be taken by the city. This would drastically reduce the depth of the estates lying near Milk Street, which included some of the most valuable land in the city, completely eating up some lots situated at the site of the proposed junction. This made property owners in the area furious, and they responded by threatening to sue the city for huge damages.

The Street Commissioners responded to this abutter opposition by debating the pros and cons of the improvement for nearly four months. Then they caved in to the opposition and drew up a compromise. The new plan involved taking the land for the widening from the other side of the street entirely. The compromise was that the Commissioners agreed to increase the widening by ten feet. After some debate, the City Council approved this proposal.[57]

As a group of protesters made clear, the compromise amounted to a complete surrender to the powerful opponents of the original plan. All the land for the improvement, including the extra ten feet, was to be taken from other property holders. The opponents of the merger were spared any sacrifice at all. Worse, the new plan did not eliminate the dead-end turn onto Milk Street, which, as noted earlier, was the cause of some of the most troublesome traffic problems in the city.[58]

The City Council played a passive role in the abandonment of the Federal and Congress merger, simply approving a decision by the Board of Street Commissioners which undermined the goals of the burnt district improvement project. The Council could play a more dynamic role in the planning process, however, for with its veto power it could kill orders already passed by the Commissioners. The Washington Street improvement fell victim to this problem.

Washington Street was one of the most important thoroughfares in the city. It ran from the North End through the financial district all the way into Dorchester. One of the oldest streets in the city, it was extremely narrow, especially within the business district. Because of the high buildings that lined it, the *Boston Globe* called it "a crooked narrow gorge." It was so cramped that truckers making deliveries brought traffic on the street to a complete halt. This had posed so severe a problem for travelers and truckers moving across the district that the city had had to pass a five-minute time limit on delivery stops. Many people had habitually found it necessary to go far out of their way to avoid the street and its congestion.[59] As a result, the widening of the street was generally agreed to be a desirable goal. The City Surveyor's November 12 map proposed widening the entire section lying inside the burnt district, the expectation being that more widenings would follow later.

The Street Commissioners and the City Council quickly approved a plan to widen the blocks between Summer and Milk Streets.[60] The controversy arose over the proposal to widen the small section between Summer and Central Court, which also fell within the burnt district. The Street Commissioners finally approved this plan in mid-March. The Board of Aldermen, however, proceeded to kill it, hypocritically arguing that the $29,400 improvement would cripple the city treasury.[61]

These problems testify to the important role that site assembly, consensus building, and institutional barriers to change played in the process of infrastructural improvement in Boston after the great fire. There was more behind the conflict and compromise that plagued the improvement process than these supply-side frictions, however. In addition, there were powerful, albeit comparatively subtle, demand-side frictions, demand frictions that went beyond the constraint of abutter influence to the problem of public apathy. Once the City Council voted to accept the City Surveyor's November 12 street redevelopment plan, most people naturally turned their attention back to their own affairs and, apparently assuming that everything was set, lost interest in the street issue. The difficulty was that their failure to continue pressing for the improvements gave abutters free sailing in their fight to force officials to compromise or drop the plans.

This public demand problem was quite different from the frictions just described. Postmaster Burt's extraordinary and ultimately successful effort to save the plan to widen Water Street documents the way that it influenced the course of street improvement. Like the plan to merge Federal and Congress Streets, the plan to widen Water Street to sixty feet was a part of the Postmaster's scheme to make the Post Office the hub of a unified and efficient central business district traffic network. It was also a linchpin of Burt's master plan to extend Beacon Street across the Boston Common and connect it with Water Street to create Boston's first major cross-town thoroughfare. Like his other plans, it initially enjoyed almost universal support. Like the others, however, it subsequently generated enormous opposition from abutters. It caused so much opposition, in fact, that the members of the Joint Committee on Streets were forced to take a unanimous stand against it, while the Street Commissioners were compelled to reject it formally twice.

Here again the abutters were among the most politically and economically powerful men in Boston. In this case, they included the trustees of the John Simmons estate and Charles G. Greene and his partners, the owners of the *Boston Post*.

The *Post*'s owners and the Simmons trustees took the lead in the fight to stop the widening. Both groups were driven to do battle against it by excruciating site assembly problems. The taking of the land threatened both properties with mutilation. It promised to leave the Simmons lot a peculiar dumbbell-shaped piece of land that would be only fifteen feet wide in the middle and hence an unsuitable building site.[62] The effect on the Greene property would be even worse. The *Post* building had been only slightly damaged by the great fire; so, of course, Greene and his partners were still using it to produce their paper. This meant that the widening not only threatened to so reduce the size of their lot as to make the paper's return to Water Street impossible but, worse, promised to do what the catastrophic fire itself had failed to do, namely, force Greene to relocate the paper completely, find and outfit a new building, and absorb all the expenses and inconveniences that such a move would inevitably entail.[63] Significantly, the Simmons trustees had not tried to stop other street widenings that had cut into their land but not damaged it so severely. This dramatizes the way that truly drastic property losses could cause abutters to view improvements as life-or-death matters, compelling them to try to stop them.[64]

Like so many other opponents of the Burt improvements, both Greene and the Simmons trustees had a great deal of power at their disposal. They had considerable economic leverage over the Street Commissioners, because they threatened to sue the city for at least $800,000 if the improvement passed, a huge sum that naturally struck terror in the hearts of the protectors of the city treasury. They also had substantial political clout to use against the widening. One of the Simmons trustees, Edward A. White, was in an unusually good position to influence the decision makers privately, because he was a former Alderman who had served on the Board of Aldermen's Committee on Streets. He not only had special access to his former colleagues but also had practice in stopping improvements, having successfully used his insider position to block improvement proposals that had seriously threatened Simmons property in the past.[65]

Greene and his partners, meanwhile, had the power of the *Boston Post* at their disposal. Ironically, they had originally wholeheartedly supported the Burt plan to widen Water Street. Indeed, the editors of the paper had gone so far as to declare that it "was universally admitted" that the fire had created an excellent opportunity for the city to widen all the streets around the Post Office to "certainly not less than sixty or eighty feet," and they had asserted that the Postmaster's plans "satisfy everybody." Only after the widening's impact on the *Post* building had become clear had they changed their tune. Then they filled the paper with vitriolic condemnations of the (as they said in one editorial) "impertinent," "presumptuous," "extravagant," and "preposterous" improvement. They also rallied support from other city newspapers, which obligingly published heated denunciations of the plan. Together the papers put city officials under extreme public pressure to drop it.[66]

Given these political and economic pressures, it is not surprising that the Street Commissioners, several of whom apparently personally supported the widening of Water Street, once again backed off, rejecting the plan, and then, after it was revived, rejecting it again on the grounds that it was not worth the cost.[67]

What sets this project off from some of Burt's other improvement proposals is the fact that it nevertheless did not go down to complete defeat. Instead, Burt managed to overcome the abutters' opposition.

It is the way that he accomplished this feat which illuminates the demand articulation aspect of the barriers to change. The Postmaster realized that one of the biggest problems he faced was the difficulty of counteracting the abutters' passionate opposition to his proposals, given the Street Commissioners' penchant for basing their deliberations almost exclusively on input gathered from abutters through hearings and private dealings. Burt's solution was to work outside established municipal decision making processes and institutions, to go over the heads of both the abutters and the Street Commissioners, as it were, so as to create new demands for the improvements that were powerful enough to overwhelm the opposition.

What Burt did first was go to Washington, D.C., to get the U.S. Congress to give city officials an unprecedented economic incentive to adopt the plan. Specifically, he got Congress to pass a bill funding the repair and enlargement of the Boston Post Office which made that funding conditional on the widening of Water Street. In order to offset the defeat of the Federal and Congress street merger, he had Congress tie the funding to a novel requirement that the city also take the triangle of land between Congress, Pearl, and Bath Streets for the creation of a plaza (Post Office Square). Needless to say, both street improvements had to be made entirely at the city's own expense.[68]

Not surprisingly, this maneuver outraged the foes of the Water Street widening, all the more so because the federal government was going to have to fund the reconstruction and renovation of the building anyway. More than ever convinced that Burt was a "crank" who had "Post Office on the brain,"[69] they sent the Mayor on a trip to Washington to demand the removal of the bill's street improvement provisions.[70] Significantly, the stratagem nevertheless got Burt what he wanted. Because the city needed the federal funds to repair and enlarge the Post Office, Burt's ploy motivated the Street Commissioners to consider once again the Water Street proposal. It also finally motivated them to approve both the widening and the plan to create Post Office Square.

Next Burt tried a more ordinary, and considerably less successful, maneuver within the regular governmental decision making process to facilitate the passage of the improvement proposals through the City Council. He got the Street Commissioners to break with custom and send their order for the improvements to the City Council without the usual itemized estimate of the expense. Although the conflict between the city's and the abutters' valuations of the land was, of course, well known, the Commissioners merely provided a low, rounded-off, aggregate $400,000 estimate of the cost, a sum that was based on the city's old assessments and no more than half of what the property holders were demanding. Burt's supporters justified this move on the grounds that a detailed estimation would give the abutters "an advantage in going before a jury and quoting the committee as to what the land was worth." They argued that because of their action, "interested parties might talk about millions of dollars," but the courts would never take their claims seriously, knowing that the total cost should amount to no more than $400,000.

Unfortunately for Burt, the members of the Common Council were not impressed. On March 20 they became the first house in the City Council to debate and vote on the proposal. Disgruntled by the Street Commissioners' failure to follow the usual practice of itemizing the expense, they voted to table the order until the Commissioners gave them a detailed estimate.[71]

Aware that it was going to be extremely difficult to get the Water Street and Post Office Square projects through the budget-conscious City Council once the full price was given, Burt cast about for another way to put outside pressure on the decision makers. This time he attempted to create popular pressure for the improvements that would overwhelm the abutters' powers. Aware that the ordinary people of the city generally passively deferred to their elected officials on such matters unless they were riled up, he moved to rewaken their interest in the street improvement problem. Cleverly, he also moved to stir up their hostility to the individual abutters fighting to block the improvement plans.

What he did was send a long, passionate open letter to the City Council in which he revived memories of the scandals that had accompanied past attempts to widen the terribly congested streets around the Post Office. He pointed out that Edward A. White, the Simmons trustee who was helping lead the fight against the Water Street widening, had, as an Alderman and member of the Committee on Streets, pulled strings to get the Post Office located across the street from the Simmons Devonshire and Water Street estates in the first place. The city had accepted the site on the condition that the part of Devonshire across from the Post Office be widened. As the land for the Post Office was being cleared, however, the Simmons trustees had begun the construction of the "Rialto" building, one of the largest and most ornate structures in Boston at the time, without setting the building back and providing for the widening as promised. While the land was vacant, Burt reminded his readers, he had beseeched the city to step in and make the improvement. White, however, had blocked the proposal in the Committee on Streets and so had left the Post Office with a "carriage way of less than twenty feet" between it and the Rialto, a passageway "almost impassable for public travel." In 1871 the Simmons trustees had begun an extension on the Rialto. And, Burt reminded his readers, again he had appealed for the widening of Devonshire Street. But again White had stopped him. Now, because that part of Devonshire was outside the burnt district, it seemed unlikely that any widening would ever be done, except in the unlikely event, as Burt put it, that the city bought the lot behind the Simmons estate and moved the Rialto back.[72]

Playing upon popular feeling against big business, Burt then launched into an attack on greedy capitalists who aggrandized their interest at the expense of the public good. "The Simmons estate sits on the new Post Office like a nightmare," Burt declared. "It is all around it and is as selfish and as inimical to the people's wants as mere property without personal ownership can be. Corporations, it is said, have no souls. What shall be said of trust estates?"[73]

Again he set out the arguments for the extension of the Post Office and the widening of the streets around it. He affirmed the need for a more capacious building, pointing out that the present one had less than one-quarter the space of Philadelphia's new Post Office and less than an eighth that of Chicago's. He noted that the federal government had originally intended to build a larger structure but had been stopped by the owners of the surrounding estates, and he commented on the tremendous increases in land values the Simmons and neighboring properties had enjoyed because of the Post Office. He discussed the safety and health benefits the creation of the square would offer the public. He also explained and justified his actions in Washington and reiterated his view that the widening of Water Street would greatly improve transportation in the city.[74]

Like his Washington, D.C., ploy, Burt's attempt to bring public pressure to bear on the decision making process was tremendously effective. City Council members and several papers gave his letter wide dissemination. Most important, however, it evidently struck a powerful chord in ordinary

people's minds, not only mobilizing public opinion in favor of the improvements but also turning it against the abutters. The papers that had been
supporting the *Post* in its opposition to the widenings suddenly stopped
publishing hostile editorials. Even the *Post* abruptly adopted a much more
moderate tone in its continuing opposition. The result was that the members
of the Board of Aldermen repeatedly referred to Burt's letter in their debates
over the improvement and then passed the order to widen Water Street and
take the triangle of land. As the editors of the *Globe* noted in an editorial
on Burt's victory, opinion had completely shifted since the Common Council
had tabled the order, and now "the general sentiment of our citizens is
strong and united in approbation of the plan."[75]

Had the letter truly changed the *public's* feelings on the issue? That is
hard to say. Clearly, however, it had changed the Aldermen's perception of
community demand.

Because the Common Council still had to vote, the Postmaster's fight to
save the widening of Water Street was not yet finished. Now, however, the
abutters were on the defensive. In a letter published in the *Post* and a
remonstrance presented to the Common Council, the Simmons trustees
attempted to defend themselves against the charge that they were capitalists
who had no souls. They reminded all who would listen that they held the
Water Street property in trust for the creation of a women's college (Simmons
College) "devoted for all time to aid thousands of Boston girls struggling to
gain an independent livelihood ... a purpose quite as important as showing
off an imaginary Post Office building." They also attacked the widening as
"an infringement of private rights," which would "destroy confidence in the
security of private property." At the same time, the owners of the *Post* again
protested against the hardships that they would have to bear if forced to
abandon the newspaper building, which "had been fitted and furnished with
specific reference to our business." Although more conciliatory in their tone
than in the past, they reiterated their intention to force the city to pay dearly
for the entire lot and building. As their desperation intensified, they and
their supporters circulated rumors that wily Congressman Benjamin Butler
and the infamous Cape Ann granite "ring" were behind Burt and the federal
law mandating the improvements, "pulling every wire."[76]

It was all to no avail, however. In the debates in the Common Council,
supporters of the improvements repeatedly referred to Burt's description of
the Devonshire Street widening fiasco and to his eloquent discussion of the
benefits that the improvements would bring. As he argued, so they argued
that the justification for the widening of Water Street and the creation of
Post Office Square boiled down to "a question of safety," to the need to
provide fresh air, light, and fire barriers to people working and shopping in
the central business district, as well as the public need to cut past selfish

private interests and take advantage of the reconstruction process to redesign
the city's antiquated streets. This time the majority of the members of the
Common Council found the arguments convincing. They passed the order
thirty-one to twenty-five.[77]

Burt's successful and extraordinary manipulation of Congress and mobilization of public opinion to save these widenings from certain death throw
light on the inner complexities of the street improvement process. They
naturally draw attention to the importance of the site assembly problem as
a barrier to change. By their extraordinary success, however, Burt's actions
also illustrate the peculiarly evanescent nature of the community demands
that called forth environmental improvement. In so doing, they draw attention
back to the institutional and economic factors which normally gave abutters
extra power to thwart improvement plans, and they suggest that this was
what made site assembly such an important barrier to environmental redevelopment.

Commercial property owners who had much to lose from street improvement found it easy to take over the planning process for three reasons. First,
they were able to participate actively in the planning of improvement through
the government hearing process. Second, they often had the economic power
and the community position to make officials pay attention to them. Third,
they expended a great deal of energy trying to influence officials, because
they had something to lose. Their dominant position meant that in the
absence of a citizens' organization committed to lobbying for some version
of the "public" interest, there were not yet any institutionalized means, aside
from a usually divided press, for people to interject more generalized views
of the community interest into the planning process. As Burt's activities
show, this meant that the planning and implementation of controversial
public improvements often required the unlikely effort of some individual
who, like Burt, was both willing and in a position to resort to unusual political
machinations and grandstanding techniques outside regular governmental
channels to force decision makers' hands.

Burt's success parallels J. Y. Scammon's equally single-handed effort to
stop the establishment of a union depot on Chicago's lakefront. It also
parallels the Northsiders' extraordinary effort to block passage of the comprehensive fire ordinance in Chicago. Burt's and Scammon's actions were
mirror images of each other, since Scammon's goal was to block, not achieve,
environmental change. Together, however, all three struggles suggest additional subtleties of the environmental redevelopment problem. They show
that the domination of the decision making process by private interests
worked both ways, individuals and corporations with much to win, as well
as those with much to lose, fighting to define the public interest in their
own terms. As events in Chicago indicate, this conflict often reflected class

divisions or the split between residential and commercial land use. As the battles between abutters in Boston show, however, it also pitted rival commercial interests against each other. It was a political competition in which the most politically and economically powerful private interests typically got what they wanted, regardless of the costs to others and the community as a whole. It was also a cut-throat competition in which people who opposed the dominant interests were able to voice their demands effectively only by moving outside normal municipal decision making channels.

Unfortunately for Burt, even the Boston City Council's decision to widen Water Street and create Post Office Square did not end the opposition to his efforts to improve the Post Office and its environs. After the city took the land to make the street improvements, Thomas and Edward Wigglesworth, the Merchant's Insurance Company, and several other property owners managed to block the federal government's taking of the land for the expansion of the Post Office building, which was the project that had legally mandated the controversial street improvements in the first place. Like J. Y. Scammon, the property owners went to court, where they won a decision which forced the government to pay the full market value for the land as of October 1873. This was $50.50 per square foot, which was over seventy percent more than the city's assessed valuation and more than twice the sum authorized by Congress. Furious, the members of the U.S. House and Senate refused to appropriate the additional money needed to undertake the expansion of the building for over two years. Even after construction finally began, however, Burt's troubles were not over. In 1876 his opponents finally forced him to resign his Postmastership over charges (never proven) that he had taken kickbacks on the improvements.[78]

In comparison with these street improvement troubles, the regrading of burnt district streets was easy. City officials achieved their goal of raising the streets quickly, ameliorating the area's flooded-basement problem with little effort. Normally, of course, street-regrading projects injured abutters almost as badly as did street widenings, since they necessitated extensive structural renovation to adapt buildings to the new street levels. Now, however, property holders eagerly embraced the opportunity to regrade the street because the buildings had already been demolished. As a result, the Massachusetts legislature had no trouble passing a law which empowered the Board of Aldermen to establish a new grade in Boston of at least twelve feet above mean low water level. The Aldermen changed their minds several times on just how many feet to raise the grade, but they approved the improvement easily, without any heated debate.[79] If the problems the city had in achieving street widenings document the inverted pyramiding of political and economic barriers to change caused by the physical difficulty of redeveloping structures and infrastructures, the ease with which this grade change was accomplished illustrates the way the pyramid collapsed when its base in property holder opposition was suddenly removed.

Other public improvements

Renovations in the street system were not, of course, the only infrastructural improvements demanded in the initial aftermath of the great Boston fire. In addition, people called for the modernization of the water system and the establishment of more accessible fire houses. On the face of it, the terrible experience of the conflagration mandated the immediate implementation of both projects. Nevertheless, here, too, people found that the old barriers to infrastructural redevelopment were still blocking necessary change.

As in Chicago, the fire made the need for improvements in the water system especially obvious. As the Fire Department's Chief Engineer, Charles Damrell, told the committee that investigated the causes of the fire, antiquated pipes and hydrants had made it impossible for the firemen to stop the flames before the fire went completely out of control. "I think we could have held the fire on the corner of Devonshire and Summer Street," Damrell said, "if we had had a sufficient supply of water, but, just at the time we got the Boston and Charlestown departments massed, the water gave out and we could not hold it." He added, "It is terribly disheartening to a man when he gets into such a position to find that his water has gone." The investigating committee's report concluded that the water system was "without a doubt" one of the main causes of the conflagration.[80]

The problem was the age of the fire hydrants, water mains, and distribution pipes. They had been laid decades earlier, when the area was still residential. The equipment was so old-fashioned that there was only one water outlet per hydrant and extra couplings were required to attach the fire hose. This caused firemen serious delays in fighting large fires by forcing them to connect several different hoses to several different hydrants, a time-consuming process. The mains and distribution pipes were just as bad. Most of the mains were only six inches in diameter to begin with, most of the branch pipes only three or four inches or less. Worse, most were thickly encrusted with an inch or more of rust. Their narrowness prevented the system from providing the water pressure needed to fight fires above the second or third stories of tall buildings, notwithstanding the adequate pressures generated by the water works.[81]

Despite the severe fire hazard these conditions posed, the city had done even less to improve the distribution system than it had done to improve the district's streets. As in Chicago, the barrier to improvement had been a lack of effective demand for improvement. Here again ordinary citizens had had very little interest in the state of these underground infrastructures, since the system served regular commercial needs adequately. More important, here again the Fire Department, the natural advocate of redevelopment, had had no power to make its demands effective. The Fire Department itself had apparently failed to recognize the nature and severity of the water problem for several years. When it had finally begun to press for new mains and hydrants, the city officials with the authority to make the changes had refused to heed its calls.

Beginning in the mid-1860s, Damrell had repeatedly demanded the provision of bigger mains and distribution pipes. He had called for the establishment of more hydrants and the introduction of modern Lowry hydrants that afforded multiple hose connections. He had also pressed for the establishment of an auxiliary saltwater supply for fire fighting purposes. He had expressed these demands in his annual reports, as well as in private dealings with officials. In 1869, in an attempt to make the need for the improvements clear to the officials, he had even depicted the crisis in the southern section of the burnt district pictorially with a map which showed the lack of hydrants and the meager dimension of the pipes in the Franklin and Devonshire Street area.[82]

Damrell's efforts had been to no avail, however, for the Cochituate Water Board, the agency which officially controlled the water supply, had refused to heed his demands. Instead, like the members of Chicago's Board of Public Works, its members had continued to concentrate on satisfying the more powerful demands for service extension created by the real estate developers and property owners building homes on the periphery of the city. In fact, apparently resenting Damrell's attempt to meddle in their affairs, the Board members had refused to have direct dealings with Damrell and the Fire Department at all. They had done nothing more in the central district than lay one new line of pipe and one new hydrant on Morton Place, and that they had offset by removing a hydrant on Hawley Street. Meanwhile, according to Damrell, they had wasted city money on such things as building a promenade around the suburban Chestnut Hill water reservoir, work that was not even necessary for service extension, frittering away funds that were desperately needed to prevent serious conflagrations in more developed areas.[83]

The members of the City Council had been slightly more receptive to Damrell's pleas, passing an order calling on the Water Board to construct the auxiliary saltwater system he wanted. Because the Board was an independent agency, however, even the Councilmen had not been able to compel the Board to make the improvement. To make matters worse, the Water Committee had completely failed to carry out its role as Council liaison between the Fire Department and the Water Board. Evidently the members of the Water Committee had not even brought the City Council's request for an auxiliary saltwater system to the Water Board's attention. According to one critical observer, the Committee had functioned altogether too much as a social club, its members forgetting their obligations to the Fire Department in the long and sumptuous dinners which frequently accompanied their meetings.[84]

Like the great Chicago fire, the great Boston fire stimulated a groundswell of criticism of the city's past failure to make improvements in the water system, as well as a burst of popular demands that the improvements finally be made. What sets the Boston experience off is that this time municipal authorities took action. Badly embarrassed by their own and the Water Board's negligence, the members of the City Council took matters into their own hands by appropriating $85,000 of city funds to force the Board to make the improvements. As a result the Board, equally embarrassed, finally began replacing the old six-inch mains and two- to four-inch rust-encrusted distribution pipes with new eight- and twelve-inch mains and new coal-tar–covered feeder pipes. It also began replacing antiquated hydrants with large new Lowry hydrants. By the spring of 1874 it had repiped almost every street in the burnt district and had replaced eighty-three of the old hydrants with one hundred thirteen Lowry hydrants, which it laid at distances never exceeding two hundred sixty feet.[85]

The fire also motivated the Cochituate Water Board to make improvements in the distribution system in the rest of Boston. After another bad fire destroyed nearly two acres close to the burnt district on May 30, the City Council requested additional improvements, and the Water Board approved a $380,000 program to lay new pipes and Lowry hydrants in the rest of the central city, South and East Boston, Roxbury, and Dorchester. This was only a little greater than half the more than $600,000 worth of improvements that Damrell had demanded the city undertake. The Water Board, however, called it a "very liberal" program. In any event, it was certainly indicative of a new attitude on the part of the Board toward the city's fire safety needs.[86]

The Water Board's remarkable turnaround demonstrates how a disastrous breakdown of an underground infrastructure could sometimes overcome traditional barriers to change by stimulating enough popular alarm to make municipal authorities take action. Significantly, however, the turnaround was not complete. The Board refused to undertake all the improvements Damrell requested. It continued to ignore the City Council's repeated demands that it consider constructing an independent saltwater system in the business district for fire fighting purposes. In 1871, as noted earlier, the City Council had ordered the Board to build such a system, but the Board had not taken action. Now it again refused to act, despite the fact that both the Common Council and the Board of Aldermen repeatedly ordered it to report on the matter and despite the fact that it apparently had investigated a similar system in Lockport, New York, that summer. It seems to have even refused to

comply with the City Council's demands that it deliver an official report on
the feasibility of such a system.[87]

These failures illuminate another underlying obstacle to change, a problem
that Bostonians shared with Chicagoans. The great fire caused enough of
a public outcry to force the Water Board to correct its most ruinous failures,
but it did not produce a shock sufficient to force the Board to adopt new
goals. Except in the immediate aftermath of the conflagration, the Board faced
the same kinds of demands it had always faced. On the one hand, as in
Chicago, most ordinary people were still unconcerned about the state of the
water distribution system for fighting fires, since the system was mostly
invisible to them and since fires were usually discrete, temporary events that
affected only a few individuals at a time. On the other hand, again as in
Chicago, most suburban property owners and real estate developers were
still insisting on the extension of water service into newly developing areas.
Unlike the Boston Fire Department, real estate developers and well-to-do
property owners still had great power to lobby and bring pressure and incentives to bear on the Water Board. As a result, they could easily overwhelm
the Board with their demands for service extension, drowning out the Fire
Department's relatively weak calls for service redevelopment. The Cochituate Water Board seems never to have reverted to its old practice of blatantly
ignoring the needs of fire fighting in the inner city. It quickly, however,
returned to its customary role as planner and constructor of huge water
works projects and facilitator of residential real estate development, which
was where the most powerful demand for its activities lay.

The effort to establish a new engine house in the burnt district also proved
to be a mixed success. Like the antiquated water mains and fire hydrants,
the lack of a local fire house was an old problem which resulted from trade-
offs made to satisfy the needs of people settling in the suburbs and other
areas outside the city center. What is interesting in this case is that the city
had not merely neglected to improve the existing inner city infrastructure
in favor of making extensions to the suburbs but had actually cannibalized
it to make extensions. The burnt district had once contained two fire engine
houses, legacies of the hand system of fighting fires. The City Council had
gradually dismantled these houses (and others in the business district) and
moved the equipment in them to the suburbs. The result was that by 1872,
the old central part of the city had only six steam engines to protect an
estimated $514,697,450 worth of property, while the recently annexed sub-
urb of Dorchester alone had six engines to protect only about $31,395,000
worth of property. The suburbs' territorial expansiveness at least partially
justified this reallocation of resources. Needless to say, however, it seriously
weakened the Fire Department's ability to fight fires in the business center,
the area of the city where the most serious fires usually took place. Unfor-

tunately, the Department had not been able to express its demands for more equipment in this district any more successfully than it had been able to express its demands for better water service.[88]

The great fire finally motivated the City Council to accede to Fire Chief Damrell's repeated demands to establish another fire house in the business center. Strange to say, however, it did not move the Council to construct the house inside the burnt district, despite the fact that in the aftermath of the fire the Common Council had passed an order for the construction of the house in the district on property the city already owned. Instead, the city built the new house on city land at Washington Square on nearby Fort Hill. The Fort Hill site was not especially accessible to the southern side of the burnt district, which was where the great fire had started. It was not, however, a bad compromise location, since it provided increased protection for parts of the North End.[89] Interestingly, the city would not construct a new fire house in the burnt district until well into the twentieth century. The Boston Chamber of Commerce would note this failure with some alarm in 1922, the great fire's fiftieth anniversary.[90]

Making buildings better

Besides inspiring these attempts at infrastructural redevelopment, the great Boston fire stimulated public officials and private property owners to initiate efforts to improve the quality of the buildings in the burnt district. Like the Chicago fire, it led to improvement in two ways. It caused a burst of interest among officials and businessmen in tightening construction standards to prevent future conflagrations. It also gave property owners the opportunity to reconstruct their properties on a larger, more modern, and more remunerative scale.

The conflagration made the old buildings' lack of fire resistance obvious. Unlike the great Chicago fire, the Boston fire had not roared through blocks and blocks of wooden shanties. It had, however, consumed sixty-five acres of mostly substantial-looking stores and warehouses, many of which had literally exploded into flames. The investigating commissioners' report on the causes of the fire concluded that one of the "principal" causes of the conflagration had been the buildings' flammable construction, especially their "great height" and "exposure of timber to the flames at a height which could not be reached by water."[91] As the investigators discovered in the course of their inquiry, the structures had been so unsafe that British insurance underwriters (still reeling from the great Chicago fire) had that very autumn begun discussing the advisability of dropping their coverage of all of the buildings in Boston's central business district.[92]

The massiveness of the destruction produced an immediate consensus that the city should not permit property owners to re-create these terrible conditions. As in Chicago, city officials turned to the law as the only instrument at their disposal for controlling the reconstruction process. The problem was that Boston's building code was not a much better tool for preventing unsafe construction than Chicago's inadequate fire limits ordinance. The regulations went considerably farther than a simple ban on frame siding. They lacked many requirements that were generally acknowledged to be essential, however, including such basic precautions as prohibitions against wooden roofs, wooden cornices, and wooden sheds. Although providing for the appointment of a building inspector, the regulations also failed to provide any truly effective enforcement mechanism.[93]

City Council members quickly moved to remedy the code's deficiencies. As before, however, they found themselves entangled in the web of frictions that had plagued their past attempts to mandate positive environmental change. The main opponents of a stronger building code were the property owners and construction industry interests who did not want to pay the cost of meeting the new safety standards. The opponents had no need to resort to the drastic, semi-insurrectionary methods Chicago workers used to block passage of that city's comprehensive fire ordinance after the great Chicago fire. Instead, taking full advantage of their wealth, social standing, and close contacts with state and city leaders, they simply continued to employ their usual private pressure tactics.

The members of the City Council played directly into their hands, for the Councilmen similarly carried on in a business-as-usual manner, despite the urgency of their mandate to strengthen the code. First, rather than attempt to revise the building code independently of hostile property owners and the building lobby, they handed the responsibility of preparing the amendments back to the "experts," the members of the Committee on Buildings, who had been working on the regulations since the beginning. Apparently these men were genuinely interested in a broad reform of the building law. Most, however, were builders and other "practical men." As a result, as David Chamberlin, the Inspector of Buildings, observed in 1873, they were "not likely to approve any measure which would be onerous or impracticable."[94]

The Committee members were urged to prepare only a few amendments for the special session of the state legislature and leave the bulk of the amendments for consideration during the regular session in 1873. Because of past experience, however, they decided to draw up a single, full set of revisions to avoid the difficulty of having to push amendments through the legislature twice. Unfortunately, they moved so quickly that the architects of Boston had no time to study the changes in detail before the proposal was sent to the State House. As a result, Chamberlin noted, the bill "was much less stringent than might have been expected." In preparing it, the committee members had been "careful not to incorporate anything which they, as builders, could not stand by."[95]

Theoretically at least, the members of the City Council might have avoided this predicament. They could not avoid, however, another institutional factor that made them subservient to the opponents of a strict building law. This was the burden of a city charter which forced them to ask the Massachusetts legislature for authority to put the code into effect. This requirement necessitated a second, difficult round of consensus building, which put the code at the mercy of the combined forces of building interests from across the state. A "clamoring clique" of builders and lumbermen, the building lobby exerted a strong influence on the proceedings through the use of paid agents. The lobby not only succeeded in persuading the legislators to strike out such important provisions of the bill as requirements for brick-enclosed elevators and self-closing elevator hatches but also managed to confuse the inexpert legislators enough to weaken or muddle many of the requirements that were not eliminated.[96]

To make matters worse, legislators themselves initiated dangerous changes in the bill for irrelevant political reasons because of their ignorance of the technicalities of architecture. One of the most seriously flawed amendments was the substitution of iron plates for stone in the bond of the piers supporting the floors and basements in buildings. The technical problem was that mortar would not form a permanent bond with iron. In a fire the iron would expand and break the bond, causing the building to collapse. Even worse, the amendment required iron plates two and a half inches thick rather than thin sheets of metal. Besides adding to construction costs, this requirement exacerbated the problem of expansion. Nevertheless, the legislators approved the change, because, as Edward C. Cabot, President of the Society of Architects, pointed out, "someone on the committee in the Legislature studying the code thought the original clause would give a monopoly to the blue stone quarriers." In Cabot's opinion, the code was useless, even dangerous, because of such problems. Some of the requirements actually prevented architects and builders from trying to improve building safety.[97]

In short, the opponents of a strict building code managed to use all of their standard tactics to prevent the passage of a strong, new law. This was not the limit of their success, however, for after the legislature approved the amendments to the old code, they managed to weaken even these less than stringent new restrictions. Using the lobbying techniques that had served them so well in the past, they succeeded in getting the legislature to pass another set of amendments in May that removed some of the "onerous" restrictions that had not been eliminated earlier.[98]

This was only one dimension of the problem, however. Closely related to and reinforcing these political and institutional constraints were some equally serious and no less inescapable technological obstacles to making buildings safer. They were caused by builders' and architects' ignorance of the best ways to design fire-resistant buildings. Architects and engineers had already discovered some of the principles of fireproofing buildings by 1872, including the principle of cladding steel and iron structural members with terra cotta tiles, a technological advance that made possible the complete and safe elimination of wood from buildings. These principles were not, however, generally settled on and accepted by the leading architects and engineers of the day, let alone by ordinary architects and builders. Quite the contrary, these groups were still hotly debating the whole issue. Unfortunately, the great fire did not clear up their confusion. It prompted a burst of interest in the subject, but all that this interest produced was more disagreement about the relative merits and limitations of brick, wood, stone, marble, slate, tin, copper, and iron in building and roofing construction.[99]

This confusion weakened the new building code in several ways. First of all, as Boston's Inspector of Buildings pointed out, it prevented even the most well-intentioned architects and builders from preparing an effective building law. In the absence of any generally accepted standards, each builder followed his own peculiar method of construction, and as a result every proposed amendment provoked a wave of criticism and condemnation "simply because" it differed from various people's personal ideas of proper construction techniques. "A provision which one builder will condemn as severe and stringent," the Inspector observed, another builder "of equally good judgement and reputation" would approve as necessary and efficient. Most of the competing but apparently equally valid opinions could not be reconciled. This made at least some of the code's flaws unavoidable.[100]

To make matters worse, the ignorance and general confusion fostered public and official complacency about the weaknesses of the code. Lacking familiarity with the technicalities of architecture, businessmen, legislators, newspaper reporters, and insurance underwriters evidently simply assumed that the amendments would effectively prohibit unsafe building practices. They did not begin to take note of and criticize the code's weaknesses until a second disastrous conflagration destroyed two acres of slums and commercial structures on the edge of the burnt district on May 30, 1873, which was after the legislature had passed the second, debilitating set of amendments to the code. This fire finally caused a public outcry against the law. But by then the issue was already dead as a legislative matter. The members of the City Council and the Massachusetts legislature had gone on to other business, leaving the belated protests to fall uselessly on deaf ears.[101]

As in Chicago, an underlying problem here was the inelastic demand for unsafe structures in the central city. Unlike the impoverished North Siders of Chicago, a large proportion of the area's property owners probably could have afforded to construct more fire resistant structures. Because they had a captive market for good-looking stores and warehouses, however, regardless of the buildings' poor resistance to fire, they had no *need* to spend extra money to make the structures safer. Not only did marginal businesses have little choice but to take up quarters in these less than ideal buildings; but in addition, because of physical and practical ties to place, the exigencies of maintaining agglomeration economies, and the limited availability of commercial space in the central city, even successful businesses had little choice but to make do with the unsafe quarters property owners provided. As critics of the insurance industry often pointed out, the ready availability of insurance gave cost-cutting property owners freedom to build unsafely, for it provided a financial cushion that enabled them and their tenants to avoid paying the full cost of their parsimonious shortsightedness.[102]

In fairness to the code, it should be pointed out that the amendments passed in December 1872 and May 1873 went considerably beyond the original law in their regulatory scope. They were also much more sophisticated than Chicago's fire limits law. To be sure, they contained numerous technical loopholes and mistakes. They also failed to mandate important changes in building design and construction techniques. They did nothing, for example, to encourage the fireproofing of the steel and iron columns and facades that were increasingly coming into use. Nevertheless, the amendments did provide for such advances as thicker walls and party walls and more fully (if not yet thoroughly) fireproofed boiler rooms, heating pipes, elevators, and stairwells. They required the separation of floor timbers by brickwork and, most important, the elimination of all wooden roofs and exterior woodwork. And, they tightened up the enforcement process somewhat by providing for the imposition of fines on violators under certain circumstances. As a comparison of pre- and post-fire insurance maps indicates, some of these provisions, particularly the ban on wooden roofs and exterior work, had a powerful impact on the burnt district's rebuilt environment. Wooden sheds and back buildings and roofs completely disappeared from the area.[103]

The disappearance of wood from the facades and roofs of the business buildings that lined the burnt district's streets links this episode of reconstruction with the reconstruction of Chicago. The key point of comparison between the two rebuildings, however, is that reconstruction in Boston produced no expansion of brick and stone and iron-veneered commercial space comparable to the huge explosion of commercial space that took place in the business district of Chicago.[104]

As in Chicago, the fire's massive destruction created an opportunity for property owners to build more modern and spacious stores and warehouses in order to satisfy businesses' burgeoning need for a greater number of bigger and better facilities. Several factors limited the extent to which Boston's property owners could take advantage of this chance to enlarge the commercial space available in the burnt district, however. In fact, certain conditions actually served to reduce their ability to create new space.

One of the most obvious constraints was the lack of technology for constructing, on Boston's slender building lots, structures more than six or seven stories tall which would have sufficiently narrow bearing walls to permit the commercial use of the valuable ground floors. This put a cap on building heights at six or seven stories, the maximum height of the buildings in the burnt district prior to the fire.

This technological problem was barely relevant to reconstruction, though, for an even bigger constraint was the widespread idea that the heights of the buildings ought not to exceed the widths of the streets on which they fronted, so that fire fighters would be able to put out fires in their upper stories. The idea made sense. But because many streets were only forty to fifty feet wide, new buildings had fewer stories than were technically feasible. In fact, as of March 29, none of the buildings for which the city had granted building permits had more than five stories, and most had only four. Before the fire many had had five or six.[105]

Vertical expansion was not the only means by which property owners could have enlarged the commercial space available in the burnt district and the central business district as a whole. Another way would have been to expand horizontally by redeveloping adjacent residential or blighted commercial areas for new commercial use. This was the method by which property owners had so radically expanded Chicago's central business district after the great Chicago fire. In Boston, however, this possibility was limited by the spatial character of the fire itself, in a manner that illustrates the importance of neighborhood effects and the physical durability of structures as barriers to change.

Unlike the Chicago fire, the Boston fire did not obliterate large residential or blighted areas on the periphery of the central business district. Instead, it burned only to the edges of the business center and, of course, in some places not even as far as that. As a result there were no adjacent burnt-out slums into which business could easily expand. The fire destroyed a few blighted areas *inside* the business district, notably on Arch and Hawley Streets, which until then had been too narrow for first class commercial development, despite their desirable central locations. In these places the fire (and the resulting street widenings) did indeed result in important structural redevelopment, with respectable stores and warehouses replacing what the *Transcript* called "a motley collection of dismantled dwellings and sheds used for mechanical work, rarely relieved by a modern structure."[106]

Beyond this, however, the fire stimulated only a small amount of new peripheral commercial construction. The reason was that it had not destroyed the buildings and lively rental market that had been physically and economically discouraging property holders from engaging in commercial development outside the business district prior to the conflagration. Nor had it eliminated the neighborhood effects that had been psychologically and economically discouraging businesses from demanding space in these areas all along. A few of the businessmen squeezed out of the burnt district by structural and infrastructural redevelopment did manage to obtain permanent new quarters outside the district, in the process dislocating existing tenants and sometimes inspiring landlords to renovate the buildings to which they moved. The amount of redevelopment this entailed was extremely small, however, and it did not significantly expand the total amount of commercial space available in the central city.

Finally, the widening and extending of streets in the burnt district prevented property owners from expanding the supply of commercial space. More than that, the land taken for street improvements actually reduced the amount of space available for commercial development in downtown Boston. The city widened seventeen of the burnt district's streets. In order to assemble the site for this massive addition to its transportation infrastructure, the city naturally had to slice swaths of land from all the lots fronting on the widenings, depriving scores of property owners of long strips of frontage up to thirty or more feet deep. The city also extended four streets. To do this it had to perform even more radical surgery on landholding patterns, excising entire (or nearly entire) lots from private ownership. When multiplied by the number of stories the buildings on the land could have contained, these acquisitions reduced the amount of space available for use in stores, offices, and warehouses by hundreds of thousands of square feet.[107]

Within these vertical and horizontal space constraints, property holders managed to redevelop their properties in ways that served to benefit business, improving the quality if not the quantity of commercial space. Like property owners in Chicago's burnt-out central business district, many built more modern stores and warehouses with new conveniences and facilities. Some constructed buildings that were designed to meet the needs of a completely different kind of tenant. They replaced burnt-out stores and warehouses with bank or insurance offices, for example, thus facilitating land use succession. Some managed to construct larger individual buildings, replacing two or more small buildings with one large business block.[108]

These property owners also confronted serious barriers to change, however. As in Chicago, the task of constructing bigger and better buildings generally required that individual property owners either assemble several adjoining lots or obtain the cooperation of several adjacent property owners in joint construction efforts. As in Chicago, a good deal of this activity occurred. Here again, however, it illuminates the way that some fundamental barriers to change had been and were still holding structural improvement in check.

The great fire stimulated a measurable increase in land transfers in the burnt district, most of which were directly or indirectly related to land assembly. Figure 7.6 displays the pattern of land transfer on Pearl, Franklin, and Lindall Streets between 1850 and 1885. The three graphs provide representative examples of *bona fide* real estate sales in the north, west, and east sides of the burnt district, which were, respectively, the boot and shoe, drygoods, and mixed business sections of the area.[109]

The graphs show that land sales shot up sharply on all three streets during reconstruction (November 10, 1872, through December 31, 1873). They also show, however, that there were more sales on Pearl and Franklin Streets in the mid- and late-1850s than during reconstruction. These early peaks resulted from the transition from residential to commercial land use. The big jumps on Franklin during 1857 and 1858 were related to the widening and extension of Franklin and Devonshire Streets. These street improvements had created a number of small parcels which people proceeded to buy and sell, simultaneously making the area attractive to real estate developers seeking to purchase land for the construction of new warehouses and stores. The large number of sales on Pearl similarly resulted from sales related to commercial development, several of the deeds making mention of the dwellings on the lots being transferred. Complicated deals involving the division and rearrangement of several adjacent lots among the owners also partially account for the large number of sales on Pearl Street at this time. Hawes and Lindall Streets, on the other hand, had been commercially developed before 1850. This probably accounts for the lack of sales there during this period.

What emerges most clearly from the graphs is the basic torpor of the land market after the commercial transitions. With the exception of the year following the fire, only two sales occurred per year on average on Pearl, less than one per year on Franklin, and virtually none on Hawes and Lindall in the 1860s, 1870s, and 1880s. A detailed examination of the transactions that occurred during reconstruction suggests a great deal about the causes of this lack of activity, shedding light on the relationship between the inflexibility of the real estate market and structural redevelopment. It thereby draws attention to some of the deepest underpinnings of environmental inertia and change, particularly the monopoly power that individual property owners wielded vis-à-vis each other in the land assembly process.

The transactions on Pearl were the most numerous and so are the most revealing. Some of the first sales appear to have been direct responses to the fire and the destruction of structures. In the first transfer, which occurred in December, Caleb Stetson sold a small, sixty-five-square-foot section of his lot to his neighbor, Samuel Atherton. This was evidently a piece of land that Atherton had had his eye on for some time but that he had found infeasible to purchase until the fire destroyed the existing buildings.[110]

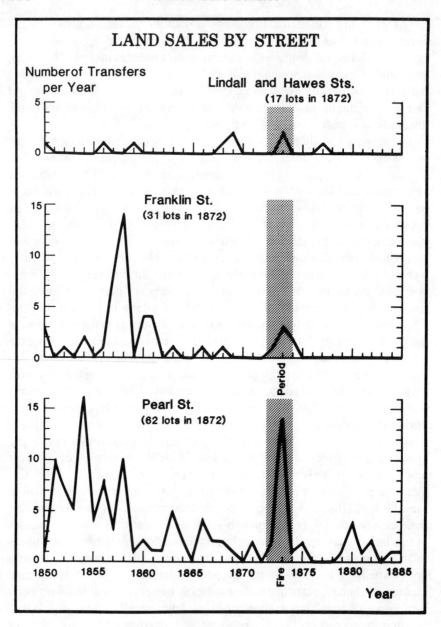

Figure 7.6.

Another sale which seems to be directly attributable to the fire's destruction took place in February when Mortimer C. Ferris sold his lot at the corner of High and Pearl Streets to Charles Dalton. The deed suggests that this was a fire sale. It states that Ferris was conveying "all that lot of land in Boston with the remains of the building thereon ... subject to the right of said McGregor [his neighbor] to occupy the brick and iron safes ... if and so far as such rights now lawfully exist, the safes themselves having been destroyed in the great fire." The words suggest the personal disaster the fire was for some landowners. Whether it was the loss of the safes that drove Ferris to make the sale is not clear. He owned other land and may have been selling the lot in order to finance the rebuilding of the other properties.[111]

The Ferris to Dalton sale is interesting not only because it illustrates the role the fire played as a force for change, but also because it suggests the incestuous nature of land transfer in the city. Dalton was related by marriage to James McGregor, the man who owned the adjacent lot and the joint interest in the burned safes. In 1877, McGregor died, and his wife and daughters, one of whom was Charles Dalton's wife, purchased his lot under the provisions of his will with the legacies he left them. Dalton was a trustee of the will. Thus, in purchasing the Ferris lot, Dalton was actually using his connection with McGregor to expand and consolidate his holdings in advance of the receipt of the McGregor property.[112]

Other transactions occurring in the aftermath of the fire underline the importance of the family basis of landownership in the business district. In May, for example, the heirs of Freeman Allen sold to Emma Casewell the 940 square feet of land remaining to them after the extension of Franklin Street consumed the other 5,442 square feet of their double lot running between Congress and Pearl. Emma (Fairbanks) Casewell was an heir of John Fairbanks. Another Fairbanks heir, Julien Fairbanks, owned the lot adjacent to the Allen estate. In order to consolidate her holdings, Casewell also purchased his property. She then entrusted the land to Juan C. DeMier, Jr.[113] Besides documenting the significance of family in land transfers, this transaction reveals the important role that street improvements played in loosening the land market. The property did not remain in the family long. In July 1875, DeMier resigned as trustee. Casewell then entrusted the land to Ellis C. Mott. He failed to pay off a mortgage, causing a mortgage foreclosure in September and the loss of that lot. It was sold to the mortgager, the Massachusetts Hospital Life Insurance Company, in 1877.[114]

The other intra-family sales that occurred in the aftermath of the fire were much more profitable. For example, in May, after the taking of land for the widening of Milk and Pearl Streets, the heirs of Abel and George A. Kendell sold their lot on upper Pearl for $23,375 to Cordelia Kendell, another Kendell heir. This seems to have been a *bona fide* sale and has been counted as such in the graph, even though it involved a price of only $8.90

per square foot. In August, Cordelia Kendell resold the lot to the Mutual Life Insurance Company of New York for $52,677, or $20 per square foot – a huge profit. She was benefiting from the expansion of the financial district. The Mutual Life Insurance Company was buying many properties at the head of Pearl Street because the street improvements near the Post Office had suddenly made upper Pearl accessible to the financial district. It is not clear if Cordelia Kendell was simply the lucky beneficiary of a fire sale and the Mutual Life Insurance Company's decision to move to upper Pearl, or if she was acting as the agent of the other heirs in preparation for the sale to the insurance company, or if she had inside information not available to the other heirs and was exploiting their ignorance for her own gain.[115]

Another profitable family-based series of transactions made possible by the fire was William Atherton's April purchase of what was left of Wales Tucker's lot after the extension of Franklin Street. William Atherton was the brother of Samuel Atherton, who in December had bought the small parcel from his neighbor, Caleb Stetson. Wales Tucker owned the lot adjacent to Samuel Atherton's lot on the side opposite from Stetson. In May, Samuel bought a one-half interest in the lot that William had just bought from Tucker for one-half William's purchase price. The brothers continued to hold the lot jointly until 1891. This was obviously a family arrangement. By making his brother a partner to mobilize family funds, Samuel Atherton managed to expand his holdings on Pearl, despite the fact that he was forced to sell for the widening of Pearl two hundred thirty-three square feet of his original lot and three hundred thirteen square feet of the new lot held jointly with his brother.[116]

Atherton's extension and consolidation of his property was an improvement made possible as much by the destruction of his neighbors' buildings and the taking of their land for street improvements as by his brother's help. Other transactions also demonstrate the way that the fire and the taking of land for street improvements facilitated land assembly. In December of 1873, for example, Mary F. and Louise Carney sold their neighbor Arthur A. Smith a small lot containing about eight hundred square feet at the corner of Pearl and Sturgis (Franklin) Streets. They had inherited the property in March 1872, and after the fire had had to turn over about twenty square feet to the city for the elimination of a jut during the improvement of the street. Their recent acquisition of the lot by inheritance, coupled with the destruction of the building on it and the loss of the small parcel, probably helped to make the land a likely candidate for sale. On the other hand, the sisters hardly unloaded it at a loss. They got $22.60 per square foot, more than any other landowners on Pearl received in such transactions on that street in the aftermath of the fire. This suggests that there may have been no customer at all for so small a lot until after the fire. Andrew Carney, the previous owner, was probably asking a very high price for the property, if he was quoting any price at all. Small as the lot was, it contained a building tenanted by three boot and shoe firms and one leather firm and was undoubtedly providing an excellent return. Furthermore, Smith, as the owner of the adjacent lot, was the only likely purchaser. He may not have wanted to add it to his own small lot earlier, since making advantageous use of it would have required a heavy expenditure, over and above the high purchase price, for the demolition of the existing structures on both lots and the construction of a large new building. The fire, however, made the sale feasible, the destruction of the buildings simultaneously making the land more attractive to Smith and less desirable to the Carney sisters, who had to rebuild. The high selling price indicates that Smith was, indeed, eager to buy.[117]

The purchase of the triangular lot at the southwest corner of Pearl and High by the adjacent landowner was similar. After the widening of High Street left this lot with only a little more than one thousand square feet of land, the owners, Jeffrey Richardson and Elisha N. Holbrook, sold out to their neighbor Jerome A. Bacon. Holbrook had inherited his interest in the property only a few months before the fire. Thus he may not have been as interested in maintaining the property as his recently deceased predecessor, Elisha E. Holbrook, probably would have been. It is likely, however, that he and Richardson sold the land primarily because they saw little profit and much expense in rebuilding on so small a lot and because Bacon saw great profit in taking advantage of the opportunity to build without demolition to expand his holdings. Like the Carney sisters, Richardson and Holbrook got a price that was high for their area of lower Pearl – $16.20 per square foot – which suggests that Bacon was eager to buy and that the owners were relatively reluctant to sell.[118]

Two other sales were the direct result of the expansion of the financial district, which was also a consequence of the great fire and the improvement of the streets, as will shortly be explained. In July, the Mutual Life Insurance Company of New York purchased two lots at the head of Pearl from the Abbott Lawrence estate of New York. Its intention was to complete the acquisition of the fairly large estate at the corner of Milk and Pearl that included the lot the company had purchased from Cordelia Kendell. The number of separate purchases the insurance firm had to make and the high price it had to pay in order to assemble this single, relatively large property reveal the problems involved in consolidating large lots in the context of a very fragmented system of landownership. The company paid about $17.50 per square foot to buy the Lawrence lots in July and $20 per square foot to purchase the Kendell property in August. This was a fifteen percent inflation in price in just one month. All of the other sales on Pearl averaged out at about $14.25 per square foot. Clearly Cordelia Kendell was making the most of her power as the owner of the only lot on Pearl adjacent to the Mutual Life Insurance Company's newly purchased properties.[119]

Only four of the Pearl Street sales were not obvious products of the fire or the street improvement process, and three of these may have been fire sales. The first was Isaiah D. Richards's sale of a lot to A. Burbank a month after the fire. This resulted in no consolidation of holdings, since Burbank owned no other property on Pearl Street. There was nothing in the deed to suggest that it was a fire sale, though it may have been, since it came so soon after the fire.[120]

The second and third sales involved Peter H. Brigham's splitting up of his two adjoining lots between High and Pearl Place in January. He sold one to his neighbor, Harvey D. Parker, and the other to J. F. Mills. Despite the division, this resulted in no increase in the fragmentation of landownership on the street, since Parker owned the adjoining lot and so doubled his holdings by the transaction. Mills owned no other land on Pearl; but he was, in general, expanding his holdings, having purchased two lots on Lindall Street the year before.[121]

These three sales may have been in the works before the fire, but they may also have been caused, or at least speeded up, by Richards's and Brigham's inability or unwillingness to finance the reconstruction of their estates. The splitting up of the Brigham lot demonstrates one of the problems of land consolidation: the high price of land. Together the lots would have cost Parker $60,000, more than he evidently felt he could afford.

The fourth sale not clearly attributable to the fire demonstrates the amorphous nature of many land transactions, which made the classification of transfers difficult. In 1873, the heirs of Charles Lane sold their several interests in a lot to Frederick D. Allen for $45,147, or $12.50 per square foot. This was a fairly typical price for their area. Only a year and a half later, however, in May 1873, the Lane heirs repurchased the lot for $50,000. Because of the appreciation in the price, this has been counted in the graph as a genuine sale, although it may simply have been some sort of straw sale stemming from a loan or other deal between the participants, possibly related to the financing of reconstruction. Whatever the case, it did not result in any permanent change in landholding patterns.[122]

The patterns of change observed on Pearl also existed on Lindall and Franklin Streets. No sales took place on Hawes. The two that occurred in this section of the burnt district were on the north side of Lindall, where land was taken for the widening of the street.[123] The fire provided the impetus for three of the four sales on Franklin Street, either directly or through the stimulus of street improvement.[124]

Taken together, these transactions reveal a number of things about the land market in the burnt district and, by implication, in business districts in general. First, they show the important role that the family played in land-ownership. Most of the land for sale was not really on the open market, but was being transferred among relatives, next-door neighbors, and relatives of next-door neighbors.

Second, the sales demonstrate the basic inertia of landholding patterns. Fifteen transactions on Pearl resulted in the entrance of only four new landowners who were unrelated to the other landowners, namely, Mills, Burbank, the Mutual Life Insurance Company of New York, and the questionable Frederick D. Allen. None of the sales on Hawes and Lindall or Franklin brought new owners permanently onto the streets. Furthermore, only twelve of the fifteen transactions on Pearl and three of the four on Franklin actually involved different lots. The others were repeat sales of lots that had already been transferred once. Similarly, with the exception of the Mutual Life Insurance Company's large-scale multiple purchases and the purchase of a large lot on Franklin by the Sears estate, all of the transfers involved only relatively small, single pieces of land, most of which were strips or triangles left over from street widenings.

Finally, and most important, the sales highlight the importance and the difficulty of land assembly activity in the area after commercialization. Together with the lack of sales in the 1860s, 1870s, and 1880s, they demonstrate that the land market was frozen by the monopoly power of property owners vis-à-vis outsiders and each other in the assembly process, while the burst of sales during reconstruction dramatizes the way the physical durability of structures reinforced the stasis of the bilateral monopoly confrontations between landowners under normal circumstances. The fire clearly prompted almost all of the twenty-one reconstruction sales. It did so either by damaging the owners' interests in the properties directly, through the destruction of buildings, or by damaging them indirectly, through the taking of land for street improvements. The ultimate result in all but four cases was land assembly. And except for the Mutual Life Insurance Company, the assemblers were all the owners of adjacent lots. In other words, entry into the real estate market in this area was so difficult and land assembly so important that owners of adjacent lots (and their relatives) were practically the only purchasers. They reaped the rewards both of their neighbors' sudden, disaster-caused willingness to sell and of their own monopoly power in the market as owners of the adjacent lots.

What is significant is that it was only through land assembly or through cooperative redevelopment that property owners were able to construct the large business blocks needed to meet individual business firms' increasing needs for larger stores and warehouses. Without architectural plans it is impossible to know how much this construction might have increased the amenities and quantity of space that new buildings offered their tenants. Certainly, however, the new arrangements would have eliminated the need for space-consuming party walls between buildings, the required thickness of which had been increased by the new building code. They would also have allowed for advantageous rearrangements of interior space, including the opening up of small rooms.

What must also be kept in mind, however, is that these transactions and agreements merely facilitated a reorganization of space. They did not enable property owners to create space. As a result, they made it possible for burnt district property holders to meet the changing needs of some individual firms. They did not, however, empower them to meet the growing needs of business as a whole.

Changes in business location patterns

The great Boston fire had an important impact on business location. As the maps in Figures 7.7 through 7.12 show, it not only burnt out and temporarily displaced hundreds of firms. It permanently changed their spatial organization. Six maps have been constructed. They show the locations of the companies in three of Boston's most important wholesale trades before and after the great fire. The three are the boot and shoe, the leather, and the drygoods wholesale trades. All three were almost entirely concentrated in the burnt district and together dominated it spatially as well as economically.[125]

As the maps indicate, Boston's commercial district was extremely crowded, even more crowded in some areas than the congested central business district of pre-fire Chicago. The number of firms in the three trades was growing, the total number of boot and shoe dealers jumping from four hundred nine to four hundred thirty between 1872 and 1875, the number of leather dealers growing from two hundred thirty-six to two hundred forty-six, that of dry-goods dealers, from one hundred twenty-one to one hundred thirty. This reflects the long-standing importance of the textile and boot and shoe industries in the New England economy and Boston's role as the premier regional marketplace for these commodities. Many businesses crowded into the same addresses, especially in the boot and shoe district.

In evaluating the fire's impact, it is important to keep in mind that unlike the great Chicago fire, the great Boston fire did not destroy the whole central business district. Quite the contrary, it spared most of the State Street financial district, as well as the wholesale produce and provisions areas in the North End and the railroad terminal facilities in the North and South Ends. It also spared the residential sections of the city. All the Boston fire did was devastate the most vital, valuable part of Boston's business center outside of the financial district. The area contained a large number of firms in retailing, light manufacturing, publishing, financial, and various professional lines of business, in addition to almost all of the city's boot and shoe, leather, drygoods, clothing, and textile wholesale activity.

The fire and reconstruction had two basic effects on the spatial distribution of firms in the boot and shoe, leather, and drygoods trades. One was a general southward migration of each trade. The other was an internal restructuring of the spatial layout of each trade.

The most conspicuous changes took place among drygoods and boot and shoe dealers. The drygoods wholesalers thinned out inside the burnt district along Franklin Street and upper Devonshire Street. They moved south onto Summer Street and beyond, many setting up shop on or near Chauncy Street, in the area where a few of their colleagues had clustered before the fire, others moving even more deeply into the South End. This brought about a southward displacement of the trade, as well as a general decentralization of it. The dealers spread out from a territory covering about one-quarter of a square mile of land and thirteen different streets into an area roughly one-half mile square that encompassed eighteen streets.

The change among burnt-out boot and shoe dealers was even more striking. The proportion of dealers with addresses in the west and northwest part of the burnt district plummeted from close to seventy percent of the trade to only thirty percent of the trade, as dozens of firms deserted the upper blocks of Pearl, Congress, Federal, and Devonshire Streets. This shift not only caused a southeastern movement of the trade, as dealers reconcentrated on lower Pearl and High and Summer Streets. It also caused a geographical decentralization of the trade. Unlike the drygoods dealers, however, the boot and shoe dealers decentralized not by dispersing over a larger area but by breaking up into three geographically isolated sub-centers. The proportion of firms on Pearl, the pre-fire center of the trade, dropped from sixty-five to thirty percent, the residual agglomeration there shrinking into the street's two middle blocks. At the same time, a new center of agglomeration emerged a quarter of a mile to the southeast near the junction of High and Summer Streets. The number of firms there doubled, the concentration of boot and shoe wholesalers in this area shooting up to thirty percent, equivalent to that on Pearl. Meanwhile, about three-quarters of a mile to the northwest of Pearl, the small node of concentration near the junction of Hanover and Elm Streets also grew. This was the location of the old Shoe and Leather Exchange, which had been a center of the trade in the 1840s and 1850s. It had contained only seventeen percent of the trade before the fire. Now it contained twenty-one percent and was one of three centers of agglomeration of roughly equal size and density.

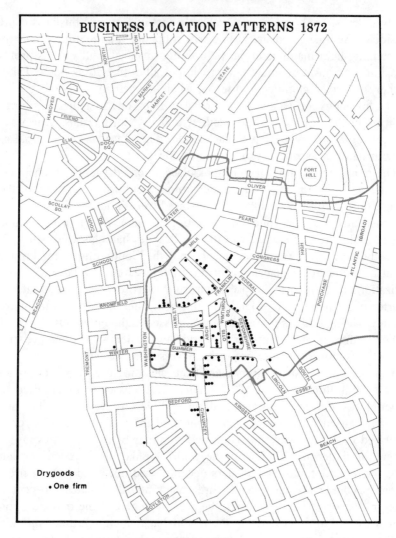

Figure 7.7.

Compared with this, the wholesale leather trade experienced little spatial reorganization. Most burnt-out leather dealers reagglomerated along the three blocks of High Street between Pearl and Federal Streets or in the immediately surrounding area, where they had been concentrated before the fire. There was some movement of the trade, however. The primary change was the disappearance of the High Street center's northeastern Pearl Street tail and the southerly stretching of the High Street center over Summer Street onto South Street. There was also a general eastward movement

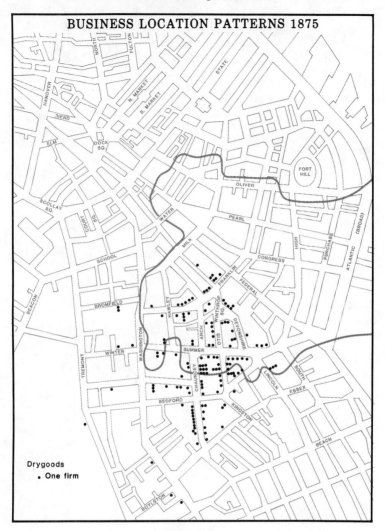

Figure 7.8.

toward the harbor, as leather dealers moved off streets in the upper sections of the burnt district onto High Street and Purchase Street. The scattering of dealers in the North End also increased slightly, from about six percent to ten percent of the trade.

In short, the location patterns of Boston's boot and shoe, leather, and drygoods trades changed in several significant ways. The shifts pall in comparison to the far more drastic shifts that took place in business location patterns in Chicago after the great Chicago fire, where the central business

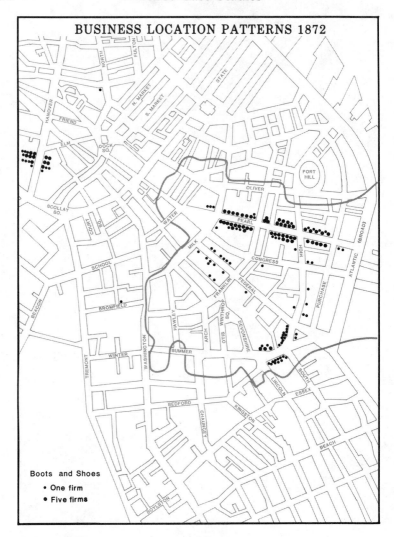

Figure 7.9.

district doubled in size. They were important developments in their own right, however. Until the fire, the drygoods trade had been concentrated around Franklin and Devonshire Streets for close to a decade. The boot and shoe dealers had been centered along Pearl for almost twenty years.[126]

Why did the fire lead to this particular pattern of spatial change? It is, of course, difficult to find materials which provide in-depth information about the location decisions of particular firms. As in Chicago, however, some newspapers and journals followed the experiences of the burnt-out wholesale

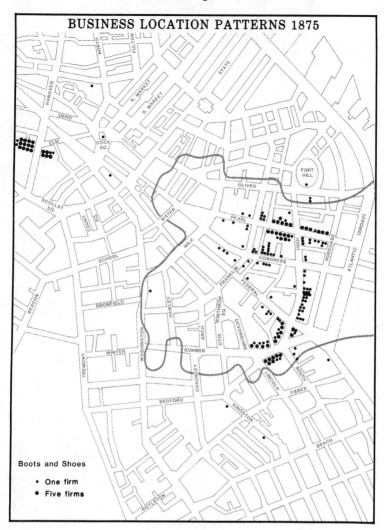

Figure 7.10.

merchants quite closely, providing many useful insights into the often conflicting dynamics of spatial change.

Like the great Chicago fire, the great Boston fire itself played only an indirect part in the establishment of the new spatial order. It suddenly uprooted hundreds of businesses from areas which had been home for them for years. Most firms, however, found temporary quarters difficult to obtain and, when finally secured, less than satisfactory. For example, many boot and shoe and leather dealers moved to corrugated iron shanties that they

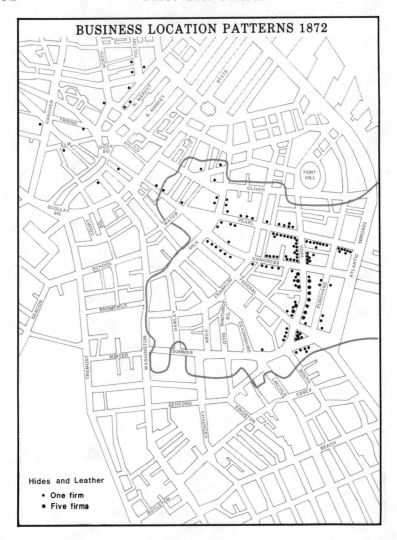

Figure 7.11.

hastily erected on Fort Hill lots set temporarily aside by the city for such use. Many others crowded in with the dealers on Hanover Street, subletting small rooms and desks at high rents in buildings like the old Shoe and Leather Exchange, which let in scores of tenants until it was completely filled.[127]

Inevitably some firms found themselves in areas that seemed to offer significant advantages over the quarters that they had had to flee. For example, two well-known drygoods firms, Sargent Brothers and Perry, Cook & Towers,

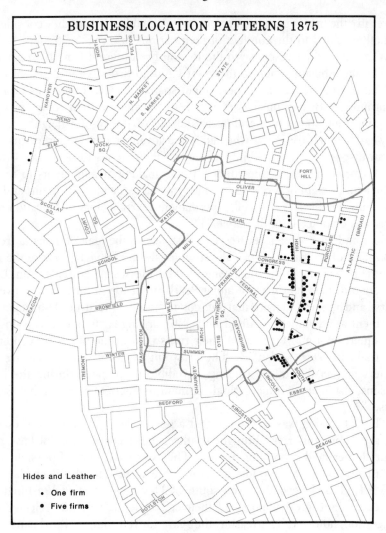

BUSINESS LOCATION PATTERNS 1875

Hides and Leather
- One firm
- Five firms

Figure 7.12.

settled in the North End on Canal and Friend Streets near Traverse Street, where they found, apparently to their amazement, a welcome combination of relatively low rents, extensive and conveniently located rail facilities, and spacious new brick and granite warehouses. Impressed by the advantages of the location, a writer in the *Daily Advertiser* declared that the firms' forced transfer had proved so fortunate "as to make it almost a matter of surprise that the desirability of the place had not been recognized before."[128] This was the exception, however. As in Chicago, most businessmen found themselves in "the most out of the way places imaginable," places they considered "wholly unfitted to the conduct of their various branches of trade."[129]

What made their response to the Boston fire different from the response of Chicago's businessmen to the great Chicago fire was the depth of their resistance to the idea of any permanent spatial change. There was no rush by prominent Boston businessmen to lead transfers of their trades by constructing new stores or warehouses outside of the ruined neighborhoods they had had to leave. A few who had found advantageous temporary quarters began discussing the possibility of moving their trades to new places. The vast majority, however, immediately began making arrangements to return to their old neighborhoods as soon as possible. For most of them, and for most outside observers as well, a permanent rearrangement of location patterns was completely unthinkable.

Boot and shoe dealers expressed resistance to the idea of a spatial reorganization of their trade especially strenuously and publicly, despite the fact that theirs was one of the most congested businesses in central Boston. Boot and shoe dealers had massed along Pearl Street for so long (nearly twenty years) and in such density that the congestion on the street had begun to put them at a competitive disadvantage by driving rents one to two dollars per square foot above the rents their rivals paid in the other big center of the trade in New York City. The crowding was not only squeezing the dealers financially but, by causing incredible traffic jams during the busy seasons, also making it increasingly difficult for them to carry on their business.[130]

The congestion was so intense that a few dealers who wished to escape the area's onerous rents brought up the subject of a change of base at a trade dinner held soon after the fire. They suggested several possible sites for a new center of the trade, including the North End, the Back Bay, the South End, and beyond, "even south of Dover and east of Washington" Streets.[131] The great majority of their colleagues vehemently rejected the suggestion, however. The reasons they gave for returning to Pearl constitute a summary of the sources of inertia in the location of the trade.

First and foremost, the foes of change pointed to the economic advantages the dealers derived from close association on Pearl Street. Fully cognizant of the benefits of what economists today call agglomeration economies, they declared that it was crucial "to individuals, to the trade, and to the city that the trade be concentrated near together." For them, proximity far outweighed the high cost of land on Pearl. Just as important, they doubted whether any other place could now be found in Boston which was "so centrally located, so near to depots and wharves and hotels," which would be large enough to accommodate the hundreds of firms that would want to cluster together in a new center.[132]

In addition, they argued against a move because the boot and shoe dealers had been concentrated on Pearl for so many years. Buyers had grown "used to" making their purchases and conducting their business in the first class warehouses and counting rooms that lined the street, they claimed. Their habit of doing business on the street had both provided the dealers with a secure market in a time of growing competition and given the street its reputation as the nation's most important and prestigious boot and shoe market. These benefits could not be easily transferred or quickly reestablished elsewhere and could not be sensibly abandoned.[133]

Finally, the advocates of a return to Pearl pointed out that there were institutional factors that bound a large number of firms to their old locations. Many dealers had long leases which they would have to break to move. Others owned the buildings they had occupied and were already busy making arrangements with their landlords for the immediate reconstruction of their stores. They had no desire to surrender their old stands, especially now that Pearl was going to be widened and so made even more attractive as a business street.[134]

The desire to return to the old spatial patterns as quickly as possible was not peculiar to boot and shoe traders. The leather dealers stayed as much as possible in their old center around High Street. Many drygoods traders returned to their old neighborhoods as well, notwithstanding the general reorganization of the drygoods district. Of twenty-one drygoods firms displaced onto Chauncy Street in the aftermath of the fire, for example, fifteen returned to the burnt district, even though Chauncy was already a relatively popular area for drygoods dealers and even though the total number of drygoods firms there would rise from sixteen before the fire to twenty-eight in 1875. Even the two drygoods firms that moved to the North End and claimed to be pleased with spacious new quarters on Canal and Friend Streets near the North End rail depots returned to their old haunt in the burnt district. In fact, one of the two, Sargents Brothers, returned to its original address.[135]

While Boston's burnt-out businessmen had many practical, economic reasons for wanting to return to their old locations, they also seem to have been driven back by a less rational inability to imagine *not* returning to the old patterns. Outside observers expressed an inability to imagine, much less welcome, any change – an attitude that reflected, and undoubtedly reinforced, the dealers' conservative desire to keep things the way they had been for their own sake. For example, the editors of the *Shoe and Leather Record* indicated in the first few months after the fire that they could not accept the idea of a transfer of the trade, because, at least in part, it did not seem natural or right. A move to the North End "may be an economic suggestion," they admitted in December, "but we are confident that it will not have much influence with the trade, who naturally, desire to see Pearl, High, and Congress Streets filled once more with magnificent warehouses especially adapted to their wants, and more beautiful as well as more enduring than those that have been destroyed." They were sure that the dealers would come together again "on their own ground." The editors of the *Daily Herald* expressed the same feeling after discussing the pros and cons of a move at some length in January. They flatly declared, "It is quite certain that the shoe and leather trade of Boston will not be changed much from its former position and five years hence the project for removal will be forgotten by everybody."[136]

Burnt-out wholesale dealers did not begin to consider seriously the possibility of permanently leaving their old neighborhoods until spring. They began to do so then, not because the economic and psychological advantages associated with agglomeration in the old locations had diminished with the passage of time but because they had no other choice.

What had changed? First of all, by spring there had been a significant decrease in the amount of space available for business use in the burnt district. As noted earlier, in the aftermath of the disaster, many property owners had a well-founded fear of constructing buildings that were taller than the width of the streets on which the buildings fronted. As a result, because the streets were so narrow, most of the new buildings consisted of only four stories, whereas before the fire many had had five or six.[137]

An even more important factor was that by spring many streets had been widened or extended. When the land taken for the streets was multiplied by the number of stories in the abutting buildings, it became apparent that the improvements had caused an additional loss of hundreds of thousands of square feet of space for use in stores and warehouses by business. This pushed many wholesale merchants out of their old locations. As the *Commercial Bulletin* put it, there was not enough space left in the burnt district for all the businesses to go back:

> But after all that can be done to economize space for commercial purposes, the hard fact must still remain that the business formerly accommodated in this burnt district can never be wholly put back here. ... after the contemplated street improvements shall have been carried out, it will be as physically impossible for them to get back bodily into their old quarters as it would be to crowd a bushel of corn into a peck measure.[138]

In addition to these physical pressures, the burnt-out wholesalers faced an economic squeeze generated by a threatened invasion of banks, brokers, and insurance companies. Boston's financial district was centered just beyond the edge of the burnt district on State Street near its junction with Congress Street. Financial concerns had clustered in this area for so long that they were now suffering, as were the boot and shoe dealers on Pearl Street, the ill-effects of serious overcrowding. As a result, the redevelopment of the streets and buildings in nearby sections of the burnt district inspired a burst of talk about the imminent, long-overdue expansion of the financial district into the area of the burnt district. As it happened no such mass migration took place. Only a few financial concerns moved in. Nevertheless, a few moves took place, and these, in combination with the talk of the impending expansion of the financial center, created a sense of change in several neighborhoods, an expectation of transition, which raised land values.[139]

As the mass migration of boot and shoe dealers off of upper Pearl Street shows, these physical and economic squeezes were powerful enough to compel the spatial reorganization of some parts of the burnt district. In the boot and shoe district, the partial widening of Pearl Street reduced the amount of available floor space by more than eighty thousand square feet.[140] Equally important, a speculative fever among landlords raised rents to such an extent that many firms could not afford to move back to the area.

The street improvements that created Post Office Square transformed Pearl Street into a major access route to the State Street financial center. This encouraged property owners to think that Pearl would soon become an extension of the financial district. In point of fact this did not happen. Pearl became home to only one major financial concern in the aftermath of the great fire, the Mutual Life Insurance Company of New York (although the firm's building actually fronted on nearby Milk Street at its intersection with Pearl). Nevertheless, the mere expectation that this transition was going to take place was enough to cause property owners to start jacking up rents. According to the *Shoe and Leather Record*, Pearl Street landlords became "dictatorial as regards the firms that had previously been located" there and began demanding "exorbitant" rents from tenants who had to negotiate new leases. In some cases, they refused to negotiate leases with the boot and shoe dealers. They preferred to delay reconstructing their estates in the hope of snaring new financial tenants whom they planned to attract by putting up office buildings instead of warehouses.[141]

Boot and shoe dealers had paid high rents to stay on Pearl Street before the fire, of course. Now, however, the "dictatorial" ambitions of the reconstructing property owners forced them to desert the street, despite their desire to remain there. The first major move took place in mid-April, when several of the biggest and most important Pearl Street firms arranged to move in tandem to the Webster Block, a large warehouse that a group of property owners were cooperatively constructing on Summer Street just beyond its intersection with High Street. The migrating firms included Clement, Coburn & Company, a concern that owned its own lot and building on lower Pearl. Evidently the firm shared the expectation of the other Pearl Street property owners that the street would soon be taken over by the financial district, and planned to build for this more lucrative use rather than construct more warehouses. In any case, the firms' collective decision to relocate to Summer Street "caused quite a sensation" among the other dealers, according to the *Shoe and Leather Record*. What it did was function as a catalyst to the other, more hesitant dealers, setting off a general migration to the Summer Street area by giving the other firms a lead to follow. It also gave notice to the press that an important spatial reorganization of the trade was finally beginning. Ironically, as soon as the firms' decision to move became known, the editors of the *Shoe and Leather Record* began to write of the shift off of Pearl as if it were a natural step in the evolution of the trade and a move that had been a "foregone conclusion several years ago." This abrupt about-face from their earlier contention that such a move would never happen is indicative of the speed with which attitudes toward leaving Pearl Street changed once a few leading firms made moving elsewhere respectable.[142]

The migration made the area around the junction of Summer, High, and Federal Streets a new center of the boot and shoe trade. Over one hundred companies moved there, while fourteen firms that had been burnt out of the neighborhood returned to their old addresses or moved into nearby buildings in the same area. Other firms mixed in with the leather dealers on High Street, while others left the burnt district entirely, primarily to establish permanent quarters on Hanover Street.

An abnormally high attrition rate has made it impossible to trace more than half of the burnt-out boot and shoe firms from the 1872 edition of the *Boston Directory* to the 1875 edition (even though the total number of boot and shoe firms jumped from four hundred nine to four hundred thirty). Of the nine traceable firms that moved from the burnt district to permanent quarters on Hanover Street, however, all but one had taken temporary quarters on the street in the aftermath of the great fire and had simply decided to stay there. The other firms that moved there were newly organized concerns. It is likely that some of these were reorganized Hanover Street firms which had absorbed some of the dealers who had taken temporary quarters in the area in the aftermath of the great fire, since the 1875 *Directory* listed forty-five new firms there, while the total number of firms in the area increased by only twenty. Whether new or old, most of these companies settled down in the old Shoe and Leather Exchange at 48 and 50 Hanover, a building whose owners were evidently more than happy to have and keep them. They had welcomed scores of displaced boot and shoe dealers after the fire, allowing them to crowd into the building until it was, according to the *Shoe and Leather Record*, "filled to overflowing."[143]

It is significant that the boot and shoe dealers responded to the changes on Pearl Street by breaking up into three geographically isolated sub-centers, rather than spilling over onto the streets adjacent to Pearl Street. The editors of the *Shoe and Leather Record* initially thought the dealers might be able to expand their territory of agglomeration by taking over adjacent streets in this way. They predicted that the boot and shoe wholesalers would "simultaneously extend their borders and *concentrate* their trade" (emphasis added) by moving out onto newly improved Milk, Water, and Franklin Streets in large numbers.[144] Needless to say, this kind of expansion would have been advantageous, since it would have enabled them to maintain the benefits of agglomerating in one area while reducing the problems of overcrowding. It was not within their power to displace the firms that already occupied these streets, however. Instead, the boot and shoe dealers were themselves the victims of displacement – displacement caused by the fire, by the city's improvement of the streets, and by the things that property owners were doing to raise rents and attract a higher class of tenants in the course of reconstructing their buildings. Ironically, the ambitious property owners on upper Pearl Street failed rather disastrously to achieve their aims. Because the expected expansion of the financial district into their neighborhoods did not take place and many boot and shoe dealers did not return, the street began to suffer a gradual decline.[145]

It is also significant that the boot and shoe dealers did not expand over the boundaries of the burnt district into the South End. This reflects these conservative dealers' unwillingness to settle down in unfamiliar areas. It also reflects the inflexibility of the building stock outside the burnt district, a condition discussed earlier. Just as most boot and shoe merchants were not interested in leaving their old neighborhoods, so most property holders outside the boundaries of the central business district were evidently not interested in redeveloping standing buildings to make them attractive permanent quarters for the trade. Actually, there was no reason for them to do so; after all, they already had tenants for the buildings.

Street improvements and the expansion of the financial district also helped cause the spatial reorganization of the drygoods trade. The city purchased more than twenty thousand square feet of land to widen Devonshire, Franklin, and Summer Streets, where sixty percent of the drygoods traders had had addresses before the fire. Multiplied by the number of floors in the buildings that would have been erected on the land, this represented a loss of more than a hundred thousand square feet of space that had been occupied by this and other trades before the fire. At the same time, financial concerns began moving to Devonshire and Winthrop Place. These changes put a squeeze on all of the firms in the area, not just drygoods dealers, pushing the wool trade from its concentration on Devonshire onto Franklin, for example, thus intensifying crowding and displacement.[146]

Like the boot and shoe firms, the drygoods traders departed from their old neighborhoods with trepidation. Afraid of becoming isolated from one another, they, too, contrived to move together, renting buildings in groups as much as possible, staying close to the old centers of concentration to the extent that this was feasible, and balking at striking out in new directions. For example, they refused to leapfrog into the North End, despite the discovery by Sargent Brothers and Perry, Cook & Towers of the cheap, conveniently located modern brick warehouses there.

The situation of the drygoods dealers differed from that of the boot and shoe traders in only one important respect. The drygoods dealers crossed the boundary of the burnt district into the South End in fairly large numbers, many clustering on Chauncy Street, a smaller number clustering on Kingston Street, and others moving even more deeply into the South End area. Wholesale drygoods merchants had begun to move to Chauncy Street before the fire. This presumably made it an attractive area for them to relocate to after the fire, in the same way that the pre-fire sprinkling of boot and shoe dealers at the corner of High and Summer Streets made that location an attractive place for boot and shoe merchants to cluster. Strangely, though, as noted earlier, most of the drygoods firms that moved to Chauncy in the immediate aftermath of the fire did so only on a temporary basis, ultimately moving back to the burnt district. But other drygoods firms replaced them, making Chauncy a permanent center for the trade.

Drygoods firms scattered onto Kingston, Essex, Washington, and two or three other streets instead of crowding together in just one place along Chauncy, perhaps because these businessmen had less need for the massive agglomeration economies that boot and shoe traders apparently required. On the other hand, it may well be that this pattern of land use is more indicative of property owners' attitudes toward renovating their existing buildings and making them available for drygoods firms than of the drygoods merchants' desire to agglomerate on Chauncy. It is likely that not all of this was actually up to the drygoods merchants – that instead, not all property owners on Chauncy and adjacent streets were willing to take them in, at least not at prices which they could afford.[147]

The remote location of the leather district accounts for its comparatively minor spatial change. Although street widening took a bite out of the space available for commercial use along High Street, the spine of the leather district, High was too far from State Street to be considered desirable for banks and other financial concerns. So only the relatively few leather dealers who had been located in the upper half of the burnt district experienced the economic dislocation that pushed so many boot and shoe dealers off Pearl Street and drygoods dealers off Devonshire and Franklin Streets. Boot and shoe firms competed with the leather dealers for space on High Street after the fire. Because they competed on roughly equal terms, however, they were not able to push the leather dealers off the street to any great extent.

Equally important, the fire's destruction of the buildings on Purchase
Street and the tip of South Street allowed the leather dealers to keep High
Street as a stable geographical center of their trade by giving them space to
spread out from High onto adjacent streets. Neither Purchase nor South
Streets presented the sort of ecological barrier to territorial expansion that
forced the boot and shoe dealers to leapfrog from Pearl Street to remote
neighborhoods after the great fire. Both Purchase and South had been lined
by lowly lodging houses and small factories and warehouses before the fire,
the inhabitants of which were in no position to keep relatively prosperous
leather dealers from bidding their locations away during reconstruction.[148]

All this movement had a neutral, even negative impact on the economic
welfare of Boston's boot and shoe, leather, and drygoods dealers. Many of
them no doubt benefited from the land assembly and cooperative construction which enabled property owners to construct buildings with larger rooms
and more conveniences. Because the great Boston fire did not clear out the
residential and slum districts adjacent to the city's business district as the
great Chicago fire had, however, the Boston fire did not produce the surplus
of commercial space that played such a crucial role in the spatial reorganization of Chicago's business. As a result, businessmen in Boston's central
business district did not enjoy the general reduction in rents that Chicago's
businessmen received. Nor were they able to expand their enterprises in the
way that businessmen in Chicago did. Quite the contrary, in the face of a
continuing increase in the total number of firms, the expansion of the financial district, and the loss of land to street improvements, they were in
the aggregate still being forced to make do with less and less total space in
the downtown area. As a consequence, many firms continued to eliminate
their inner city warehousing operations entirely. As they turned these functions over to the manufacturers in the countryside, Boston's wholesale district
became more and more a high-rent district of showrooms, more and more
a place where wholesalers specialized solely in marketing their goods.[149]

Nor did the Boston fire have the massive impact on residential land use
patterns that the great Chicago fire had had. Only the few people living in
the small number of lodging houses burnt on Purchase Street were dislocated
by the Boston fire. And because reconstruction resulted in no more than a
slight expansion of the commercial district, there was little additional displacement of non-commercial land users from the central city. The basic
spatial effect of the Boston fire was not the setting off of a chain reaction
of land use change in which commercial expansion caused peripheral movement and increased crowding of the residential population. Instead, the
outcome was the redistribution and increased crowding of wholesale and
financial activity largely within the existing confines of the business district.

Thus a combination of physical and economic forces caused a variety of changes in the spatial organization of the businesses affected by the Boston fire. Significantly, city officials and property owners played as important a role in determining the final pattern of land use in the burnt district as the businessmen themselves. Their interaction with the burnt-out businessmen brought this episode of reconstruction full circle, dramatizing once again the interconnectedness of structural, infrastructural, and spatial frictions in the process of environmental development.

Conclusion

It is not easy to compare the rebuilding of Boston with the rebuilding of Chicago, since the two events differed in so many important ways. As disastrous as it was, the Boston fire was much less catastrophic than the Chicago fire, demolishing but a part of Boston's central business district rather than almost four square miles of densely built up residential and industrial as well as commercial land. Moreover, because Boston's burnt district suffered from environmental problems that Chicago did not have, such as crooked and narrow streets, Bostonians had some improvement goals in which Chicagoans had little or no interest.

There are obvious similarities between the two rebuildings, of course. Not only did Bostonians and Chicagoans share some environmental problems and improvement goals, but in addition, people in both cities ran up against constraints that limited what they could do to solve their problems and achieve their goals. The importance of these constraints in the process of reconstruction in both places provides extensive supporting evidence for the conceptual framework outlined in Part I of this book. Clearly a host of frictions mediated in an extremely powerful and intimate way the stimulus-response relationship by which the people in these two cities obtained the environmental redevelopment required to satisfy the needs created by economic and population growth. The frictions both held back environmental improvement that might have prevented the great fires and distorted and deflected improvement undertaken during reconstruction.

The frictions did not affect reconstruction in the two cities in identical ways, however. For example, the primary impediments to the institution of an effective fire law in Chicago were the poverty and political power of the working class people who could not tolerate restrictions on their right to build houses of wood. In the face of working class protest and lack of debate about proper techniques for protecting the environment against fire, ignorance of the technology for building fireproof buildings, though widespread, was a relatively unimportant constraint on the improvement process. In Boston, however, such ignorance created a significant barrier to improvement, as did the political power wielded not by workers but by wealthy, well-connected central business district property owners and builders who opposed a strong law. Such discrepancies in the frictions constraining the improvement process were partly results of differences in the historical development of the building laws of the two cities and partly the consequence of the much larger scale of the Chicago fire. The Boston fire did not affect working class homeowners in Boston, nor did the proposed changes in the building law. So workers in Boston had no reason to participate in the conflicts over structural improvement as workers in Chicago did. Much more serious than the constraints caused by the opposition of Boston's business property owners and builders, the frictions caused by the power and poverty of Chicago's North Siders led to a far more sweeping weakening of controls on buildings in Chicago than in Boston.

A comparison of the two rebuildings repeatedly reveals such juxtaposition and intertwining of similarity and difference. This interpenetration of resemblance and divergence is evident at all levels of analysis, even the most microscopic, as the process of spatial change in the two cities shows. In both places the private and public developers of the land in question interacted with the users of the land to establish the new land use pattern. Although both landowners and land users played critical roles in the process of spatial change in both cities, however, the particular role each group played was different. Although businessmen in both cities had attachments to their old locations, Bostonians generally displayed a much deeper reluctance to leave their old neighborhoods than Chicagoans. This demand-side barrier to spatial change was largely overwhelmed by the behavior of property owners in Boston as in Chicago. In Boston, however, property owners did not stimulate the rearrangement of business location patterns by slashing rents and racing to build luxurious new buildings as property owners in Chicago did. Instead, they stimulated spatial change by raising rents and delaying reconstruction, pushing rather than pulling land users in new directions. In Boston, the lack of available open space on the periphery of the existing business district created a powerful supply-side friction, which severely restricted the ability of land users to respond to this stimulus by relocating to rationalize land use patterns. This friction simply did not exist in Chicago during reconstruction, the territorial extensiveness of the Chicago fire having given burnt-out businessmen a great deal of room in which they could spread out. Such differences help explain why the two fires had contrasting impacts on the spatial organization of business in the two cities.

Even where the frictions involved in the process of change were in a categorical sense the same, their precise manifestations and impacts on environmental redevelopment varied. In the two cities, similar mixtures of political demand articulation frictions and government decision making frictions impeded and complicated the improvement of water, street, and other infrastructures. But in Boston much more was done to improve street and water infrastructures than in Chicago, the frictions leading to compromise rather than complete inertia.

Such differences should not obscure the underlying importance of the frictions. Despite the differences, frictions were an intrinsic component of the process of environmental development and redevelopment in both cities. Nor do the differences decrease the heuristic usefulness of the concept of friction as a means of explaining the problems of growth in nineteenth century cities. Instead, they illustrate the analytic utility of the concept.

Perhaps the most significant testament to the importance of the frictions is the way the elimination of one, the physical durability of structures, provoked the chain reactions of land use change previously described. In Boston, as in Chicago, a measure of this domino effect was the large amount of money spent to redevelop the built environment. In less than two years, property owners spent an estimated $25 million to construct new buildings in Boston's burnt district, a sum that was more than a third higher than the estimated value of the buildings they were replacing.[150] The Cochituate Water Board spent $89,000 installing Lowry fire hydrants and new water mains and pipes in the burnt district and several hundred thousand more upgrading the water system in the rest of the city.[151] There is no saying how much the burnt-out businessmen spent to find, furnish, and move to their permanent new quarters, but in the aggregate it was probably in the hundreds of thousands of dollars. What is especially remarkable, though, is the huge sum the city spent to widen, straighten, and extend burnt district streets. In the forty-eight years between 1822 and 1870 the City Council had spent a little more than $8 million on all of the widenings and extensions it had made of all of the streets in the entire old part of the city. In 1872 and 1873, it spent more than $6 million on burnt district streets alone.[152]

As in Chicago, the city financed these massive expenditures entirely through regular credit channels. People and cities from across the nation sent Boston many thousands of dollars to provide help in the immediate aftermath of the fire. With great pride, as well as a certain amount of controversy, however, the City Council returned all of the money. To pay for the street improvements, it raised $5 million by taking out a twenty-year, five percent, £1 million loan through a company in London. It also raised the tax rate.[153]

As usual, landowners helped finance the street improvements by paying betterment assessments, still quite unwillingly it must be said. They had contributed $836,482.11 by this method as of 1880.[154]

Property owners also financed the reconstruction of their buildings in the usual way, through private mortgages. Despite the financial panic that began in the middle of 1873, they managed to raise enough private capital to rebuild almost all of the burnt district with ordinary mortgages, "without assistance from abroad and without apparent withdrawal of capital from active business," in a little over a year.[155] The City Council made an effort to aid property owners with municipally financed, low-interest mortgage loans. Strange to say, however, many landowners did not welcome the help. Some simply thought that the aid was unnecessary, while others considered it a threat to the capitalist system and a personal insult to their integrity as self-sufficient owners of property. A court injunction permanently halted the program before any money was actually loaned out. An attempt by the city to mitigate the cost of rebuilding by securing drawbacks on the cost of lumber from the federal government also failed.[156]

Did the massive expenditures help to rationalize land use in the burnt district? The conclusion must be mixed. Certainly the fire did not provoke the rationalization of commercial, industrial, and residential land use patterns that the great Chicago fire had. (Of course, that transformation had already taken place in Boston many decades before.) In Boston, burnt-out businessmen clung to their old neighborhoods as much as possible. What changes they made were not necessarily beneficial. The spatial reorganization of the burnt district did not bring about a general reduction in rents. Nor did it enable most firms to enlarge their enterprises or enjoy better agglomeration economies.

Moreover, the new buildings bore a marked resemblance to the buildings they replaced. Wooden exterior work disappeared, a significant improvement. But the new buildings still contained serious fire hazards, something the Fire Department would soon be complaining about again.[157]

Even the new street system showed an enduring resemblance to what had gone before, as did the traffic jams the system continued to suffer. The only completely new additions to the system were the creation of Post Office Square and the extensions of three other streets. Post Office Square was nothing but a small triangle of land, and of the three extensions, only one street, Franklin Street, was lengthened more than one block. Seventeen streets were widened; all but two, however, were widened to no more than forty, fifty, or sixty feet, at a time when in other cities, such as Chicago and Philadelphia, streets eighty and one hundred feet wide were already badly overcrowded. The most ambitious improvement, the widening of Broad Street to one hundred feet, was undertaken many blocks away from the most congested sections of the business center. This was indicative of the limits of the street improvement process in general. Because of the high cost of condemning valuable land and the intensity of opposition, the city had not been able to make the most ambitious improvements where they were most needed. With the exception of Congress Street, all of the widenings stopped at Milk Street, in one of the central business district's most jammed up areas. Even Congress Street narrowed just one block up from Milk at Water Street, in an area where four streets intersected.[158]

In short, there was enough inertia in the burnt district to make the re-development of the area seem more like a perpetuation of enduring patterns than a solution to enduring problems. What is significant, however, is that most Bostonians at the time thought that reconstruction had produced an improvement in the environment of the burnt district that was nothing less than spectacular. They heralded the first anniversary of the disaster with a public showing of flags, speeches, and a parade through the new streets to celebrate what they perceived to be an exceedingly beneficial environmental transformation. Several newspapers commemorated the anniversary with long feature articles that described the new buildings and the widened streets in glowing terms.[159] The *Evening Transcript* summed up the feeling that prevailed with these words:

> A year ago the man who had presumed to prophesy what are now accomplished facts ... hardly imagined it possible to change within twelve months such a mass of smoking, jagged, and unsightly ruins into fine and symmetrical structures.... The improved aspect of the entire district shows that occurrences calamitous in their first effects sometimes result in important material good. That great fire, forming so lurid a page in the history of Boston ... furnished the opportunity for rebuilding the metropolis at its very center of operation on a comprehensive scale.[160]

People were especially impressed by the architectural beauty of the new buildings. It was, they believed, "vastly superior to that of the old." They admired the "remarkable" variety of building styles and materials being used. "Not a street will show the uniformity of grey granite" which some had exhibited before the conflagration, the papers happily declared, praising build-ers' subtle juxtapositions of different shades of marble, granite, and sand-stone for "very rich and beautiful effect."[161] People also commented on the structural superiority of the new buildings. The *Advertiser* declared that they had "a beauty and an elegance combined with a thoroughness of construction which will substantiate Boston's claim of possessing the finest architecture of any American city." Even the Building Inspector said that the structures showed "great superiority, both as regards to strength and safety, to those which were destroyed by the fire," although he also pointed out that they were something less than satisfactorily fireproof.[162]

The street improvements also excited great admiration. The *Advertiser* pointed out to its readers that of the thirty-one streets, eight places, and one court in the burnt district, seventeen, or well over a third, had been widened, and four had been extended. Among the most prominent improvements, Hawley and Arch had been transformed from "mere alleyways" into "first class business streets." Other street widenings and extensions had opened up new cross-town thoroughfares that connected the South End to the financial district and the North End.[163]

Both the *Advertiser* and the *Transcript* found these and other changes so exciting that they devoted several pages to describing the improvements, street by individual street.[164] For the *Advertiser*, even the fact that the city had not been able to straighten the streets to any great extent was an accomplishment. The paper argued that the crooked course of the avenues made it possible for observers to see the beautiful new buildings to their "best advantage," and it applauded the city's success in keeping the district "free from the tedious and prosaic system of streets common to most cities." At "every corner, every turn, and every sweeping curve some new feature and architectural surprise unlike anything before will strike and gratify the eye." The *Transcript* went so far as to assert that the improvements in the streets and the buildings not only enhanced the city's "architectural display" but also made the streets more efficient transport routes, increasing "the convenience and facilities of extensive mercantile transactions." Thus the improvements were advances in economic as well as aesthetic terms.[165]

For many Bostonians, the combination of physical reconstruction and the spatial reorganization of business seemed a transformation of almost Rip Van Winkle proportions. Indeed, in a poem announcing his new address, a local insurance man made that very comparison in describing the change he had experienced. "Van Winkle slept for twenty years, / And twenty years he thought a day," he wrote.

> Suppose he'd looked the other way,
> And slept one year ago today,
> When fiery demon held full sway,
> And filled men's hearts with dire dismay.
>
> And saw those grand imposing fronts
> Which imposed upon insurance once,
> And saw those millions lost because
> Of disrespect to building laws.
>
> And now should he walk forth w'me,
> And through these self same streets should see
> How o'er all Enterprise has hovered,
> Until the district's 'most recovered;
>
> And warehouses far more secure
> And proper for me to insure,
> I think he'd say, " 'Tis passing strange
> That one short year could see such change."[166]

Although hindsight makes the conservative nature of these changes apparent, the excitement they provoked among people at the time emphasizes the extent to which the fire had indeed speeded up the environmental redevelopment process simply by temporarily eliminating the one barrier to redevelopment posed by the physical durability of structures. The first domino knocked down by the destruction of structures was the public's apathy toward change. As in Chicago, the other dominoes fell in a chain reaction of land use redevelopment that produced what was, to contemporary eyes, truly a major physical transformation of the environment.

As in Chicago, however, the fact remained that this environmental transformation had not been accompanied by a comparable reduction in environmental problems. Vulnerability to fire, crowding, high rents, and traffic snarls and collisions – all of these problems remained.

The celebratory self-congratulations of the first anniversary notwithstanding, even contemporary observers acknowledged and bemoaned this fact. After the second major fire occurred in May, for example, insurance underwriters, newspaper editors, and other people lamented the weaknesses of the building code and the edifices being constructed under it.[167] People also expressed disappointment in the street improvements. In July, for example, the editors of the *Advertiser* gave up on the possibility of transportation's ever being significantly improved through street widening: "Widening streets is an excellent protection from conflagration, but it is too costly and too partial to depend upon for curing our interrupted communications," they dolefully declared. They suggested that the city give up trying to change the pattern of the streets and instead attempt to reduce the area's traffic congestion by establishing one-way streets, prescribing certain routes for heavy teaming, and regulating the routes of streetcars.[168]

There was a good reason why reconstruction had not eliminated these and other problems. It was that a wide variety of physical, technological, economic, and political frictions had played important roles in obstructing the redevelopment process. As reconstruction in Baltimore after the great fire of 1904 would show, city dwellers would gradually find ways to circumvent some of the political and administrative problems that had hampered improvement in Boston and Chicago. At this point, though, there was little that anyone could do to avoid the full range of barriers to change that persistently limited people's ability to adapt their cities to their needs.

8

The rebuilding of Baltimore

The great fire of Baltimore began just before 10:45, Sunday morning, February 7, 1904, in the basement of a six-story brick building occupied by J. E. Hurst & Company, a wholesale drygoods firm. Fire engines immediately responded to an automatic, thermostatic alarm. Before they could be put into service against the flames, however, the building mysteriously exploded, and suddenly six adjacent buildings were also fiercely burning. Soon there were more explosions. These created a skyful of sparks and firebrands that set fire to still more buildings, sending the flames leaping from street to street.

Scarcely hindered by the more than twelve hundred firemen ultimately called in to fight it, the fire became a conflagration that roared for more than twenty-five hours, engulfing most of Baltimore's central business district. Like the great Boston fire, it never grew to more than a fraction of the size of the great Chicago fire. It still, however, consumed nearly one hundred and forty acres, more than twice the acreage of the Boston fire, in less than two-thirds of the time (see Figure 8.1). It gutted eighty-six city blocks containing 1,526 buildings, burning out more than 2,400 businesses, including twenty banks, eight large hotels, nine newspapers, dozens of large corporate offices, and hundreds of wholesale and retail grocery, produce, boot and shoe, clothing, and drygoods dealers. It barely touched the residential city. It decimated the major portion of downtown Baltimore that stretched from Liberty Street in the west to Jones Falls in the east and from Fayette Street in the north to the Inner Harbor in the south, however, turning this normally bustling section of the city's business center into a wasteland.[1]

Despite the extent of the destruction, Baltimoreans greeted the disaster with an intense determination to undertake a redevelopment of the burnt district that would make it better than before. In fact, like the victims of the Boston conflagration, they began discussing possible improvements almost before the flames were out. As in Boston, their first thought was for street widenings and extensions. Soon, however, the city's business and civic leaders were calling for a wide range of additional environmental changes, in-

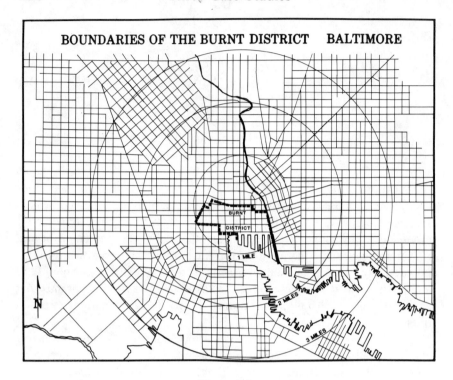

Figure 8.1.

cluding stricter building standards, the elimination of above-ground electric utility poles and wires, and the establishment of business district public parks. Within a few days they were also demanding extensive redevelopment of the dock and wharf facilities of the burnt-out Inner Harbor. On February 12, the Mayor responded by appointing a sixty-three-member Citizens' Emergency Committee to develop a comprehensive plan of environmental redevelopment. Within a week, the Committee had drawn up a program of improvements that included a dozen street widenings and extensions, several park proposals, a plan for a stricter building code, a far-reaching dock and wharf improvement project, and a sewerage improvement plan.[2]

As in Boston, many factors drove people to embrace ambitious redevelopment goals. One was undoubtedly a psychological need to make a benefit of the disaster. Another, however, was a deep-seated practical need to ameliorate environmental problems which had been threatening to choke Baltimore's central business district to death for years. Like Bostonians in 1872, Baltimoreans were suffering from the effects of narrow, poorly connected, traffic-jammed streets that had been creating safety hazards and travel inconveniences for decades. Needless to say, they were also suffering from the fire hazards caused by antiquated buildings, narrow water mains, and a paucity of fire hydrants, problems which had been plaguing them for decades. In addition, they were enduring environmental problems that Bostonians had hardly dreamed of back in 1872. Tens of thousands of easily broken overhead electric wires were adding to their fire problems, for example, while a multitude of utility poles were crowding them off their sidewalks. They were also suffering from the pollution and miasmatic smells emanating from the business district's poorly drained, unsewered streets and from the stagnant, sewage-filled waters of the nearby Jones Falls and Inner Harbor. Moreover, they were enduring the ill effects of an aging building stock that was increasingly incapable of adequately meeting business needs, as well as the undesirable consequences of an antiquated Inner Harbor that was completely incapable of accommodating the city's shipping trade. All were serious problems that the city had been unable to resolve despite decades of frustration and complaint. Like the Bostonians, Baltimoreans seized on the idea of redeveloping the burnt district in the hope of redressing these problems at last.

Finally, there was also in Baltimore a spirit of reform igniting the explosion of demand for change. Most of the people calling for the improvements were self-styled reformers. The great fire inspired them to try to rebuild better than before as a way of extending the progressive ideals of municipal efficiency and civic beauty to the city's physical environment.

Progressive reformers had taken control of Baltimore's city government in 1895, after almost twenty years of sustained crusading against the political machine that had ruled the city since 1871. They had consolidated their power in 1898 by instituting a new city charter which restructured the city administrative apparatus along progressive lines. Once in power they had repeatedly tried to do something about the city's mounting environmental problems. But because they were split by inter-party and intra-party rivalries and opposed at every turn by utility companies and the still-lively state Republican and Democratic political machines, they had never managed to complete a single plan.[3]

Now, however, the fire inspired them to renew their efforts, for it had finally given them a "golden opportunity" to bring their long-postponed plans to fruition, and they believed that they now had the political and administrative power to achieve these changes. Like Bostonians in the immediate aftermath of the Boston conflagration, many Baltimoreans were filled with the sense that the fire had cleared away many of the most important physical barriers to redevelopment and so had made it relatively easy for the city to widen streets, bury utility wires, acquire land for parks, lay sewers, and establish the legislative groundwork needed to ensure the construction of a modern, fire-resistant commercial building stock. Unlike Bostonians in 1872, they were quick to acknowledge the difficulties of obtaining voluntary cooperation from the individuals affected by improvements. Embued as they were with progressive reform zeal, however, they believed that the property holders, corporations, and other private interests which had traditionally blocked improvements might very well embrace the unique opportunity suddenly before them to make Baltimore a better city, despite the private costs. They believed that they might now, as the President of the Merchants and Manufacturers Association put it, with "pleasure ... set aside" their "personal interests where they conflict with the evident welfare of the whole community" and join in pursuing the improvement goals.[4]

Most important, the reformers believed that the city government would no longer permit private interests to stand in the way of public improvements. An editor of the *Baltimore Sun* wrote in regard to the need for underground electrical utility conduits, "The ground is cleared. There is no business in the area under consideration and even the interests that have hitherto resisted the burying of the wires may no longer protest. *But whether they do or not,* the city authorities should resolutely take advantage of the opportunity at hand and remove a capital nuisance and danger" (emphasis added).[5] Reformers had finally gained significant power in both political parties, as well as mastery of administrative machinery designed along progressive lines. This, in combination with the destruction of the built environment, promised to make it possible for government officials to make the long hoped for improvements, no matter what the opposition. This promise, in itself, inspired the chorus of demands for change.

It is this reform context that sets the reconstruction of Baltimore off from the reconstructions of Boston and Chicago. As in the other two cities, the traditional barriers to environmental redevelopment quickly made their presence felt. Unlike Bostonians and Chicagoans, however, Baltimoreans found ways to circumvent some of the barriers. As a result they went much farther toward achieving planned comprehensive redevelopment than did the residents of either of the other cities.

What is important is that they overcame barriers not only as Boston's Postmaster Burt had done, by working outside the city government, but also by working inside it to take advantage of the institutional reforms and philosophical principles of the urban progressive reform movement. Their achievements testify to the effectiveness with which municipal progressive reform alleviated certain of the traditional, political, economic, and institutional obstacles to environmental change. Paradoxically, however, their successes also testify to some of the weaknesses of the progressive solution to the problem of maladaptive urban growth.

The burnt district improvement plan

Baltimoreans embarked on a remarkably effective campaign to renovate and add on to nearly every infrastructure in Baltimore in the aftermath of the great fire, outside as well as inside the burnt district. In the burnt district, the improvements they took up first were street widenings and extensions, sewers and new parks, and new docks and piers for the wharves along the burnt out Inner Harbor.

A wide range of pressing business and community needs stimulated an outpouring of demand for change in these infrastructures. The streets in the burnt district were a source of particularly widespread complaint, since, like Boston's crooked and narrow thoroughfares, most had been laid down in the colonial period. The municipal government had done almost nothing to improve them since the Civil War, aside from paving and repaving them. As a result, most were fewer than fifty feet wide and encumbered with traffic-stopping dead ends and inconvenient jogs. Several had steep grades that made heavy hauling prohibitive. Some were crowded with multiple streetcar lines in addition to carriages, trucks, and other private traffic. To make things worse, the poor connections, steep grades, and narrow, often uneven widths together shunted most of the city's growing vehicular and streetcar cross-town traffic onto already heavily congested Baltimore and Pratt Streets, which were the only streets which offered comparatively straight and level passage through the area between the industrial and residential regions on the city's north, south, west, and east sides. This exacerbated the difficulties that shoppers, teamsters, and businessmen experienced as they tried to maneuver within the area, in addition to complicating travel for the people who merely wanted to cut across the district. The traffic jams in the area burdened the entire city.[6]

The wharf facilities in the Inner Harbor were in even worse condition. The Inner Harbor had last been extensively redeveloped in the 1820s, when the city had filled in the old waterfront in order to extend Pratt and Lombard Streets to Jones Falls. All the burnt-out piers and docks dated from that time. Having been intended for small sailing craft, they were much too narrow to provide properly for modern sailing ships, let alone accommodate the coastal and international steamship business. To complicate matters, the Inner Harbor was too shallow for most modern ships. Never more than twenty feet in depth originally, it was constantly silted up, as well as polluted, by sewage-laden run-off from Jones Falls, despite repeated dredging. Worse, most of the old docks were so narrow that the city's dredging machines could not enter to either clean or dredge them. The result was that they were, in the words of an editor at the *Sun*, "blind canals" that were "open foul smelling sewers," as well as archaic transport infrastructures. Conditions were so bad that they were undermining the economic vitality of the southern section of the business district itself. Most of the city's harbor-related businesses were simply deserting the area for the Middle and Outer Harbors, where they were developing modern wharf facilities. Thus they were abandoning the old piers and docks and associated warehouses to continued deterioration and spreading blight.[7]

The burnt district's sewerage system was just as primitive. Strictly speaking, Baltimore had no formal sewerage infrastructure at all, only a loose and in many places ancient network of storm drains which discharged storm runoff into Jones Falls and the Inner Harbor (which health officials called the Back Basin). People depended on a honeycomb of tens of thousands of cesspools, on the storm drains (which was illegal), and on street and sidewalk gutters to dispose of kitchen slops, bath water, and other human and industrial waste, even in the business center. Rain, gravity, and constant street cleaning saved the elevated sections of the city from the worst effects of this rudimentary way of handling sanitation. Because most of the waste poured down the long hill on which the city was built through storm and surface drains and underground streams into Jones Falls and the Back Basin, however, serious sanitation and drainage problems plagued the central business district and the other low-lying areas of the city. The pollution of Jones Falls and the Back Basin created a terrible stench that pervaded parts of the business center during the summer. It also contributed to major flooding problems, since silted-up Jones Falls often overflowed its banks. The overflows not only deluged adjacent areas with contaminated water, but also backed up the storm drains emptying into the lower falls, thereby causing flooding as far away as Calvert Street.[8]

To complicate matters, the burnt district suffered the negative effects of an extremely primitive storm drainage system. Private property holders had constructed most of the drains haphazardly when the area was first being built up. As a result, the drains were of all shapes and sizes. In fact, some were nothing more than old stream beds that property owners had long ago arched over with brick or stone. The drains generally followed extremely circuitous routes which ran primarily under private property. Many even ran directly under buildings. The city had repeatedly attempted to repair and replace sections of most of them. Because, however, there were so many miles of antiquated conduits in the central city as a whole, and because the drains were inaccessible and the grades of some streets too low to admit the construction of new drains of adequate dimensions, the work of cleaning, repairing, and replacing them had always been a Sisyphean task which had not served the burnt district well. The result was that at the time of the great fire most were filled with filth and garbage. Many of those with old wooden floors and walls were also physically rotted out, while many of those with old stone or brick arches were in danger of collapsing.

Needless to say, all these conditions exacerbated the district's flooding and summer stench problems. They also created dirt, dust, and ice, which indirectly increased the district's street congestion. As the Board of Health noted in a report, they forced the city to employ "brigades of scrapers, sweepers, and carts" to keep the streets from being buried in the filth, "to the great hindrance of general traffic, and the infinite annoyance and discomfort of all passersby."[9]

Finally, the burnt district (and the rest of the central business district) suffered from a lack of open space. People complained of an inability to escape the "miles of brick and mortar" which surrounded them, a suffocating sensation which street congestion and the area's pervasive dust and bad smells undoubtedly exacerbated. Many civic boosters also felt a need for more open space to show off the City Hall and the area's other public buildings.[10]

The movement to redress these environmental problems began on February 9 at a meeting in the home of reform-minded businessman William Keyser, during which a number of the city's leading "capitalists, financiers, and merchants" discussed the desirability of widening the burnt district's streets. The participants developed a street improvement plan, which they submitted to Mayor Robert L. McLane. They suggested that he appoint a committee to consider planning the reconstruction of the city in more detail. On February 11, the Mayor officially sanctioned their proposals by appointing them and a number of their fellow business and civic leaders to a Citizens' Emergency Committee and formally charging them with the responsibility of planning the reconstruction of the burnt district.[11]

At the time, Baltimoreans were most excited by the possibility of taking advantage of the fire's destruction to widen and extend streets. As a result, one of the Emergency Committee's first acts was to create a special Sub-Committee on Streets to recommend a plan of street improvements for the city to institute. The members of the Sub-Committee promptly immersed themselves in this task. As people began demanding additional improvements, however, the Sub-Committee members broadened their agenda and developed additional proposals related to the establishing of public parks, the redevelopment of the Inner Harbor, and the creation of a sewerage system.

The members of the Sub-Committee worked "day and night" to devise the improvement plans. What they came up with was a wide-ranging program of street widenings and extensions, a recommendation that the streets be regraded, three park proposals, an ambitious harbor redevelopment plan,

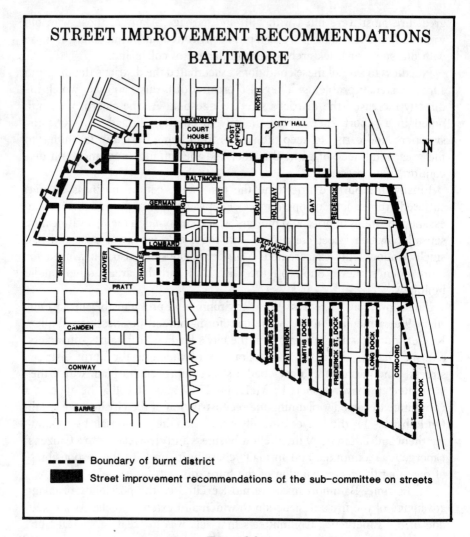

Figure 8.2.

and a vague but ultimately even more ambitious sewerage plan. The proposals made clear their deep desire to solve the burnt district's many infrastructural problems as comprehensively and systematically as possible.[12]

The Sub-Committee's street improvement proposals were especially detailed. They are shown on the map in Figure 8.2. The suggestions for improving the north-south streets primarily concerned the particularly congested and poorly connected thoroughfares in the burnt district's northwest corner. They included the widening of St. Paul Street from Lexington to

Fayette to one hundred sixty feet (in order to create a plaza opposite the Court House which would balance the existing plaza on the other side of the Court House), the widening of St. Paul Street past Fayette Street to Baltimore Street to sixty-six feet, and the widening of Light Street (the continuation of St. Paul) from Baltimore to Pratt to one hundred two feet. They also included widening Charles Street where it ran inside the burnt district, extending Hanover Street through Baltimore to Fayette Street, widening Hopkins Place from Lombard Street to German Street, and extending Hopkins north from German to Liberty Street.

The Sub-Committee's suggestions for improving the district's east-west streets called for widening all of the major thoroughfares. The Sub-Committee recommended widening Pratt Street from Light Street to Jones Falls (except between O'Donnel's and Dugan's Wharfs, where the United Railway and Electric Company's powerhouse was located), widening Lombard Street from Charles Street to Jones Falls, widening German Street from Liberty to Light Street, and widening Baltimore from Liberty to Jones Falls. In conjunction with these suggestions, the Sub-Committee further recommended that the City Surveyor revise the grades of the streets "without delay" to reduce steep grades.[13]

The Sub-Committee members had two primary goals in making these proposals. One was to reduce the congestion caused by the growing crush of cross-town traffic on Pratt and Baltimore Streets. The other was to eliminate bottlenecks and generally facilitate traffic flow on the narrow and heavily traveled streets in the western half of the district.[14] As the map of the improvements in Figure 8.2 indicates, the Sub-Committee's solution to the problems was not nearly as farnreaching as the radical plan of street redesign that Bostonians first contemplated after their conflagration. A few people did talk of more drastic changes initially. City Engineer Benjamin Fendall, for example, prepared a plan that would have imposed a perfectly straight grid of eighty-foot-wide streets, closing all alleys in the area and eliminating German Street.[15] The members of the Sub-Committee never seriously considered such a radical revision of the system, however. Instead, well aware of the difficulties of implementing drastic changes, they confined themselves to proposing improvements in the area's existing streets. By treating traffic flow as an integrated system, they tried "as far as reasonably practicable" to improve the facilities of travel "in every direction."[16]

The Sub-Committee's park and harbor recommendations were just as comprehensive and, if anything, more radical. They are displayed in Figure 8.3. Both proposals required sweeping use of the city's powers of eminent domain. The park recommendations involved taking nine of the eighty-six blocks in the burnt district completely out of private hands. The Sub-Committee's first suggestion was that the city acquire the seven blocks

LAND TO BE CONDEMNED
BALTIMORE

- - - - **Boundary of burnt district**

▬▬▬▬ **Land to be condemned** under the street and the park and harbor
recommendations of the sub-committee on streets

Figure 8.3.

bounded by Baltimore Street, Marsh Market Space, Lombard Street, and
Jones Falls for "park and other purposes." Its second suggestion was that
the federal government acquire the block bounded by Calvert, Baltimore,
North, and Fayette Streets and, if that worked out, that the city also acquire
the adjacent block bounded by North, Baltimore, Holliday, and Fayette
Streets. The goal was to create an open green space in the heart of the
commercial center and simultaneously to provide a "proper" aesthetic setting
for the Court House and the City Hall.[17]

The Sub-Committee's harbor improvement proposals were even more extensive. Its recommendations were, first, that the city take possession of all the docks and piers between Bowley's Wharf and West Falls Avenue (except the United Railway and Electric Company's powerhouse, which the Sub-Committee deemed too expensive for the city to purchase); and second, that the city completely redesign the area, establishing "proper" bulkheads and pier lines and otherwise redeveloping the property "exclusively for dock and pier facilities." This truly drastic improvement entailed condemning and redeveloping roughly sixty-five acres of property, about as much acreage as Boston's whole burnt district.[18]

The Sub-Committee's sewer recommendations were much less detailed and never became an official part of the city's burnt district improvement plan. Because the district's sanitary problems could not be solved without the passage of a multi-million dollar public bond referendum that would enable the city to build a city-wide sewerage system, something that most people did not believe would happen any time soon, the Sub-Committee merely advised that the city repair and make necessary additions to the district's existing storm drains. Even here, however, the members' ultimate goal was comprehensive change. In the hope of coming close to the attainment of a city-wide sewerage system, they recommended that the Mayor and members of the City Council resolve their long-standing dispute over what kind of sewerage system the city should build. They suggested that the city lay small service pipes for the future system now, so that it would not have to tear up the streets again when construction of the system at last began.[19]

As the sweeping character of these proposals suggests, the people serving on the Sub-Committee on Streets had high hopes that city officials would take advantage of the fire's destruction to improve the quality of life in the burnt district. In effect, they were recommending nothing less than an almost overnight resolution of environmental problems that had been accumulating in the area for over half a century. In a move which demonstrated how widespread their hopes were, the members of the Citizens' Emergency Committee quickly adopted the Sub-Committee's suggestions *in toto*. In order to implement the changes, the committee members also adopted a plan to finance them. Specifically, they recommended that abutting property owners and the city share the cost of the street improvements, abutters paying a third of the cost through betterment assessments. They called on the city to fund the rest by floating a $6 million bond issue and spending $4 million of the money it had received from selling the municipally owned Western Maryland Railroad in 1902.[20]

According to Mayor McLane, the precedents for his creation of the Citizens' Emergency Committee were similar citizens' committees established in Boston and Chicago after their great fires. In fact, however, McLane's appointment of the Emergency Committee was the first substantive event to set the reconstruction of Baltimore off from the reconstructions of Boston and Chicago. Both the Mayor of Boston and the Mayor of Chicago had created citizens' committees. Their purpose had been to organize the distribution of charity and job relief, however, not to plan the environmental redevelopment of the burnt district.

Despite their unique approach to physical reconstruction, however, Baltimoreans could not avoid sharing an important bond with the citizens of fire-stricken Boston and Chicago, even at this early stage. This was the inescapable presence of frictions in the process of environmental redevelopment. From the start, members of the Sub-Committee on Streets were unable to circumvent these barriers to change.

The first meeting of the Sub-Committee established the dialectic that would become the leitmotif of all of reconstruction in Baltimore. It revealed the hopes people had for achieving far-reaching environmental improvement. More important, it illuminated the unyielding reality of the barriers to improvement lurking just beneath the members' progressive determination to overcome the barriers.

Most of the talk at the meeting concerned the possible street widenings and extensions the city might make. Part, however, concerned the difficulties of implementing the improvements. In this regard, the suggestion of one man, Emanuel Greenbaum, is particularly important. Greenbaum proposed that property owners and businessmen join together to make enlightened, progressive self-interest a solution to the age-old difficulty of assembling land for street widenings and extensions. What he did was volunteer to *donate* to the city a strip of frontage ten feet deep from his own lot on German Street on the condition that all the other property owners on both sides of the street do the same, in order to make possible the widening of German Street by twenty feet from Sharp Street to Charles Street. The suggestion was a dynamic (albeit naive) attempt to come to grips with the problems that traditionally obstructed street improvement by putting the public interest ahead of selfish private interests. Impressed, several of Greenbaum's neighbors agreed to join him in his offer. Several of his other neighbors, however, immediately spoke out against him, some refusing to sacrifice their land without fair compensation and others, especially those with shallow lots, protesting having to cut their properties up at all. Needless to say, the exchange promptly punctured hopes that there might be such an easy, noble way to avoid the site assembly problem.[21]

At this point, a naively upbeat dynamic characterized the improvement process, as people focused on deciding what improvements the city ought to make and generally ignored or minimized the problems epitomized by the Greenbaum squabble. As the days passed, however, their optimism soured, for the problems were inexorably grabbing more and more of the their attention. On the day the Sub-Committee disclosed its street and park improvement proposals, for example, intractable site assembly problems came to the fore. The members of another Sub-Committee announced that they were having difficulty obtaining Congressional support for the plan to have the U.S. government purchase the block of land on Fayette Street, dimming hopes for the two-block park across from the Court House and City Hall. On the same day, abutting landowners began publicly protesting street widenings that threatened serious damage to their properties. They warned that the list of improvements was "so large in its scope" and required "such an immense outlay" of funds that "there was danger of the whole plan falling to the ground and none of the improvements being accomplished."[22]

Soon property owners and businessmen were voicing their opposition to the Sub-Committee's other plans. Fish and produce dealers, for example, staged a meeting to protest against the proposal to turn the Marsh Market Space area into a public park. They spoke out against "any such attempt to use the space for any purposes as are prejudicial to the interests of business." Pointing to the overcrowded conditions of the old market, they demanded the land be taken to enlarge their marketing facilities.[23] In the meantime, the merchants who had occupied the warehouses on the old piers in the Inner Harbor began protesting against the plan to redevelop the harbor, objecting that it would deprive them of direct access to the waterfront. They feared that this would throw them at the "mercy" of the avaricious railroads by forcing them to run tracks from the piers to their warehouses in order to move their goods from port to storage.[24] To complicate matters, spokesmen for the city's railroad and steamship interests also began speaking out against the harbor improvement plan. They protested that it would interfere with their business activities along the Inner Harbor.[25]

While these people were pressuring municipal decision makers to stop implementation of the plans, other kinds of barriers to change began making themselves felt. One of the most serious was a legal problem. As members of the Sub-Committee on Streets had pointed out as early as February 17, state condemnation laws created "major difficulties" in achieving street and park improvements by adding legal complications to the already convoluted site assembly process. The laws threw obstacles in the way of redevelopment in two ways. First, like most such laws, they required the city to compensate abutters fully for both the loss of their property and the loss of the economic use of their property, thus compounding the cost of making the improvements. Since land in Baltimore was encumbered with irredeemable ground rents, this created serious problems. Second, and more important, unlike the condemnation laws in most other states, Maryland law prohibited the city from taking possession of any land needed to construct improvements until after all injured property holders had completely satisfied their rights to full compensation in the courts, no matter how much time all the necessary court proceedings might take. This created the potential for extremely long delays, which, if past experience was any guide, could postpone the implementation of the improvements (and thus the rest of the reconstruction itself) for years. The mere prospect of such a wait gave many burnt district improvement boosters cold feet.[26]

As the days passed, the problem of financing the park and street and harbor improvements also began to weigh heavily on the improvement process. On the one hand, abutters protested against the proposal that they contribute a third of the cost of the street improvements through betterment assessments, adding another dimension to the growing political opposition to the plans.[27] On the other, the plan's supporters faced the difficulty of raising the public monies to pay for the improvements. The city would have to submit a $6 million bond referendum to the voters, as well as spend several million dollars of its Western Maryland Railroad funds. One problem was that Baltimoreans had a nasty habit of turning down bond referendums. This led some people to question the advisability of delaying reconstruction until after the referendum was held. It also, of course, threatened to limit the amount of money that could be spent on improvements to the $4 million available from the Western Maryland Railroad funds. An even more serious problem, though, was that the reformers pushing the burnt district plans had several other expensive public improvements on their agenda, including ambitious sewerage, park, school, pavement, and fire engine house projects. These projects also involved the passage of bond referendums and use of the limited Western Maryland funds. Since most civic leaders thought it unlikely that the voters would approve more than one multi-million dollar bond issue, paying for the burnt district improvements threatened to deprive the city of its ability to undertake other desperately needed municipal improvements dear to progressive hearts. Needless to say, this created even more conflict.[28]

Finally, throwing additional obstacles in the path of change were institutionally based collective decision making problems and city officials' growing awareness of them. First of all, the advocates of improvement faced the difficulty of obtaining the enabling legislation from the state that was necessary to undertake and finance the burnt district plan. Second, and more important, they faced the difficulty of maneuvering the plan through Baltimore's own government. The problem was that the authority for planning and implementing public works was terribly fragmented in Baltimore, much more divided, in fact, than in Boston's government in 1872.

Like Boston's City Council, Baltimore's contained two independent houses.

Called the First and Second Branch, both had to approve public improvements before the city could put them into effect. In the context of the public's disagreement over the improvement plans, this institutional division was, of course, enough to create stalemating dissension in the government decision making process. To complicate matters, there was also a political division between the houses. The last municipal election had put the First Branch in the hands of the Democratic party and the Second Branch in the hands of the Republican party. The rivalry between the two parties enhanced improvement's foes' ability to play the houses against each other to block individual improvement plans. And there were still more institutional divisions that fragmented government decision making authority. Unlike Boston's Common Council and Board of Aldermen, Baltimore's First and Second Branches did not have to cooperate with an independently elected agency responsible for proposing and budgeting improvement plans like Boston's Board of Street Commissioners. They did, however, have to work with not one but two, separate executive departments, the Board of Estimate and the Board of Public Improvements, which had these duties. Mayor McLane charged the Citizens' Emergency Committee with the responsibility of formulating the burnt district improvement plans. Even before the Emergency Committee had a chance to take its recommendations to the state legislature, however, the members of the Board of Estimate and the Board of Public Improvement began intervening in the planning process. They promptly demonstrated their independence both by objecting to several of the Emergency Committee's key proposals and by making recommendations of their own.[29]

This institutional division of power not only complicated the planning of improvements, but also threatened additional decision making delays that appalled the people advocating environmental reform. As one man pointed out at a hearing on the improvements, past experience had shown that "the more bodies through which a measure has to pass, the longer it is becoming a law." He expected that the two Boards and the two houses of the City Council would disagree on many of the improvements, foresaw the Mayor vetoing some of the amendments that the City Council might make, and, along with many other people, generally feared "a wrangle that would continue indefinitely." William Cabell Bruce, the City Solicitor, worried that the different governmental bodies might debate the plans for so long that property owners would give up on them and "rebuild along the old street lines and the proposed improvements would be lost."[30]

Together these political, economic, and institutional problems caused a rapid loss of support for the improvements. The first signs of popular retreat from the goals of redevelopment appeared as soon as abutters began publicly protesting against various proposals. Just two days after the Sub-Committee on Streets announced its list of street widenings and extensions, property owners began objecting to them. For example, the editors of the *Baltimore Sun* backed off from their enthusiastic endorsement of comprehensive change. Until then they had been steadily running editorials and articles on the critical need to take advantage of the opportunity for comprehensive environmental redevelopment. They had even called on the city fathers to consider adopting Haussman's wide-ranging redevelopment of Paris as a model for the city. Now, however, they changed their tune, bowing to abutters' protests. Cautioning that it was "not practicable now to put into effect the entire scheme of improvements proposed by the committee," they solemnly declared that "it would be the part of wisdom to adopt such of its recommendations as are feasible and to drop the rest."[31]

Even the members of the Citizen's Emergency Committee were quickly backtracking from the improvement plans. The federal government's refusal to finance the acquisition of the park across from the Court House forced them to abandon their plans for both that park and the municipal park adjacent to it almost as soon as they proposed them. Although they stubbornly clung to their list of street improvements, intransigent opposition from abutters, businesses, the Board of Estimate, and the Board of Public Improvement also forced them to forsake their proposal to make the area between Marsh Market Space, Baltimore Street, Lombard Street, and Jones Falls a park. They replaced it with a plan to redevelop the area for fish and produce market purposes. A report in the *Sun* that members of the Sub-Committee on Streets denied they had ever made any park recommendations and that they had all along intended the area around Marsh Market Space to be used for market and street purposes is a graphic indication of the kind of pressure they were under on these matters.[32]

Further retreat came in late February when the members of the Board of Public Improvement and the Board of Estimate caved in to an intense lobbying campaign against the harbor redevelopment. Arguing that the harbor improvement would be too expensive, the Boards decided that the city should not ask the state for the enabling legislation it needed to float the $6 million loan recommended by the Emergency Committee to pay for the improvement. This meant abandoning the ambitious harbor redevelopment plan, as well as any other improvements that could not be financed by the Western Maryland Railroad funds.[33]

What is interesting is that despite these setbacks, the improvement plans generally escaped defeat. The city instituted all but one of the Citizens' Emergency Committee's street improvement recommendations, essentially as the Committee had formulated them. Although it did not build any parks, the city constructed a large, modern marketplace that became a model for other cities. It also laid new sewerage drains in preparation for the new municipal sewerage system. It even implemented the Emergency Committee's entire harbor redevelopment plan.

The advocates of the improvement plan achieved all this by finding ways to sidestep some barriers to change. They circumvented the barriers both by organizing themselves and by reorganizing the institutions and procedures of government decision making to make it extremely difficult for their opponents to dominate the improvement process in traditional ways. In so doing, they took the progressive political reforms instituted a few years earlier under the new City Charter one step farther, coming closer to completely replacing the old, chaotic, but democratic from-the-bottom-up mode of municipal public policy making with a new, bureaucratic from-the-top-down system. Somewhat paradoxically, they also developed methods of progressive mass political mobilization to full advantage. Their institutional and political maneuvers by no means eliminated the barriers to infrastructural redevelopment. They were actions deliberately undertaken to circumvent the barriers, however, actions which were far more sophisticated than Emanuel Greenbaum's conditional offer to donate the land for street widenings, moves which, in the end, proved remarkably successful. What is significant is that the things that Baltimoreans did to get around the barriers to change, by their very nature, demonstrated the great importance of the barriers in both environmental redevelopment and political reform.

It was the critical decision by the Boards of Estimate and Public Improvement to abandon the plan to redevelop the Inner Harbor that forced business and civic leaders to begin taking actions which would ultimately enable them to hurdle the barriers to change and bring the improvement plans to fruition. Up to this point, they had done little but worry about the problems threatening the plans. Now, however, they began to act to keep the improvements from slipping through their fingers.

At first the harbor plan's supporters moved in very traditional ways to try to force the McLane administration to heed their demands. Representatives of the city's municipal Harbor Board combined forces with representatives of the River and Harbor Committees of the Chamber of Commerce, the Merchants and Manufacturers Association, and the Board of Trade and quietly stepped up the pressure on the Mayor and the members of the Boards of Estimate and Public Improvement to retain the plan.[34]

This influence tactic worked, but only temporarily. It persuaded the Boards of Estimate and Public Improvement to hold another meeting. The Boards then reversed themselves, agreeing to request the enabling legislation for the $6 million loan. Within two days, however, the Boards were once more caving in to the demands of the harbor plan's opponents and threatening to abandon the loan.[35]

This prompted the plan's supporters to take more extreme steps to save the plan. First they went to work to silence and discredit the opposition by attempting to change the minds of the opposition's most influential spokesmen. They convinced at least three, Chamber of Commerce Chairman James C. Gorman, Board of Trade President James Foard, and Pennsylvania Central Railroad agent George C. Wilkens, to reverse themselves, apparently by bringing up the possibility of having the federal government undertake a project to deepen the shipping channel in the Inner Harbor. This improvement was irresistibly attractive to most business leaders because, in combination with the proposed dock improvements, it promised to make the Inner Harbor a truly important regional ship and railroad transportation center.[36]

More important, the supporters went public with their lobbying effort, attempting to manufacture a louder collective demand for the improvement by staging a public rally. They called a hundred of the city's most important business and professional men to the rally. They also enlisted several of Baltimore's most influential business and civic leaders (including Gorman, Foard, and Wilkens) to give speeches on why it was essential that the city undertake the harbor redevelopment. This not only gave the supporters the means to promulgate their views but also offered a forum from which they passed a resolution "heartily favoring" the implementation of the plan. The passage of the resolution gave the harbor redevelopment an official stamp of community approval.[37]

This produced a realignment of demand which completely drowned out the voices of the opposition. Not only did the newspapers run full reports on the rally and, inspired, begin publishing editorials in support of the improvement, but the City Council also passed a joint resolution which called on the Boards of Estimate and Public Improvement to request the enabling legislation, further fortifying and legitimating the demand for the improvement. Duly impressed, the Boards approved preparation of the enabling bill to authorize the floating of the $6 million loan. They transmitted the bill to Annapolis independently of their request for the enabling legislation for the other improvements, apparently holding it in abeyance until after the main bill could be passed, in order to make sure that residual opposition to the loan or the harbor redevelopment would not destroy the street improvement plan.[38]

In manipulating public opinion, the organizers of the rally were attempting to achieve a public good by generating an irresistible public demand for it. As such, their actions paralleled Postmaster Burt's mobilization of popular support in behalf of the widening of Boston's Water Street through his open letter to the City Council. They also mirrored the North Siders' demonstration of popular opposition to Chicago's comprehensive fire limits ordinance through their march on City Hall. In all three cases, individuals or groups with deep interest in the outcome of a government decision went outside normal governmental channels to articulate their policy demands in an effective way. In each case, they had previously attempted to obtain their goals through less public, more traditional methods of influencing decision makers but, because of their opponents' greater influence, had failed. They had then coped with their weakness by transforming the demand competition which had put them at a disadvantage. In each case, they had interjected into the demand competition the explicit force of community opinion. In this way they had thrown their opponents on the defensive, overpowering with numbers and the extraordinary character of their activity the influence that their opponents wielded by virtue of their special access to decision makers, their community position, or their economic clout. The tactic could be used by either an improvement's proponents or its foes, of course. In this case, what enabled Chicago's North Siders to kill a proposed improvement enabled Baltimore's business leaders to save one.

This would not be the only time that Baltimoreans would try to influence the outcome of the infrastructural improvement process by manipulating public demand. What makes the redevelopment of Baltimore so special, however, is that the advocates of improvement went much farther than these attempts to restructure the demand side of the improvement process as they labored to get the improvements passed. In addition, they worked on the supply side, attempting to sidestep the barriers to change by restructuring the institutions and procedures of government decision making.

First, good progressive reformers that they were, they moved to concentrate control of the improvement process in the executive branch of the city government, the most bureaucratic, least democratic section of government. They did this by creating an independent executive agency, the Burnt District Commission, to plan and execute all of the improvements.

The formation of such an agency had not been one of the Citizens' Emergency Committee's original proposals. In fact, the Commission's appearance on the scene came so late that it was a total surprise to people who were not closely following the preparation of the enabling legislation. City officials and other advocates of the improvements decided to create it only after the members of the Board of Estimate and the Board of Public Improvement repudiated the $6 million loan, dramatizing city officials' vulnerability to the insistent voices of opposing forces. Their desire to minimize the opportunities that abutters and other interested parties had to block the improvements by pressuring government decision makers initially led some city officials to consider writing the Emergency Committee's proposals directly into the enabling law. This was, of course, a move which would have stopped the planning process right there. The difficulty of accurately describing the new street lines prior to a proper survey made it impossible, however. As a result, those in favor of the improvements turned to the special commission idea as the next best way to protect the plans' integrity.[39]

People debated a bit about how to organize the Burnt District Commission. As the enabling law finally constituted it, however, the agency was an evenly balanced, bipartisan, four-member body composed of two Democrats and two Republicans, with the Mayor serving as an *ex officio* member. The law gave the Mayor, who happened to be an enthusiastic supporter of the improvements, the power to appoint the voting members, subject to approval by a majority of the members of the Second Branch of the City Council. In order to ensure the Commissioners' independence from the ongoing politics of the city government, it prohibited the Mayor from appointing any person who was already a paid or non-paid legislative or administrative official of the city. It also, however, gave him the power to appoint the members without the Second Branch's approval if the Second Branch rejected two of his nominations in succession. To prevent the Commission from becoming the basis of a new political machine, it also provided for the agency's demise once its work had been completed.[40]

The enabling legislation gave the executive branch of the city government command over the improvement process by granting the Commissioners control of both the planning and the implementation of the improvements. It did this by giving the Commissioners the responsibility both of fixing the new street, alley, lane, sidewalk, and building lines and laying out the new market and wharf and dock facilities and of acquiring the land for the improvements, awarding damages (subject, of course, to property owners' constitutional right to seek fair compensation in the courts), and assessing betterments. The act required the Commissioners to consult with the members of the Board of Estimate and the Board of Public Improvement, to whom it gave authority to approve, disapprove, or suggest changes in the plans. It limited the City Council's involvement in the planning process to approving the Commission's plans, however, denying the Council any power of amendment. Thus it stripped the Council members of their traditional policy-making functions. It also prohibited the Council members from participating in the execution of the improvements in any way, beyond the role of enacting any ordinances needed to enable the Commission to carry out its duties. To secure executive control of the improvements, it prohibited the City Council from passing any ordinance to deprive the Commission of its powers.[41]

The Maryland legislature passed the enabling act on March 11, 1904. The next day Mayor McLane appointed the four members. They were Charles K. Lord, the Chairman of the Board of Directors of the Consolidated Coal Company, former Vice-President of the Baltimore and Ohio Railroad, and Chairman of the Emergency Committee's Sub-Committee on Streets;

Sherlock Swann, a former City Councilman, member of the Sub-Committee on Streets, and stepson of ex-Mayor Ferdinand Latrobe; Reuben Foster, President of the Chesapeake Steamship Company and another member of the Sub-Committee on Streets; and John T. Graham, a real estate broker and former President of the city's Taxpayers Association.[42]

As the non-elected, bipartisan character of the Commission and its stripping of the traditional authority of the City Council suggest, the Burnt District Commission was a typical product of what historians have labeled "structural" or administrative progressive reform – reform that focused on changing the structure of municipal government rather than the content of public policy. Despite the appointment of three business elites to the four-member body, however, the reformers' goal in creating the Commission was not simply to put more businessmen in office or to give the business community more political power at the expense of the working class or a political machine, as the historians of this kind of progressive reform typically suggest. After all, "Good Government" politicians supported by Baltimore's business interests and its middle and upper classes already dominated the City Council and ran all the city's executive departments. Nor was the reformers' goal to make the planning and execution of the improvements more "efficient" for the sake of affirming business values or for the sake of cutting costs.[43]

Instead, their purpose was to centralize government decision making in order to facilitate the redevelopment of the burnt district. Their aim was to alleviate the impediments to improvement posed by the existing fragmentation of decision making authority in Baltimore's city government. Their underlying goal was to avoid the political manifestations of the site assembly problem that resulted from the power that abutters and other affected parties had to sway government officials to oppose improvement plans.[44]

The commission idea was not, of course, the perfect solution to the problem of the fragmentation of authority. As the man who first proposed the Burnt District Commission, Richard Venable, later admitted, rather than necessarily centralize power, the new agency ironically raised the specter of yet another division of authority, yet another point at which officials could turn down proposed improvements at the behest of the plans' opponents. Venable became so concerned about this that he suggested that the Commission stage be bypassed and the Boards of Estimate and Public Improvement empowered to formulate the plans.[45]

The creation of the Commission was nevertheless a significant institutional innovation. The framers of the enabling act made sure that it enhanced supporters' power rather than played into the opposition's hands. First, they gave the Democratic Mayor the power to appoint enthusiastic friends of the improvements to the Commission, even over a potentially hostile Republican Second Branch's veto. Thus they made sure that the Commission itself would not become a weak point in the planning process. Second, they merged the Board of Estimate with the Board of Public Improvement to make a single "Joint Board." In this way they reduced by one-half these two agencies' ability to disrupt and divide the planning process. Finally, as noted earlier, they denied the City Council the power to amend the Commission's plans. Apparently counting on the Councilmen's basic enthusiasm for the improvement goals to prevail over their frustration over their inability to modify individual proposals, they gave them only the power to approve or disapprove the plans. Thus they limited the options Council members had for responding to the pressure from opponents.[46]

With these institutional changes in hand, the people in favor of the plans went on to consolidate their control over the improvement process. They did this by modifying the traditional hearing procedure by which officials formally gathered the information they needed to formulate policy decisions. They restructured the hearing process on both the executive and the legislative levels.

This effort was even more blatant an attempt to deprive the opponents of the improvements of their influence than the creation of the Burnt District Commission. First, on March 12, the same day their appointments were confirmed, the members of the Burnt District Commission officially adopted the Citizens' Emergency Committee's list of improvement recommendations "in toto," completely skipping the public hearing procedures which traditionally preceded and helped shape official adoption of public works plans. Neither they nor the Emergency Committee nor the Board of Estimate nor the Board of Public Improvement had ever invited the people who would be injured by the improvements to any formal hearings on them in the government's customary manner. The Burnt District Commissioners finally held a public meeting three days after they had adopted the Emergency Committee's recommendations. Despite the fact that many of the people who attended brought suggestions and remonstrances, however, they continued to refuse to hold a hearing on the plans. Instead, they conveyed the improvement proposals directly to the Joint Board. The Joint Board followed the same procedure, also adopting the improvements without holding any public hearings.[47]

The decision by the Burnt District Commission and the Joint Board to refuse to hold hearings was part of a larger decision by the improvement plans' supporters to confine formal public debate over the improvements to a single series of hearings before the City Council's Joint Committee on Highways. As such, it was a crucial part of their attempt to centralize decision making and thus make it difficult for opponents to fight the plans. "We do not want to take three bites at the cherry," Mayor McLane said, aptly summing up their strategy.[48]

With this procedural innovation established, the officials pushing the improvements began to work on the City Council. First, supporters on the Council's Joint Committee on Highways scheduled the Committee hearings in such a way as to rush the proposals through the only stage of the decision making process in which property owners and others were now allowed to voice their disagreements with the plans. The Committee completed the hearings in less than a week, a remarkable feat made possible only by their adherence to a strict timetable under which they heard arguments for and against each improvement one at a time in quick succession, several improvements per night, each night, for six nights straight (with one break over Sunday night). The advantage of this was that it left all the people objecting to the plan for a given street no more than about an hour, on average, in which to state collectively all of their objections.[49]

Second, the plans' supporters engineered the hearings so that the plans' patrons would not be overwhelmed by opposition. This was necessary only in the case of the proposal to widen Baltimore Street, a particularly unpopular improvement. Property owners and businessmen who opposed the widening showed up at the scheduled hearing in such large numbers and made such impassioned arguments against it that they completely swamped the supporters, who seem to have barely shown up at all. Strictly speaking, such unmitigated opposition should have forced the members of the Committee to abandon the plan. Rising to the challenge, however, the Committeemen simply declared an extension of the debate. Ignoring their tight schedule, they allocated an hour at the beginning of the next night's hearing for the supporters to make their case, making sure that this time several prominent allies appeared to argue in favor of the widening.[50]

These maneuvers were implemented with such skill and doubletalk that it was not until well into the week of the joint committee hearings that most City Council members discovered that they did not have any power to amend the improvements.[51] The McLane administration did not begin trying to explain the new rules until it became essential that the City Council members be informed that they no longer had their traditional right to change the plans.[52]

The ploys were much more than mere political expedients, however. Their significance rests in the new conception they contained of the organization and purpose of city planning and government decision making and the ordinary citizen's proper relationship to both. Implicit, and even at times explicit, in them was a new idea about the way government ought to handle the barriers to environmental redevelopment, particularly the site assembly barrier to change.

Progressive Baltimoreans who wanted the government to take action on long-needed improvements were not only tired of the city's prolonged inability to act on their demands but also completely fed up with "pointless" Councilmanic debates, time-consuming administrative procedures, and the other trappings of the government's role in the improvement process. Galled by apparently weak-willed, incompetent, and possibly corrupt politicians who seemed to be personally incapable of achieving change and exasperated by the decision making practices which seemed to be responsible for much of the inaction, they wanted change.[53] Their solution was to abandon the city's traditional from-the-bottom-up decision making process in order to free officials from their obligation to try to please abutters. What they did was what municipal reformers all over the country were doing, which was to attempt to forge a new, less "political," less democratic, more from-the-top-down process. The editors of the *Baltimore Sun* summed up their appraisal of the situation, pointing to the futility of trying to achieve the "public good" on the basis of the conflicting voices of a host of "inconsistent private individuals." Changes in the street were necessary, the *Sun* declared. "The difficulty is that the objecting property holder, while approving the proposed changes affecting property holders on other streets, is unwilling to have them on his own streets. *But it is impossible to devise a plan that will please all, and a waste of time to try*" (emphasis added).[54] With their new procedures the reformers stopped wasting time trying to appease the opposition.

The new top-down dynamic of government decision making is clear in the creation of the Burnt District Commission and the other institutional changes made to concentrate power in the executive branch of government. It is also evident in the improvement supporters' frequent attempts to justify the improvement plans in terms of the "expertise" and "trained insight" that supposedly informed them (a necessity now that they could no longer legitimize the plans on the traditional basis of community participation in public policy formulation). It is especially clear, however, in the things supporters did to cut off their opponents' access to decision makers. These tactics were epitomized by their decision to confine formal public debate on the street proposals to a single set of hearings before the City Council's Joint Committee on Highways *after* they had already taken away the City Council's power to amend the plans. With this combination of maneuvers, those in favor of the plans cunningly tried to limit opponents to contact with officials who had almost no power to respond to their demands.

Significantly, the new approach to government decision making was evident in the McLane administration's handling of all the other burnt district improvements, including the preparation of the plans to redevelop the Inner Harbor and regrade burnt district streets. Because the Sub-Committee on Streets had not developed any detailed recommendations for either the harbor or the street grades, the enabling act charged the Burnt District Commission with the responsibility of preparing the wharf and dock improvement plans and the City Surveyor's office with the responsibility of preparing the regrading plans. Both the Commissioners and the Surveyor followed the top-down model of public policy making, largely developing the plans internally and using hearing procedures in highly non-traditional ways.

The Burnt District Commissioners designed their harbor improvement along the lines of the sketchy plans outlined by the Sub-Committee on Streets. In the process, they held a public hearing. Again, however, they refused to use the hearing procedure for the customary purpose of listening to abutters' complaints. The hearing was "not for the purpose of protesting against the plans," Chairman Swann flatly told the property owners and businessmen in attendance, despite the fact that many had brought objections and remonstrances. "We have decided upon that point," he said.[55]

What the hearing's real purpose was is not completely clear. Swann said that it was to have the participants "assist" the Commissioners by making positive suggestions that would help, not interfere with, the formulation of the plans. This may have been at least one of the Commissioners' genuine reasons for holding the meeting, but it does not appear to have been their only or indeed their primary motivation. The fact was that Mayor McLane used the hearing to describe the benefits of the redevelopment and calm fears that it would force small businesses off the waterfront. Alternative plans proposed by prominent business interests had no perceptible impact on the final product, and the final allocation of wharf and dock space had next to nothing to do with what the small businessmen at the meeting suggested. This indicates that the Commissioners' real intention was to use the gathering to sell the improvement to the people who would be affected by it and, by giving them at least a sense of participation in the planning process, to co-opt the opposition.[56]

Using the hearing process to sell a plan was, of course, a drastic departure from the traditional practice of using it to gather information to aid in formulating a plan. Even holding it to garner citizen "assistance" was a break with tradition, given that the Commissioners had prohibited the citizenry from complaining.[57]

The preparation of the street regrading plan followed a top-down dynamic that was even more extreme. The City Surveyor and the City Engineer and their staffs prepared a broad-ranging set of grade revisions, the most ambitious of which included plans to level the "hump" on Lombard Street between Charles and Hopkins Place, to reduce the steep grades near the intersection of Fayette and St. Paul, and to fill in the low-lying area around Marsh Market Space and the dip on Light Street near Balderson.[58] They prepared the plan completely bureaucratically, proceeding so privately that they left the rest of the community, including most city officials, entirely in the dark about what they proposed to do. This forced them to embark upon a campaign to sell the plan. To this end, they did not even try to co-opt opposing property owners and businessmen, but instead used the hearing process to gain the support of government leaders. What they did was to hold a meeting for the Mayor and other important executive branch officials and City Council leaders at which they explained the virtues of the plan. Then they took the officials on a tour of the streets to be regraded to demonstrate the plan's advantages.[59]

Neither the City Surveyor nor the City Engineer made any attempt to hold public hearings for the purpose of involving abutters in either the planning of the changes or the campaign to sell them. Because some of the deepest cuts affected streets at the edge of the burnt district and so affected many buildings that had not been damaged by the fire, they knew that the abutters who attended any public hearing would inevitably make objections to the plans, objections that they had no intention of considering, since there was no way to satisfy the abutters and still achieve the changes that they believed were necessary. As an unnamed "prominent" member of the Second Branch pointed out while attempting to explain why he hoped that the City Council would refuse to hold hearings on the plan, the predictability of abutters' protests meant that it would be a "waste of time" to invite the people who would be injured by the changes to a meeting to discuss them, since officials could not both heed the protests and make the changes. "I am in a position to appreciate the fact that drivers will not go on streets where there are heavy grades," the Councilman said, "and it seems to me that we are bound to consider the good to be accomplished to the community at large, rather than the few people or firms that will be damaged." He added, "As this is the case, I cannot for the life of me see why it should be necessary to hold public hearings."[60]

What makes these institutional and procedural "reforms" so important is that they indicate the lengths to which the people who favored the burnt district improvement plans felt it necessary to go to achieve implementation of the improvements. The maneuvers represented attempts to deactivate the site assembly issue by institutionally and procedurally sealing the improvement process off from interference by the people who made site assembly such a serious political obstacle to infrastructural change.

What is also important about the ploys is that they facilitated the improvement process, but not as well as those in favor of the plans wanted or expected. In fact, they came close to completely backfiring and causing the defeat of almost half of the proposals. The bitter conflict they inspired testifies to the extent to which the problems of adapting the urban environment to demographic and economic change inevitably generated strife.

That the maneuvers might not have stopped opponents from obstructing the improvement process as well as supporters hoped was indicated by rumors circulated during the hearings that some City Councilmen were making deals with property owners to vote against certain plans. The code name for this activity was "party politics," a reflection of the progressive tendency to identify politics with the vulnerability of politicians to the high-powered importuning of vested interests. On March 26, the *World*, for example, called attention to the "orators – paid orators at that," with whom the "enemies of the Commission report" were "flooding" City Council rooms to lobby against certain improvement proposals.[61]

On March 24, the Committee on Highways finished its hearings amid reports that things had gone so smoothly that it expected to approve every improvement easily.[62] Just four days later, however, on March 28, the Committee delivered majority and minority reports which spelled out the full dimension of the abutters' irrepressible influence. In that short interval the Committee had become, as the minority report put it, "hopelessly divided on nearly all of the respective propositions."[63]

The Committee on Highways had just six members, Stephen C. Little (the Chairman), George Konig, and Albert M. Sproesser from the First Branch and William D. Platt, George W. Howser, and John Hubert from the Second Branch. Chairman Little now opposed the plan to widen Baltimore Street, as did his First Branch colleagues Sproesser and Konig. In addition, Sproesser now opposed the extension of Hopkins Place and the improvement of Marsh Market Space, as well as the plans to widen Charles Street and to create the plaza on St. Paul Street. Platt, Howser, and Hubert joined the First Branch members in disapproving the Baltimore Street widening. Now, however, Hubert also opposed the plans to widen Charles Street and to create the St. Paul Street plaza. Howser opposed the plans to widen Pratt and Lombard Streets, as well as the plan to widen Charles Street. And Platt opposed the plans to create the St. Paul Street plaza, to extend Hopkins Place, and to widen German and Light as well as Charles Street.[64]

The six disagreed on so much that there were only two improvements which a majority agreed to reject, namely, the plan to widen Charles Street, which four rejected, and the plan to widen Baltimore Street, which they unanimously disapproved. As the minority report noted, they were so divided that "very few" of the improvements that they had approved had received "a majority endorsement from the same alignment of members."[65]

As this sudden, idiosyncratic, indecisive burst of opposition shows, neither the creation of the Burnt District Commission nor the scheduling of speedy, carefully engineered hearings had served to isolate members of the Committee on Highways from the cross-pressures exerted by the opponents of the improvement plans. By all their institutional and procedural maneuvering, the plan's supporters had, indeed, deprived their foes of meaningful *formal* access to the members of the Committee and the City Council as a whole. They had not, however, eliminated the opposition's *informal* access to officials, nor had they changed the economic and social conditions that gave wealthy and politically influential property owners and businessmen the power to sway officials through private contact. As a result, instead of sidestepping political conflict over the improvements, they had merely succeeded in shifting conflict out of formal settings into the City Hall corridors and back rooms.

What is more, the opponents' irrepressible influence was not the only problem the plans' supporters faced. As the members of the Committee on Highways made clear, the men behind the institutional and procedural "reforms" had also badly miscalculated when they had tried to facilitate the improvement process by stripping the City Council of its power to amend the improvement plans. As noted earlier, members of the McLane administration had been very slow to reveal how they were restructuring the city government to speed passage of the improvement plans. City Solicitor Bruce had announced the Council's loss of amendment-making power to the members of the Committee on Highways in the form of a legal opinion delivered halfway through the hearings. Now that the Committeemen had experienced the brunt of the hostile property owners' and businessmen's efforts to block the plans, they were furious at this blatant sleight of hand.

Speaking for his colleagues, Committee on Highways member George Konig addressed the First Branch, bitterly attacking the Burnt District Commission and the McLane administration for the way they were trying to manipulate the improvements through the City Council. The McLane administration had gotten legislation appointing a Burnt District Commission passed in Annapolis, "robbing this Council of any voice in the rebuilding of the city," Konig angrily declared. They had tried to stack the deck against abutters in every way, he charged. "Let us look at the gentlemen who came before the Committee and argued for the Burnt District Commission. Who are they? None but the Burnt District Commission, itself," he cried; "on the other hand, who came to argue against some of the things laid down by the Burnt District Commission? A large number of property owners with their attorneys representing thousands – I might say millions – of dollars worth of property in the same burnt district." Pointing to the city's filthy sewers, its inadequate schools and fire houses, its lack of suburban pavements, and its hungry families, Konig called on his fellow Council members to consider the other demands on the city's budget, urging them to do what was in the "best interest of the taxpayers in general." Condemning the McLane administration for forcing the Council to veto entire improvements rather than letting it modify them in comparatively small ways, he also urged them to approve or disapprove each proposal on its individual merits. "I hope that the Council will pass the things that they have recommended that are for the good of the community and I hope that they will have the courage to turn down those things they think are not good."[66]

After a stormy debate, the members of the First Branch voted seventeen to four (with three abstentions) to print the speech in full in the Council journal. Thus they gave Konig's attack "official standing," prompting some observers to declare that the Democratic First Branch had put itself in "open revolt" against the Democratic McLane administration and its efforts to railroad the improvements through the City Council.[67]

Together with the Committee on Highways' reports, Konig's speech made clear that the improvement plans still faced a gamut of obstacles created by the site assembly problem and the institutional division of municipal decision making authority. Nevertheless, the advocates of the improvements continued to fight valiantly for the plans' passage, and largely because McLane's Democratic party controlled the Branch, they managed to guide the proposals through the First Branch relatively unscathed. Disgusted with the Committee on Highways' confusion, a majority of the members of the First Branch refused to accept either the Committee's majority or its minority report. First Branch President Evan Morgan, however, rescued the entire plan by ruling that it would be given its first reading the next night anyway, "precisely" as it came from the Burnt District Commission. The next night's meeting got off to an ominous start, with a swarm of property holders and lawyers in the hallway buttonholing members as they walked into the meeting amid "persistent rumors in the corridor" that the anti-reform Democratic organization had passed the word that Democrats should vote against the Baltimore Street widening. Again, however, the McLane-allied Democratic leadership of the house saved the improvements, this time by stationing City Solicitor Bruce inside the First Branch chamber to render opinions to help President Morgan sidestep the technical and procedural arguments of the opponents. The Councilmen who opposed the various plans barraged the meeting with a stream of "amendments, substitutes for amendments, motions, counter motions, resolutions, and questions." In the course of rendering at least twenty-five opinions, however, Solicitor Bruce managed to defuse every potentially lethal attack. Then, with both the Democrats and Republicans badly divided, the members proceeded to approve every improvement in the plan except one, the plan to widen Charles Street.[68]

In the Second Branch the next night, however, the ax fell. As most of the newspapers put it, the members of this Republican-controlled house of the City Council proceeded to "murder" the improvement ordinance. They slashed out the St. Paul Street plaza, the Baltimore Street widening, the Light Street widening, the German Street widening, and the Commerce Street widening and tried to eliminate the Calvert Street widening, the extension of Hopkins Place, and the harbor improvement as well. In the overwrought words of the outraged *Morning Herald*, they "threw the ordinance up, shot at it with double-barreled weapons, stamped on it when it hit the floor, and mauled it right and left," all but one of the nine members "displaying a fiendish desire to rip at least one recommendation out."[69]

Once again the friends of the improvements had attempted to defuse the situation. Solicitor Bruce, as well as Mayor McLane, other administration officials, and several of the city's most prominent business leaders took seats in the Second Branch chamber to lobby the Councilmen privately and make speeches to keep them from vetoing the plans. This time, however, they failed to stem the tide. Led by Branch President Clay Timanus, the Republican members spearheaded the attack, proposing all but one of the many motions to eliminate given improvements. Like their colleagues in the First Branch, the members of both parties were randomly divided in the final voting. Together, however, they mustered enough of a consensus to disapprove the five plans. Added to the First Branch's veto of the Charles Street widening, this brought the total number of vetoed improvements to six.[70]

As the Councilmen repeatedly pointed out, the perpetrators of the institutional and procedural "reforms" had, because of the nature of the reforms, contributed to the fiasco. They had done so not simply because they had not stopped opponents from articulating their opposition, but because by denying the City Council the right to amend plans, they had forced Councilmen to veto whole improvements, no matter what they might have wanted to preserve. The transparency of the situation prompted hoots of derision from frustrated improvement supporters, who cried that the Councilmen were "crucifying the city for petty jealousy" and trying to take over the planning themselves "pretty much on the rule or ruin principle."[71] To make their opposition and power perfectly clear, however, the members of the Second Branch spelled out their refusal to rubber-stamp the Burnt District Commission's plans with a resolution in which they requested that the Burnt District Commission send them "supplementary ordinances concerning the improvements which have been stricken from the ordinance as recommended by them." Thus they, in effect, demanded that the Commissioners either give them amendatory powers or lose the rejected improvements completely.[72]

The full significance of the Second Branch's actions did not at first impress the plans' supporters. Mayor McLane, for example, responded with threats to veto the entire "mangled" ordinance, arguing that it was "better to abandon the present scheme altogether than to widen two or three streets." Digging in his heels, Burnt District Commission Chairman Swann also attempted to "stand pat." "Compromise?" he asked. "Why should we compromise? That plan was the result of no snap judgment, but was the result of earnest thought and discussion on the part of the Citizens' Emergency Committee, comprising more than forty of the most intelligent and representative citizens of the community." Some officials even began discussing the possibility of repealing the section of the enabling legislation that gave the City Council its veto power. Two state legislators proposed replacing the provision with a new enactment that would leave all power to pass on the improvements in the hands of the Board of Estimate and the Board of Public Improvement. This suggestion represented the ultimate extension of the reformers' anti-democratic bias.[73]

Nevertheless, the result was that the City Council got the power to amend the improvements it had demanded. After taking their disagreements into a conference committee, the members of the First and Second Branches hammered out a compromise that restored the Light and Commerce Street widenings that the Second Branch had struck out. After much bickering, they also passed resolutions which requested that the Burnt District Commissioners submit supplementary ordinances providing for the creation of a St. Paul Street plaza, the widening of Charles Street, and the widening of German Street to their own specifications. The resolutions called on the city to construct a plaza on St. Paul Street which would be one hundred twenty-six rather than one hundred sixty feet wide; to widen Charles Street through only three blocks, from Commerce Street to Fayette Street, rather than four blocks to Lexington Street; and to widen German Street through only three blocks, from Light Street to Hopkins Place, rather than four blocks to Liberty. Rather than lose all three improvements, the Burnt District Commissioners acceded to the Council's wishes and submitted the supplemental ordinances; and the Mayor approved them.[74]

In short, the members of the Second Branch called the McLane administration's bluff. Their success in obtaining the power to amend the Burnt District Commission's plans shows that the site assembly impediment to street improvement could not be eliminated by mere institutional and political manipulations, at least not completely eliminated. It thereby underlines the fact that the barriers to infrastructural redevelopment went much deeper than the surface politics of the redevelopment process, extending down to the physical character of the infrastructures themselves.

At the same time, however, as the remarkably positive outcome of the conflict indicates, the people behind the institutional and procedural maneuvers had met with at least some success in their efforts to facilitate the improvement process. They had succeeded in depriving abutters of at least some of their power to thwart the improvement plans. They had won passage of the plans less than one month after passage of the enabling legislation, less than two months after the great fire itself. Furthermore, they had accomplished this with little modification of the Citizens' Emergency Committee's original proposals. They lost only one improvement in its entirety, the widening of Baltimore Street, and only tiny fractions of three others.

This achievement stands in stark contrast to the city's ineffective handling of ambitious public improvement projects in the past. It also stands sharply apart from the Boston city government's ineffective six-month compromising battle over its burnt district street improvement plans back in 1872 and 1873. Thus it illuminates the way that these progressive reforms of city government facilitated, at least to some extent, the achievement of public policy initiatives.

The passage of the supplementary ordinances did not end the conflict over the burnt district street improvements. Despite the remarkably successful compromise, a number of civic, business, and government leaders kept on struggling for ambitious change. Their goal was to resurrect and achieve the widening of Baltimore Street, the one street improvement that had been lost in its entirety. The battle that ensued pushed the conflict over street improvement to new levels. The contention it inspired further demonstrates the futility of the McLane administration's attempt to eliminate traditional processes of demand articulation from government decision making. By the same token, however, it also helps to explain why people tried so hard to do just that.

The attempt to rescue the widening of Baltimore Street makes clear how very much the city's most prominent progressive leaders wanted to improve traffic flow in the business district. Baltimore Street was the business center's most important, but also most congested, thoroughfare. The people who had to use it were constantly inconvenienced and delayed by its incessant traffic jams. They therefore tried everything in their power (short of trying to reform further the institutions and procedures of government decision making) to take advantage of this unprecedented one-time opportunity to widen the street without having to assume the heavy cost of demolishing and paying damages for abutting buildings. They pressured and petitioned members of the City Council for the improvement. They also proposed alternative methods of reducing congestion on the street. These included removing streetcar tracks, widening the street by six feet on both sides instead of ten feet on the north side only, and straightening it by prohibiting stair-cases, bow windows, showcases, and pillars that would be likely to disrupt traffic by projecting over the sidewalks. Most creatively, some who owned property on the street offered to donate land to the city to facilitate land assembly.[75]

The appeals renewed the public's and the City Council's interest in the improvement. The result was that new resolutions calling for the widening of Baltimore Street were introduced in both houses of the City Council, resolutions which requested the widening of the street by six feet on both sides instead of the ten-foot widening on the north side that had been rejected earlier.[76]

This was not enough to save the plan, however. On April 9, the First

Branch approved the resolution to widen the street six feet on both sides. On April 11, however, the Second Branch defeated it.[77]

The defeat in the Second Branch seemingly dealt the improvement a death blow. Burnt District Commission Chairman Swann declared that the question of widening Baltimore Street had been "settled forever." Mayor McLane agreed. Fearing that any further attempts to revive the plan would open a Pandora's box of threats to the other street improvements, McLane declared that the Burnt District Commission would not consider any more proposals to add, amend, or eliminate street widenings and extensions in the burnt district. "This means that Baltimore Street will not be touched," he emphasized.[78]

This did not stop the business and civic leaders who favored the improvement, however. What they did was organize to lobby for the widening in a much more public, much more coordinated, and, they hoped, much more effective way. Their organizational tool was the Municipal Art Society, Baltimore's influential, prestigious, and highly active City Beautiful organization. Hoping to generate a mighty community-wide demand for the widening of Baltimore Street, they called a meeting of the Society to which they invited delegates from business and neighborhood improvement associations from across the city.

They held the meeting on April 16 at the Hotel Rennert. Representatives of twenty-one organizations attended, including men from the Board of Trade, the Merchants and Manufacturers Association, and other smaller local improvement and business associations. The delegates gave the organizers of the meeting precisely what they wanted: a unanimous vote to ask the city to widen Baltimore Street by six feet and one inch on both sides. (The extra inch was added to enable the City Council to reconsider the proposal.)[79]

The organizers of the meeting were explicit about what they hoped to accomplish by this. As Charles Oehm explained in a letter published in the *Baltimore World*, they intended to force the City Council to approve the widening by demonstrating that public opinion was united in favor of the plan. Business organizations "from every section of the city" endorsed the widening at the Hotel Rennert meeting, said Oehm. Confident that eight out of every ten voters in the city favored the improvement, Oehm wrote, "If the City Council represents the vast majority of our people, they will respond to their wish and widen Baltimore Street one way or another." As the editors of the *Morning Herald* put it, the City Council member "who is chosen by popular vote has no right to set up his judgment against that of the majority if he has good evidence to think that a large proportion of the community desires to have what he does not want." For the plan's supporters, of course, the meeting was the evidence of the community's desire.[80]

Their strategy worked. On April 18, both houses of the City Council voted overwhelmingly to ask the Burnt District Commission to prepare a supplementary ordinance providing for the widening of Baltimore Street by six feet and one inch on both its north and south sides.[81]

Like the rally to prevent the Boards of Estimate and Public Improvement from killing the plan to modernize the Inner Harbor, this extraordinary lobbying maneuver represented an attempt to overcome the opposition to an infrastructural improvement by realigning patterns of demand. Having failed to restructure the institutions of government decision making enough to silence the opposition and, no less important, having failed to offset the opposition's voices with their own exhortations, the community leaders favoring the widening of Baltimore Street finally managed to drown out the opposition's demands with the shout of community opinion.

The City Council's overwhelmingly positive response seemed virtually to guarantee achievement of the controversial Baltimore Street improvement. Even opponents agreed that by voting so strongly in favor of asking the Burnt District Commission to prepare the supplemental ordinance, the members of the City Council had "pledged" themselves to approve the widening.[82]

Getting the City Council to approve the supplemental ordinance turned out to be a much more difficult task than the supporters of the improvement had anticipated, however. The additional Council vote gave the opposition one last chance to thwart the plan. They responded by orchestrating a lobbying effort that completely dwarfed the Hotel Rennert meeting.

The problem was that the plan to widen the street on both its north and its south sides affected roughly twice the number of property holders as the original plan to widen the street only on its north side. Worse, it antagonized some of the city's most powerful individuals and corporations.

It continued to draw protests from the principal opponents of the original plan, namely, the owners of the small stores and shops that had lined the north side of the street before the fire. They objected to it because of the tiny sizes of their lots (many of which had unusually shallow depths of only seventy, sixty, even fifty feet and less). They feared that even a six-foot shrinkage of the lots would ruin property values by preventing them from rebuilding in a satisfactory manner.[83]

In addition, however, the new plan now drew the opposition of some very powerful owners of large properties who had not been opposed to the original plan. Unlike the north side, the south side of Baltimore Street contained three large steel frame office buildings: the Continental Trust Building, the International Trust Building, and the Alexander Brown and Sons Building. Because the great fire had only partly destroyed these edifices, leaving their steel frames largely intact, the new plan necessitated extensive and expensive renovations of these standing buildings. As a result, it ran up against the

barriers to infrastructural change caused by the physical durability of structures, making enemies of three powerful corporations that had not been
unfavorably disposed toward the original, one-sided widening. The new plan
also involved the taking of land owned by the *Baltimore American* and the
Baltimore Sun publishing companies. Although they had supported the original widening, now they, too, switched sides, adding their influential voices
to the opposition forces.[84]

Outraged by the City Council's overwhelming endorsement of the new
plan, these well-connected and extremely powerful property owners embarked upon a sophisticated and intense campaign to force the Council to
repudiate the widening. Their strategy was to show the Council that they,
not the widening's supporters, had public opinion and the public interest
behind them.

First, they organized a new citizens' association to counter the Municipal
Art Society and the Hotel Rennert meeting so as to articulate "public"
opposition to the widening. They called the organization the Burnt District
Association and promptly framed a series of public interest organizational
"objectives" to establish its credibility as a public interest group. The objectives included the admirable goals of encouraging the implementation of
public improvements in the burnt district, of encouraging the "wise and
economic expenditure of public money," and of opening up public discussion
of "the questions now before the authorities...which are being crowded
on our City Council without giving that body and the public at large the
necessary data and figures." The Association's leaders used the organization
as a means of mobilizing community opposition to the widening by getting
as many interested property holders, businessmen, and concerned citizens
as possible to join. They claimed that they enrolled five hundred members.[85]

Second, like Chicago's North Siders, the opponents of the widening staged
a march on City Hall to demonstrate the intensity of their opposition as
directly and dramatically as possible. They held the demonstration on the
evening of April 21, during the Burnt District Association's first public
meeting. The leaders of the Association led those in attendance into City
Hall and the First Branch chamber. As a reporter for the *American* put it,
they "marched" down Calvert Street, "invaded and overran the chamber of
the City Council," and then "in brief interviews with the members of the
First Branch...conclusively demonstrated the rashness of the proposed plan
to railroad the ordinance through to enactment."[86]

Third, the leaders of the opposition began a campaign to discredit the
Hotel Rennert meeting. They pursued this course of action by making
speeches and by publishing vitriolic editorials in the *American* and the *Sun*
in which they characterized the meeting's organizers and participants as
"aesthetes" and "outside agitators" who not only did not represent the

interests of the community but did not even represent the interests of the business and neighborhood associations whose delegates attended the Hotel Rennert meeting.[87]

Fourth, they organized a postcard campaign to barrage City Council members with constituent mail expressing opposition to the widening. They printed thousands of postcards with this message:

> Dear Sir – You are earnestly requested to vote against and use your influence to defeat the ordinance now before the City Council as unnecessary and calculated to entail a serious burden upon the taxpayers of Baltimore.

By distributing the cards to workers who labored in factories or lived in precincts that they and their allies owned or controlled, they managed to flood most City Councilmen with hundreds of these communications. Thus they added still more legitimacy to their claim that the community was united in opposition to the widening.[88]

Finally, the leaders of the opposition exerted as much private pressure as they could muster to change City Council members' minds. They consulted personally with the Councilmen. They also dispatched lawyers and professional lobbyists to consult with them on their behalf. According to the pro-widening *World*, they created a lobby that "resembled the old Annapolis days" (before the triumph of progressive reform) in both its membership and its activities. They marshaled many of "the old guard," machine-linked lobbyists, according to the *World*. These included influential and highly respected lawyers such as Bernard Carter and retired, machine-associated government officials such as ex-Mayor Ferdinand C. Latrobe and former Governor William Pinkney White, as well as such less reputable but no less influential ward bosses as William Riggs, "Billy" Hamilton, "Cooney" Dickhart, and other apparently notorious characters. These people discussed the terrible effects the widening would have on property holders and on the city as a whole, working the economic angle for all it was worth, jacking up the price of the improvement day by day. They also made political deals and, according to widespread rumor, offered monetary bribes to City Councilmen in order to "convince" them that voting against the widening of Baltimore Street was in the public interest.[89]

As the *American* explained, the purpose of all these pressure tactics was to show the City Council that the opposition to the widening of Baltimore Street was "as a mountain to a molehill, compared to the selfish few who favor the widening of the street." The strategy succeeded.

The turning point came with the march on City Hall. As one of the leaders of the march, the publisher of the *American*, gleefully declared, the action turned the tables on the Hotel Rennert crowd:

Oh! What a demonstration it was, and oh! how the sledgehammer blows
fell upon the poor little ordinance which the Councilmen had been led
to believe was the popular offspring of a conference of representatives
of businessmen gathered at the hotel [sic] Rennert. Oh! How the truly
and really representative men of the city did show that conference up
last night! They swarmed into the Council Chamber and vehemently
put their stamp of disapproval on the widening project.[90]

As a demand articulation mechanism, the demonstration had obvious
parallels with the North Siders' march on City Hall in opposition to Chicago's
comprehensive fire limits plan. Not surprisingly, however, Baltimore Street's
elite and mostly well-to-do property owners neither viewed themselves, nor
were perceived by others, as radicals engaged in a semi-insurrectionary act.
Their rhetoric shows that they undertook the march in order to regain
authority that they felt was rightfully theirs because of their economic wealth
and high social position. They expected the City Council to heed them and
were outraged by its failure until then to pay them the attention they felt
they deserved. This is evident in the Burnt District Association's statement
of its organizational objectives, which declared that the Association's purpose
was to give "those of our citizens who represent millions of dollars of investment" the opportunity that had so far been denied them to express their
opposition to the widening of Baltimore Street. It is also clear in statements
made by Charles D. Fisher before the demonstration. Fisher complained
that Baltimore Street property owners had not been "properly consulted"
on the issue, "much" to their "disrespect," and had therefore been "re-
pressed." "We are important members of this community, men who have
been known always as men that were worth listening to," he declared with
a proud self-righteousness. The same attitude underlay the *American*'s gleeful
comment about the invasion of the Council chamber: "Oh! how the truly
and really representative men of the city did show that conference up last
night!"[91]

As the ease with which these wealthy property owners reasserted their
domination suggests, their sense of their own importance was shared by
many city officials. The members of the First Branch responded to them by
scheduling not one but three hearings on the subject in the Committee on
Highways: the first on the next night, Friday, April 22, for the opponents
to make their case; the second on the night after, Saturday, April 23, for
the supporters to make their case; and the last on Monday, April 25, to
which both sides were invited.[92]

The people who supported the improvement promptly moved to counteract the opposition's sudden resurgence. They lobbied the Councilmen.
They gathered petitions in favor of the plan. They placed advertisements in
the city's newspapers to mobilize their allies for the April 23 hearing. And

they appeared in force to make their case before the Committee on Highways. They also assailed the leaders of the opposition, attacking them as selfish "croakers," "calamity howlers," and "boodlers and bulldozers" who had supported the widening of Baltimore Street until it affected their own property and now were using unfair, even corrupt, methods to block it.[93]

Now, however, they were on the defensive. Articles in the *American* put them on the spot by pointing out that many of the delegates to the Hotel Rennert meeting had taken a stand in favor of the widening in the name of their respective associations without formal authorization from the members of the association. Embarrassed, some of the associations were forced to disassociate themselves from the meeting, and Mayor McLane found it necessary to disclaim any desire to "dictate" to the City Council.[94]

The tension mounted as both sides formally presented their cases to the Committee on Highways and informally battled for influence in the back rooms and corridors of City Hall. Signs of the opponents' upper hand came in the final April 25 hearing, when the Committee on Highways gave the opposition two hours to make its final arguments and gave supporters only half an hour. The next night, the Committee reported negatively on the improvement. In an act that defied most observers' expectations, however, and that testified to the supporters' as yet unbested lobbying strength, the First Branch proceeded to vote thirteen to zero in favor of substituting the supplemental ordinance for the Committee's negative report. It gave the supporters this taste of victory despite the "graceful flop" of one of the improvement's most stalwart allies to the opposition forces.[95]

The First Branch still had to vote to approve or reject the improvement, however. That vote was postponed until the next night, and the opposition forces intensified their pressure on wavering supporters of the measure. As the *World* commented, "If there were no chips left, then rumor goes for nothing." By 10:00 the next morning, two more supporters had "flopped." By evening, two more had also gone over to the other side. The result was that the First Branch proceeded to reverse itself and kill the widening. Its members voted fourteen to nine to postpone consideration of the ordinance "indefinitely." They also passed several other motions to ensure that the improvement would never be revived.[96]

How far the opposition pushed its struggle to convince City Councilmen to vote against the widening is not clear. It may be that they simply overwhelmed the supporters with their numbers, their social standing, and the power of their arguments. East Baltimore Councilman William H. Weissager's official explanation for his "graceful flop" on the May 26 vote is suggestive in this regard. "Mr. President," the *Evening Herald* reported he told the President of the First Branch, "if de constituents in my ward wot wants de street widened don't come and consult me dat's deir fault if I vode

de odder way. Both sides was presented, and dey don't need no more grace."
In all likelihood, however, the opposition went considerably farther than this,
as Weissager's unofficial explanation for his switch suggests. "Dey got me
bughouse.... Dey come to my house after me last nide," he was reported
to have said.[97]

The conflict culminated in the spectacle of some of the city's most prominent citizens hurling accusations of evildoing at each other, opponents of
the widening condemning those in favor of it for their unfair "lobby methods,"
those in favor condemning those opposed for their politicking and bribery.[98]
Whether the accusations were true or not, the important point is that the
opposition succeeded by whatever means in drowning out the advocates of
the improvement in the demand articulation competition. The accusations
reflected what people thought was happening and were symptomatic of the
terrible divisiveness that paralyzed the infrastructural improvement process
in nineteenth and early twentieth century cities.

Once again, the fundamental problem was the finitude of urban space
and the land use trade-offs that site assembly for street improvements therefore entailed in a congested inner city. What is interesting about the problem
from the viewpoint of this study is that the great fire relaxed the barrier to
site assembly caused by the physical durability of abutting structures enough
to inspire city leaders to stop complaining about their traffic problems and
try to do something about them. Unfortunately, the fire did not, of course,
relax the institutional and political conditions that made consensus building
so difficult, nor did it alleviate the underlying, property-based obstacles to
redevelopment enough to permit the necessary assembly of the land.

The fruitless, bitter conflict over the plan to widen Baltimore Street demoralized the advocates of the burnt district improvement project. It was a
harsh reminder to the McLane administration of the futility of trying to
silence opponents of improvements with institutional and procedural maneuvers that merely denied them formal access to government decision
makers. More disheartening to supporters, it suggested that stifling debate
on a controversial improvement in the early planning stage could only lead
to time-consuming, improvement-defeating excesses of debate and political
wheeling and dealing later. Abashed, Mayor McLane hastily began backtracking from the City Engineer's top-down approach to planning the revisions of the street grade. Declaring that he wanted to know "just what the
people prefer that one should do in the matter of the grade," McLane urged
the City Engineer to hold public hearings on the regrading plan to forestall
multiple hearings and vetoes on the issue by the City Council later. The
Engineer responded by compromising on one of his most unpopular cuts.[99]

Where this demoralized movement toward open planning and compromise
might have taken the burnt district improvements is not clear. Things were

so bad that the retreat might have continued on several fronts. At this point, however, people suddenly remembered the impending May 17 referendum on the $6 million harbor loan. It was barely two weeks away. The work of getting it passed rallied the supporters of the burnt district improvement plans, renewing interest in the seemingly abandoned task of finding ways to circumvent the barriers to environmental redevelopment.

Public opposition to raising the money to pay for the harbor redevelopment rose on many grounds. As usual, the reluctance of taxpayers to vote for anything that might necessitate an increase in the tax rate was a particularly important source of resistance. In addition, however, the measure drew the ire of many ward bosses, who feared that rival politicians might control the disbursement of the funds and the harbor project patronage. It also drew the opposition of labor leaders, who feared that politicians would allocate jobs on the basis of party affiliation, as was the custom in the city, and the opposition of residents of the suburban Annex, who feared that the loan's passage could delay or even prevent passage of their much desired Annex road improvement loan, which was to be considered at some later time. It also rankled the small wholesale merchants who had occupied the warehouses on the old piers. They feared that the redevelopment of the wharves would push them off the waterfront. Finally, the measure faced the problem of public apathy. Most ordinary people had minimal interest in the harbor. They had little idea of what the city's elite merchants, financiers, railroad interests, industrialists, and government officials had planned and even less sense of the benefits the plans might bring. As the advocates of the project realized, their disinterest could kill the loan by giving its many opponents a free hand to vote it down.[100]

The need to overcome the combination of widespread indifference and extensive opposition to the loan and the harbor improvement was the sort of friction that had frequently derailed municipal improvements in the past. Forging a majority community consensus in favor of the loan in less than two weeks' time was an especially serious challenge. The strategy of Baltimore's business, civic, and government leaders was once again to mount a public lobbying campaign to restructure the pattern of community demand. In this case, however, they had to do more than simply create an appearance of community support to impress some City Councilmen. Instead, they had truly to reshape the public's thinking on the matter, and do so very quickly.

Their first move was to organize another association, the Dock Improvement Association, to lobby for the redevelopment. Their second, almost simultaneous move was to call a mass meeting to mobilize and demonstrate popular interest in the improvement. They sent out six hundred invitations to the meeting, summoning representatives from business organizations, neighborhood organizations, and labor organizations from across the city.[101]

They held the meeting two days later, on May 6. Several of the city's most influential business and government leaders addressed the assemblage, including Dock Improvement Association Chairman Frank A. Furst, Mayor McLane, and Congressman Frank Wachter. In order to convince any waverers that the $6 million loan was indeed worth fighting for, the speakers described the terrible condition of the old docks and piers and explained why it was essential to condemn them and reconstruct them according to a bold, new plan. More important, they described the problems threatening the passage of the bond referendum, including the opposition of ward politicians, the Annex problem, taxpayers' fears of higher taxes, and the concern of the working class that jobs would be provided on the basis of political affiliation.[102]

The strategy they outlined had two basic elements. The first was to bally-hoo the many community benefits of the harbor redevelopment and debunk the opposition's arguments against it.[103] The second was to work through the city's ward political clubs, business organizations, neighborhood associations, and labor organizations to communicate the arguments in favor of the loan to the electorate. In essence, explained the officers of the Dock Improvement Association, the plan was to get their message across to Baltimore's mass of workers at the grass-roots level by getting the voters' own leaders to promulgate it. Obtaining the support of labor organizations was especially important because it was the key to getting around ward politicians' opposition.[104]

The meeting apparently served its education-mobilization function very well, for the delegates promptly moved out into the neighborhoods and began proclaiming the Association's message to their friends and to their business, neighborhood, and labor organizations. The groups responded by publicly endorsing both the harbor plan and the $6 million loan. Although there were rumors that both the Democratic and Republican organizations secretly opposed the improvement, even most ward politicians and ward political clubs came out in favor of the loan. By May 12, the papers were publishing long lists of these organizational endorsements, further disseminating and legitimizing the Association's message.[105]

In the meantime, the leaders of the Dock Improvement Association stepped up their own efforts to mobilize support for the bond referendum. They got the Mayor and the City Council to proclaim May 17 a municipal holiday in order to draw attention to the election and make it easier for people to go to their polling places and vote. They placed advertisements in all of the city's newspapers and printed and distributed circulars. They got the editors of the papers to publish editorials and articles which described the need for the improvement and exhorted people to vote in favor of the loan. To calm fears that the project would be used for political patronage, they had the

Mayor promise that the city would distribute jobs without regard to political affiliation. Finally, they organized two more mass meetings to drum up popular support for the bond issue.[106]

They directed the first mass meeting at Baltimore's middle and upper class voters, holding it at Ford's Opera House on May 13. The rally featured speeches by various community leaders and a letter from Cardinal Gibbons strongly endorsing the $6 million loan. The speakers pitched their pleas for the loan to fit their listeners' genteel sensibilities, stressing the public interest to be served and appealing to their patriotism and civic pride.[107]

They directed the second mass meeting at East Baltimore's working class voters. They held this meeting on May 16, the night before the election, in Broadway Market Hall, which was the armory of the First Naval Brigade. It featured performances by the Fourth Regiment Band before the meeting and between speeches, a grand entrance by the Second Ward Active Republicans Club, and speeches by a number of locally popular politicians and government officials. These speakers also pitched their arguments for the loan to suit the interests of their audience. They stressed the jobs that the harbor redevelopment would generate and argued that the improvement might lower taxes.[108]

The Dock Improvement Association's well-orchestrated campaign to sell the loan worked. Baltimoreans went to the polls and approved the bond by a landslide vote of 31,720 to 9,218. They passed it by a large majority of votes in every ward, defeating it in only 11 of the city's 308 precincts.[109]

The $6 million dock improvement loan was not the first multi-million dollar bond issue that Baltimore's business and civic leaders had managed to get the people of the city to approve since the passage of the new City Charter and the ripening and consolidation of the progressive reform movement in Baltimore. In 1902, they had won approval of loans to expand the water supply and to create an electric utility subway system.[110] By the extremity of its hard sell, however, the Dock Improvement Association's intense, many-faceted, sophisticated campaign to win passage of the dock loan attests to the ongoing power of the barrier to environmental redevelopment embodied in the ordinary voter's right to vote down the bond issues needed to finance redevelopment. It also throws light on the convoluted set of problems behind this barrier to change: the rivalries among competing politicians and political organizations; the opposition of negatively affected parties; the electorate's fear of higher taxes; and the public's distrust of the government officials who disbursed the funds and controlled the construction of improvements. It particularly highlights the difficulties civic leaders faced in creating popular, community-wide constituencies for spending multimillion dollar sums to construct public improvements that would directly affect only small sections of the city. These problems had put an end to or seriously delayed most past attempts to enlarge the water supply, construct sewers, bury electric utility wires, build schools and fire houses, pave streets, and make the other improvements in the city's infrastructures needed to adapt its built environment to economic and population growth. They were so endemic and so strong that the advocates of the harbor loan had had to take extraordinary measures to combat them effectively.

As important as it was, however, the passage of the $6 million harbor loan was just one victory in a long war, for serious barriers to change still stood in the way of achieving the burnt district improvements. The fundamental friction in the improvement process remained the problem of site assembly. Even the unlikely achievement of a perfect community consensus in favor of the harbor loan would not have eliminated this barrier to change.

As noted earlier, abutter opposition to the City Engineer's plan to reduce some of the steep street grades in the burnt district and its environs began building the minute Fendall publicly announced what the plans were. His decision in late April to compromise on the controversial cut near the intersection of Fayette and St. Paul Streets mollified some of his critics. It did not calm the several hundred property owners and businessmen who were still threatened by his proposal to level the Lombard Street "hump," however. On May 6, the same day the Dock Improvement Association staged its first mass meeting on the $6 million loan, a large group of these abutters mounted a demonstration to communicate their protests to the members of the City Council. In response, the Committee on Highways held a public hearing in which the angry property holders and businessmen swamped the Councilmen with protests and remonstrances against the hump regrading.[111]

The result of this was that the City Council proceeded to enact a nearly disastrous replay of the conflict and contention that had marked its earlier handling of the street widening plans. There were only two major differences. First, the Second Branch played the role of advocate for the improvement, while the First Branch played the role of foe. Second, the members of the Second Branch held so stubbornly to their position that the hump regrading was an essential part of the whole burnt district project that they almost refused to pass the other grade changes without it, very nearly sacrificing the City Engineer's entire plan. The two Branches were deadlocked over the grade ordinance for over a week, despite several attempts by conference committees to reach a compromise. In the end the Second Branch capitulated, refusing to defeat the entire project and accepting the First Branch's "riddled" ordinance.[112]

It is unclear why the Second Branch suddenly emerged as the patron of improvement, after repeatedly killing so many other burnt district street improvements. Nor is it clear why the First Branch similarly switched sides. What is important, however, is that the episode was another demonstration of the barrier to change posed by the fragmentation of authority in the legislative branch of the city government. Baltimore's City Council had two houses, and it took the veto of just one to defeat an important environmental improvement.

Again, beyond this problem was the much more fundamental problem of site assembly and the scarcity of urban space. Like the abutters who fought the widening of Baltimore Street, the abutters who fought the hump regrading project were the real barriers to redevelopment.

Significantly, abutters were also an obstacle to change after officials had finally agreed to institute improvement plans. The site assembly problems that they caused hampered the execution of the plans, prolonging the improvement process greatly and adding to its expense.

The burnt district improvement enabling act gave the Burnt District Commissioners complete responsibility for acquiring the land for the improvements. The Commissioners had to determine the value of the land in question and then take title to it. The problems they faced in trying to carry out these functions partially explain why the city had done so little to redevelop infrastructures in the decades prior to the fire.

Many things made the work of appraising the land frustrating and time-consuming. The Burnt District Commissioners had to have exact measurements to compute the prices legally. As they discovered to their dismay, however, the city government lacked even "one single map" providing this information. There were no cadastral maps of property lines in the central city. There were not even many plats of individual lots available, and many of those that could be had were out of date. Even the measurements on property deeds were too frequently inaccurate to be of use. This meant that the Burnt District Commissioners had to have all the land involved in the improvements surveyed from scratch.[113]

Giving the individual properties a monetary value was even more troublesome. Most of the land was encumbered by ground rents. In the harbor area it was burdened by a profusion of wharf rights, riparian rights, easements, and other interests. Simply untangling the welter of competing claims was difficult. Worse, in many areas no interests in property had changed hands in years, so past sale prices offered little guide to present values. Aside from sales prices, the only existing sources of information on property values were the city's property tax assessment records. But they were not of much use, either. They had rarely been updated and so were badly undervalued. Even worse, as the Commissioners were outraged to discover, some of the property and property rights were not on the city's books at all. These conditions forced the Commissioners to try to determine the values of the properties through negotiations with the owners, who all too often demanded clearly exorbitant prices in the hope, as the Commissioners said, of making a "killing" off the improvements.[114]

Even worse, the difficulty of appraising land was just a prelude to the even more complicated and prolonged job of taking title to it. Four progressive-minded property owners donated the first four pieces of land the Burnt District Commissioners acquired.[115] Most of the other property owners resisted turning over their property interests and land, however. Many demanded exorbitant prices, ranging from two to a hundred or even a thousand times the assessed valuation. Still others refused to sell out at all.[116]

This forced the Burnt District Commissioners to obtain the properties through condemnation proceedings. Condemnation was a stumbling block because of a provision in the Maryland Constitution which gave property owners the right to retain ownership of property condemned for public improvements until the owners had exhausted their right to appeal the condemnation in the courts. Unlike the laws of most other states, Maryland law did not permit government authorities to take possession of land by means of posting bond before a condemnation proceeding was consummated by the cash payment of damages. As a result, as the editors of the *Baltimore American* put it, there was nothing that the Burnt District Commissioners could do to bring "unreasonable property owners to terms" or to "cut off their unalienable right to 'delay the game' by appeals." By law the city had to wait to take possession of the land "until the gauntlet of the courts" had been run.[117]

Finally, the Burnt District Commissioners had to deal with the so-called strip problem. Their land acquisitions often mutilated building lots, leaving property owners with misshapen or extremely narrow remnants of their original estates. Few owners in these situations owned enough adjoining property to construct first class commercial buildings, and they inevitably found themselves in monopoly confrontations, unable to buy adjoining lots and asking too much to sell their strips to any adjacent owners. This produced a general fear that many leftover strips would be made available for "billboards, peanut or fruit stands, or small, stunted buildings," structures which would blight the entire burnt district. In the past, property owners in this situation had in fact thrown up billboards and constructed deliberately ugly buildings in order to force their neighbors to purchase their strips at exorbitant prices. This increasingly popular form of blackmail still blighted the stretch of Lexington Street east of the Court House that had been widened in the 1890s. Now it created all sorts of tensions that complicated the Burnt District Commission's work.[118]

This morass of impediments to site assembly helps explain why so little had been done to redevelop the harbor in the decades before the fire. The confusion over titles, ground rents, wharf rights, water rights, and easements combined with property owners' insistence on the payment of exorbitant prices for giving up such rights to make it almost impossible for either the city or private individuals to assemble the land needed to modernize the wharves.[119]

What is interesting about the way that city officials carried out the burnt district improvements is that they showed the same willingness to deal with these discouraging barriers in untraditional ways as the planners of the improvements had. As they had during the planning process, the Burnt District Commissioners personally behaved in especially innovative ways.[120] First, they cut red tape to speed up the technical and bureaucratic chores of site assembly. In the past the city had always delayed condemnation proceedings to acquire land for public improvements until all the necessary surveys had been made, all the required damage and benefit plats had been completed, and all the relevant titles had been searched. Now, however, the Commissioners waited for none of these things and began posting the legal notices of their intentions immediately. They also found a way to purchase land before the necessary surveys had been made, by arranging to buy it at certain rates per square foot or front foot, as ultimately determined by the survey, rather than at some fixed price.[121]

They also managed to defuse the "strip" problem. They bought out entire lots if property owners believed that their holdings would be mutilated by partial takings. In order to undercut the bilateral monopoly problem that ordinarily discouraged adjacent owners from buying the parcels and incorporating them into larger properties, they later sold the remnants at public auction. They also helped persuade the members of the City Council to pass a "billboard" ordinance which outlawed the construction of unsightly billboards on the strips.[122]

In perhaps their most innovative step, the Commissioners found a way to get around the State Constitution's time-consuming legal condemnation requirement under certain circumstances. A special provision of the enabling act authorized them to take possession of land before condemnation proceedings were concluded, if they could negotiate the voluntary "surrender" of the land from its owners.[123] This "surrender" clause did not give the Commissioners the means to avoid condemning land when the owners refused to give up their interests voluntarily. Nonetheless, where agreements could be reached, and many were, their use of the clause sped up the pace of execution considerably.[124]

Moreover, in order to use the surrender clause as much as possible, the Commissioners adopted an unusual carrot-and-stick approach to convincing reluctant property owners that it was in their best interest to sell their lots at less than exorbitant prices. The Commissioners tried to appeal to the owners' sense of civic and personal pride by publishing a "Roll of Honor," which listed all the names of the people who voluntarily transferred property to the city by sale or surrender. They also used tax assessments as a "weapon" to scare owners into selling out at acceptable prices. With the judges of the Appeals Tax Court acting as their allies, they threatened the owners with higher taxes based on the inflated prices that the owners demanded the city pay them.[125]

These maneuvers enabled the Burnt District Commissioners to complete the site assembly process in what was, for Baltimore, record time. Site assembly for the city's last major downtown street improvement, the widening of a few blocks of Lexington Street, had taken nearly ten years.[126] It took the Commissioners only nine months to acquire the 443,770 square feet of land needed for the twelve street widenings (excluding a few appeals). And it took them just three years, seven months, and twelve days to take possession of all the land needed for all the improvements, including the sites for all the street widenings and extensions, the construction of the new marketplace, and the redevelopment of the Inner Harbor. What is more, they ended up paying *less* than they had initially expected. They obtained the property for a net cost of roughly $6 million. This was a third less than the $10 million that the City Council had appropriated for the work and a much smaller sum than anyone had originally thought possible.[127]

These innovations put the execution of the improvements on a par with the progressive planning of them. As the nearly four-year time span in which the Commissioners labored to take possession of the land demonstrates, they did not eliminate the underlying barriers to infrastructural redevelopment caused by property owners' unwillingness to give up their property, any more than the McLane administration's institutional and procedural maneuvers had. Nor did they enable the Commissioners to make the changes without depriving many people of their land against their will. Nor did they enable them to make the changes without displacing, or at the very least, inconveniencing many land users. They did, however, enable the Commissioners to undercut property owners' and businessmen's power to delay and block threatening change. This political achievement, as much as the physical achievement of the improvements, was what set the reconstruction of Baltimore off from the reconstructions of Boston and Chicago.

The greater Baltimore

Infrastructural improvement after the great fire did not stop with the improvements proposed by the Citizens' Emergency Committee. Inspired by the clamor of demand for change, city officials made a number of improvements in the burnt district that the Citizens' Emergency Committee had not formally suggested that they make. Significantly, they also began an ambitious $20 million program to modernize, enlarge, and extend public services in the rest of Baltimore.

In the burnt district, the great fire stimulated a chorus of demand for improvement of both the water system and the electrical utility system. The interest in these improvements was so strong and so general that if the Municipal Water Board and the Electrical Subway Commission had not already been working on the projects for several years, the members of the Citizens' Emergency Committee probably would have made them part of its agenda. Instead the demand put pressure on the agencies to step up their work and make the changes immediately.

The downtown electrical utility system was a serious problem and had been for many years. The Fire Department and at least fifteen private companies had been erecting utility poles and stringing wire for so long without coordinating their activities that they had turned Baltimore's downtown streets into a forest of poles and a maze of cross-arms and telephone, telegraph, and electric power wires. The thick meshes of wire had been a constant fire hazard since at least the 1880s, because the wire often broke and sparked and burned. They had also been a hindrance to fire fighting, since in some places they were so dense that they obstructed the flow of water from the fire hoses and entangled and electrically charged ladders so badly as to make them useless. Even the poles had created problems, by serving as unsightly, pedestrian-blocking "encumbrances to the sidewalks."[128]

City officials had begun trying to get the electric streetcar and utility companies to move the wires underground in the mid-1880s. When their efforts failed, they got state authorization to undertake the task themselves in 1892. They did not manage to obtain authority to issue the first bonds to pay for the work until 1896, however. The voters did not approve the bonds until November 1896, and work did not begin until February 1901. By the time of the great fire in 1904, the city had laid conduits for the system in only a few blocks in the center of the city (including a portion of the burnt district), and it had removed only two hundred and thirty of the thousands of poles in the business center.[129]

The barriers to change that accounted for this slow pace of progress ranged from the opposition of the powerful transportation and utility companies whose poles and wires had to be moved, to taxpayers' unwillingness to raise taxes to pay for such improvements, to the physical difficulty of planning and constructing municipally owned electric subway systems. As bad as the political problems were, the physical problems were in some ways worse. The Subway Commission faced a twofold predicament in trying to develop the new system. First, the Subway Commissioners had to reorganize and systematize the power grids of a large number of competitive private companies (some no longer in existence) that had over the years "lost all semblance of a system" because of the rapid development of electric streetcar railroads, the frequent relocation of power stations, and the lack of any common engineering standards. To complicate matters, they had to do this under the constraint of many companies' reluctance to provide necessary information and insistence that they had the right to construct their own conduits. Second, the Commissioners had to introduce the new system to an underground Baltimore that was, in the central city at least, almost as congested as the surface of the city. The question was, as the Commissioners put it, "how to provide room under the streets for additions to gas, water, electrical and sewer service," when most of the space was already filled. The only answer was to fit all of the underground infrastructures into an integrated system. This involved rearranging the conduits of a host of other municipal agencies and private utility companies, which needless to say, compounded the already severe economic, political, and engineering difficulties of rationalizing and burying the electric utility wires.[130]

The great fire did not eliminate any of these difficulties. It did, however, at least temporarily solve the problem of removing the poles and wires in the burnt district by burning them down. The Electrical Subway Commissioners moved to make this situation permanent by prohibiting the erection of new poles and the stringing of new overhead wires in the district for any purpose except street railways. Despite pleas by several utility companies that temporary poles and wires be allowed, the Commissioners stuck to their ban.[131]

The fire also cured the "mysterious paralysis" that had kept city officials from forcing utility companies to take down their poles and wires in the district where the subway system had already been constructed.[132] The companies had not done much to remove their infrastructures from the areas where they were no longer needed, and the fire had not done all of their work for them. As a result, on October 4, Building Inspector Preston issued a warning that in three days his Department would begin cutting the offending wires down. Three days later, amid editorial cries that the best way to remove the wires was "to take them down, and do it at once.... to do it and not talk about it,"[133] the Department actually began cutting the wires. It was not the first time that officials had threatened to do this. But it was the first time they had followed through with their threat. Oddly enough, the Building Inspector had invited utility company officials to a hearing to discuss the new policy, but none of the officials appeared, apparently because they assumed that the warning was just another idle threat. They protested strenuously once the wires began coming down. Preston and the Mayor held firm, however, and the wires stayed down.[134]

The result of this aggressiveness was that in less than ten months' time, the city managed to eliminate permanently thousands of overhead wires and 486 poles from the burnt district and a part of the surrounding area. The Electrical Subway Commissioners also laid 683,310 new feet of main and distribution conduits in just two years' time, which was 64,742 feet more than the 618,568 feet that had been constructed in the five years since the first conduits in the city were laid in 1899.[135]

The mere opportunity for environmental redevelopment did not guarantee that officials would embrace new attitudes toward getting things done, however, even in progressive Baltimore. The most notable laggard was Alfred M. Quick, the Chief Engineer of the city's Water Board. Unlike the Building Inspector and the Electrical Subway Commissioners, Quick responded very slowly and reluctantly to demands that the water system be improved for fire fighting purposes, notwithstanding the recent disaster of the fire. In fact, he initially responded to suggestions that improvements be made with angry denials that there were any problems with the water supply in the business center at all, denials that prompted criticism of his "supersensitiveness" and unwillingness to take "timely and proper criticism."[136] His less than enthusiastic reaction to the demand for change was symptomatic of the problems and constraints that had prevented the introduction of more water and hydrants in the district earlier, problems that the fire had plainly failed to rectify.

As in Boston and Chicago, it was the Fire Department, not the public, that was most interested in achieving improvements in water service for fire fighting purposes. Unfortunately, like its counterparts in pre-fire Boston and Chicago, Baltimore's Fire Department had had no authority to take the action necessary to satisfy its needs. This power rested with the city's Water Board, an autonomous agency that, like Boston's Cochituate Water Board and Chicago's Board of Public Works, spent most of its time and money developing new water supplies and extending water service to the periphery of the city. Baltimore's Fire Commissioners had repeatedly complained about the Water Board's lack of interest in their needs. With but a few exceptions, however, the Water Board had stubbornly refused to listen to the Fire Commissioners' demands for over thirty years. It was not until 1901 that the Board had finally begun to heed the Fire Department's calls and embarked upon a major program to modernize the distribution system in the central city. Armed with a $2 million loan, it then began cutting out old three-, four-, and six-inch mains, laying larger new mains, and establishing new fire hydrants in the central business district.[137]

Making up for more than thirty years of neglect was an immense task, however. As of 1902, there were still only 2,703 fire hydrants in the entire city, only 238 more than the 2,375 that Boston had had in 1872, the year of the great Boston fire. And as of April 21, 1904, water pressure in the business center was still only a "steady" forty to fifty pounds, less than what it had been in Chicago's near South Side slums before the modernization of that city's water distribution system after the second great Chicago fire in 1874.[138]

The great fire did not erase the tension between the Water Board and the Fire Department. It did inspire the Water Board to turn its attention to improving the mains and hydrants in the badly neglected manufacturing district along East Baltimore's waterfront.[139] Strangely enough, however, it did not prompt any concerted effort by the Board to modernize the system in the burnt district. Perhaps because he had already laid a few new mains and erected a few new hydrants there, Chief Engineer Quick refused to acknowledge the weaknesses of the system in the area, notwithstanding the fire's obvious demonstration of them. In fact, at one point, he proudly cited the forty to fifty pounds of pressure in the district as evidence that nothing was amiss.[140]

Not until 1905, after many more complaints by the Fire Department, did Quick finally initiate a major program to upgrade hydrants and distribution mains and pipes in the burnt district. And even then the tension between the Board and the Fire Department remained. Chief Engineer Quick continued to refuse to acknowledge publicly that the improvements were needed to redress the weaknesses of the system for fighting fires. Instead, he described the new installations as products of the Board's pragmatic response to "the necessity of changing our distribution system in the Burnt District because of the widening of streets and changing of the grades there," which, he implied, necessitated the renovation of the system anyway.[141]

Quick's reluctance to redevelop the water distribution system in order to protect the business center from future conflagrations serves to highlight the personal and political factors that mediated Baltimore's progressive response to its disaster. Significantly, however, Quick's negative attitude was unusual. Most city officials embraced the goal of improvement as eagerly as the members of the Citizens' Emergency Committee, Mayor McLane, and the Electrical Subway Commissioners. The result of this was that they completely transformed the infrastructural face of the burnt district. Besides instituting the street, market, harbor, electric utility, and water service improvements, they outlawed brick sidewalks, prohibited open street and sidewalk drains, replaced all the old cobblestone pavements, and began the construction of a sewerage system in the district.[142]

City officials also embarked upon an ambitious project to establish, extend, and modernize infrastructures in the city as a whole, improvements that were more vast and, if anything, even more impressive than the remarkable improvements they instituted in the burnt district. Baltimore's progressive government, business, and civic leaders had been trying to achieve a wide range of public improvements in the rest of the city for years and, in many cases, decades prior to the great fire. These included a modern sewerage system, new schools, new fire houses, new parks, new highways, and paved streets. At first they feared that they would have to postpone them because of the cost of financing the burnt district improvements.[143] The success that the Dock Improvement Association had had in mobilizing popular support for the $6 million harbor loan inspired them to push ahead, however. As a result, they "struck the iron while it was still hot" and succeeded in achieving the improvements in short order.

Ironically, Clay Timanus, the man who had presided over the defeat of five of the burnt district street improvements in the Second Branch, led the campaign to win approval of these projects. He did so in the capacity of Mayor of the city, an office he assumed after Democratic Mayor Robert McLane committed suicide on May 29, apparently in response to a combination of family problems and the strain of managing the reconstruction and redevelopment of the burnt district. The succession put the Republicans in control of the city government. It is indicative of the breadth of support for the goals of environmental redevelopment, however, that it did not deflect the course of municipal improvement in any way. It merely put Timanus in charge of directing the improvement process, a role that, as it turned out, he grasped as eagerly as had McLane.[144]

Two factors stood in the way of building sewers and highways and instituting the other city-wide improvements, as they had for years. One was getting the state legislature to pass the enabling legislation. The other, more serious obstacle was getting the voters to approve the necessary bond issues. To hurdle these barriers, Timanus held a "Municipal Improvement Conference" on December 5, to which he invited representatives of the City Council and thirty-nine business, trade, and neighborhood associations. The Municipal Improvement Conference was modeled on the Citizens' Emergency Committee and the Dock Improvement Association. Timanus used it not only to draw public attention to his plan but also to flesh out the details of the improvements, to mobilize grass-roots support for them, and to overcome the sectional and political rivalries that had traditionally obstructed the implementation of general improvement projects. He appointed delegates to various committees to map out in detail what the city ought to do. Then he sent the delegates out to proselytize on behalf of the proposals.[145]

The newspapers labeled the campaign "the movement for a Greater Baltimore." Like the Dock Improvement Association's campaign to sell the public the $6 million loan, it was one part organization and one part propaganda, the leaders' goal being to convince the public of the desirability of the improvements. Since two of the biggest stumbling blocks to instituting ambitious public improvements in Baltimore had always been and still were their great cost and taxpayers' unwillingness to vote for projects that would raise taxes, the key to achieving the plans was finding a way to persuade voters that they could afford to pass the bonds. The solution developed by the Conference leaders was to propose that the improvements be financed not by taxes, as was the custom in the city, nor by relatively short-term loans, as was more and more the practice, but by long-term fifty-, seventy-five, or one-hundred-year loans. This enabled supporters to argue, innovatively and persuasively, that a large part of the costs of the projects would be distributed to "posterity," which they insisted would be "in a better position to meet its apportionment of the improvement assessment than the present generation." Members of the Conference's finance committee also figured out ways to juggle city accounts in order to lower the costs of the improvements on paper. This enabled them to advocate the plans, as the Dock Improvement Association had so successfully advocated the harbor redevelopment, as great and necessary public improvements that taxpayers would not actually have to pay for, that "would not add to taxes" but would "on the contrary, when completed . . . add to the taxable basis of the city," and so possibly even reduce taxes and save them money.[146]

The delegates invited to the Conference took this message to the people of the city. By their very participation in the Conference, they also spread the word that Baltimoreans were united in favor of the plans, that, as the editors of the *Sun* put it, they were joined together "for a long pull, a strong pull, a pull all together" to achieve the improvements.[147]

Once again the hard sell worked. In 1906 and in the next several years the state legislature passed a series of enabling acts authorizing the city to issue its credit for the construction of the improvements. More important, the voters of Baltimore proceeded to approve the necessary bond referendums. As a result, the city implemented nearly $20 million worth of new infrastructures in addition to the burnt district improvements, including the construction of a modern sewerage system, the paving of the city's cobblestone streets, the opening and paving of streets and other improvements in the Annex, the construction of new schools and fire houses, the enlargement of the park system, the enlargement of the water supply, the enclosure of Jones Falls in a sewer and the construction of a wide boulevard above it, the establishment of a central system of wholesale and retail markets, and many other, lesser undertakings.[148]

Thus did the great Baltimore fire both directly and indirectly stimulate infrastructural improvement across the city, not just by creating a physical opportunity for environmental redevelopment but also by galvanizing the spirit of progressive reform and thus creating new attitudes toward public policy making and new techniques for achieving change. After thirty years of frustrating failure, the city's business and government leaders had finally found a way to circumvent some of the frictions that had been holding back improvement.

Structural redevelopment

Like the great fires of Chicago and Boston, the great fire of Baltimore destroyed a large number of buildings, in addition to obliterating many infrastructures. And like the other two fires, it consumed many structures that were antiquated tinderboxes. Many of the area's oldest, most unsafe buildings had been crowded along the Inner Harbor, where dilapidated wooden sheds and warehouses had covered ancient wharves. The whole district, however, had contained old brick structures that were burdened with wooden roofs and rear attachments. There had even been assemblages of detached wooden sheds, wooden stables, and wooden houses in the center of some centrally located blocks at the rear of more substantial buildings. Old fire-vulnerable buildings had lined even the most prestigious and centrally located business streets, newly constructed steel frame office buildings and well-built brick edifices butting up against smaller buildings that were old, in some cases dilapidated, and made partially of wood.[149]

As in Chicago and Boston, the destruction ignited an explosion of demand that property owners take advantage of the disaster to replace their ruined buildings with bigger, more modern, much safer structures. As in the other cities, the movement to improve the buildings crystallized into a movement to reform the city's building law. And here again, what made Baltimore's response to the demand and opportunity for change distinctive was the ability of the people of Baltimore to circumvent some of the barriers to change that had stymied past improvement efforts.

Baltimoreans did all they could to ensure that the revision of the building code would not be handled in the usual manner. First, rather than let the City Council once again fumble the task of drawing up a new and better building code, Building Inspector Preston drew up a new code himself without input from a hearing process and presented it to the members of the Council as a *fait accompli*. Second, the progressive leaders of the City Council aggressively pushed the ordinance through the Council without holding public hearings. The members of both Branches of the City Council passed the new law in Preston's form on March 18, just a little over a month after the great fire.[150]

The new code was extremely strict. It covered all buildings in the central business area, imposing more rigorous though still comparatively minimal strictures on buildings fewer than eighty-five feet in height while requiring that all buildings more than eight-five feet high be totally "fireproof through-out" and prohibiting construction of any building more than one hundred and seventy-five feet in height.[151]

Needless to say, both the strictness and the swift passage of the new code stand in sharp contrast to the handling of similar codes after the great fires in Boston and Chicago. This is not the only thing that made the process of structural redevelopment in Baltimore distinctive, however. Another factor was the availability of a modern construction technology for building fireproof steel frame and reinforced concrete structures. This technology was still in its infancy – but it existed. The Baltimore fire did not exacerbate confusion in the architectural and engineering communities as to the worth of such technology, as the Boston fire had. Instead it dispelled confusion. Architects and engineers rushed to Baltimore to investigate the ruins. Their research showed that both reinforced concrete and structural steel encased in portland cement or hollow tile had fire-resistant qualities that were superior to those of such traditional materials as brick. Their findings received a great deal of publicity in local newspapers and business journals, as well as architectural publications. This information not only persuaded many property owners to use the new materials and technology to make their buildings safer but also encouraged them to use them to make their buildings bigger and taller, by demonstrating that skyscrapers could be safely built.[152]

These technological advances combined with the quick passage of the strict new building code to put the structural redevelopment of Baltimore's burnt district on a different footing than the structural redevelopment of either Boston or Chicago. Needless to say, however, here again, they did not put reconstruction on a completely different footing. Serious barriers to structural improvement remained.

One major problem was the cost of using the new technology to construct buildings that would meet the requirements of the strict new building law. The requirement that all buildings more than eighty-five feet tall be completely fireproof, or in the language of the code "fireproof throughout," was vague, but Building Inspector Preston meant the requirements to be taken literally to the extent that modern building technology permitted. Neither the owners of downtown property nor the members of the City Council had apparently appreciated this at the time the Council passed the ordinance. By mid-May, however, Preston had made the significance of the term "fire-proof throughout" clear. The owners and would-be owners of tall buildings discovered that the rule outlawed all wood in buildings over eight stories high, including wood in interior and exterior window frames and interior and exterior trim, partitions, floors, and doors. They also discovered that the rule outlawed the use of ordinary glass. In other words, they found out that the ordinance mandated the use of concrete or tile floors, as well as metal doors, window frames, and partitions, in addition to wired glass in all interior and exterior windows. Most of the prospective owners of downtown sky-scrapers were apparently willing to make use of fireproof steel frame con-struction technology to erect their tall buildings, this being the only feasible way to construct them. The requirement that they use metal and other "fireproof" materials in their doors, floors, windows, and trim was unac-ceptable to them, however. Whether fairly or unfairly, they considered these rules to be "prohibitively expensive."[153]

Angered, powerful property holders like the owners of the Merchants' National Bank, the *Baltimore American*, the Continental Trust Company, the Equitable Building, and the Calvert Building began to protest against the strictures of the new law to the Mayor and the members of the City Council. Like the opponents of the plan to widen Baltimore Street (some of whom were one and the same, of course), they had enough influence in City Hall to make their protests effective. The response they got was much like the responses that government officials had made to similar protests in Chicago and Boston. Baltimore's officials began backing off from their insistence on strict new controls, only in this case after, rather than before, they had enacted a new building code. Preston soon retreated from his requirement that no wood or ordinary glass be used in any interior partitions, doors, floors, trim, or windows. When he continued to insist that all exterior window frames and doors be made of metal and that all exterior windows be fitted with wired glass, City Councilman John E. Semmes introduced an ordinance to repeal these offending rules. Semmes's code specifically permitted the use of ordinary glass in all windows and the use of wood in all "sub and surface floors, window and door frames, sashes, standing finish, such as architectural trim, handrails for stairs, . . . and for isolated furring blocks embedded in the plaster." The City Council passed this new law on June 17.[154]

The amendments gave property holders most of what they wanted but in the process increased the risk of fire in the business center. Unfortunately for the property holders, however, the loopholes did not eliminate all the economic problems that made it difficult for them to build the tall buildings which many of them wanted. Not only did ambitious commercial real estate developers still have to deal with the high cost of obtaining the credit, materials, and labor needed to finance the construction of towering twelve- and fifteen-story buildings, but they also had to handle serious site assembly problems.[155]

Steel frame skyscrapers could be built on single lots because the stress resistance of the slender steel skeleton made it possible to carry the height and weight of such a building in a small space. The problem was that few people wanted to build this way, because such structures would be very tall and skinny – which to many minds meant wasteful and ugly. This brought ambitious real estate developers face to face with the dilemma of convincing adjoining landowners, ground rent owners, and other title holders to sell their property at mutually acceptable prices. Although some property owners wanted to sell out in order to avoid having to rebuild themselves, most exploited their monopoly position in the real estate market in the usual way, by greedily jacking up their asking prices whenever they believed that they had a serious buyer at their mercy (to the dismay and sometimes cynical clucking of the press, not to mention the frustration of the prospective buyers). Others refused to sell out at all. The newspapers reported that ground rent owners were especially recalcitrant, as one might have expected. Because some real estate developers insisted on building only on land which they owned in fee, the obstinacy of the ground rent owners stopped the construction of some tall buildings even when developers had been able to obtain deeds to the land in question.[156]

Those developers who were especially devoted to the idea of constructing large, tall structures tried not to let these assembly problems stop them. The managers of the powerful Baltimore and Ohio Railroad, for example, tried every trick they could think of in order to assemble a large enough piece of property at a reasonable price at the corner of Baltimore and Charles Streets so that they could erect a huge fifteen-story office building there for their company headquarters. Their efforts included using out-of-town agents to acquire the land, spreading rumors that the company intended to build their new headquarters elsewhere, and, when all else failed, arranging special long-term leases with hold-outs so that they could use the land even when stubborn property owners refused to sell. In this case, they succeeded in their endeavors. Needless to say, however, many property owners could not go to such lengths and so had to settle for constructing buildings that were much smaller than they had originally planned.[157]

In short, a number of constraints still limited what property owners could do to take advantage of the opportunity the fire had provided for structural improvement, despite reform and technological progress. As a consequence, like property owners in Chicago and Boston, property owners in Baltimore's burnt district constructed hundreds of new buildings that were for the most part larger, more modern, and safer than those the fire had ruined and yet not quite as large, good, or safe as they, their tenants, Building Inspector Preston, and other outside observers might have liked.

The new buildings in the burnt district differed from the old ones in four important respects, some negative, some positive. First of all, they were safer than the old buildings. Although buildings fewer than eight stories tall were considerably less than completely fireproof because of the looseness of the new building code, and although those more than eight stories tall were less fireproof than Building Inspector Preston's original building code revision would have required, the new buildings were far more fireproof than those they replaced. Gone were the wooden sheds and other frame buildings that had covered the old piers in the Inner Harbor. Gone also were the wooden buildings that had filled the backs of many lots in the burnt district proper, as well as the old wooden roof-top structures, frame siding, wooden porches, wooden cornices, and other flammable attachments that had decorated many brick buildings before the fire. In their place were hundreds of substantial brick structures. There was also a dramatic increase in the number of steel frame buildings that the Sanborn Insurance Company deemed completely fireproof. According to Sanborn Insurance atlases, property owners erected over one hundred fireproof steel frame buildings of various sizes in the years following the fire. These structures took up nearly a third of the area of the burnt district proper.[158]

Second, many of the new buildings were taller and larger than those they replaced. By February 7, 1906, property owners had constructed fifteen buildings with ten stories or more, eight of which contained the building-code-mandated maximum of sixteen stories. True, most buildings were still in the three- to five-story range, and there were not as many skyscrapers as real estate developers would have liked. Costs had forced the Gaither estate, for example, to abandon its plans for a ten-story office building in favor of an eight-story building. Costs had also forced the Maryland Casualty Company to give up its plans for an eleven-story building and erect a three-story structure instead. Nevertheless, on average, buildings in the burnt district were larger than those they replaced. The average amount of floor space rose from less than 7,200 square feet of space per building before the fire to over 9,900 square feet in September 1906.[159]

Third, the buildings contained many structural and architectural amenities that the old buildings had lacked. Many contained larger, better arranged, better ventilated rooms. Many also had the much larger windows that steel frame construction made possible. Businessmen liked the windows because they let in more sunlight and so made better display cases for their wares.[160]

Finally, there were far fewer buildings in the burnt district after the fire than there had been before it. In the part of the district north of the waterfront, the number dropped from 1,343 to 702, as of September 1906. The area was only eighty-five percent rebuilt at the time, but observers predicted with confidence that the number of buildings would remain under 800 after the area was completely rebuilt. On the wharves the drop was even more drastic, over a hundred small, mostly wooden structures giving way to only 31 buildings of mixed character and a great deal of vacant space.[161]

The decrease in the number of buildings was partly the consequence of the increase in the number of buildings that covered more than one lot. In the harbor area it was also the result of the way the city handled occupancy of the wharves after the harbor improvements had been completed. The Harbor Board leased all but one of the new piers to the highest bidders, enabling a small number of large transportation firms to bid them away from the multitude of small businessmen who had owned and tenanted the many buildings that had crowded the wharves before the fire, the city retaining control of only one pier, which became a public pier that was off limits to regular development as well.

The biggest cause of the decrease, however, was the taking of land for street improvements. As in Boston, environmental improvements to benefit the users of downtown streets were made at the expense of the vested interests of the users and owners of downtown buildings. The Burnt District Commissioner took more than fifteen acres of land out of private hands for street and market improvements and another sixty-five acres of property for dock improvements. In the process nearly seven hundred lots were permanently lost to property owners for use in building structures.

The result of this was that while the new buildings were on average bigger than those they had replaced, they nonetheless provided much less floor space overall. The total amount of floor space in the burnt district shrank by close to one-third. Before the conflagration, the structures in the burnt district proper had contained 9,746,000 square feet of floor space. As of September 1906, however, the new buildings in this area provided only 6,958,460 square feet of space, a loss of nearly 3 million square feet, to which must be added the indeterminate losses that resulted from the drastic reduction of buildings on the wharves along the Inner Harbor.[162] As in Boston and Chicago, only the territorial enlargement of the central business district, only the commercial redevelopment of surrounding mixed and residential areas, could have produced enough additional floor space to bring about an increase in the total amount of space available for business. And as in Boston this did not happen, because the fire did not cross the boundaries of the central business district to destroy residential buildings in the surrounding areas, as the great fire of Chicago had.

Spatial change

Finally, like the great fires of Chicago and Boston, the great fire of Baltimore affected business location patterns. The maps in Figures 8.4 and 8.5 show the spatial organization, before and after the fire, of several trades that were concentrated in the area of the burnt district before the fire took place. The trades include the city's banks, wholesale drygoods merchants, and retail jewelers.[163]

The maps provide a glimpse of the sorts of spatial reorganization the

Figure 8.4.

area's office, retail, and light wholesale trades experienced during reconstruction. What is interesting is that compared with the dramatic spatial
changes that took place among businesses in Chicago and Boston, these
trades experienced only very incremental movement. A few jewelers migrated
to the north and west. Most, however, continued to cluster on Baltimore
Street within a block or two of Charles Street, the same area in which they
had been concentrated before the fire. A few drygoods dealers also dispersed
to the north and west. Most continued to center around Baltimore Street
between Hanover and Howard Streets, however, where they, too, had been
concentrated before the fire. Only the banks experienced any notable spatial
reorganization, and even they exhibited considerable geographical stability
in the midst of change. The banks were clustered before the fire in two sub-
centers of agglomeration, the largest and most densely concentrated of which
was on the eastern side of the burnt district between Baltimore, Lombard,

Figure 8.5.

South, and Fredrick Streets. This center shifted slightly west after the fire, with most banks leaving the area between Gay and Fredrick Streets but remaining in the area around South and Commerce Streets. Most of the other banks were scattered about in another center on the western side of the burnt district and the adjacent areas beyond the northern and western boundaries of the district. After the fire, most of these banks moved out of the burnt district altogether in order to join the other banks in the adjacent area.

According to the available evidence, this pattern of slight dispersion into the surrounding areas and slight movement within the burnt district itself was the general pattern of spatial change during reconstruction. For example, retailers engaged in the sale of drygoods and women's clothing continued to concentrate outside the burnt district around Lexington Street west of Charles Street. Retailers engaged in the sale of menswear, art supplies, books, and similar goods continued to concentrate inside the burnt district along Baltimore Street. The part of the burnt district south of Baltimore and west of Fredrick Streets remained a mixed office and wholesale center, while the part of the district east of Fredrick Street around Marsh Market Space remained a grocery and wholesale produce center.[164]

Only one group of businesses experienced radical spatial change, and that was the large group of mixed warehousing and wholesale firms that had concentrated around the waterfront, on or adjacent to the wharves in the Inner Harbor. As noted earlier, after redeveloping this area, the city leased the space on the new wharves to a few large transportation companies, despite having promised to make the space available to the small wholesale and warehouse firms that had clustered there before the fire. This forced the small companies to scatter to railroad sidings and wharves in South and East Baltimore.[165]

With this one notable exception, however, the pattern of land use in downtown Baltimore was generally quite stable during reconstruction. It is more difficult to describe the location decision making that led to this stability than to describe the decision making that led to the spatial changes that took place in Boston and Chicago, because newspapers in Baltimore did not follow the process of spatial change as closely as papers and journals in the other two cities did, probably because not much was happening which was worthy of comment. The newspapers did discuss the subject in considerable detail in the first few months after the fire, however. This was because, ironically, at that time many people believed that business was standing on the threshold of exciting spatial transformation.

Most of this anticipation centered on the future of the city's retail center. The expectation was that Baltimore Street would cease to be the city's premier retail shopping street. Baltimore Street had been the center of the city's retail trade for decades. Movement out of the area had begun several years before the fire, many womenswear shops, for example, having already left for an area to the north along Lexington Street between Charles and Eutaw Streets. Now that the fire had uprooted the remaining firms, observers predicted that the migration would accelerate, purveyors of menswear, books, and other retail goods following the womenswear shops to the greener pastures to the west and north until they had all gone. A *Baltimore American* reporter confidently declared two weeks after the fire, "It is generally agreed that Baltimore Street as a shopping thoroughfare may be finally and completely doomed."[166]

Several factors accounted for the widespread presumption that far-reaching and permanent spatial change was in the offing for the city's retailers. First, the new shopping district held powerful attractions to the retailers who had not yet moved. The retailers who had stayed on Baltimore Street were well aware of the migration of their colleagues and, more important, their colleagues' customers. The movement had upset the status quo, making the retailers psychologically more receptive to the idea of a transfer, while the success of the new shopping center had given them some economic incentives to move, incentives that were perhaps stronger now that they had to consider seriously the possibility of making temporary moves permanent.[167]

Second, Baltimore Street suffered powerful negative externalities. All the conditions that inspired people to demand that the street be widened constantly impinged on the retailers' stores, encouraging them to leave the area. Heavy, noisy streetcar and vehicular traffic; overcrowded, difficult to navigate, narrow sidewalks; and an increasing number of view-obstructing, shadow-throwing skyscrapers were making their establishments less attractive places to shop. As a writer in the *Sun* commented, this was causing retailers to experience "enforced change," putting them under pressure to move elsewhere whether they wanted to leave the street or not.[168]

Finally and, it would seem, most tellingly, a number of retail firms were publicly searching for permanent new quarters off of Baltimore Street. Like the Fields, Farwells, and Coolbaughs of Chicago in the aftermath of the great Chicago fire, several of the retail businessmen who had been burnt out of Baltimore Street purchased buildings or acquired long leases on stores located on other streets, apparently in the hope of sparking spatial change. They announced their intention to resettle permanently in their new locations with great fanfare, lending credence to the idea that the last retailers on Baltimore Street were deserting the old center of the retail trade in mass. This created a sense of movement that, as a writer in the *Sun* pointed out, made it "reasonable to conjecture that, even after the burnt wastes are rebuilt, the business area will be largely expanded."[169]

As it turned out, of course, the "general" assumption that Baltimore Street was "doomed" as a shopping street was a mistake. The street remained an important retail center. In fact, some of the firms that had bought or acquired long-term leases on property on other streets ultimately decided to return. The owners of the jewelry firm Hennegan, Bates & Company, for example, bought a large new store at 318 North Charles soon after the fire and declared their expectation that North Charles would become the "retail center for jewelry at least." Just two years later, however, the company was back on Baltimore Street, a few doors down from where it had been before the fire.[170]

It is not completely clear why the early expectations of change proved to be wrong. It is likely, however, that after pondering for several weeks the prospect of a permanent transfer to some new location, many retailers realized that they had deep psychological and economic ties to Baltimore Street that they did not want to break. Some had probably been there for so many years that they found it difficult to move. Others, especially those involved in the sale of men's clothing, hats, and shoes, no doubt remembered that they had a ready market in the mostly middle class men who worked in nearby offices and stores.

As previously noted, the retail district had already undergone a period of spatial reorganization; it may well be that through the natural evolutionary process of ordinary location decision making, retailers had before the fire already sufficiently overcome the frictions in the process of spatial redevelopment to have adjusted to the geographical stress of growth. If this is true, however, many people nonetheless expected that retailers would continue deserting Baltimore Street, including some retailers who were certain enough of this to buy or take long leases on quarters elsewhere for themselves. These expectations suggest that there was no general recognition that a permanent new land use equilibrium had indeed been established before the fire, something that again indicates that there was a complicated collective psychological dimension to the process of spatial change which transcended any "objective" measure of economic self-interest.

Whatever the case, as in Boston and Chicago, the former occupants of the burnt-out buildings were not the only people whose decision making helped determine the course of spatial change. As might be expected, the talk of a mass desertion of Baltimore Street by retail firms alarmed property owners, especially those whose small lots were suitable only for the construction of small shops and stores. In the hope of countering talk of the attractions of other streets, they began agreeing to rebuild to meet their tenants' special needs. They also began publicly boosting Baltimore Street, ballyhooing its advantages as a shopping center and bad-mouthing the alternatives. Some even joined in calling for the widening of the street, arguing that this would seal its importance as a first class retail thoroughfare. Others fought the widening all the more strenuously, fearing that it would hasten the street's decline.[171]

Significantly, there are no reports of property owners on other streets offering incentives such as low rents to lure retailers from Baltimore Street. If they had, as property owners in Chicago had, they might have caused a much more radical spatial reorganization of the retail district. Because they had not, however, the efforts by Baltimore Street property owners to keep retailers on the street helped create an excitement about it that ultimately transformed the feeling that Baltimore Street was "doomed" into a pervasive sense that it would become, as one paper put it, "an even greater shopping center than in the past." This helped bring the street's burnt-out retailers flocking back, despite its many disadvantages.[172]

The resurrection of Baltimore Street as a retail center stands in odd contrast to the spatial reorganization that affected the city's banks. In this case, observers initially predicted that there would be *no* spatial change. In late February, the editors of the *American* proclaimed that it had become "a practical certainty" that "every" financial institution affected by the fire would return to its old location. They asserted this with the same assurance as that with which as a writer in the same paper had earlier asserted that Baltimore Street was "doomed" as a retail thoroughfare. "The financial center will not change, and the visitor a year to two hence ... will be able to find the same institutions in the same locations as formerly, although in newer and handsomer buildings."[173]

Was the editorial in the *American* an accurate reflection of the banks' location decision making at the time? Or was it a promotional effort of some type, an attempt to encourage the banks to return to their old locations, or perhaps a call to property owners to do what was needed to lure them back to their old sites? There is, unfortunately, no way to tell. It certainly is not clear why the banks deserted their old stand around Gay and Fredrick Streets while remaining in force just two blocks west on South Street. They may have been pulled this short distance to the west by the equally mild shift of retail, wholesale, and office businesses in this direction. Or it may be that they were responding to the behavior of their landlords. In any case, they did desert part of their old center, despite predictions that they would remain there, but they did not move very far. A significant number of banks continued to cluster in the southeast corner of Baltimore's central business district, despite the growing importance of business on streets that were many blocks to the north and west.

If it is impossible to know exactly what the burnt district bankers felt about the desirability of migration, it is obvious how the wharfside wholesalers felt. They vehemently opposed the idea of a change of base. Waterfront warehousers and wholesalers tried to stop the redevelopment of the Inner Harbor precisely because they feared that the improvement project would permanently displace them. They protested against the scheme when it was in the planning stage and, after it was passed, continued resisting it by refusing to sell or surrender their properties to the Burnt District Commissioners. They expressed their unwillingness to move so powerfully that, as noted earlier, the McLane administration twice decided to drop the harbor redevelopment plan. Once committed to the improvement, the Burnt District Commissioners assured the small wholesalers that they would be able to return. Other officials apparently promised to give them preference in the leasing of the new wharves. Nevertheless, the small waterfront businessmen could not go back. City Solicitor Bruce announced that the city was legally required to lease the piers to the highest bidders just a month after the voters approved the loan, a decision that guaranteed that large transportation companies would be able to appropriate the new wharves. It is indicative of the political significance of the wholesalers' unwillingness to relocate, however, that the McLane administration had had to accommodate to their resistance as much as it did. The near abandonment of the project reveals the extent to which the wholesalers' ties to place created barriers both to spatial and to infrastructural change.[174]

What all this points to is the same thing that the analysis of spatial change in the burnt districts of Boston and Chicago illuminated: the ongoing importance of a wide variety of demand- *and* supply-side frictions in the process of spatial redevelopment. In Baltimore, as in Boston and Chicago, the things property owners did that affected the supply of space available for land users worked in combination with the land users' demand for particular locations to determine the final pattern of land usage.

Supply-side frictions were also evident in other aspects of redevelopment, notably in the spatial effects that resulted from the construction of tall buildings. The erection of tall buildings contributed to the stability of land use patterns in the burnt district because the new structures provided floor space that at least partially compensated for the loss of land to street improvements. Because most of the tall buildings constructed in the district were office buildings with stores and wholesale showrooms on their lower floors, they particularly encouraged territorial stability on the part of office, retail, and light wholesale trades. Without the space these buildings provided, the demand-side frictions that contributed to the stability of land use patterns in the burnt district would have come to nothing, and a much more dramatic spatial reorganization of downtown businesses would almost certainly have taken place.

Even while the area's new skyscrapers made possible a degree of spatial continuity, they simultaneously produced a different kind of spatial change, namely, change that was vertical rather than horizontal in character. As a writer in the *American* noted, tall buildings caused a "condensation of population within a limited area." Each skyscraper constituted a "condensed town and not a small town either."[175] This vertical change was at the heart of the overall territorial stability of business location patterns in the area. Like the buildings themselves, the shift was a product of the new construction technology that helped set the reconstruction of Baltimore off from the reconstructions of Boston and Chicago.

At this point the conceptual distinctions between spatial change and the frictions that constrained the process of spatial change blur. This is, analytically speaking, precisely the point. The conceptual distinctions have always been blurred. In Baltimore, as in Boston and Chicago, a tangle of frictions mediated the relationship between the factors that necessitated environmental redevelopment and the adaptation responses that constituted redevelopment. The frictions mediated this relationship between stimulus and response so intimately, so fundamentally, that they must be seen as organic components of the process of environmental redevelopment. They were critical determinants of the process by which structures, infrastructures, and land use patterns were adapted to people's needs, as essential to the dynamic of change as the stimulus and the response that produced change; hence, they were as much a part of change as they were causes of inertia.

The reconstruction of Baltimore and progressive reform

In sum, the reconstruction of Baltimore stands both in comparison and in contrast to the reconstructions of Chicago and Boston. Each rebuilding was unique in all its particulars: The cities were different; their political situations varied; different people were involved in the rebuildings; the fires burnt different amounts of land and different things. And yet it is clear that beneath the diversity of this historical circumstance, there was in all three cities a common experience. In each city, the massive destruction of the built environment temporarily eliminated an important friction holding back environmental redevelopment – the physical durability of structures – long enough and thoroughly enough to cause a chain reaction of structural, infrastructural, and spatial change. And despite this change, all three cities continued to be affected by the presence of the other frictions in the process of environmental redevelopment. These other frictions continued to make it difficult for people to obtain the improvements they wanted, in many instances preventing them from adapting location patterns, buildings, streets, water service, and other infrastructures to their needs. In neither Chicago, Boston, nor Baltimore was success automatic, simple, or complete, even after the destruction by the fires.

It is not surprising that a study that combines theoretical and narrative approaches to the examination of urban problems would find such a blend of similarity and difference in its analysis of these rebuildings. Theory is attuned to sameness; history, to uniqueness. What is clear, however, is that even at the abstract level of analysis which provides insight into the common processes and constraints exhibited by the three rebuildings, there are differences which set the reconstruction of Baltimore apart from the reconstructions of Chicago and Boston. To be specific, an analytical comparison of the three cases indicates that in Baltimore the development of progressive reform and the use of a new construction technology alleviated some of the common barriers to change. As a result, the environmental improvement process went much farther in Baltimore than in either Boston or Chicago, not in the sense that Baltimoreans redeveloped a larger proportion of their environment (needless to say, much more was redeveloped in Chicago, where the fire had destroyed twenty times more land) but in the sense that Baltimoreans achieved more of their improvement goals more fully than the others and consequently solved more problems.

Historical comparisons are difficult to make because of the singularity of every place, person, problem, and event in history. The comparison in this study is especially difficult because the epiphenomenal variety must be multiplied by three. There are, accordingly, contradictions and complexities at every analytical turn, even when it comes to drawing the ostensibly simple conclusion that environmental improvement went farther in Baltimore because Baltimoreans pursued and were able to achieve a wider range of improvement goals. Baltimoreans undertook a major redevelopment of their harbor facilities, but they did not attempt to redevelop their rail facilities as the people of Chicago did. Baltimoreans achieved all but one of their original street improvement plans, but the widenings and extensions were not as extensive as those in Boston, and Baltimoreans did not even seriously consider taking their burnt district by eminent domain and redeveloping their streets on a comprehensive scale as Bostonians first did. On the other hand, the city of Baltimore used its power of eminent domain successfully to acquire all of the wharves along the Inner Harbor, an area that was about the size of Boston's entire burnt district. Baltimoreans made impressive improvements in their electrical utility infrastructures, and yet such infrastructures barely existed in Chicago and Boston at the time of their great fires. Baltimore was not only a unique city, but its fire took place more than thirty years after the other fires, after three decades of far-reaching political, economic, technological, and cultural change. So how can a fair comparison be made?

It is complicated, but relationships can nevertheless be drawn, particularly if the focus of analysis is shifted (as it has been in this study) from the physical product of environmental redevelopment to the underlying processes of redevelopment, to the human activity that caused environmental change and the constraints that influenced that activity. It is the distinctiveness of the process of redevelopment that sets the reconstruction of Baltimore off from the reconstructions of Chicago and Boston.

Even Baltimoreans were aware that they had somehow managed to surmount some of the problems that had continually hampered their attempts to improve the city in the past. They were, needless to say, extremely pleased by the results of reconstruction. Like the residents of Boston and Chicago, they congratulated themselves on all the benefits they had achieved.[176]

What is important is that they were also impressed by the *way* they had obtained these benefits. They recognized that the fire had vitalized their community in such a manner as to facilitate the process by which they achieved many long-hoped-for but heretofore unobtainable improvements. For example, the editors of the *Sun* called attention to the "mighty force" aroused by the great fire which was enabling Baltimoreans to achieve environmental advances "which arouse the admiration of the world." They pointed out that this "mighty force" was the new approach that city leaders were taking to planning and implementing redevelopment goals. "Just as the furnace flames separate the gold from the ore," they said, so the fire had separated Baltimore and its people "from the ore of old ideas, of old methods, and of old appliances, which served well in their day of a generation or two ago, but which were not and never would have been able to compete with the methods, ideals, and mechanical appliances which go to make successful competition" in the modern world. As another writer said in 1912, the conflagration had been a "staggering blow," but a "blow that awoke the fighting spirit." Baltimoreans had approached the opportunity of the disaster with an unprecedented willingness to experiment with new methods for achieving their improvement goals, and this had enabled them to accomplish "far-reaching change," including improvements in the burnt district's buildings, public market facilities, streets, sidewalks, electrical utilities, water service, and sewerage.[177]

Technological advance and political reform provided the new "methods, ideas, and mechanical appliances" that helped make this possible. In constructing tall steel frame buildings, Baltimoreans were not making innovations in construction technology so much as they were exploiting innovations that had already been made. They were being innovative, however, when they reformed the procedures of municipal government decision making in order to push their improvement plans through City Hall. Early twentieth century disasters were the birthing grounds for a number of important progressive reforms of city government, the devastating Galveston hurricane and tidal wave of 1900 giving rise to the commission form of government, the destructive Dayton flood of 1912 providing part of the stimulus for the first adoption of the commission-manager form of government by a major city.[178] Baltimore's progressive leaders never went so far as to restructure radically the overall form of their government in the aftermath of the great fire. They did, however, make significant changes within the system which had much the same effect. For example, they appointed the Burnt District Commission and concentrated all power to plan and implement improvements in the Commission's hands. They used the law to deprive the members of the City Council of their traditional power to participate in and control the planning and implementation of the improvements. And they restructured the public hearing process so as to make it more difficult for abutters to block improvement plans. They also used the city's credit in innovative ways by juggling the city's accounts and spreading out the repayment schedules of the city's debt so as to reduce the cost of the improvements to the city's taxpayers, all of which was also very much in keeping with the mainstream thrust of the urban progressive reform movement.

Historians have been debating the significance of municipal progressive reform for some time now. For the most part, they have been arguing over whether it was a victory for American democracy and the public interest or whether it was a miserable defeat for both – a victory for middle class taxpayers, business elites, and government bureaucrats which was wrapped up in a mantle of hypocritical democratic rhetoric. The historiographical controversy has grown out of the discovery in the 1960s that the municipal progressive reform movement was much more than the liberal social reform movement heralded by the progressives themselves by which do-good reformers wrested power from entrenched, corrupt machine politicians and instituted broad-minded social reform policies, restoring democracy to the urban political system. New research led to the discovery that there was another, more ambiguous side to the movement, an administrative reform side by which reformers attempted to increase the efficiency of urban government by instituting civil service reform, by modernizing financial accounting practices, by replacing ward elections with at-large elections, and by taking power from the legislative branch and concentrating it in the hands of officials ensconced in the executive branch of government.[179]

Historians have generally agreed that the bulk of the social reform programs and public works projects instituted by the progressives to help the poor were genuinely democratic and liberal. As a result, most of the controversy has boiled down to a debate over the question of whether the administrative reforms were liberal or conservative, democratic or undemocratic, good or bad. It is an issue that many historians have settled in the negative, on two basic grounds: First, the administrative reforms were essentially undemocratic because they undercut the institutional basis of popularly elected government by shifting power from officials who were elected through ward elections to officials who were elected through at-large elections or not elected at all (being bureaucrats hired under civil service laws). Second, the reforms were intrinsically conservative because they served the interests of the middle and upper classes at the expense of the working class by turning practical control of public policy making over to the middle class professionals and business elites who dominated the bureaucracies and commissions the reforms had created.[180]

The question has been and still is an interesting and provocative one for students of American political development. It is more than a question of semantics, of properly defining "liberal" and "democratic." As this chapter indicates, the institutional side of progressive reform was indeed undemocratic in Baltimore. The city's progressive business and political leaders restructured the institutions and procedures of government decision making in such a way as to reduce drastically the formal participation of both the public and the public's elected Council representatives in the making and implementation of public policy. Although the city's leaders worked hard to mobilize public opinion behind their improvement plans, even this activity was extremely manipulative in character. It was a from-the-bottom-up effort to convert and exploit public opinion much more than a from-the-bottom-up attempt to read it.

On the other hand, as this chapter also shows, these undemocratic methods of pushing public policies through government were not necessarily connected to conservative policy goals. The administrative reforms were not ends in themselves. They were means to ends, instruments for achieving practical goals which could be either liberal or conservative goals, which in this case included a wide variety of much needed, long-overdue environmental improvements that benefited the entire Baltimore community. The new techniques and institutional arrangements for maneuvering policies through City Hall were useful tools for achieving environmental improvement because they enabled people to circumvent some of the frictions in the process of environmental redevelopment, frictions which resulted from the economic and ecological costs that made traditional approaches to achieving improvement frustratingly divisive and defeating. Unlike the great fire, the reforms did not *eliminate* any of the frictions, even temporarily. The economic costs and site assembly and displacement problems of improvement remained an integral part of the process of redevelopment, as did the anger of the injured property owners and land users. The reforms did, however, give city leaders a more effective way to *handle* such frictions. They gave them the means to avoid at least some of the political compromise and stalemate these barriers to change traditionally caused. This enabled them to secure a wide variety of public improvements not only in the burnt district but also in the city as a whole, under the rubric "The movement for a Greater Baltimore."

The irony is that even with the reforms and technological advances, Baltimoreans did not overcome the frictions to the extent that they were actually able to "solve" all the environmental problems they wanted to solve. Baltimoreans achieved a great deal of significant improvement as a result of the fire's destruction and their new approach to effecting change. The new buildings in the burnt district were substantially better than those they replaced, as were the renovated water distribution system, the modernized Marsh Market Space, and the new underground electrical utility system. The street improvements, harbor improvements, and sewerage and drainage improvements were also very impressive achievements.

The fact remains, however, that even with the street widenings, traffic congestion in the downtown area remained a serious problem. The increasing use of the motor car (another product of technological innovation) soon began to make up for the city's failure to regrade the area's horse-defying hills. Needless to say, however, the proliferation of motor vehicles brought additional traffic problems to the area, problems that were even more serious than those the city had hoped to solve during reconstruction. Nor did the redevelopment of the wharves along the Inner Harbor, as massive as it was, do much to stem the decline of the Inner Harbor as a shipping center. The wharves simply could not be modernized enough and the harbor dredged deeply enough to compete successfully on a long-term basis with the much more extensive and advantageously situated ocean and rail transport, warehouse, and industrial facilities located in the area of the Outer Harbor and elsewhere in the city. As a result, the eastern section of the burnt district continued to decline as a business area, despite the widening of streets, the improvement of the market area, and the redevelopment of the wharves.[181]

By the same token, the burnt district continued to suffer from small fires, despite the improvement of buildings. Even the modernization of the drainage and sewerage system was less successful than it appeared to be. The construction of a system of sanitary sewers and the establishment of a sewage treatment plant in Anne Arundel County were indeed magnificent accomplishments, albeit long overdue. This new sewerage system significantly improved drainage and sanitation in the lower sections of Baltimore, including the burnt district and working class East Baltimore, for it reduced the flow of industrial and household waste water from cesspools down Baltimore's long hill, alleviating the filth and flooding problems that had plagued these areas for years. The improvements also reduced the pollution in the Inner Harbor. Unfortunately, however, for decades many of the benefits of the system were not fully realized in the poorer sections of the city (where they were most needed), because the poor could not afford to pay.[182]

In short, powerful barriers to environmental improvement continued to exist in Baltimore, as in Boston and Chicago. As the relative success with which Baltimoreans met the challenges of redevelopment indicates, the Progressive Era's new "methods, ideas, and mechanical devices" provided the means to get around some of the frictions in the process of environmental improvement, at least in part. As observers often said, there was a new spirit in the city, a spirit that made itself felt in the willingness of city leaders to try new techniques and strategies for keeping the opponents of improvement at bay and convincing the larger population of the necessity and promise of far-reaching change.

As the failures of the improvement process also show, however, and as the struggles that characterized the process of improvement indicate, many barriers to change remained. They expressed themselves during reconstruction in the conflict over street widenings, the legal and practical difficulties of site assembly, the juggling of city accounts, the gutting of the new building code, the anger of the waterfront businessmen trying to resist displacement, and the lengths to which city leaders had to go to secure approval for the bonds to finance the improvements. As future battles over urban renewal would show, they would continue to impede the process of environmental improvement, not only in Baltimore but also in Boston and Chicago and in the rest of America's big cities, through the rest of the twentieth century.

PART III

Conclusion

9

Power in the city

Fires were common in American cities in the nineteenth and early twentieth centuries. Their destructiveness constantly prompted environmental redevelopment on a small scale. Great fires like those in Chicago, Boston, and Baltimore took place comparatively rarely. They were, however, common enough to constitute an important natural force for urban renewal on a major scale in many large cities in this period. As this study indicates, they temporarily eliminated an important barrier to change, the physical durability of structures. This lifted a wide variety of other powerful demand- and supply-side barriers to environmental improvement, stimulating extensive structural and infrastructural redevelopment and, depending on the timing and extent of the destruction, considerable spatial redevelopment as well.

Clearly, great fires played an important part in the environmental development of many American cities. The purpose of this book has not been to identify and analyze precisely the role that these disastrous conflagrations played in the process of city growth, however. Instead, its goal has been to explain the *frictions* impeding the process of environmental development, the *difficulties* of environmental adaptation, which account for the terrible fire, pollution, congestion, housing, and other environmental problems cities suffered in this era. The great fires and reconstructions of Chicago, Boston, and Baltimore have merely provided the historical context in which these barriers to improvement have been described.

I have made a conceptual and historical analysis of the frictions in the process of urban redevelopment the focus of this study because I believe that they provide an extremely useful tool for understanding the multiple causes of the environmental problems that plagued America's Victorian cities. The analysis helps fill a void in the literature on urban growth and city planning by providing a comprehensive examination of the overlapping problems of structural, infrastructural, and spatial redevelopment. Perhaps more important, it integrates this explanation of the problems of city growth into a general interpretation of the political, economic, and physical processes of environmental development.

But what else, if anything, does this study do? As I ponder the task of finally summing up, what strikes me is the way this book raises questions about the role that people, not abstract political and economic forces, but people, played in city growth. Any study which puts together conceptual, narrative, and comparative analysis is bound to make one wonder about the connection that exists between personal action and the impersonal economic, political, and social forces that influence such action. The more that historians move toward social science (and the more that social scientists move toward narrative history), the more both groups find that they must consider the meaning and significance of human agency and will in a world in which so much of what we human beings do seems to have been predetermined (or at the very least constrained) by forces beyond our reach. With its emphasis on barriers and limits, this study draws attention to this issue.

Even with the joining of theory and narrative history, it is not easy to reach a general conclusion about the relative significance of human agency and larger structural conditions in the building of American cities. It is not even clear how we should separate the roles played by individuals in the redevelopment of their cities from the roles played by the economic, political, social, and environmental forces which prompted them to do as they did and which limited and delimited their accomplishments. How, for example, are we to assess the significance of the part that J. Y. Scammon played in the defeat of the union depot plan in Chicago, given the larger site assembly and economic problems that in a deeper sense also led to this defeat? What is the significance of the political reform undertaken by the McLane administration in the successful institution of street and harbor improvements, given the impetus and opportunity for this change provided by the fire?

These questions bring us to one of the central problems of this study: the problem of describing and evaluating the nature of power in cities. The subject of power is a broad one. It is also controversial, and rightly so, for practical as well as analytical reasons. The historians and social scientists who have examined the issue in its American urban context have usually concentrated on a single dimension: the question of who has held power in cities. But even this narrow topic has provoked much disagreement. Generations of historians and political scientists have examined the distribution of political power in urban communities in the United States in the hope of settling a larger debate over whether American local governments are truly democratic. Simply put, their dispute has hinged on the question of whether American cities have in general been ruled in an autocratic, elitist fashion by small, stable groups of wealthy, politically influential individuals or whether they have been governed in a relatively democratic, participatory, pluralistic manner by a comparatively large number of people organized in large but shifting coalitions.[1]

The question is important, even in this narrowly defined form, and as the debate has matured, the terms have broadened. Few historians and political scientists view power in purely governmental terms any longer or seek simply to identify which people and interest groups wielded overt political power in particular situations. Instead, most scholars consider power to be the product of bilateral and multilateral relationships among people, all of which are shaped by a wide variety of social and cultural as well as political and economic factors. They accordingly examine the way external institutional arrangements and social values help determine the outcome of conflict over public and private goals, giving individuals and groups a wide range of different kinds of influence over other individuals and groups.

This increasingly abstract way of construing power has shifted attention to the impersonal conditions that constrain the exercise of power by individuals and groups, defining government and public agendas and structuring political battles. Significantly, however, even as debate over power in cities has moved into this new realm, historians, political scientists, and other scholars have continued to focus on the old problem of the distribution of power. They have continued to devote the bulk of their energy to searching for answers to new versions of the same underlying question: Have elites dominated their communities, or have they shared power with other interest groups, their influence fragmented and offset by cultural values, institutional factors, and the countervailing activity of other groups participating in the government decision making process?[2]

The present study has taken this sophisticated analytical perspective on power as one of its starting points. What I have simply tried to do is pursue the implications of applying this kind of analysis to an examination of the difficulties of environmental development and redevelopment in American cities. In order to follow up this concern, however, I have had to shift my focus away from the traditional questions that have entranced so many generations of scholars about *who* has held power in cities to the related but less thoroughly debated issue of *what* power has been *used for* and what has *prevented* its use. Thus, in attempting to explain the problems of city growth in terms of the physical, economic, technological, and institutional factors that shaped the process of environmental change, I have raised questions about the extent to which people have had the capacity to achieve certain objectives, to meet certain needs, whether or not they enjoyed politically, economically, socially, or culturally defined positions of power and influence in their communities.

The basic concern is to some degree a metaphysical one. Indeed it bears a resemblance to the old religious query about the relationship between predestination and free will, a controversy that centered on the Calvinist contention that mere mortals had no power to save their souls through personal endeavor. Are substantial improvements in the human condition in some ultimate sense beyond the reach of humankind? Posed in this way, the question seems so extreme as to be of marginal academic interest. In this case, however, it has a practical side because it casts doubt on the ideals and purpose of modern city planning, a discipline which is based on, and legitimized by, the belief that people can have *both* the expertise and wisdom to improve the urban environment in an optimal way *and* (under the right conditions at least) the capacity to achieve these improvements through deliberate personal and collective endeavor.

This study provides a bleak answer to its urban version of this metaphysical question. It suggests that because of physical, economic, political, and technological constraints, city dwellers did *not* have the power they needed to adapt their environment to their multi-faceted, ever changing needs in an effective way. Moreover, it suggests that people still do not have this power. The theoretical chapters describe an abstract, three-dimensional process of environmental redevelopment composed of stimuli, adaptation responses, and frictions. In other words, these chapters posit a redevelopment process in which a large number of physical, economic, political, and technological limits on power were – and are – inherent because of the very nature of the environment itself and the nature of the political process, society, and the market in America. These constraints constantly held back environmental improvement. Indeed, they constantly held back most kinds of environmental change, negative as well as positive, forcing people to make do with over-crowded, unsafe, and inconvenient living, working, and traveling conditions, whether they were rich and powerful or poor and weak, in both the ordinary circumstances of city growth and the extraordinary circumstance of reconstruction after a disaster.

The practical limits of power should not be overstressed. People made significant improvements in their environments during all three of the reconstruction processes examined here, especially in Baltimore. And what is important is that they achieved these improvements not only because the fires temporarily eliminated certain constraints but also because they exercised power by spending money, manipulating public opinion, building political coalitions, reforming political institutions, using the court system, and so forth. Moreover, people redeveloped and improved their environments under the normal circumstances of city growth. Cities continually grew and evolved in the absence of great fires because people continually modified structures, infrastructures, and residential and commercial land use patterns to accommodate economic and population growth through a natural process of renovation, demolition, reconstruction, and, in the case of land use patterns, migration. To say that their power was limited is not to say that they had no power to improve the urban environment at all.

The fact remains, however, that the achievement of such positive change usually lagged behind the need for change. This lag is what links my explanation of the process and problems of environmental improvement to a more general investigation of the process and problems of exercising power in cities. Power always seems to be a potent end in itself as well as a potent means to ends, at least until one begins to consider what it *fails* to enable people to do. Even an examination of the improvements achieved during the fluid conditions of reconstruction ultimately draws attention back to this, back to the physical, economic, technological, and institutional conditions that limited what people could do to adapt their surroundings to their needs.

Such a consideration of power is a far cry from studies that treat it as if it were in some obvious and complete way *powerful*, as if it were something that a person holds by virtue of property ownership, social class, position in government, or participation in successful political coalitions, which once grasped gives one practical control over things and people. Ownership would seem to be the most potent instrument of power, something that gives one legal as well as practical mastery over real estate, objects, and, in the case of slavery, people. As recent examinations of slavery demonstrate, however, even outright ownership did not give slaveholders complete control over enslaved people.[3] This is also true of real estate. As this study shows, the ownership of land, buildings, and infrastructures did not give private individuals, corporations, or governments enough power to enable them to adapt what they owned to everyone's environmental needs. Nor did it necessarily give them, either individually or collectively, enough power to prevent change they did not want. It did not, because market conditions, demand factors, technological constraints, physical conditions, institutional factors, and site assembly problems limited what they could do to use, improve, and protect these inanimate forms of property, just as surely as the resistance of individual slaves and the psychological and ethical inhibitions of individual slaveowners limited what slaveowners could do to exploit their human property.

But what about the distributional issue? In the case of slavery, no one doubts that the owners of slaves had more power over slaves than the slaves over their owners, the limits of this power notwithstanding. There was a skewed distribution of power inherent in the master-slave relationship. By the same token, power imbalances shaped the process of environmental redevelopment. As the case studies in this book show, individuals, business corporations, and governments exercised power in cities in order to do one of two things: to redevelop the environment or to block redevelopment. And in every instance, there were those people who succeeded in achieving their goals and those who did not, those who benefited from their achievements and those who were disadvantaged by them. What light does this shed on the old question of who holds power in cities?

This study cannot provide a definitive answer to this query, focused as it is on a completely different problem, namely, the process and problems of city growth. It does provide some insight into the subject, however, insight that illuminates the limits of power in cities. At the very least, it demonstrates that a few business elites did not monopolize power in Boston, Baltimore, or Chicago, at least during the periods under study here. Instead, as the cases show, power was widely distributed.

Many people participated in the process of environmental improvement by influencing government policy. Moreover, as the proponents of the pluralist theory of power argue, they often did so by organizing political coalitions through which they collectively and sometimes at cross-purposes struggled over improvement plans at many levels of government, manipulating, lobbying, and otherwise jointly pressuring government decision makers in the executive as well as the legislative branches of local and state government. People also influenced government decision making by such comparatively *ad hoc* and highly personal means as private consultations with officials and participation in hearings, presenting their demands on an individual rather than collective basis. For example, property owners who opposed street widenings attempted to stop them by presenting formal, personal remonstrances at public hearings. Transportation and utility company executives pushed for lucrative rights of way and franchises through participation in public hearings and through individual contact with officials. Suburban real estate developers pushed for public service extensions in the same personal ways.

In addition to pressuring government officials in the executive and legislative branches of government, people went to court and sued to influence the course of environmental improvement. Some litigated over the statute and common law of property, nuisance, and regulation in order to compel the owners of structures and infrastructures to make improvements that they would not voluntarily undertake. Alternatively, others used the courts to fight regulations forcing them to make improvements they did not want to make. In either case, like J. Y. Scammon, who used the courts to prevent the Illinois Central Railroad from building a union depot in Chicago's Lake Park after the great Chicago fire, and like the transportation and utility companies that staved off expensive regulations with spirited legal defenses based on the doctrine of vested interest, they often found the law a potent weapon.

People also exercised a great deal of power over the environment outside the political arena altogether. They did so by operating in the real estate market, by buying and selling property, and by constructing and furnishing buildings and leasing space within them. They also did so by transacting with utility and transportation companies for various kinds of services.

The desire to use these tools of power was as important as an ability to do so. Great silences shaped the evolution of urban landscapes in the nineteenth and early twentieth centuries. Time and time again, people, rich and poor alike, seem to have taken for granted the inconveniences, inadequacies, and dangers of the buildings, streets, sanitary services, and other infrastructures in their neighborhoods. Ignorant of the technical complexities of serious environmental problems and apathetic, even complainingly complacent, about what was in their own self-interest, they often failed to try to exercise economic or political power to achieve critical environmental improvements, even after disaster struck.

Needless to say, though, certain groups of people had more opportunity to exercise the various instruments of power than others. To be specific, as a class, wealthy businessmen had more power in the private market than the less privileged members of the communities. They also had superior access to government officials and good lawyers, as well as a greater ability to back up their political demands with compelling *quid pro quo*s. This inevitably tipped the balance of power in their favor.

Significantly, however, it does not appear that any one elite group monopolized power in these cities, the tipping of the balance of power toward the business class notwithstanding. Quite the contrary. The case studies in this book substantiate the findings of the pluralists that the distribution of power, while skewed, was both extremely fragmented and broad. First of all, the cases show that disputes over land use often pit members of the middle and upper classes against each other, frequently dividing even the relatively few members of a city's business elite against themselves. Second, they show that working class people as well as middle and upper class people took part in conflicts over land use, participating in coalitions and even organizing them when their personal interests were visibly at stake.

All of the fires examined in this book were central business district fires, all but the great Chicago fire exclusively so. Thus it is not surprising that in Boston and Baltimore, influential newspaper publishers and central business district businessmen and property owners controlled the redevelopment of the burnt districts, dominating the struggles over land use change in both the real estate market and City Hall. Nor is it surprising that working class people were relegated to the sidelines, doing little to influence the course of reconstruction in either city besides contributing their labor to the rebuilding. However, in Baltimore, working class people participated in the coalition politics of the city business leaders as they battled over the improvement of streets and other infrastructures, by sending postcards to their City Council representatives to protest the widening of Baltimore Street and by voting in favor of the $6 million bond issue. Was their support critical to the outcome of these conflicts? That is not clear. It is, however, significant that Baltimore's business leaders found it necessary to seek it.

The Chicago fire was different. It destroyed more buildings owned by workers than middle and upper class stores, warehouses, and homes. Here, accordingly, working class people as well as middle and upper class people participated in struggles over reconstruction on a comparatively equal footing. As a class, Chicago's workers did much more to influence reconstruction than simply labor on the rebuilding for wages and contribute secondary support to coalitions organized by business leaders. Indeed, like middle and upper class people, they independently helped give shape to large parts of the city's new built environment by buying and leasing land and constructing their own buildings. They also helped determine the layout of Chicago's much expanded railway system by struggling on a neighborhood basis with other groups of middle, upper, and working class homeowners over where the new rights of way would be put, by petitioning City Council members, and by making protests at public hearings. Most remarkably, they managed to prevent the passage of the comprehensive fire limits ordinance demanded by the city's business elite. In an effort to protect their homes, impoverished North Side homeowners and would-be homeowners organized a public protest movement to stop passage of the law to extend the fire limits to the city limits. They organized the movement in much the same way that Baltimore's far more wealthy and influential business leaders would later organize a movement to stop the widening of Baltimore Street. And they enjoyed the same success.

In short, the case studies show that even before labor unions rose to political power in the twentieth century, working class people, like middle and upper class people, took part in conflicts over land use development by engaging in coalition politics, sometimes in cooperation with members of the other classes, sometimes in opposition to them. And working class status and lack of economic wealth did not necessarily prevent them from having an impact on the improvement process, even when their interests clashed with the goals of business elites. What mattered in any struggle to influence the outcome of a land use policy dispute was a comparative ability to bend the governmental ear. In this, success was frequently a matter of carrying off some grandstand ploy, like organizing a protest march on City Hall, a political gambit in which the poor, no less than the rich, were capable of engaging.[4]

The present study indicates that power was more widely distributed than this. To be specific, it suggests that like the members of the middle and upper classes, working class people exercised power by means other than political coalition building, power that gave them additional ways to influence the course of environmental improvement in their cities.

It was not just that poor people were capable of influencing municipal land use policy by manipulating machine politicians on an individualistic, *ad hoc* basis. The residents of urban slums were neither as motivated nor as well positioned to do this as suburban real estate developers and transportation and utility company executives and other powerful elites, because of apathy, the cost of betterment taxes, the cost of effective demand articulation, and the reward structure of machine politics which paid off working class constituents with jobs on public works projects rather than by locating the public works to meet workers' needs. But there is little doubt that on occasion slum dwellers did individually and collectively press their ward politicians for action on specific environmental problems and meet with some success.[5]

Nor was it simply that working class people exercised a great deal of economic control over the environment through their transactions in the real estate market. As the owners or tenants of a large proportion of the land and buildings in most cities, they determined to a large extent what got built in urban America. And this did indeed affect the process of environmental improvement, albeit in an often negative way, since their poverty continually prevented them from making many desirable improvements in the buildings they owned or rented. Poor people built hundreds of thousands of small, unsanitary, firetrap houses and other structures in American cities. This was as much an exercise of power as the building of tenements and the erection of million dollar skyscrapers by well-to-do land speculators and real estate developers.

These things are important. They do not, however, reveal the full complexity of the situation, the full extent to which power over the environment was distributed across urban populations in a broad-based and disjointed manner. Power is a peculiar thing when one examines it from relational angles. It is generally treated as something that people actively and deliberately exercised to control situations and people in order to achieve certain goals. As the material in this book indicates, however, there was also a passive dimension to the exercise of power. People shaped the course of city growth without taking any overt economic or political action to effect or prevent change, because their inaction, their inertia, discouraged *other people* from making changes. People passively influenced the demand for land and the development and redevelopment of structures and infrastructures simply by living and working in particular areas. They did so because the way in which they used space in their neighborhoods generated positive and negative externalities, neighborhood effects, which had an impact on the perceptions and well-being of others. These neighborhood effects sometimes encouraged property owners to renovate or reconstruct their buildings for new uses. More often than not, however, they prejudiced expectations about the desirability and profitability of change in such a way as to discourage redevelopment.

In this regard, some of the most powerful members of urban society were perhaps those ostensibly powerless people who resided in the slums that were crowded along the edges of most central business districts. Their miserable poverty gave them the means to passively stave off the disruptions and dislocations that commercial redevelopment of their neighborhoods would have caused. On the one hand, their impoverishment made them a lucrative captive market for existing buildings in these areas, which discouraged land-lords from making the land available to central business district firms. On the other, by turning the areas into slums, their poverty discouraged pros-perous businessmen engaged in central business district trades from seeking space there. In this way, as the examinations of spatial change in Chicago and Boston show, poor people slowed the inexorable expansion of their cities' central business districts. They forced businessmen who had the economic power to bid their locations away to pay high rents and suffer the inconveniences of overcrowding in the central city, despite the fact that they, the inhabitants of slums, had very little ability to resist displacement by actively exercising political or economic clout.[6]

Is it reasonable to call such a passive and uncalculated influencing of the process of environmental development an exercise of "power"? Some se-manticists might argue that it is pushing the definition of the word a bit far. Yet in these situations certain groups of city dwellers did in subtle ways control the behavior of others in such a manner as to suggest the existence of a power relationship between them. As noted earlier, social scientists and historians who study the distribution of power in urban communities now emphasize the social and cultural factors that enabled certain groups to influence the behavior of others in covert, sometimes even subconscious ways through their everyday interactions with them. This is a clear parallel to the situation here. In environmental development, as in social development, the exercise of power involved far more than the spending of money and the overt use of legal authority and political force.[7]

In short, this book suggests that power in nineteenth and early twentieth century cities was simultaneously more complexly distributed and more wide-spread than either the pluralist or elitist theories traditionally would have it. This is one of the reasons why power to improve the environment was *limited*. Because of neighborhood effects, site assembly problems, the public goods character of infrastructures, and a host of other problems, many of the most important kinds of environmental improvement could not be undertaken without the cooperation of a large number of people. Because of the way the real estate market and the American political system worked, most people had the ability, individually or collectively, to prevent other people, including government officials, from achieving these kinds of change. At any rate, they had the ability to try to stop them from making changes. Needless to say, they did not always desire to do so. Because of the costly and disruptive nature of many kinds of redevelopment, however, they often did. And they frequently succeeded.

An assumption of most pluralist evaluations of power in American society is that pluralism is inherently beneficial and desirable for society. The argument is that a broad distribution of power reflects the success with which our political system incorporates democratic principles, allowing many diverse interests to participate in government decision making. The idea is that participation is in and of itself a good thing. The implication of this study is slightly different. It is that a broad distribution of political and economic power could at times be detrimental to the public interest because it limited in practical and complex ways society's ability to take action to solve problems. Ironically, one of the limits of power was its broad and complex distribution. So many people had so much power that it was often difficult for anyone to accomplish what was required to adapt the urban environment to rapid economic and population growth.

The broad distribution of power revealed in this study was only one of many barriers to environmental improvement, of course, only one of many constraints on power. Technological problems, budgetary limits, the scarcity of centrally located space, the fact that many improvement goals were thus mutually exclusive, and all the other problems described in this book also limited what people could do to adapt the environment to their needs. Indeed, the broad distribution of power was a friction in the process of environmental development in large part because of these other problems. By itself, however, the broad distribution of power was a constraint. And as such it was one of the reasons why the progressive reform of municipal government did so much to speed up the pace of environmental improvement in many twentieth century cities. It was also one the reasons why, with the aid of massive federal subsidies, city planners began using the government's power of eminent domain in increasingly sweeping ways to redevelop inner city slums in the 1950s and 1960s.

Government officials have in the twentieth century imposed an unprecedented degree of control over the private redevelopment of the environment through the strengthening of building codes, the tightening of utility and transportation regulations, and the establishment of zoning regulations. They have also cleared many inner city slums of their old buildings, infrastructures, and residents and made the areas available for public and private redevelopment on a scale that was unheard of in the nineteenth century. Progressive reform helped make this possible by restructuring the institutions of city government in order to make it much more difficult for ordinary people to fight change effectively in City Hall. The government's increasing use of its power of eminent domain also made it much harder for people to resist disruptive and displacing change in passive, apolitical ways. City dwellers could no more passively resist the use of eminent domain than they could passively resist the destruction of great fires.

These legal and institutional developments facilitated the process of environmental improvement because they served to strip ordinary businessmen, property owners, and residents of some of their power to delay and thwart improvement. What is the significance of this? Does it mean that from the perspective of solving environmental problems, this strengthening of the hand of government was inherently beneficial, that it necessarily promoted the public interest?

No, not necessarily. These reforms reduced the impact of this one barrier to improvement. They did not, however, eliminate it or any other barrier completely. Nor did they guarantee the wisdom of the proposals of city planners, eliminating the opportunity for vested interests to distort official definitions of the public interest. As a result, the reforms increased the ability of government to initiate land use policies and programs which *hurt*, as well as helped, the communities they were supposed to benefit. As the problems of city planning in the twentieth century show, government officials often used their powers in ways that exacerbated the problems of their cities by making them less desirable places in which to live and work. Indeed, in many places the experience with zoning and urban renewal was so painful that by the late 1960s and 1970s a backlash had developed. An explosion of neighborhood and other grass-roots activism took place, the aim of which was to restructure the institutions and procedures of city government and civil litigation so as to give ordinary citizens a *stronger* voice in the process of environmental improvement, to give them *more* power to *prevent* private property owners and government officials from initiating environmental redevelopment.[8]

This said, the fact remains that there are still problems with the urban environment that need solving. Engineers, city planners, public interest groups, and even private developers sometimes devise sound plans for rectifying them. When this happens there are significant advantages to legal and administrative arrangements that strengthen the ability of government to institute the improvements by reducing the ability of other groups to thwart their institution. Even the most objectively necessary improvements are economically costly and physically disruptive for at least some of the businessmen, residents, property owners, and taxpayers in a community. If such improvements are to be achieved, people must be made to bear the costs, something that often requires force. One of the lessons of the nineteenth century is that when government cannot or will not apply this force, the result is an accumulation of serious environmental problems.

Because of advances in the law of land use regulation and eminent domain, city officials today have far more power to force people to bear the costs of environmental improvement than their nineteenth century counterparts. Their task is to use this power responsibly, to make sure that it is used to implement land use policies with benefits that *do* outweigh the costs. The question is whether they will have the power to use their power wisely and effectively. Unfortunately, if the past is any indication, the answer is that in all likelihood they will not.

It has been common for historians and other analysts to explain the environmental problems that have plagued our cities over the past two centuries in terms of the misuse of power, to blame them on the abuse of power by greedy real estate developers and corporate executives and corrupt, easily co-opted politicians. The probability that government officials will continue to abuse their power is one good reason for being pessimistic about our ability to solve urban environmental problems in the future. It is not the only reason, however. City growth is an immensely complicated process. As this study has shown, it is plagued by a host of social, economic, political, technological, and physical conditions that not only tend to blind us to our problems but also hamstring our attempts to solve them. These frictions in the process of environmental improvement function as constraints on power. They are no more easily eliminated from city growth than the greed that leads to the abuse of power. If the past is indeed an indication of the future, political reform movements will come and go, but these frictions will remain. They will always make environmental improvement a slow, difficult upward struggle in which the achievement of improvement lags behind the need for change.

Notes

Chapter 1. Introduction

1 For an excellent discussion of the value of integrating theoretical analysis with historical narrative in historical studies, see Philip Abrams, "History, Sociology, Historical Sociology," *Past and Present*, 87 (May 1980), pp. 3–16.

2 Chicago Plan Commission, *Chicago Population 1900–1950 by Square Mile for Each Decade* (map, Chicago Municipal Research Library).

3 Alan Anderson, *The Origin and Resolution of an Urban Crisis* (Baltimore, 1977), p. 62.

4 Carroll D. Wright, *Analysis of the Population of the City of Boston as Shown in the Census of May 1885* (Boston, 1885), p. 9.

Chapter 2. The barriers to structural improvement

1 Leo Grebler, *Housing Market Behavior in a Declining Area* (New York, 1952), pp. 25, 120, 165–68.

2 Edith Abbott, assisted by Sophonisba P. Breckinridge and two other associates in the School of Social Services Administration of the University of Chicago, *The Tenements of Chicago 1908–1935* (Chicago, 1936), pp. 183–204. The widespread moving of wooden buildings in Chicago is well known. Notices of application for permission to move wooden buildings appeared every day in the "Corporate Notices" column of the *Chicago Evening Post*.

3 Census and municipal tax records document the existence of huge concentrations of poor workers and marginal businesses in inner city locations. Historical materials compiled by Dun & Bradstreet Co., available at the company's New York City offices, also provide financial information on marginal businesses.

4 Reformers often claimed that slum owners received forty percent and more per year. See Citizens' Association of Chicago, *Report of the Committee on Tenement Houses of the Citizens' Association of Chicago* (Chicago, 1884), p. 9; Marcus T. Reynolds, *The Housing of the Poor in American Cities* (New York, 1969, reprint of 1893), p. 31. See also Anthony Jackson, *A Place Called Home* (Cambridge, Mass., 1976), pp. 146–47.

5 *Baltimore Sun*, July 13, 1904.

6 Edward S. Philbrick, *American Sanitary Engineer* (New York, 1881), p. 109.

7 *Baltimore Sun*, February 17, 1904.

8   Abbott, *The Tenements of Chicago*, pp. 363–400.

9   Elizabeth Blackmar, "Housing and Property Relations in Antebellum New York City" (unpublished Ph.D. dissertation, Harvard University, 1980).

10 References to this form of landholding abound in the literature on slum housing. The important thing is that it was also a characteristic form of ownership in business areas. See James Ford, *Slums and Housing, with Special Reference to New York City* (Cambridge, Mass., 1936), pp. 95, 450; Grebler, *Housing Market Behavior in a Declining Area*, pp. 26, 98, 217; and Part II, this book. See also Richard M. Hurd, *The Principles of City Land Values* (New York, 1905), p. 111.

11 References to this form of landholding also abound in the literature on slum housing. See Jackson, *A Place Called Home*, pp. 146–48; Abbott, *The Tenements of Chicago*, pp. 182, 190; Ford, *Slums and Housing*, p. 448.

12 R. Joseph Monsen, "Who Owns the City?" *Land Economics*, 37 (May 1961), pp. 174–78. Monsen examined transfer deeds in detail to arrive at his figures and demonstrated that identifying trust beneficiaries is the key to determining "beneficial" ownership, as opposed to nominal or "record" ownership, since title abstracts and other public records often record titles in the names of trustees and agents and not the actual owners. About twenty-six percent of the property in the business district and about twelve percent of the residential property was trust owned. Grebler estimated that about ten percent of the property on the Lower East Side was held by trust estates during the 1900–20 period. He does not appear to have tried to establish "beneficial" ownership but points out a problem that Monsen ignored, namely, that when an estate is distributed among the heirs, it then appears as a parcel that is owned by individuals, rather than as an estate. He suggests that his estimate thus underestimates the true proportion of inherited estate ownership (Grebler, *Housing Market Activity in a Declining Area*, pp. 95–101, 214–18).

13 *Baltimore Sun*, April 23, 1904. Blackmar traces the development of this form of ownership in New York City in "Housing and Property Relations in Antebellum New York City."

14 Ford, *Slums and Housing*, pp. 104–5, 131–32, 148–50. See also Blackmar, "Housing and Property Relations in Antebellum New York City."

15 These concepts were developed by economists in the early 1960s to explain the origins of slums and to justify urban renewal. They have been subject to considerable criticism, but the chapters of this study on the rebuilding of cities after great fires will show that they provide valuable insights into the process and problems of city growth in the nineteenth century. See Otto A. Davis and Andrew B. Winston, "The Economics of Urban Renewal," *Law and Contemporary Problems*, 2 (Winter 1961), pp. 105–17; Jerome Rothenberg, *Economic Evaluation of Urban Renewal* (Washington, D.C., 1967), pp. 39–42; James Heilbrun, *Urban Economics and Public Policy* (New York, 1974), pp. 277–81. The discussion of market imperfections in the text is based on these sources, although it emphasizes certain concepts and problems more than these writers do and deemphasizes others.

16 For a more extended definition of the externality concept, see Robert L. Bish

and Hugh O. Nourse, *Urban Economics and Policy Analysis* (New York, 1975), pp. 111–16. For a very extensive analysis, see Robert J. Starf and Francis X. Tannin (eds.), *Externalities: Theoretical Dimensions of Political Economy* (New York, 1973).

17 Hurd, *Principles of City Land Values*, pp. 124–25.

18 Cadastral atlases of landownership reveal the fragmentation of landholding patterns most graphically. See, for example, atlases published by G. W. Bromley Co. for Boston, Chicago, and Philadelphia.

19 Davis and Winston, "The Economics of Urban Renewal," pp. 106–11; Rothenberg, *Economic Evaluation of Urban Renewal*, p. 40.

20 Rothenberg, *Economic Evaluation of Urban Renewal*, p. 41; Davis and Winston, "The Economics of Urban Renewal," p. 110.

21 *Baltimore Sun*, April 26, 1904.

22 Carl Condit, *American Building: Materials and Techniques from the First Colonial Settlements to the Present* (Chicago, 1968), pp. 64–75, 114–18; Condit, *American Building Art: The Nineteenth Century* (New York, 1960), pp. 47–48; T. Ritchie, *Canada Builds, 1867–1967* (Toronto, 1967), p. 260.

23 Condit, *American Building*, pp. 114–30; Frank A. Randall, *History of the Development of Building Construction in Chicago* (Urbana, Ill., 1949), pp. 11–21.

24 Hurd, *Principles of City Land Values*, pp. 97–98. Building heights were effectively limited to five or six stories until the 1870s, when hydraulic elevators were introduced.

25 Condit, *American Building Art*, pp. 286–87, 223–40.

26 Ibid., p. 39. See *Transactions of American Society of Civil Engineers* and *American Architecture and Building News* for material relating to the technical difficulties of technological advancements.

27 Condit, *American Building Art*, pp. 43–50.

28 Ibid., pp. 48–49.

29 "Lessons of the Baltimore Fire," *American Architect and Building News*, 85 (July 9, 1904), pp. 11–13; "Effects of Fires on Building Stones," *American Architect and Building News*, 8 (September 4, 1880), p. 118. See also Chapter 7 of this book.

30 Philbrick, *American Sanitary Engineering*, pp. 109–20ff.; William Paul Gerhard, *House Drainage and Sanitary Plumbing* (New York, 1881), pp. 74, 152–53, 171; Gerhard, *Sanitation and Sanitary Engineering* (New York, 1909), p. 120. See also Robert Hunter, *Tenement Conditions in Chicago* (Chicago, 1901), pp. 105–7.

31 *The Plumber and Sanitary Engineer, Public Health, Drainage, Water Supply, Ventilation, Heating, Lighting* (hereafter referred to as *Sanitary Engineer*) and the *American Architecture and Building News* are excellent sources of information on this subject. Eugene S. Ferguson, "An Historical Sketch of Central Heating, 1800–1860," in Charles E. Peterson (ed.), *Building Early America: Contributions Toward the History of a Great Industry* (Radnor, Pa., 1976), pp. 165–85, provides a very interesting description of the problems and processes involved in the development of central heating.

32 Gerhard, *House Drainage and Sanitary Plumbing*, pp. 7, 17. One of the reasons

for the scare seems to have been Prince Albert's death from typhoid contracted from sewer gas leaking into his library. Sewer gas was not the only problem behind the "plumbing scare." The woodwork in which Victorians habitually enclosed bathroom fixtures was also a dangerous germ trap. See Gerhard, *House Drainage and Sanitary Plumbing*, p. 199; and "Annual Report of the Board of Health," *Baltimore City Documents*, 1885, p. 415.

33 Gerhard, *House Drainage and Sanitary Plumbing*, pp. 17, 68–85; Philbrick, *American Sanitary Engineering*, pp. 109–11.

34 William Ripley Nichols, "On the Use of Lead for Conveying and Storing Water," *Sanitary Engineer*, 9 (December 6, 1883), p. 13.

35 Along with the lack of sanitary facilities and overcrowding due to the inadequate size of the housing stock as a whole, this was the most important problem with slum housing. See Ford, *Slums and Housing*, p. 12.

36 Robert W. DeForest and Lawrence Veiller (eds.), *The Tenement House Problem* (New York, 1903), Vol. 1, p. 37.

37 *Harpers Weekly*, December 19, 1857; *Sanitary Engineer*, 6 (June 8, 1882), p. 21. Even housing reformers did not try to apply the European designs until very late. As a result of their early "model," tenements were as bad as the worst slums built by speculators. See, for example, DeForest and Veiller, *The Tenement House Problem*, p. 86.

38 Jackson, *A Place Called Home*, pp. 58–81; *Sanitary Engineer*, 6 (June 8, 1882); Ernest Flagg, "The New York Tenement House Evil and Its Cure," *Scribners Magazine*, 16 (July 1894), p. 109.

39 See the *Sanitary Engineer* and *American Architecture and Building News*, both of which constantly emphasize the need to educate builders and the public. Occasionally they also refer to "crooked" contractors (e.g., *Sanitary Engineer*, 3 [September 1, 1880], p. 370). The quote is from the same issue of the *Sanitary Engineer*, p. 378.

40 Flagg, "The New York Tenement House Evil and Its Cure," pp. 109–11.

41 *Report of the Committee on the Expediency of Providing Better Tenements for the Poor* (Boston, 1846), pp. 16–17, 18.

42 Citizens' Association of Chicago, *Report of the Committee on Tenement Houses*, pp. 7–18.

43 Quoted in Jackson, *A Place Called Home*, p. 3.

Chapter 3. The barriers to infrastructural improvement

1 "Mains and Subways," *New York Evening Post*, reprinted in *Engineering Record*, 41 (June 23, 1900), p. 601.

2 Charles Zueblin, *American Municipal Progress* (New York, 1916), p. 19. For a general summary of the research done by historians on the various aspects of infrastructural development, see Joel Tarr, "The Evolution of the Urban Infrastructure in the Nineteenth and Twentieth Centuries," in Royce Hanson (ed.), *Perspectives on Urban Infrastructure* (Washington, D.C., 1984), pp. 4–60.

3 *Report of the Street Railway Commission to the City Council . . .* (Chicago, 1900), p. 17.

4 Ibid.; see also Thompson King, *Consolidated of Baltimore: A History of Consolidated Gas, Electric Light and Power Company of Baltimore* (Baltimore, 1950), pp. 49–90; Nicholas B. Wainwright, *History of the Philadelphia Electric Company 1881–1961* (Philadelphia, 1961), pp. 26–33ff.; John Bauer and Peter Costello, *Public Organization of Electric Power: Conditions, Policies, Programs* (New York, 1949), pp. 16–17. See also Edmund J. James, "The Relation of the Modern Municipality to the Gas Supply," *Publications of the American Economics Association*, 1 (May 1886), pp. 17–23.

5 See Chapter 8 of this book.

6 Robert O. Bish and Hugh O. Nourse, *Urban Economics and Policy Analysis* (New York, 1975), pp. 116–19; Richard A. Musgrave and Peggy B. Musgrave, *Public Finance in Theory and Practice* (New York, 1973), pp. 52–56; Neil M. Singer, *Public Microeconomics* (Boston, 1972), pp. 94–96; Peter O. Steiner, "Public Expenditure Budgets," in Alan S. Blinder, Robert M. Solow, George F. Break, Peter O. Steiner, and Dick Netzer (eds.), *The Economics of Public Finance* (Washington, D.C., 1974), pp. 244–51; Robert Haveman, *The Economics of the Public Sector* (New York, 1970), pp. 32–43; James M. Buchanan, *Public Finance in Democratic Process: Fiscal Institutions and Individual Choice* (Chapel Hill, N.C., 1967), pp. 114–15.

7 Bish and Nourse, *Urban Economics and Policy Analysis*, pp. 116–19; Musgrave and Musgrave, *Public Finance in Theory and Practice*, pp. 52–56; Singer, *Public Microeconomics*, pp. 94–96; Steiner, "Public Expenditure Budgets"; Haveman, *The Economics of the Public Sector*, pp. 32–43; Buchanan, *Public Finance in Democratic Process*, pp. 114–15.

8 Nelson Manfred Blake, *Water for the Cities: A History of the Urban Water Supply Problem in the United States* (Syracuse, 1956), pp. 58, 67, 106, 122, 190. The same was true in other cities, including Philadelphia (pp. 35–36, 82–83). For descriptions of central Baltimore's antiquated sewers, see the annual reports of the City Commissioner in *Reports of the City Officers and Departments to the City Council of Baltimore* (hereafter abbreviated *BRCOD*), 1869–1900. The old sewers were repeatedly repaired and extended but not replaced and, despite name changes, can be traced through the reports.

9 "Annual Report of Health Department," *BRCOD*, 1887, p. 1009.

10 See, for example, "Annual Report of Board of Health," *BRCOD*, 1880, pp. 511–12; 1881, pp. 411–12.

11 Quoted in King, *Consolidated of Baltimore*, p. 52.

12 Robert L. Bish and Robert Warren, "Scale and Monopoly Problems in Government Services," *Urban Affairs Quarterly*, 8 (September 1972), pp. 97–100.

13 See Chapters 6, 7, and 8 of this book for more detailed analyses of this problem. Engineering journals, city government records, and municipal reform journals are filled with discussions of the problem. See, for example, Captain William Brophy, "History of the Solution of the Wire Problem in Boston," *City Government*, 5 (May 1898), pp. 25–26. "Annual Report of Wire Department," *Boston City Documents*, 1897, No. 33, contains excellent photographs of the many underground infrastructures encountered during the construction of the city's electrical subways.

14	It took decades to fill in the Back Bay in Boston, for example. See Walter Muir Whitehall, *Boston: A Topographical History* (Cambridge, Mass., 1968), pp. 150–59. The work on leveling Fort Hill had to be halted for three years until a place to deposit the earth was obtained. Including this delay, the project took six years. See Charles Phillips Huse, *The Financial History of Boston from May 1, 1822 to January 31, 1909* (Cambridge, Mass., 1916), pp. 127–28.

15	Harry Scheiber, "The Road to Munn: Eminent Domain and the Concept of Public Purpose in the State Courts," *Perspectives in American History*, 5 (1971), pp. 329–402; Scheiber, "Property Law, Expropriation, and Resource Allocation by Government: The United States 1789–1920," *Journal of Economic History* (March 1973), pp. 232–251; Morton J. Horwitz, *The Transformation of American Law, 1780–1860* (Cambridge, Mass., 1975), pp. 63–85.

16	Henry Demarest Lloyd, *The Chicago Traction Question* (Chicago, 1904), pp. 8–29; William T. Stead, *If Christ Came to Chicago: A Plea for the Union of All Who Love in the Service of All Who Suffer* (Chicago, 1894), pp. 173–189, 196–201. On occasion railroad companies were even able to obtain rights of way on public streets without the permission of the City Council members – indeed, despite their vehement opposition. See Edwin A. Gere, Jr., "Dillon's Rule and the Cooley Doctrine: Reflections of the Political Culture," *Journal of Urban History*, 8 (May 1982), pp. 272–76.

17	"Annual Report of Commissioner for Opening Streets," BRCOD, 1877–99. The general problem is discussed in detail in Chapters 5, 6, and 8 of this book and in Flavel Shurtleff and Frederick Law Olmstead, *Carrying Out the City Plan: The Practical Application of American Law in the Execution of City Plans* (New York, 1914).

18	Huse, *The Financial History of Boston*; Jacob Harry Hollander, *The Financial History of Baltimore* (Baltimore, 1899); Howard Kimball Stokes, *The Finances and Administration of Providence* (Baltimore, 1903). See also Sherry Olson, "Baltimore Imitates the Spider," *Annals of the Association of American Geographers*, 69 (December 1979), pp. 557–74.

19	Blake, *Water for the Cities*, pp. 63–77; "Electrical Subways," *Engineering Record*, 83 (February 8, 1896), p. 165.

20	At any rate, companies sometimes used this as a justification for their demands for very long term franchises. See Chicago Street Railroad Company, *The Humphry Bills* and *Comparisons of American Street Railways* (Chicago, 1897).

21	Huse, *The Financial History of Boston*, passim; Hollander, *The Financial History of Baltimore*, passim; Edward Dana Durand, *The Finances of New York City* (New York, 1898), passim.

22	Huse, *The Financial History of Boston*, pp. 222, 224, 328; Hollander, *The Financial History of Baltimore*, pp. 195, 345–46; Bessie Louis Pierce, *A History of Chicago* (New York, 1937), Vol. 1, pp. 355–63, Vol. 2, p. 349. States sometimes imposed ceilings on tax rates as well. See Huse, *The Financial History of Boston*, p. 320.

	On the problems in New Orleans see "Sanitary Reform in New Orleans," *Engineering Record*, 40 (June 17, 1899), p. 45; "New Orleans Sewerage Ordinance," *Engineering Record*, 40 (July 15, 1899), pp. 146–47; and "The Drainage Problem of New Orleans," *Engineering Record*, 40 (September 16, 1899), pp. 360–61.

23 Bish and Nourse, *Urban Economics and Policy Analysis*, pp. 117–18; Musgrave and Musgrave, *Public Finance*, pp. 52–56; Singer, *Public Microeconomics*, p. 95; Haveman, *Economics of the Public Sector*, pp. 32–43; Buchanan, *Public Finance in Democratic Process*, pp. 114–15.

24 Quoted in Blake, *Water for the Cities*, p. 228.

25 Economists have been discussing the problems of monopoly power in the private sector since Adam Smith's day. For a summary, see Richard G. Lipsey and Peter O. Steiner, *Economics*, 4th ed. (New York, 1975), pp. 326–44. For a particularly vivid contemporary study of monopolistic profiteering based on quantitative data, see Civic Federation of Chicago, *The Street Railways of Chicago* (reprinted from *Municipal Affairs*, 1901), pp. 9–23. For an example of monopolistic inefficiency, see King, *Consolidated of Baltimore*, pp. 124–25, 129–34. On New Orleans see *Second Report of the Sewerage Commission* (Baltimore, 1899), p.76; and "Sanitary Reform in New Orleans," p. 45.

26 Blake, *Water for the Cities*, passim; King, *Consolidated of Baltimore*, pp. 44–52.

27 King, *Consolidated of Baltimore*, pp. 64, 72–74, 84–86; Wainwright, *History of the Philadelphia Electric Company*, p. 26.

28 Newspapers, municipal reform publications, and government documents are the best sources of information on this sort of problem. "Annual Report of the Wire Department," *Boston City Documents*, 1897, No. 33, pp. 2–16, for example, discusses the overhead electric utility wire problem in Boston (and also mentions gas pipe problems). In Baltimore, after almost twenty years of growing official and public protest in this area, the city finally took care of corporate resistance to underground subways by cutting down the firms' illegal overhead wires on its own. See "Mayor's Address," *BRCOD*, 1885, p. 25; 1886, pp. 40–44; 1889, p. 68; "Annual Report of Board of Fire Commissioners," *BRCOD*, 1886–1903; *Baltimore Sun*, October 8–22, 1904.

Criticism of gas companies tends to focus on gas rates, but regulatory commission reports and newspaper articles often reveal the existence of physical problems as well: *Baltimore Sun*, March 18, 1904; *Engineering Record*, 41 (June 23, 1900), p. 601; *First Annual Report of the Commission of Gas and Electricity of the State of New York* (New York, 1906), pp. 22, 56, 64, 70–71; see also Stead, *If Christ Came to Chicago*, pp. 194–207.

For discussion of transportation company resistance to demands for improvement, see, for example, *Report of the Street Railway Commission to the City Council of Chicago* (Chicago, 1900), pp. 21–24; Lloyd, *The Chicago Traction Question*, pp. 30–34; Edwin Jones Clapp, *The Port of Boston: A Study and a Solution of the Traffic and Operating Problems of Boston . . .* (New Haven, Conn., 1916), passim; Commission on Metropolitan Improvements, *Public Improvements for the Metropolitan District* (Boston, 1909), pp. 17–30, passim; Joint Board on Metropolitan Improvement, *Final Report* (Boston, 1911), pp. 46–78. See also Edward M. Bassett, *Report on the Grade Crossings in New York and the Need of Change in the Grade Crossing Law* (Albany, N.Y., 1910), p. 8; Stead, *If Christ Came to Chicago*, pp. 194–96.

29 Bish and Nourse, *Urban Economics and Policy Analysis*, pp. 121–25. See also James M. Buchanan and Gordon Tullock, *The Calculus of Consent: Logical Foundations of Constitutional Decisionmaking* (Ann Arbor, Mich., 1965), pp. 92–116ff.

30 Sam Bass Warner, Jr., *The Private City: Philadelphia in Three Periods of Its Growth* (Philadelphia, 1968).

31 For some good pictures of this problem see Whitehill, *Boston: A Topographical History*, pp. 83, 138; Harold M. Mayer and Richard C. Wade, *Chicago: Growth of a Metropolis* (Chicago, 1969), pp. 94–95. For the legal dimension of the problem see Horwitz, *The Transformation of American Law*, pp. 71–74. Even government agencies fought to protect their investments in the status quo. See, for example, Clapp, *The Port of Boston*, pp. 16, 28–37, 50, 79–80, 251ff; "Mains and Subways," *Engineering Record*, 41 (June 23, 1900), p. 601; *Second Report of the Sewerage Commission* (Baltimore, 1899), p. 31. See also Chapter 8 of this book.

32 "Annual Report of the Superintendent of Streets," *Boston City Documents*, 1867, No. 6, p. 14. See also Chapters 6, 7, and 8 of this book.

33 See Chapters 6, 7, and 8 of this book for extended descriptions of this problem.

34 Samuel W. Bates, *Proposed Highland Railroad: Arguments of Samuel W. Bates for the Remonstrants* (Boston, 1872), p. 4.

35 An excellent, in–depth discussion of these problems in the context of actual redevelopment efforts is in Blake, *Water for the Cities*, passim. See also Chapters 6, 7, and 8 of this book.

36 Blake, *Water for the Cities*, pp. 63–77, 172–247.

37 For progressive reformers like Frank J. Goodnow, this powerlessness was one of the main reasons for the failure of city governments to deal constructively with urban ills: See his *City Government in the United States* (New York, 1904), pp. 89–99, 303–04; *Municipal Problems* (New York, 1907), pp. 34–38, 61–62, 73–79; and *Municipal Home Rule: A Study in Administration* (New York, 1895). See also Chapters 7 and 8 of this book.

38 Huse, *The Financial History of Boston*, pp. 73–74, 127–29.

39 This is a very abbreviated summary of the Chicago traction problem. For more detailed histories, see Lloyd, *The Chicago Traction Question*; and Board of Supervising Engineers, Chicago Traction, *Twentieth Annual Report* (1927), pp. 4–28.

40 Bish and Nourse, *Urban Economics and Policy Analysis*, pp. 126–27; Steiner, "Public Expenditure Budgeting," pp. 272–75.

41 Seymour J. Mandelbaum, *Boss Tweed's New York* (New York, 1965), pp. 58 and passim. See also Chapter 8 of this book.

42 Perhaps because they were so much closer to the action (and not as accustomed as we are to assuming that government is the natural source of public policy making), nineteenth century muckrakers realized that this was the direction in which most "boodle" flowed. See, for example, Lincoln Steffens's *The Shame of the Cities* (New York, 1904) and "Who, or What, Started the Evil?" reprinted in Edward C. Banfield, *Urban Government* (Glencoe, Ill., 1969), pp. 248–51. See also Stead, *If Christ Came to Chicago*, pp. 178–87.

43 Victor Rosewater, *Special Assessments: A Study in Municipal Finance* (New York, 1898).

44 Roger David Simon, *Expansion of an Industrial City: Milwaukee 1880–1910* (unpublished Ph.D. dissertation, University of Wisconsin, 1971); "Street Paving in Chicago," *Municipal Engineering*, 15 (October 1898), p. 254.

45 See Chapters 6, 7, and 8 of this book.

46 The detailed reports of municipal engineers and of departments and boards of public works make this very clear. For an interesting mapping of the outward expansion of certain public services in Baltimore, see Olson, "Baltimore Imitates the Spider," pp. 559–60, 568–72. See also Samuel P. Hayes, "The Changing Political Structure of the City in American History," *Journal of Urban History*, 1 (November 1974), pp. 14–15.

47 "Mains and Subways," *New York Evening Post*, reprinted in *Engineering Record*, 41 (June 23, 1900), p. 601.

48 See Chapters 6, 7, and 8 of this book.

49 For example, the Tweed Ring delayed the building of badly needed sewers and street improvements in aging inner city areas in favor of constructing them in the developing middle class periphery. See Mandelbaum, *Boss Tweed's New York*, pp. 59–67, 73, 103; and Eugene P. Moehring, *Public Works and the Patterns of Urban Real Estate Growth in Manhattan, 1835–1894* (New York, 1981), pp. 31–324. See also Chapter 6 of this book.

50 For material on the self-image of the Citizens' Association of Chicago and the scope of its activities, see *Addresses and Reports of the Citizens' Association of Chicago* (Chicago, 1874–90); and *Manual of the Citizens' Association of Chicago* (Chicago, 1886).

51 Theodore Cooper, "The Use of Steel for Bridges," *Transactions of the American Society of Civil Engineers*, 8 (October 1879), p. 264. The best primary sources for studying the gradual and hard-won development of modern civil engineering techniques and ideas are the reports of municipal engineers and public works commissioners and the engineering journals of the day, such as the *Transactions of the American Society of Civil Engineers*, *The Sanitary Engineer* (after 1887, *The Engineering Record*), and *Engineering News*. Typical of articles dealing with the problems of technological development are R. Hering, "Brick Arches for Large Sewers," *Transactions of the American Society of Civil Engineers*, 7 (September 1878), pp. 252–57, and discussion, pp. 258–63; Edward P. North, "The Construction and Maintenance of Roads," *Transactions of the American Society of Civil Engineers*, 8 (May 1879), pp. 95–148; and discussion, *Transactions of the American Society of Civil Engineers* (December 1879), pp. 333–72. Department of Public Works, City of Chicago, *Chicago Public Works* (Chicago, 1873), and King, *Consolidated of Baltimore*, also emphasize the trial-and-error nature of technological development in the public works and public utility areas. For further discussion see Joel Tarr et al., "Water and Wastes: A Retrospective Assessment of Waste and Water Technology in the United States, 1800–1932," *Technology and Culture*, 25 (April 1984), pp. 226–63.

52 Lemuel Shattuck, *Letter from Lemuel Shattuck in Answer to Interrogatories in Relation to the Introduction of Water in the City of Boston* (Boston, 1845), pp. 14–

15. For an interesting "I told you so" on the dire results of heeding the advice of "croakers" rather than farsighted civic leaders, see Josiah Quincy, *Atlantic Avenue: Its Relation to Mercantile and Economic Interests of the City* . . . (Boston, 1873), p. 10. A related problem that greatly complicated planning was the fact that in some of the older cities, infrastructures had been established in such a haphazard, *ad hoc* way that by the late nineteenth century, no one was sure where they were or what condition they were in. For example, as late as 1898, engineers in New York City complained that many of the streets in the solidly built up parts of Manhattan were still unsewered and that "many of the buildings on them are drained by means unknown to the department" ("Care and Maintenance of the New York Sewerage System," *City Government*, 4 [May 1898], pp. 167–69). For further discussion of these sorts of problems, see Tarr et al., "Water and Wastes."

53 Board of Sewerage Commissioners, *Report and Plan of Sewerage for the City of Chicago, Illinois* (Chicago, 1855), pp. 6–8. The Chief Engineer discussed the problem in retrospect in E. S. Chesbrough, "The Drainage and Sewerage of Chicago," *Public Health Reports and Papers*, 4 (1877), pp. 20–21.

54 Annual Report of the Board of Public Works to the City of Chicago, 1862, pp. 40–43; Thomas D. Garry, *History of Chicago Sewers* (Chicago, typescript in possession of Chicago Municipal Research Library, 1941).

55 Board of Sewerage Commissioners, *Report and Plan of Sewerage*, p. 8. See also David H. Pinkney, *Napoleon III and the Rebuilding of Paris* (Princeton, N.J., 1958), pp. 143–45. For an example of the debate over separate sewer systems, see *Transactions of the American Society of Civil Engineers*, 10 (February 1881), pp. 23–52.

56 Board of Sewerage Commissioners, *Report and Plan of Sewerage*, p. 15. This is *much* smaller than the up to 8- by 14.5-foot elliptical, hydraulic cement collecting mains introduced in Paris at the same time (Pinkney, *Napoleon III and the Rebuilding of Paris*, pp. 132–34).

57 Garry, *History of Chicago Sewers*, pp. 29–66; Department of Water and Sewers, *1856–1956: The Chicago Sewerage System: 100 Years of Protecting Chicago's Health* (Chicago, 1956); George W. Jackson, "An Address on Underground Chicago" (Chicago, 1906), p. 6.

58 Denise DeClue, "Deep Tunnel," *Chicago Reader* (June 24, 1977). According to Garry, the health and flooding problems climaxed in August 1885, after a storm flooded the Chicago River and carried decades of accumulated septic sludge far out into the lake, past the city's water intake crib, causing a typhoid epidemic (*History of Chicago Sewers*, pp. 17–18). According to DeClue some 90,000 people died of various diseases during this epidemic within days of the storm. In *Sanitation Strategy for a Lakefront Metropolis: The Case of Chicago* (DeKalb, Ill., 1978), p. 64, Louis P. Cain repeats the charge, apparently on the basis of a report published in 1915 by George Soper, John Watson, and Arthur Martin, *A Report to the Chicago Real Estate Board on the Disposal of Sewage and Protection of the Water Supply of Chicago Illinois*. I could find no data to support this astounding claim (which would have nearly doubled the death rate for the year), however. Strangely, neither the Health Department (1885)

nor the *Chicago Tribune* (August 2–October 5, 1885) mentioned an epidemic. A more accurate view of the heavy health costs of the system can be found in Edwin Oaks Jordan, "Typhoid Fever and the Water Supply in Chicago," reprint of article in *Journal of the American Medical Association* (December 20, 1902) in the possession of the Chicago Historical Society.

59   The city has, with the help of a huge infusion of federal aid, finally begun construction of a massive storm drainage system that the original engineers decided not to build. The multi-billion dollar improvement involves drilling one hundred and twenty-five miles of fifteen- to thirty-five-foot-wide tunnels through solid rock about two hundred feet beneath the city and building huge underground reservoirs to store the run-off from heavy storms until it can be pumped up to local treatment plants to be purified and safely returned to local rivers. Ironically, however, even this immense new system is not completely separate from the original unified storm and sanitary drains and so will still mix raw sewage with storm run-off. Critics worry that the mix of sewage and rainwater in the deeply submerged tunnels and reservoirs will ultimately pollute Chicago's aquifer. Thus the creators of this expensive infrastructural improvement may have also unwittingly designed it to cause as many problems as it solves. See DeClue, "Deep Tunnel."

60   A city's failure to appropriate sufficient funds for necessary engineering work could be disastrous. See, for example, D. M. Stauffer, "Fall of the Western Arched Approach to South Street Bridge, Philadelphia, Pa.," *Transactions of the American Society of Civil Engineers*, 7 (September 1878), pp. 264–73.
       The corrupt misappropriation of funds could be equally disastrous. See Stanley K. Schultz and Clay McShane, "To Engineer the Metropolis: Sewers, Sanitation, and City Planning in Late Nineteenth Century America," *Journal of American History*, 65 (September 1978), p. 397.

61   King discusses the rise of regulation in the public utility area in Baltimore in *Consolidated of Baltimore*. For a more general discussion see Richard Hofstadter, *The Age of Reform: From Bryan to FDR* (New York, 1955), pp. 238–56.

62   Martin J. Schiesl, *The Politics of Efficiency: Municipal Administration and Reform in America 1800–1920* (Berkeley, 1977).

63   Samuel P. Hays and Melvin G. Holli spearheaded the attack on the so-called structural or administrative reformers. See Hays, "The Politics of Reform in Municipal Government in the Progressive Era," *Pacific Northwest Quarterly* (October 1964), pp. 157–60; Holli, *Reform in Detroit: Hazen S. Pingree and Urban Politics* (New York, 1969), pp. 161–81.

64   Schiesl, *The Politics of Efficiency*.

Chapter 4. The barriers to spatial change

1   For a brief theoretical summary of the nature and function of agglomeration economies in location decision making, see James Heibrun, *Urban Economics and Public Policy* (New York, 1974), pp. 12–17. For a fuller discussion, see Edgar M. Hoover, *Location Theory and the Shoe and Leather Industries* (Cambridge, Mass., 1937).

Although it is no longer completely up to date, a good bibliographic review of the research by urban geographers on land use patterns and spatial change in nineteenth and twentieth century cities is contained in Harold Carter, *The Study of Urban Geography* (London, 1972), pp. 160–286. It surveys work done on European city development as well as that done on American city development.

Some important studies of the spatial evolution of American cities include David Ward, *Cities and Immigrants: A Geography of Change in Nineteenth-Century America* (New York, 1971); Martyn Bowden, "The Dynamics of City Growth: An Historical Geography of the San Francisco Central District, 1850–1931" (unpublished Ph.D. dissertation, University of California, Berkeley, 1967); Sam Bass Warner, Jr., *The Private City: Philadelphia in Three Periods of Its Growth* (Philadelphia, 1968); Warner, Jr., *Street Car Suburbs: The Process of Growth in Boston, 1870–1900* (Cambridge, Mass., 1962).

2 Sam Bass Warner, Jr., *The Urban Wilderness: A History of the American City* (New York, 1972), pp. 81–84; Warner, Jr., *The Private City*, pp. 3–22.

3 More detailed examinations of the impact of the specialization of land use patterns on community life can be found in Elizabeth Blackmar, "Housing and Property Relations in Antebellum New York City" (unpublished Ph.D. dissertation, Harvard University, 1980) for the antebellum era; and in Warner, Jr., *Street Car Suburbs*, for the second half of the nineteenth century.

4 This fact comes up in almost every study of social and geographical mobility in nineteenth century cities. For a summary of the findings and a qualification, see Theodore Hershberg, "The New Urban History: Toward an Interdisciplinary History of the City," *Journal of Urban History*, 5 (November 1978), pp. 18–20ff and note 39, p. 38. Historians are only beginning to follow business locations through city directories. My own (unfortunately very fragmentary) research indicates a fairly high rate of geographical mobility within definite territorial limits, as well as high firm birth and death rates.

5 Oscar Handlin, *Boston's Immigrants: A Study in Acculturation* (New York, 1972), p. 105; see also pp. 100–109. Handlin's maps of the distribution of Irish, non-Irish foreigners, and blacks in central Boston in 1850 (pp. 90, 92, 95) make an interesting comparison with Walter Firey's map of the residences of the city's most wealthy citizens (persons worth over $100,000) in 1846 (Firey, *Land Use in Central Boston* [Cambridge, Mass., 1947], p. 56). Taken together they dramatize the filling in and interspersal patterns quite vividly. For an interesting verbal description of a middle to upper class neighborhood in the process of being filled in with less well to do residents, see Richard Sennett, *Families Against the City: Middle Class Homes of Industrial Chicago, 1872–1890* (Cambridge, Mass., 1971), p. 36.

6 See Chapter 7 of this book.

7 Theodore Hershberg et al., "The 'Journey to Work': An Empirical Investigation of Work, Residence, and Transformation, Philadelphia 1850 and 1880," in Theodore Hershberg (ed.), *Toward an Interdisciplinary History of the City: Work, Space, Family, and Group Experience in Nineteenth Century Philadelphia* (New York, 1979).

8   This is evident in any downtown insurance map of the period. See also Chapters 6 and 7 of this book.
9   Raymond L. Fales and Leon N. Moses, "Thunen, Weber, and the Spatial Structure of the Nineteenth Century City," in Mark Perlman, Charles J. Leven, and Benjamin Chinitz (eds.), *Spatial, Regional and Population Economics: Essays in Honor of Edgar M. Hoover* (New York, 1972), pp. 137–68; Allan R. Pred, "The Intrametropolitan Location of American Manufacturing," in Larry S. Browne (ed.), *Internal Structure of the City: Readings on Space and Environment* (New York, 1971), pp. 380–90. As Pred points out, most manufacturing in cities remained concentrated in the *core* of the city until 1900, the relative increase of industry in the suburbs not becoming noticeable (except in a few unusual places like Pullman) until about 1910 (p. 385).
10 Hershberg et al., "The 'Journey to Work' "; Blackmar, "Housing and Property Relations in Antebellum New York City"; Thomas Tucker, *Bannisters Lane, 1708–1899* (Boston, 1899), p. 18.
11 The telephone, of course, made its first appearance quite early, in the 1870s. It did not become a common means of intra-city communication for some time, however. Indeed, as late as 1898, all the Bell companies together still had fewer than 500,000 subscribers. Thus telephone communications did not really begin to free up urban land use patterns until the end of the nineteenth century. See *Manufacturers Record* (Baltimore, July 14, 1904), p. 584.
12 For an overview, see Douglas Pocock and Ray Hudson, *Images of the Urban Environment* (New York, 1978), pp. 68–86.
13 Firey, *Land Use in Central Boston*.
14 Ibid., pp. 87–113, 170–97. Firey's example of a geographically stable working class neighborhood was Boston's Italian North End. South Boston has been just as stable for an even longer period for the same reasons and is a more appropriate example for the era covered here.
15 Edward Ewing Pratt, *Industrial Causes of Congestion of Population in New York City* (New York, 1911), p. 105; S. Seymour Curry, *Manufacturing and Wholesale Industries of Chicago* (Chicago, 1918), p. 438.
16 Firey, *Land Use in Central Boston*, pp. 136–55.
17 Thomas Lee Philpott, *The Slum and the Ghetto: Neighborhood Deterioration and Middle Class Reform, Chicago, 1880–1930* (New York, 1978), pp. 146–200. See also Chapters 6 and 7 of this book.
18 Pocock and Hudson, *Images of the Urban Environment*, pp. 25–35, 48–52; Christian Norberg-Schultz, *Existence, Space, and Architecture* (London, 1971), pp. 17–27. See also Kevin Lynch, *The Image of the City* (Cambridge, Mass., 1960), pp. 46–90, passim.
19 For a more elaborate theoretical discussion of these problems, see Julian Wolpert, "Behavioral Aspects of the Decision to Migrate,"*Papers of the Regional Science Association*, 15 (1965), pp. 161–66.
20 See Chapters 6, 7, and 8 of this book.
21 Richard M. Hurd, *Principles of City Land Values* (New York, 1905), pp. 18, 41; Bowden, "The Dynamics of City Growth," pp. 276–300, 323.
22 Hurd, *Principles of City Land Values*, p. 35.

23 Bowden, "The Dynamics of City Growth," pp. 276–300.

24 Hurd, *Principles of City Land Values*, p. 35.

25 "A Communication from the City Physician on Asiatic Cholera...," *Boston City Document*, 1886, No. 21. "Final Report of the Committee on Streets," *Boston City Document*, 1866, No. 120, pp. 23–24.

26 Bion J. Arnold, *Report on the Re-arrangement and Development of Steam Railroad Terminals of the City of Chicago* (Chicago, 1913), pp. 58–59.

27 "Report of a Majority of the Committee on the Extension of Devonshire Street," *Boston City Documents*, 1857, No. 60; *Sketches and Business Directory of Boston and Vicinity for 1860 and 1861* (Boston, 1860), pp. 156–61.

28 "Mayor's Address," *Report of the City Officers and Departments to the City Council of Baltimore* (hereafter referred to as *BRCOD*), 1890, pp. 34–35.

29 "Annual Report of the Board of Health," *BRCOD*, 1878, p. 458.

30 Warner, Jr., *The Urban Wilderness*, pp. 28–37.

Chapter 5. Theory and narrative history

1 Oscar Handlin, "The Modern City as a Field of Historical Study," in Oscar Handlin and John Burchard (eds.), *The Historian and the City* (Cambridge, Mass., 1963), p. 26.

Chapter 6. The rebuilding of Chicago

1 The best description of the fire is in Elias Colbert and Everett Chamberlin, *Chicago and the Great Conflagration* (Cincinnati, 1871). For statistics on the destruction see pp. 270–76, 285–303, 315–18.

2 Ibid., pp. 320–21.

3 Ibid., pp. 321–24. See also F. B. Wilkie, "Among the Ruins," *Lakeside Monthly*, 7 (January 1872), pp. 50–51. Chicagoans' inability to think in terms of re-development in the first few days after the conflagration is also evident in the newspapers' coverage of the fire's aftermath. This chapter draws primarily on three of the city's papers, the *Chicago Tribune, Chicago Times,* and *Chicago Evening Post,* for its analysis of environmental redevelopment during recon-struction. Except in rare cases, letters did not prove to be a useful source of information on the process and problems of redevelopment for either Chicago, Boston, or Baltimore, perhaps because people were too busy to write about anything more than the horror and anguish they felt immediately after the fires and the relief they felt after reconstruction. City newspapers proved to be an excellent source of information on the city building (and rebuilding) process, however, one that more urban historians should consider tapping.

4 *Chicago Tribune,* October 14, 1871.

5 *Chicago Tribune,* October 15, 1871.

6 *Chicago Tribune,* October 20, 1871; *Chicago Times,* October 18, 1871.

7 *Chicago Tribune,* October 20, 1871.

8 *Chicago Tribune,* October 22, 1871.

9 *Chicago Times,* October 21, 1871; *Chicago Tribune,* October 31, 1871.

10 *Chicago Tribune*, October 22, 1871.

11 *Chicago Tribune*, October 27, 1871; November 23, 1871.

12 *Chicago Tribune*, October 31, 1871; November 10, 1871.

13 *Chicago Tribune*, October 23, 1871.

14 *Chicago Tribune*, November 14, 1871.

15 *Chicago Tribune*, November 1, 1871; *Chicago Times*, October 23, 1871.

16 *Proceedings of the Common Council of the City of Chicago* (hereafter referred to as *PCCC*), October 23, 1871, p. 331; *Chicago Times*, October 29, 1871.

17 For descriptions of this effort see *Chicago Tribune* and *Chicago Times*, October 23–November 8, 1871. The fusionist mayoral candidate was Joseph Medill, editor of the *Tribune*.

18 *Chicago Tribune*, November 6, 1871.

19 *Chicago Tribune*, November 9, 1871; November 11, 1871.

20 *Chicago Tribune*, November 13, 1871; November 14, 1871; *Chicago Times*, November 12, 1871; *PCCC*, November 27, 1871, pp. 356–57.

21 *Chicago Times*, January 7, 1872.

22 *Chicago Tribune*, January 19, 1872; February 1, 1872.

23 *Chicago Tribune*, January 15, 1872; February 3, 1872; *Chicago Evening Post*, December 30, 1871; "Mayor's Inaugural Address," *PCCC*, December 4, 1871, p. 8.

24 The editors of the *Chicago Times* particularly emphasized the housing reform angle. Since the *Times* later came out in support of legalizing house moving as a necessity for the landless homeowner (while the *Tribune* never evinced any sort of concern for the problems of the poor at all), the *Times*'s concern here seems to have been genuine. See *Chicago Times*, November 12, 1871; November 16, 1871; November 19, 1871; December 11, 1871; January 7, 1872; January 10, 1872; January 16, 1872; January 19, 1872; February 10, 1872. Compare with *Chicago Tribune*, November 13, 1871; November 16, 1871; November 23, 1871; January 7, 1872; January 15, 1872; January 19, 1872; February 1, 1872.

25 *Chicago Tribune*, November 23, 1871; January 15–19, 1872; *Chicago Times*, January 14–16, 1872; January 21, 1872; February 10, 1872. See also Chicago Board of Health, *Annual Report*, 1875, p. 94; Chicago Relief and Aid Society, *Report of the Chicago Relief and Aid Society: First Special Report* (Chicago, 1873), p. 8. The *Chicago Evening Post* listed house-moving announcements almost daily.

26 *Chicago Times*, December 11, 1871; January 10, 1872; *Chicago Tribune*, November 23, 1871.

27 These facts were conveyed to the newspapers and the city as a whole in letters written by A. C. Hesing, a leader of the German community, after the January demonstration. See *Chicago Tribune*, January 18, 1872; *Chicago Evening Post*, January 17, 1872. They were corroborated by an architect, a respectable, "neutral" source, in an article in the *Times* on January 21, 1872.

28 *Chicago Tribune*, November 23, 1871; *Chicago Times*, November 16, 1871; November 19, 1871; January 10, 1872.

29 *Chicago Times*, November 29, 1871; January 17, 1872.

30   Colbert and Chamberlin, *Chicago and the Great Conflagration*, pp. 286–87, 345–46.

31   The description of the organization and events of the demonstration in the text is based on articles that appeared in the *Chicago Times*, January 14–17, 1872; the *Chicago Tribune*, January 15–18, 1872; and the *Chicago Evening Post*, January 16–17, 1872. These are, admittedly, biased sources. The editorial biases are, however, offset by the fact that the editors were so biased (or perhaps so blind with rage) that they often printed reports the details of which failed to fit their interpretation of what was going on. They are also offset by the fact that the editors attempted to give both sides of the controversy an airing (if only to debunk the other side more dramatically). The *Evening Post*, for example, ran an interview with A. C. Hesing, an organizer of the march, which the *Tribune* reprinted. Both papers also published letters from Hesing. The *Times* conducted interviews with some of the participants in the protest, while the *Tribune* published a translation of the *Staats Zeitung* report on the event, a report that was as biased positively as the *Tribune*'s was negatively.

32   No copies of the petitions apparently have survived, but the *Times* and the *Tribune* contain extracts from them, different extracts as it happens. The first quote is from the *Chicago Tribune*, January 15, 1872; the second from the *Chicago Times*, January 13; the third from the *Chicago Times*, January 15. See also Hesing's letters in *Chicago Evening Post*, January 17, 1872, and *Chicago Tribune*, January 18, 1872.

33   *Chicago Times*, January 15, 1872.

34   *Chicago Tribune*, January 16, 1872; *Chicago Times*, January 16, 1872; *Chicago Evening Post*, January 16, 1872.

35   *Chicago Times*, January 17, 1872; *Chicago Tribune*, January 15–17, 1872. ("Bummer" seems to have been the local code word for corrupt machine politician.)

36   *Chicago Tribune*, January 29, 1872; *Chicago Evening Post*, January 29, 1872.

37   Hesing letter, *Chicago Evening Post*, January 17, 1872; and *Chicago Tribune*, January 18, 1872.

38   Hesing letter, *Chicago Evening Post*, January 17, 1872; and *Chicago Tribune*, January 18, 1872. See also newspaper accounts of the gathering at Alderman Carney's grocery store preceding the demonstration; *Staats Zeitung* report translation, *Chicago Tribune*, January 17, 1872.

39   Hesing interview, *Chicago Evening Post*, January 16, 1872; *Chicago Tribune*, January 17, 1872. See also *Chicago Times*, January 21, 1872.

40   *Chicago Evening Post*, January 17, 1872.

41   *Chicago Tribune*, January 21, 1872.

42   *Chicago Times*, January 19, 1872.

43   *Chicago Times*, January 21, 1872.

44   *Chicago Times*, February 3, 1872.

45   *Chicago Tribune*, February 1, 1872.

46   *Chicago Tribune*, January 18, 1872; January 28, 1872; January 25, 1872; January 28, 1872; January 30, 1872; February 1–3, 1872; February 6, 1872.

47   *PCCC*, February 12, 1872, pp. 83–85.

48 *Chicago Tribune*, November 14, 1871. See also *Chicago Evening Post*, December 30, 1871.

49 *Chicago Tribune*, March 3, 1872; June 30, 1872; October 9, 1872; November 17, 1872; October 9, 1873; [*Chicago Times*,] *New Chicago* (Chicago, 1872; referred to hereafter as *New Chicago*), pp. 72, 81–82. See also Everett Chamberlin, *Chicago and Its Suburbs* (Chicago, 1974); Local Community Research Committee, *Documentary History of North Center Community*, Document No. 9 and passim.

50 Robert Hunter, *Tenement Conditions in Chicago: Report by the Investigating Committee of the City Homes Association* (Chicago, 1901); Edith Abbott, *The Tenements of Chicago 1908–1935* (Chicago, 1936).

51 See three reports of the Chicago Relief and Aid Society: *Report of the Chicago Relief and Aid Society: First Special Report*, pp. 7–9; *Annual Report . . . for the Year 1872* (Chicago, 1873), p. 12; *Report of the Chicago Relief and Aid Society of Disbursement of Contributions for the Sufferers by the Chicago Fire* (Chicago, 1874), pp. 183–95.

52 John H. Rauch, *A Report to the Board of Health of the City of Chicago on the Necessity of an Extension of the Sewerage of the City* (Chicago, 1873), p. 15.

53 Ironically, the Citizens' Relief and Aid Society noted this fact with pride. Chicago Relief and Aid Society, *Annual Report for the Year 1872*, p. 12.

54 *Chicago Tribune*, October 19, 1871.

55 Chicago Relief and Aid Society, *Report of Disbursement of Contributions*, p. 440.

56 Homer Hoyt, *One Hundred Years of Land Values in Chicago: The Relationship of the Growth of Chicago to the Rise of Its Land Values* (Chicago, 1933), pp. 81–90; *A Handbook for Strangers and Tourists to the City of Chicago . . .* (Chicago, 1869), pp. 33–34; Chicago Building and Loan Association, *Statistical and Historical Review of Chicago: Rise and Value of Real Estate, Parks, Tunnels, Buildings, etc.* (Chicago, 1869), pp. 34–41. Hoyt's book is the best work on land prices and real estate development in Chicago for this period. Unfortunately, he generalizes the pre- and post-fire periods and so fails to take into account the impact that the fire and reconstruction had on the physical expansion of the central business district. His claim that State Street was completely transformed by 1871 is mistaken. In fact, Palmer was unable to bully many of his neighbors into moving their wood houses back on their lots (to complete the widening of the street), let alone replace the houses with commercial structures. It took the fire to get them to finish up his commercial redevelopment scheme. See *Palmer, Potter 1826–1902 (Five Different Sketches of Potter Palmer)* (Chicago, circa 1902; typescript in possession of the Chicago Historical Society). For a vivid description of the slums on Madison Street before the fire, see *Chicago Tribune*, April 28, 1872. See also Sanborn Map Company, *Insurance Maps of Chicago, Illinois, 1868–1869* (copy corrected to about 1871; and compare with copy corrected to about 1872, both in the map collection of the Chicago Historical Society).

57 Charles Randolph (for Chicago Board of Trade), *16th Annual Report of the Trade and Commerce of Chicago for the Year Ending December 31, 1873* (Chicago,

1873); *Chicago Evening Post*, March 2, 1872; April 12, 1872; *Chicago Tribune*, October 9, 1872; July 18, 1874. Everett Chamberlin, "Five Months After," *Lakeside Monthly*, 7 (April 1872), p. 321.

58   *New Chicago*, pp. 29–32, 54–59; *Chicago Tribune*, February 1, 1872; April 28, 1872.

59   *New Chicago*, pp. 48–51; *Chicago Times*, March 3, 1872; *Chicago Tribune*, October 9, 1872.

60   *The Landowner: A Journal of Real Estate, Building & Improvement* (hereafter referred to as *Landowner*), (February 1872), p. 23; (April 1872), p. 55; (July 1872), p. 109; Robert Twyman, *History of Marshall Field & Company* (Philadelphia, 1954), pp. 43–44; *New Chicago*, pp. 21–59, 94; Frank Gilbert, "The Rebuilding of the City," *Lakeside Monthly*, 8 (October 1872), p. 294; John Villiers Farwell, *Some Recollections of John V. Farwell* (Chicago, 1911), pp. 69–71; Chamberlin, "Five Months After," pp. 314–15.

61   Cook County Registry of Deeds (hereafter referred to as CCRD), Blocks 79, 80, 81, 82 (School Section Addition to Chicago of Section 16–39–14, Ante-Fire), *Index*, Book 466, pp. 72–155.

62   *Chicago Tribune*, February 11, 1872; February 18, 1872; February 25, 1872; *Chicago Evening Post*, April 12, 1872; *Landowner* (July 1872), p. 118.

63   *Chicago Tribune*, February 11, 1872; *Chicago Times*, January 28, 1872. Coolbaugh's building was the first business block completed in the burnt district (*New Chicago*, p. 59).

64   *Chicago Times*, March 30, 1872; *Chicago Evening Post*, April 12, 1872; *Chicago Tribune*, May 5, 1872; *Landowner* (July 1872), p. 118; Gilbert, "The Rebuilding of the City," p. 306.

65   *Chicago Times*, March 30, 1872; *Chicago Evening Post*, April 12, 1872; *Chicago Tribune*, May 5, 1872; *Landowner* (July 1872), p. 118; Gilbert, "The Rebuilding of the City," p. 306. An examination of deeds relating to land transfers on Lake Street between Michigan Avenue and State Street after the fire makes clear the landowners' paralysis and also testifies to the importance of leaseholds and trusteeships on the street. See CCRD, Blocks 7, 8, 9, 10 (Fort Dearborn Addition to Chicago of Section 0–39–4, Ante-Fire), *Index*, Book 460–A, pp. 174–224, and Book 460–B, pp. 4–44.

66   CCRD Block 9, *Index*, Book 460–B, p. 16; *Landowner* (July 1872), p. 118; Gilbert, "The Rebuilding of the City," p. 306; *Chicago Tribune*, May 5, 1872; *Chicago Times*, March 30, 1872.

67   CCRD Block 9, *Index*, Book 460–B, p. 16; *Landowner* (July 1872), p. 118; Gilbert, "The Rebuilding of the City," p. 306; *Chicago Tribune*, May 5, 1872; *Chicago Times*, March 30, 1872. See also *Chicago Tribune*, March 24, 1872; *Chicago Times*, March 3, 1872.

68   CCRD Block 9, *Index*, Book 460–B, p. 16; *Landowner* (July 1872), p. 118; Gilbert, "The Rebuilding of the City," p. 306; *Chicago Tribune*, May 5, 1872; *Chicago Times*, March 30, 1872; *Chicago Tribune*, March 24, 1872; *Chicago Times*, March 3, 1872; *Chicago Tribune*, February 11, 1872; February 18, 1872. See also Chamberlin, "Five Months After," pp. 314–15; Gilbert, "The Rebuilding of the City," p. 294; *Landowner* (February 1872), p. 23; (April 1872),

p. 54; (July 1873), p. 119; *Chicago Times*, January 28, 1872; January 31, 1872; February 4, 1872; February 13, 1872; February 16, 1872; February 17, 1872; March 3, 1872; *Chicago Tribune*, September 15, 1872.

69   *New Chicago* listed all the empty lots on each street in the central business
·   district at the end of 1872 (see Figure 6.4). See also Gilbert, "The Rebuilding of the City," p. 219.

70   *Chicago Tribune*, July 7, 1872; "One Year After," *Lakeside Monthly* (October 1872), pp. 245–47; *New Chicago*, pp. 19, 29ff., 84.

71   *Chicago Times*, March 30, 1872; April 1, 1872; *New Chicago*, p. 84.

72   Chicago Evening Post, April 12, 1872; Chamberlin, "Five Months Later," p. 321.

73   *Chicago Times*, February 10, 1872.

74   *Chicago Tribune*, October 15, 1871.

75   *Chicago Times*, December 31, 1871. The problems with the pipes were ignored until after the second great fire in July 1874.

76   *Chicago Times*, December 12, 1871; *Chicago Tribune*, October 12, 1871; November 14, 1871; February 27, 1872. Some of these suggestions were made in letters to the editor: *Chicago Tribune*, October 31, 1871; December 19, 1871; March 11, 1872; *PCCC*, December 4, 1871, pp. 8–9; *Report of the Board of Police in the Fire Department…for the Year Ending March 31, 1872*, p. 21. Henceforth all references to departmental annual reports will be shortened to name of department, *Annual Report* (year ending date).

77   *Chicago Tribune*, October 27, 1871; January 1, 1872; March 2, 1872; *Chicago Times*, December 31, 1871.

78   Board of Public Works (BPW), *Annual Report* (years ending March 31, 1872; March 31, 1873; March 31, 1874). Many of the BPW's failures came to light in a dramatic way when a popular reform movement to modernize the water system began after the second conflagration in 1874.

79   BPW, *Annual Report* (year ending March 31, 1872), pp. 63, 79.

80   *Chicago Times*, December 12, 1871; the Fire Department's annual reports for 1868–71 bear this claim out.

81   Citizens' Association of Chicago, *Addresses and Reports of the Citizens' Association of Chicago 1874 to 1876* (Chicago, 1876), pp. 3–4.

82   *Chicago Times*, December 12, 1871. For evidence relating to the political reform movement's purpose as a demand articulation mechanism, see *Chicago Tribune*, July 18–19, 1874; July 26, 1874; August 27, 1874; and Citizens' Association of Chicago, *Addresses and Reports 1874 to 1876*, pp. 7–8.

83   Citizens' Association of Chicago, *Addresses and Reports 1874 to 1876*, p. 3.

84   *PCCC*, December 4, 1871, pp. 3–7; December 2, 1872, pp. 1–3.

85   *New York Herald*, October 16, 1871; *The World* (New York), October 14, 1871.

86   H. W. S. Cleveland, *Landscape Architecture as Applied to the Wants of the West* (Chicago, 1877), edited by Roy Lubove (reprint, Pittsburgh, 1965), pp. 9–28.

87   *Chicago Times*, October 26, 1871; *Chicago Tribune*, October 20, 1871.

88   Measurements computed from figures in BPW, *Annual Report* (years ending March 31, 1872; March 31, 1873; March 31, 1874). The total length of sidewalks constructed was approximately one hundred ninety-six miles. This

included sidewalks reconstructed in the burnt district. One hundred twenty-one miles of sidewalks were burnt up by the fire, but not all were replaced by 1874 – hence the estimation (*PCCC*, December 4, 1871, p. 4).

89 *PCCC*, December 4, 1871, pp. 5–6; December 2, 1872, p. 3. BPW, *Annual Report* (year ending March 31, 1873), p. 23.

90 Rauch, *Report on the Necessity of an Extension of the Sewerage of the City*, pp. 18–19. The haphazardly scattered character of all the extensions is plain in the lists of extensions undertaken each year in the BPW's *Annual Reports*.

91 Rauch, *Report on the Necessity of an Extension of the Sewerage of the City*, pp. 17–20. See also Hoyt, *One Hundred Years of Land Values in Chicago*, p. 94 (see Figure 6.15).

92 *Chicago Tribune*, May 25, 1872; June 30, 1872; August 2, 1874; August 27, 1874; September 29, 1874; *Chicago Evening Post*, May 25, 1872.

93 *Chicago Times*, December 16, 1871. The railroad history of Chicago is amazingly difficult to decipher because of the large number of companies involved and the incestuous use of rights of way. For example, the *Times* said in this article that six "grand" lines then entered the city. The *Tribune* (January 14, 1872) said that twelve routes operated by twenty-five companies entered the city. Colbert and Chamberlin said that thirteen lines entered the city in 1871 and implied that each operated a separate route (*Chicago and the Great Conflagration*, pp. 170–72). The fact was that many of the companies operated under franchises held by other companies and that they all leased the use of rights of way to and from each other.

94 *Chicago Times*, December 16, 1871; January 20, 1872; February 8, 1872; *Chicago Evening Post*, December 19, 1871; *Chicago Tribune*, October 13, 1871; November 1, 1871; November 23, 1871; January 13–14, 1872.

95 *Chicago Evening Post*, December 19, 1871; *Chicago Times*, December 16, 1871.

96 *Chicago Times*, December 16, 1871.

97 *Chicago Times*, February 8, 1872; *Chicago Tribune*, October 19, 1871; January 13–14, 1872; February 21, 1872; *Chicago Evening Post*, January 9, 1872; *PCCC*, February 19, 1872, pp. 96–97.

98 *PCCC*, April 1, 1872, p. 146; May 13, 1872, p. 225; June 12, 1872, p. 295; November 11, 1872, p. 566; September 22, 1873, p. 428; D. C. Brooks, "Chicago and Its Railways," *Lakeside Monthly* (October 1872), p. 278.

99 *Chicago Tribune*, October 13, 1871; October 17, 1871; *Chicago Evening Post*, March 4, 1872.

100 *Chicago Evening Post*, December 19, 1871; *Chicago Times*, December 16, 1871; *Chicago Tribune*, October 19, 1871; December 4, 1871.

101 *Chicago Evening Post*, December 19, 1871; *Chicago Times*, December 16, 1871; *Chicago Tribune*, October 19, 1871; December 4, 1871. See also, *Chicago Evening Post*, January 12, 1872; March 4, 1872; *Chicago Tribune*, October 17, 1871; John F. Stover, *The History of the Illinois Central Railroad* (New York, 1975), pp. 179–81; Carlton J. Corliss, *Mainline of Mid-America: The Story of the Illinois Central* (New York, 1950), pp. 163–64.

102 *Chicago Tribune*, October 17, 1871; October 19, 1871; December 19, 1871; *Chicago Evening Post*, December 16, 1871.

103   *Chicago Evening Post*, January 12, 1872; February 7, 1872; March 1, 1872;
      March 4, 1872. For more on Scammon see Thomas Wakefield Goodspeed,
      "Jonathan Young Scammon," *The University of Chicago Biographical Sketches*
      (Chicago, 1925), Vol. 2, pp. 237–54.
104   *Chicago Evening Post*, January 12, 1872; *Chicago Times*, January 12, 1872; March
      3, 1872; *Chicago Tribune*, October 19, 1871; January 21, 1872.
105   "An Act to Provide for the Exercise of the Right of Eminent Domain," *Illinois
      Laws, 1871–1872*, Chapter 47. The *Tribune* called this the Union Depot Law
      (April 28, 1872; June 2, 1872).
106   *Chicago Tribune*, October 19, 1871; January 13–14, 1872; *Chicago Evening Post*,
      December 16, 1871; January 9, 1872; Brooks, "Chicago and Its Railways,"
      p. 278.
107   Corliss, *Mainline of Mid-America*, pp. 163–67.
108   *Chicago Evening Post*, February 7, 1872.
109   *Chicago Times*, March 3, 1872; *Chicago Tribune*, November 27, 1871; December
      3, 1871. See also *Chicago Evening Post*, January 3, 1872; January 15, 1872;
      February 7, 1872.
110   *Chicago Evening Post*, January 3, 1872.
111   *Chicago Times*, February 8, 1872; February 10, 1872; *Chicago Tribune*, February
      21, 1872; *PCCC*, February 19, 1872, pp. 96–97. Other reports of committee
      hearings and petitions and remonstrances against the proposed rights of way
      are heavily scattered through the newspapers. They are also mentioned (though
      only in one case published in full) in *PCCC*, February–April 1872.
112   *PCCC*, February 19, 1872, pp. 96–97.
113   Ibid.
114   *Chicago Times*, January 13, 1872; February 10, 1872; *Chicago Evening Post*,
      March 8, 1872.
115   *Chicago Times*, January 13, 1872; February 10, 1872; *Chicago Evening Post*,
      March 8, 1872.
116   *Chicago Tribune*, February 25, 1872; March 2, 1872.
117   *Chicago Tribune*, June 30, 1872; *Chicago Evening Post*, June 26, 1872; *PCCC*,
      August 19, 1872, p. 422.
118   *PCCC*, February 26, 1872, pp. 108–109; *Chicago Tribune*, March 7, 1872. The
      City Council made a show of dealing with this problem by adding an amend-
      ment to the ordinances which provided for binding arbitration on damage
      awards by three individuals, one to be appointed by the property holder, one
      to be appointed by the railroad company, and one to be appointed by the
      Committee on Railroads.
119   *Chicago Times*, December 16, 1871; *Chicago Evening Post*, March 25, 1871.
120   *Chicago Times*, January 13, 1872; *Chicago Tribune*, January 14, 1872; *PCCC*,
      March 11, 1872, p. 122.
121   *PCCC*, February 26, 1872, pp. 108–109.
122   *Chicago Evening Post*, March 2, 1872; March 8, 1872.
123   *Chicago Evening Post*, March 25, 1872. See also Bion J. Arnold, *Report on the
      Re-arrangement and Development of the Steam Railroad Terminals of the City of
      Chicago* (Chicago, 1913).

124   *Chicago Evening Post*, December 16, 1871; January 27, 1872; February 1, 1872;
      February 3, 1872; February 17, 1872; Chamberlin, "Five Months After," p.
      318.

125   Arnold, *Report on the Re-arrangement and Development of the Steam Railroad
      Terminals*.

126   The best summary of the spatial organization of Chicago in the late 1860s and
      early 1870s is that of Hoyt, *One Hundred Years of Land Values in Chicago*, pp.
      89–111, but as noted earlier, a serious problem is that Hoyt frequently sum-
      marizes the period, mixing up pre- and post-fire developments. See also San-
      born Map Company, *Insurance Maps of Chicago, Illinois, 1868–1869* (copy
      corrected to about 1871 and copy corrected to about 1872 in Chicago Historical
      Society). See also *New Chicago*; Chamberlin, *Chicago and Its Suburbs*; CCRD,
      Sectional Plat Maps and Deed Indexes; and *Documentary History of Chicago
      Prepared for the Chicago Historical Society and the Local Community Research
      Committee*, Vols. 1–6, especially Vol. 4, Document No. 2, in possession of
      Chicago Historical Society; and *Chicago Tribune*, June 2, 1872. See also the
      real estate columns of the local newspapers. The papers gave extensive coverage
      to land use change and real estate development in Chicago. They are an
      excellent, barely tapped primary source for examining the dynamics of spatial
      change in this and many other nineteenth century American cities.

127   The maps are based on addresses given in the business section of *Edwards
      14th Annual Directory of the City of Chicago* (Chicago, 1871) and the *Lakeside
      Annual Directory of the City of Chicago* (Chicago, 1874–75), under "Banks,"
      "Grocers Wholesale," "Drygoods Commission," "Drygoods Wholesale,"
      "Drygoods Wholesale and Retail" (1874–75 only); "Drygoods Fancy" and
      "Fancy Goods Wholesale." Each firm address is represented by one symbol,
      regardless of how many contiguous street numbers the address contained. This
      was the only fair way to draw the maps, since the directories listed many firms
      only by street corner. Because some firms occupied large buildings, however,
      the maps do not show the actual amount of territory covered by a trade.

128   Elias Colbert, "Business of the Year," *Lakeside Monthly*, October 1872, p. 258;
      W. A. Croffert, "Reconstruction," *Lakeside Monthly*, January 1872, pp. 54–56;
      Chamberlin, *Chicago and Its Suburbs*, p. 91.

129   Gilbert, "The Rebuilding of the City," p. 294; *Landowner* (February 1872),
      p. 23; (April 1872), p. 54; (July 1872), p. 109.

130   *Landowner* (February 1872), p. 23; (April 1872), p. 54; Twyman, *History of
      Marshall Field & Co.*, pp. 41–42. See also Farwell, *Some Recollections*, pp. 69–
      70.

131   *New Chicago*, p. 32.

132   *Chicago Tribune*, February 11, 1872; February 18, 1872; February 25, 1872;
      March 24, 1872; May 5, 1872; June 2, 1872; *Chicago Times*, March 3, 1872;
      March 30, 1872.

133   *Chicago Tribune*, February 11, 1872; February 18, 1872; February 25, 1872;
      March 24, 1872; May 5, 1872; June 2, 1872; *Chicago Times*, March 3, 1872;
      March 30, 1872. Quote is from *Chicago Tribune*, February 25, 1872. See also

Chicago Tribune, May 19, 1872; *Landowner* (July 1872), p. 118; Gilbert, "The Rebuilding of the City," p. 306.

134 *Chicago Tribune*, February 25, 1872.

135 *Chicago Tribune*, October 13, 1872; *Landowner* (July 1873), p. 109, and frontpiece, p. 119.

136 *Chicago Tribune*, October 27, 1871; November 23, 1871; February 11, 1872; *Chicago Times*, November 23, 1871; January 31, 1872.

137 *Chicago Times*, January 28, 1872; *Chicago Tribune*, February 11, 1872. Farwell was on the Board of Directors of Coolbaugh's bank, while Coolbaugh was trustee of some of Farwell's land in the burnt slums.

138 *Chicago Times*, January 31, 1872; February 4, 1872; *Chicago Tribune*, February 4, 1872; February 11, 1872.

139 *Chicago Times*, January 31, 1872; February 4, 1872; *Chicago Tribune*, February 4, 1872; February 11, 1872.

140 *Chicago Tribune*, February 4, 1872; February 11, 1872; *Chicago Times*, February 17, 1872.

141 *Chicago Times*, January 1, 1872.

142 *Chicago Evening Post*, March 2, 1872; April 12, 1872; *Chicago Tribune*, October 9, 1872; Randolph, *Report of the Trade and Commerce of Chicago 1873*. Chamberlin, "Five Months After," pp. 314, 321.

143 *Chicago Evening Post*, March 2, 1872; *Chicago Times*, March 30, 1872.

144 *Chicago Evening Post*, April 1, 1872; *Chicago Tribune*, March 31, 1872; Twyman, *History of Marshall Field & Co.*, pp. 43–48. See also *New Chicago*, p. 94.

145 *Chicago Evening Post*, March 2, 1872. See also *Chicago Times*, January 31, 1872.

146 The maps are based on descriptions of the location of Chicago's manufacturing activity in S. S. Schoff, *The Glory of Chicago: Her Manufactories: The Industrial Interests of Chicago…* (Chicago, 1873), pp. 8–9; and Chamberlin, *Chicago and Its Suburbs*, pp. 138–41. Only the areas in which industry was heavily concentrated are shown. See also Hoyt, *One Hundred Years of Land Values in Chicago*, p. 379.

147 Chamberlin, *Chicago and Its Suburbs*, pp. 139–40.

148 Schoff, *The Glory of Chicago*, passim. Limited time and money make it impossible to plot Chicago's industries on a firm-by-firm basis; this conclusion is based on a large sample of the manufacturers listed in Schoff, which were informally traced through the city directories. See also Hoyt, *One Hundred Years of Land Values in Chicago*, p. 379.

149 Chamberlin, *Chicago and Its Suburbs*, pp. 129, 131, 141–43; Schoff, *The Glory of Chicago*, p. 8.

150 *Chicago Tribune*, November 14, 1871; *PCCC*, February 12, 1872, pp. 84–85.

151 *Chicago Evening Post*, December 13, 1871; March 16, 1872; *Chicago Tribune*, March 20, 1872.

152 *Chicago Evening Post*, March 16, 1872.

153 *New Chicago*, p. 104; *Landowner* (October 1872), p. 167; Schoff, *The Glory of Chicago*, pp. 91–92.

154 Chamberlin, *Chicago and Its Suburbs*, pp. 139–40.

155   Chamberlin claimed that three of the thirteen factories were built before the great fire. This statement may not be accurate, however. Writers often made inaccurate statements about the establishment of firms there. More important, the 1871 directory did not show any of the thirteen in the district. According to the writers of *New Chicago*, "all this region was given over to the cultivation of bullfrogs" before the conflagration. In any event, what is important is that the McCormick Reaper Works gave the district visibility and respectability as an industrial area. Reports describing its "rise" almost always began with some mention of the company – even before the McCormicks had officially decided to relocate! See *Chicago Tribune*, January 14, 1872; March 3, 1872; September 8, 1872; *Chicago Tribune*, January 14, 1872; March 3, 1872; September 8, 1872; *New Chicago*, pp. 81, 104–8; Chamberlin, *Chicago and Its Suburbs*, p. 139; William T. Hutchinson, *Cyrus Hall McCormick: Harvest 1856–1884* (New York, 1935), pp. 495, 511.

156   *Landowner* (June 1872), p. 90.

157   Hutchinson, *Cyrus Hall McCormick*, pp. 494–95.

158   Ibid., pp. 441–42, 493–511.

159   Ibid., p. 511; Stella Virginia Roderick, *Nettie Fowler McCormick* (Rindge, N.H., 1956), p. 100.

160   *New Chicago*, pp. 105–6; Schoff, *The Glory of Chicago*, pp. 82, 145. Many others are also listed in Schoff.

161   The maps give the locations of firms listed in Schoff, *The Glory of Chicago*, pp. 109–13, 156–59 (traced back through the 1871 city directory), only.

162   Schoff, *The Glory of Chicago*, pp. 109–13, 156–59. See also *New Chicago*, "Map of Structures Constructed or Under Construction," reproduced in Figure 6.4.

163   Schoff, *The Glory of Chicago*.

164   *New Chicago*, pp. 81–82, 110–11; Chamberlin, *Chicago and Its Suburbs*. The shifts are also discussed in the real estate and "New Chicago" columns of newspapers like the *Tribune*, particularly after May 1872 (references for which will be found in notes at relevant points in the text).

165   Hutchinson, *Cyrus Hall McCormick*, p. 511. Other manufacturers also faced the problem of housing their workers when they constructed factories in previously undeveloped areas. See Chamberlin, *Chicago and Its Suburbs*, p. 367.

166   *Chicago Tribune*, June 30, 1872; November 17, 1872. See also advertisements in Chicago Building & Loan Association, *Statistical and Historical Review of Chicago* (Chicago, 1869).

167   Gilbert, "The Rebuilding of the City," pp. 283, 292.

168   *Chicago Tribune*, April 28, 1872.

169   *New Chicago*, p. 31.

170   *Chicago Tribune*, February 14, 1875.

171   *Chicago Tribune*, December 3, 1871.

172   *Chicago Tribune*, March 7, 1872; June 2, 1872.

173   *Chicago Tribune*, October 9, 1872.

174   *Chicago Times*, March 3, 1872; *Chicago Evening Post*, March 30, 1872; May 16, 1872; *Chicago Tribune*, October 14, 1872; November 3, 1872; November 17, 1872.

175 *Chicago Times*, February 23, 1872; *Chicago Tribune*, April 21, 1872; May 5, 1872; May 17, 1872; Gilbert, "The Rebuilding of the City," p. 292.

176 *Chicago Tribune*, February 25, 1872; March 2, 1872.

177 *Chicago Evening Post*, May 16, 1872.

178 M. E. Blatchford and E. W. Blatchford, *Memories of the Chicago Fire* (Chicago, 1921); Anna E. Higginson to friend (Mrs. Mark Skinner), Elmhurst, November 10, 1871, in *The Great Chicago Fire, October 8–10, 1871, Described by Eight Men and Women Who Experienced Its Horrors* . . . (Chicago, 1871; 1971, enlarged ed.), p. 2. For a similar expression of woe, see Mahlon D. Ogden to Charles Binter, October 14, 1871, *Ogden Papers*, Chicago Historical Society.

179 *Chicago Tribune*, August 25, 1872; October 15, 1872; Croffert, "Reconstruction," pp. 54–56; *New Chicago*, pp. 49–50; Richard Sennett, *Families Against the City: Middle Class Homes of Industrial Chicago* (Chicago, 1970), pp. 30–40.

180 *Chicago Evening Post*, June 16, 1872; *Chicago Tribune*, June 30, 1872.

181 Croffert, "Reconstruction," p. 54.

182 *PCCC*, August 19, 1872, p. 422; *Chicago Evening Post*, June 26, 1872; *Chicago Tribune*, June 30, 1872.

183 *New Chicago*, p. 81; Chamberlin, *Chicago and Its Suburbs*, pp. 241–43, 344ff *Chicago Tribune*, July 28, 1872; September 15, 1872; October 6, 1872; December 22, 1872.

184 *Chicago Evening Post*, February 24, 1872; March 9, 1872; *Chicago Tribune*, March 17, 1872; March 24, 1872; May 19, 1872; July 14, 1872; July 28, 1872; August 25, 1872; December 22, 1872; Chamberlin, *Chicago and Its Suburbs*.

185 *Chicago Times*, October 21, 1872; *Chicago Tribune*, June 2, 1872; Gilbert, "The Rebuilding of the City," p. 292; *New Chicago*, p. 72ff. See also John Drury, *Old Chicago Houses* (Chicago, 1941), pp. 89–109.

186 *Chicago Tribune*, October 6, 1872; *New Chicago*, pp. 72–73. A map of the 1863 cholera-erysipelas epidemic shows that aristocratic Cass, Rush, and Pine Streets suffered as severely from the epidemic as Chicago's unsewered slums. Medical authorities attributed the epidemic to the pollution generated by the slaughterhouses on the South Branch and showed that it was carried by the river, affecting a slightly wider section of the city northeast of the river because of southwesterly prevailing winds. See *Report of Board of Health of the City of Chicago for 1867, 1868, 1869 and a Sanitary History of Chicago from 1822 to 1870* (Chicago, 1871), pp. 67–68.

187 *New Chicago*, p. 81; Chamberlin, *Chicago and Its Suburbs*; Sennett, *Families Against the City*, pp. 30–34. The developer was none other than Samuel J. Walker; see *Chicago Tribune*, April 16, 1884. The great fire of 1874 finished off the "near" South Side as an upper class district; the depression of 1873–77, the Union Park district. Ironically, the success of Walker's "Canalport" manufacturing center helped bring about the decline of his Union Park development by drawing heavy traffic through it.

188 Thomas L. Philpott, *The Slum and the Ghetto: Neighborhood Deterioration and Middle Class Reform, Chicago, 1880–1930* (New York, 1978), pp. 19–20.

189 See BPW, *Annual Report* (years ending March 31, 1873; March 31, 1874; March 31, 1875).

190 Hoyt, *One Hundred Years of Land Values in Chicago*, p. 91.
191 Rauch, *A Report on the Necessity of an Extension of the Sewerage of the City*, pp. 17–20; *Chicago Tribune*, May 25, 1872; June 30, 1872. See also *Chicago Evening Post*, May 25, 1872; and *Report of Board of Health for 1867, 1868, 1869*, p. 230; Board of Health, *Annual Report* (1874 and 1875), p. 94.
192 Sennett, *Families Against the City*.
193 J. B. Bradford, *The Strangers' Guide to the City of Chicago* (Chicago, 1873), p. 29.
194 See, for example, *Chicago Tribune*, July 7, 1872; "One Year After," pp. 245–47; *New Chicago*, pp. 83–84.
195 "Effect of the Fire upon Real Estate," *Lakeside Monthly*, October 1872, p. 261; *Chicago Tribune*, September 1, 1872.
196 See, for example, *Chicago Tribune*, April 28, 1872; October 9, 1872; Chamberlin, *Chicago and Its Suburbs*.

Chapter 7. The rebuilding of Boston

1 Interesting contemporary accounts of the fire can be found in Boston's newspapers and in *Report of the Commissioners Appointed to Investigate the Cause and Management of the Great Fire in Boston* (Boston, 1873); Col. Russell H. Conwell, *History of the Great Fire in Boston, November 9 and 10, 1872* (Boston, 1873); and James M. Bugbee, "Fires and Fire Departments," *North American Review*, 117 (July 1873), pp. 115–28. Also useful are John Harris (ed.), *The Great Boston Fire* (Boston, 1972); Diane Tarmy Rudnick, "Boston and the Fire of 1872: The Stillborn Phoenix" (unpublished Ph.D. dissertation, Boston University, 1971); and John W. Decrow, "The Great Boston Fire," in Boston Chamber of Commerce, Bureau of Commercial and Industrial Affairs, *The Boston Fire November 9, 1872...* (Boston, 1922).
2 Report of the Commissioners, quoted in *Boston Daily Advertiser*, January 28, 1873.
3 Estimations are based on a map in Harris (ed.), *The Great Boston Fire*, p. 19.
4 Edward Stanwood, *Boston Illustrated* (Boston, 1872), p. 55.
5 *Boston Daily Advertiser*, November 11, 1872; Conwell, *History of the Great Fire in Boston*, pp. 90–99.
6 *Report of the Commissioners*, p. iii; F. E. Frothingham, *The Boston Fire* (Boston, 1873); Conwell, *History of the Great Fire in Boston*, pp. 222–35. It is not clear how many dwellings were destroyed. J. Martin, *A Century of Finance* (Boston, 1898), says thirteen (p. 39), while Conwell says sixty-seven (p. 235).
7 *Reports of Proceedings of the Boston City Council* (hereafter referred to as *PBCC*), November 11, 1872, pp. 343–45; November 12, 1872, p. 346; Boston newspapers, November 11–15, 1872.
8 *PBCC*, November 11–18, 1872, pp. 342–59; Massachusetts General Court, *Senate Documents*, 1872, Extra Session, Document No. 1; *Massachusetts Acts and Resolves*, 1872, Extra Session, Chapters 366, 377. The newspapers reported on all of the various improvement suggestions and demands made by officials, citizens, and business and public interest groups.

9   *PBCC*, November 11–18, 1872, pp. 342–59; Massachusetts General Court, *Senate Documents*, 1872, Extra Session, Document No. 1; *Massachusetts Acts and Resolves*, 1872, Extra Session, Chapters 366, 377. See also the city newspapers, November 11–18. *The Nation*, 15, November 14, 1872, is an example of New York City–based media which expected the city to make improvements.

10 Excerpts of sermons preached on November 17, 1872, appeared in most newspapers on November 18 and in Conwell, *History of the Great Fire in Boston*, pp. 106–51. The *Boston Globe*, November 14, 1872, and *Boston Post*, November 16, 1872, had editorials headlined "The Bright Side."

11 Walter Muir Whitehall, *Boston: A Topographical History* (Cambridge, Mass., 1959), p. 34.

12 *A Professional and Industrial History of Suffolk County* (Boston, 1894), Vol. 3, p. 325; *Shoe and Leather Record: A New England Journal Devoted Especially to the Interests of Book and Shoe Leather Manufacturers and Dealers* (hereafter referred to as *Shoe and Leather Record*), April 21, 1873, p. 388; *Boston Daily Advertiser*, April 19, 1873.

13 Charles S. Damrell, *A Half Century of Boston's Buildings* (Boston, 1895), p. 116; *Report of the Commissioners*, pp. 20–23.

14 *Report of the Commissioners*, pp. 101–5; Damrell, *A Half Century of Boston's Buildings* (Boston, 1895), pp. 112–17.

15 *Report of the Commissioners*, pp. 105–6, 165, 433–34, 521, 556, 592.

16 *Boston Daily Advertiser*, December 10, 1972; February 26, 1873; November 8, 1873; *PBCC*, February 19, 1873, pp. 79–80; *Boston Globe*, December 24, 1872; February 19, 1873; *Boston Post*, November 15, 1873.

17 Samuel Adams Drake, *Old Landmarks of Boston* (Boston, 1876), pp. 254, 264; Nathaniel B. Shurtleff, *A Topographical and Historical Description of Boston* (Boston, 1872), p. 112. For flooding and drainage problems at time of the fire, see *Boston Globe*, December 24, 1872.

18 *Boston Post*, November 16, 1872.

19 *Boston Globe*, November 15, 1872.

20 Ibid. See also *Boston Post*, November 19, 1872.

21 Drake, *Old Landmarks of Boston*, pp. 254, 264; Shurtleff, *A Topographical and Historical Description of Boston*, p. 112. See also the Bonner map of Boston of 1769 and the V. G. Hale map of Boston of 1814.

22 "Unaccepted Streets," *Boston City Documents* (hereafter referred to as *BCD*), 1845, No. 6; Whitehall, *Boston: A Topographical History*, pp. 52–54; *PBCC*, December 30, 1872, p. 420.

23 "Unaccepted Streets."

24 "Exchange Street," *BCD*, 1852, No. 38; "Report . . . on the Widening of Water Street," *BCD*, 1859, No. 54; "Second Report . . . on the Widening of Water Street," *BCD*, 1859, No. 73; "Closing Report of the Committee on Streets," *BCD*, 1862, No. 97.

25 "Exchange Street," *BCD*, 1852, No. 38; "Report . . . on the Widening of Water Street," *BCD*, 1859, No. 54; "Second Report . . . on the Widening of Water Street," *BCD*, 1859, No. 73; "Closing Report of the Committee on Streets," *BCD*, 1862, No. 97. See also "Mayor's Inaugural Address," *BCD*, 1857, No.

1, pp. 13–16; "Report . . . on the Extension of Devonshire Street," *BCD*, 1857, No. 60; "Report of a Minority of the Committee on the Extension of Devonshire Street," *BCD*, 1857, No. 62; Charles P. Huse, *The Financial History of Boston from May 1, 1822 to January 31, 1909* (Cambridge, Mass., 1916), pp. 127–35.

26   See the city newspapers for November 12–14, 1872, for reports and editorials concerning the demands for street improvements. See also *Boston Daily Advertiser*, January 7, 1873.

27   *Boston Post*, November 13, 1872.

28   *PBCC*, November 12, 1872, p. 346; November 15, 1872, p. 353; Thomas Wood Davis, *Map of the Burnt District Showing Proposed Improvements in Streets* (November 12, 1872) in possession of Map Collection of the Boston Public Library.

29   *Boston Globe*, November 12, 1872.

30   Carl Wilhelm Ernst, "The Postal Service in Boston 1639–1893," *Professional and Industrial History of Suffolk County* (Boston, 1899), Vol. 2, pp. 477–78; *Boston Evening Transcript*, April 21, 1882.

31   *Boston Daily Advertiser*, November 16, 1872; *Report of the Fire Commissioners*, p. 407.

32   "Report of a Committee of Conference with a Citizens' Committee on the Subject of New Street and a City Loan," *BCD*, 1872, No. 112.

33   *Boston Daily Advertiser*, November 13, 1872; November 16, 1872; November 22, 1872; *Boston Post*, November 16, 1872; November 19, 1872; Stanwood, *Boston Illustrated*, p. 59.

34   *PBCC*, November 18, 1872, pp. 357–58.

35   Ibid.; *Boston Daily Advertiser*, November 16, 1872.

36   *PBCC*, November 18, 1872, pp. 357–58; *Boston Daily Advertiser*, November 16, 1872; *Boston Post*, November 19, 1872; *Shoe and Leather Record*, November 25, 1872, p. 136; "Report of a Committee of Conference with a Citizens' Committee."

37   *PBCC*, November 18, 1872, p. 357.

38   Ibid; *Boston Daily Advertiser*, November 16, 1872.

39   *Boston Daily Advertiser*, November 27, 1872.

40   Ibid; *PBCC*, November 18, 1872, p. 357.

41   *Boston Daily Advertiser*, November 27, 1872; *PBCC*, November 18, 1872, p. 357.

42   *Boston Daily Advertiser*, November 27, 1872; *PBCC*, November 18, 1872, p. 357. See also Davis, *Map of the Burned District Showing Proposed Improvements in Streets*.

43   "Annual Report of the City Surveyor," *BCD*, 1873, No. 5, p. 21.

44   Huse, *The Financial History of Boston*, pp. 161–69; *Boston Globe*, January 25, 1873.

45   *Boston Post*, November 13, 1873; *Boston Daily Advertiser*, March 21, 1873. Many leases still had many years to run and would be very expensive to break.

46   "Report upon the Proceedings of the Street Commissioners for 1873," *BCD*, 1874, No. 6, pp. 3–4; *Boston Globe*, December 24, 1872; February 22, 1873.

47 Huse, *Financial History of Boston*, pp. 154–55; "Report on the Collection of Assessments for Sewers etc.," *BCD*, 1867, No. 117, p. 3; *Boston Globe*, December 24, 1872. Businessmen began publicly demanding relief from assessments at the committee of conference held November 15, 1872. See "Report of a Committee of Conference with a Citizens' Committee."

48 This chapter relies primarily on the reports of the hearings provided by the *Boston Globe*, which the writer found most useful and easy to follow. The *Advertiser* and *Transcript* also reported on the hearings. Only one hearing, that held January 24 on Postmaster Burt's plan, seems to have been open to the general public. The hearing was held jointly by the Commissioners and the Joint Standing Committee on Streets of the City Council (*Boston Globe*, January 24, 1873). See also *PBCC*, February 26, 1873, pp. 79–80.

49 "Report upon the Proceedings of the Street Commissioners of 1873," pp. 3–4.

50 Huse, *The Financial History of Boston*, pp. 130–31.

51 The hearings of the City Council were recorded in *PBCC* (having originally appeared in the *Transcript*). The *Globe* also covered the City Council hearings. Its reports are even more condensed than *PBCC*, but they occasionally bring out points missed by the latter and so help to flesh out the City Council's deliberations. Both are used in this chapter.

52 "Report of the Board of Street Commissioners," *BCD*, 1873, No. 4, p. 11.

53 "Inaugural Address," *BCD*, 1873, No. 1.

54 *Boston Globe*, January 11, 1873; January 23, 1873; *Boston Daily Advertiser*, January 30, 1873.

55 See Figures 7.4 and 7.5.

56 *Boston Globe*, January 25, 1873.

57 *Boston Globe*, February 27, 1873; *PBCC*, February 26–27, 1873, pp. 79–83.

58 *Boston Globe*, February 27, 1873; *PBCC*, February 26–27, 1873, pp. 79–83.

59 *Boston Globe*, April 17, 1873; February 19, 1873.

60 *PBCC*, December 16, 1872, p. 388.

61 *PBCC*, March 17, 1872, pp. 112–113.

62 *Boston Post*, April 5, 1873.

63 *PBCC*, March 10, 1873, p. 101.

64 *PBCC*, March 31, 1873, p. 141.

65 "Communication from William L. Burt..." *BCD*, 1873, No. 55, pp. 10–13. Simmons had been one of the prime movers behind the Devonshire Street improvement in the late 1850s. His and his trustees' land and mortgage transactions take up over twenty pages in the Grantee and Grantor Indexes in the Suffolk County Registry of Deeds.

66 *Boston Post*, November 16, 1872. Almost every day after March 10 the paper made some sort of negative comment about Burt or the Post Office area improvements. It also reprinted anti-Burt editorials from the *Boston Herald*, the *Journal of Commerce*, the *Gazette*, the *Courier*, and the *New York Sun* (see the March 13 and March 24, 1873, issues of the *Post*).

67 *PBCC*, March 31, 1873, p. 141.

68 "Communication from William L. Burt," pp. 9, 14–18.

69 *Boston Globe*, January 24, 1873.

70 *Boston Globe*, January 25, 1873; *PBCC*, March 20, 1873, pp. 123–24.

71 *PBCC*, March 20, 1873, pp. 123–24.

72 "Communication from William L. Burt."

73 Ibid.

74 Ibid.

75 *PBCC*, March 31, 1873, pp. 143; *Boston Globe*, April 3, 1873.

76 *PBCC*, April 4, 1873, pp. 144–47; April 10, 1873, pp. 155–58; *Boston Post*, April 2, 1873; April 5, 1873; April 7, 1873.

77 *PBCC*, April 10, 1873, pp. 155–58.

78 U.S. Congress, House Committee on Appropriations, *Report on the Enlargement of the Boston Post Office*, H. R. Rept. 1, 43rd Congress, 1st Sess., 1874, p. 3. See also *Justice of a Public Officer: Addresses etc. at the Complimentary Dinner Tendered to General William L. Burt* . . . (Boston, 1876).

79 *Boston Post*, November 15, 1873; *Mass. Acts and Resolves*, 1872, Special Session, Chapter 377; *PBCC*, January 2, 1873, pp. 422–23; March 10, 1873, p. 103; September 1, 1873, p. 327.

80 *Report of the Commissioners*, pp. xvii, 115.

81 *Report of the Commissioners*, pp. 101–5; Damrell, *A Half Century of Boston's Buildings*, pp. 112–17.

82 "Fire Department Annual Reports," *BCD*, 1867, No. 36, pp. 7–8; 1868, No. 2, pp. 6–7; 1869, No. 37, pp. 9–10; 1870, No. 27, p. 12; 1871, No. 37, pp. 9–10; *PBCC*, June 3, 1873, p. 233; *Report of the Commissioners*, pp. 102–4, 224; *Boston Globe*, December 20, 1872; Damrell, *A Half Century of Boston's Buildings*, pp. 112–15.

83 "Fire Department Annual Reports," *BCD*, 1867, No. 36, pp. 7–8; 1868, No. 2, pp. 6–7; 1869, No. 37, pp. 9–10; 1870, No. 27, p. 12; 1871, No. 37, pp. 9–10; *PBCC*, June 3, 1873, p. 223; *Report of the Commissioners*, pp. 102–4, 224; *Boston Globe*, December 20, 1872. See also Damrell, *A Half Century of Boston's Buildings*, pp. 112–15.

84 *Boston Globe*, December 20, 1872.

85 "Auditor's Annual Report," *BCD*, 1874, No. 56, pp. 31–32.

86 "Report . . . on a Supply of Water for Extinguishment of Fires," *BCD*, 1873, No. 112.

87 *PBCC*, June 30, 1873, p. 268; October 6, 1873, p. 409; October 9, 1873, p. 417; October 13, 1873, p. 419.

88 *Report of the Commissioners*, pp. 105–6, 165, 433–34, 521, 566, 592.

89 *PBCC*, June 3, 1873, p. 233.

90 Boston Chamber of Commerce, Bureau of Commercial and Industrial Affairs, *The Boston Fire, Nov. 9, 1872* . . . (Boston, 1922).

91 *Report of the Commissioners*, p. xviii.

92 Ibid., pp. 542–47. *Boston Daily Advertiser*, November 12, 1872.

93 *Report of the Commissioners*, pp. 22–24.

94 *PBCC*, February 24, 1873, pp. 72–73.

95 Ibid.

96   *Boston Daily Advertiser*, June 6, 1873; *Report of the Commissioners*, pp. xix–xx, 436, 542, 545, 629–33.

97   *Report of the Commissioners*, pp. 629–33.

98   *Mass. Acts and Resolves*, 1873, Chapter 298; *Boston Daily Advertiser*, March 29, 1873.

99   Carl Condit, *American Building: Materials and Techniques from the First Colonial Settlements to the Present* (Chicago, 1968), p. 116; *Boston Globe*, January 10, 1873. See the testimonies of architects A. C. Martin and Gridley F. Bryant in *Report of the Commissioners* for a glimpse of the debate.

100 *PBCC*, February 24, 1873, p. 73.

101 *Boston Daily Advertiser*, June 6, 1873; June 19, 1873; *PBCC*, June 23, 1873, pp. 260–61.

102 Damrell, *A Half Century of Boston's Buildings.*

103 *Mass. Acts and Resolves*, 1872, Special Session, Chapter 371; 1873, Chapter 298; *PBCC*, June 23, 1873, pp. 260–61. Compare Sanborn Map Company, *Insurance Maps of Boston*, Vol. 1, 1867 and 1885.

104 The lack of any significant territorial expansion of Boston's commercial building stock during the reconstruction period has been deduced from the absence of any mention of it in the newspapers and from patterns analyzed in the next section of this chapter.

105 *Boston Daily Advertiser*, March 29, 1873. One unpassed amendment to the building code would have limited building heights to levels deemed safe for particular street widths. Also indicative of this fear of tall buildings is the fact that two buildings on the *Advertiser*'s March 29 list of building permits were to be only one story in height. The Beebe Building, which was located at Winthrop Square, is an example of a structure which suffered the loss of a story, from six stories to five. For a full architectural description, see Gay Baratha, David Browlee, and Victoria Glynn, "Winthrop Square: The Beebe Block" ("Seklar Papers," Harvard School of Design, December 1872).

106 *Boston Transcript*, November 8, 1873; *Boston Daily Advertiser*, November 8, 1873.

107 *PBCC*, March 10, 1873, p. 99; *Boston Daily Advertiser*, November 8, 1873.

108 *Boston Daily Advertiser*, March 29, 1873; Sanborn Map Company, *Insurance Maps of Boston*, Vol. 1, 1867 and 1885.

109 Researchers working in the Suffolk County Registry of Deeds are burdened by an antiquated and unwieldy indexing system which makes the tracing of a property from one owner to the next quite difficult.

110 Suffolk County Registry of Deeds, liber 1139, folio 53 (hereafter referred to as SCRD, lib., fol.).

111 SCRD, lib. 1145, fol. 102.

112 SCRD, lib. 1366, fol. 274.

113 SCRD, lib. 1160, fol. 77; lib. 1161, fol. 228; lib. 1160, fol. 80.

114 SCRD, lib. 1280, fols. 295, 296; lib. 1288, fols. 217, 218; lib. 1392, fol. 281; lib. 1399, fols. 59, 62.

115 SCRD, lib. 1158, fol. 124; lib. 1170, fol. 216.

116 SCRD, lib. 1154, fol. 120; lib. 1157, fol. 207.

117 SCRD, lib. 1190, fol. 133; lib. 1094, fol. 142.

118 SCRD, lib. 1170, fol. 243.

119 SCRD, lib. 1170, fols. 126, 211, 217.

120 SCRD, lib. 1139, fol. 105.

121 SCRD, lib. 1142, fols. 147, 149.

122 SCRD, lib. 1186, fol. 124.

123 SCRD, lib. 1150, fol. 108; lib. 1162, fol. 178; lib. 1171, fol. 33.

124 SCRD, lib. 1138, fol. 171; lib. 1141, fol. 145; lib. 1171, fol. 132; lib. 1140, fol. 51.

125 The maps are derived from the business sections of the *Boston Directory* published by Sampson and Murdock Company for 1872–73 and 1875–76. Unless otherwise indicated these and all subsequent references to the trades' locations are based on the lists of firm names and addresses in the *directory* classified under the following headings: "Dry Goods – Wholesale Merchants – Importers and Jobbers," "Hides and Leather," "Leather Dealers," and "Boot and Shoe Dealers – Wholesale."

Names and addresses under "Leather Dealers" and "Hides and Leather" have been cross-checked to eliminate duplication. A cross-check of "Leather Dealers," "Hides and Leather," and "Boot and Shoe Dealers – Wholesale" turned up only an extremely small, irregular amount of overlap, which has been ignored, since it was impossible to assign the firms to one category or the other and important to include them all. Each firm is signified by one symbol, even if the directory gave a series of consecutive addresses (e.g., 21–27 Pearl), unless the addresses were clearly for shops in different locations, in which case each location is signified.

126 *Boston Directory*, 1850–72.

127 *Shoe and Leather Record*, December 2, 1872, p. 148; *Boston Evening Transcript*, November 12, 1872; *Boston Daily Advertiser*, February 10, 1873; *Boston Directory*, 1873–74.

128 *Boston Daily Advertiser*, February 10, 1873.

129 Ibid; *Shoe and Leather Record*, December 2, 1872, p. 148.

130 *Boston Daily Herald*, quoted in *Shoe and Leather Record*, January 13, 1873, p. 220.

131 *Boston Daily Herald*, quoted in *Shoe and Leather Record*, January 13, 1873, p. 220. See also *Boston Daily Advertiser*, April 19, 1873; *Shoe and Leather Record*, December 2, 1872, p. 148.

132 *Boston Daily Herald*, quoted in *Shoe and Leather Record*, January 13, 1873, p. 220.

133 Ibid.

134 Ibid.

135 *Boston Daily Advertiser*, February 10, 1873. The advertisements are scattered through the *Daily Advertiser* and other papers.

136 *Shoe and Leather Record*, December 2, 1872, p. 148; *Boston Daily Herald*, quoted in *Shoe and Leather Record*, January 13, 1873, p. 220.

137 *Boston Daily Advertiser*, March 29, 1873.

138   *Boston Commercial Bulletin*, quoted in H. W. S. Cleveland, *Landscape Architecture as Applied to the Wants of the West* (Chicago, 1873), edited by Roy Lubove (reprint, Pittsburgh, 1965), pp. 29–30. For takings, see Boston Safe Deposit and Trust Company, *Plan of the Burnt District Showing Improvements as Adopted by Board of Street Commissioners and City Council* (1873), in possession of Map Collection of the Boston Public Library.

139   U.S. Congress, House Committee on Appropriations, *Report on the Enforcement of the Boston Post Office*, p. 3; *Shoe and Leather Record*, April 28, 1873, p. 400. See also "Banks," "Bankers," "Insurance Companies," "Brokers," etc. in *Boston Directory*, 1872–73 and 1875–76; and Perry Walton, *Devonshire Street* (Boston, 1912), pp. 45–46.

140   *Plan of the Burnt District*, 1873; *Shoe and Leather Record*, May 19, 1873, p. 436.

141   *Plan of the Burnt District*, 1873; *Shoe and Leather Record*, April 21, 1873, p. 400; May 19, 1873, p. 436; *Boston Globe*, April 18, 1873; *Boston Daily Advertiser*, April 19, 1873.

142   *Plan of the Burnt District*, 1873; *Shoe and Leather Record*, April 21, 1873, p. 400; May 19, 1873, p. 436; *Boston Globe*, April 18, 1873; *Boston Daily Advertiser*, April 19, 1873. Also SCRD, lib. 1450, fol. 309. Clement, Coburn & Co. kept the lot until 1879.

143   *Shoe and Leather Record*, December 2, 1872, p. 148.

144   *Shoe and Leather Record*, January 13, 1873, p. 220.

145   Compare Sanborn Map Company, *Insurance Map of Boston*, Vol. 1, 1867 and 1885. See also "Property Tax Records of the City of Boston, Massachusetts," 1872–80, in the Boston Public Library Attic Archives.

146   See *Plan of the Burnt District; Boston Directory*, 1872–73, 1875–76, under "Wool Dealers," "Banks," "Insurance Companies," "Brokers," etc. See also Figures 7.6 and 7.7.

147   Sanborn Map Company, *Insurance Map of Boston*, Vol. 1, 1867.

148   Ibid.

149   Joel Page, *Recollections of Sixty Years in the Shoe Trade* (Boston, 1916), pp. 28–29.

150   *Boston Evening Transcript*, November 8, 1873.

151   "Auditor's Annual Report," *BCD*, No. 56, 1874, pp. 31–32.

152   The total spent on street improvements in the burnt district as of April 30, 1880, was $6,362,450, exclusive of paying expenses and grade damages. See "Auditor's Annual Report," *BCD*, 1873, No. 79, p. 64; 1874, No. 56, p. 64; 1875, No. 72, p. 86, No. 56, p. 58; 1877, No. 52, pp. 58, 238; 1878, No. 55, p. 66; 1879, No. 70, p. 59; 1880, No. 86, p. 55. The 1822–70 sum is taken from "Auditor's Annual Report," 1870, No. 60, pp. 241–83. It, too, excludes the cost of grading as well as the costs of laying out and grading the new streets in the annexed areas on the city's public land in the South End, Back Bay, and other areas. Thus it applies only to the older parts of the city.

153   Conwell, *History of the Great Fire in Boston*.

154   For figures, see "Auditor's Annual Report," *BCD*, 1873–80.

155   "Mayor's Inaugural Address," *BCD*, 1874, No. 1, p. 9.

156   *Boston Post*, November 14, 1872; *Boston Evening Transcript*, November 14, 1872;

Diane Tarmy Rudnick, "Boston and the Fire of 1872: The Stillborn Phoenix" (unpublished Ph.D. dissertation, Boston University, 1971) pp. 226–28, 237–60. (Although it is not as detailed or as comprehensive as this chapter, Rudnick's dissertation provides a good overview of the fire and street improvement in Boston.)

157 "Fire Commissioners' Annual Report," *BCD*, 1881, No. 59, pp. xiv–xv.

158 *BCD*, No. 79, 1873, pp. 23–24. There is some confusion over the width of Congress Street. *BCD*, No. 79, published on April 31, indicates that it was to be widened to sixty and seventy feet, while the *Advertiser*, November 8, 1873, states that it was widened only to fifty-four and sixty feet. I could find no city document to support the *Advertiser*'s claim, but it may be that the Street Commissioners were forced to compromise on the width after the April publication of the Auditor's report.

159 Scrapbook of newspaper articles published on the first anniversary of the great fire, Boston Public Library.

160 *Boston Evening Transcript*, November 8, 1873.

161 Ibid.; *Boston Daily Advertiser*, November 8, 1873.

162 *PBCC*, June 23, 1873, p. 261; *Boston Daily Advertiser*, November 8, 1873.

163 *Boston Daily Advertiser*, November 8, 1873.

164 Ibid.; *Boston Evening Transcript*, November 8, 1873.

165 *Boston Evening Transcript*, November 8, 1873; *Boston Daily Advertiser*, March 29, 1873.

166 *Boston Evening Transcript*, November 8, 1873.

167 *Boston Globe*, June 5, 1873; June 6, 1873; *Boston Daily Advertiser*, May 31, 1873; June 6, 1873; June 19, 1873.

168 *Boston Daily Advertiser*, July 2, 1873.

Chapter 8. The rebuilding of Baltimore

1 Fire Department, "Annual Report," *Reports of the City Officers and Departments to the City Council of Baltimore* (hereafter referred to as *BRCOD*), 1904, pp. 18–19. Harold A. Williams, *Baltimore Afire* (Baltimore, 1954), and the city newspapers provide the most detailed accounts of the fire and its destruction.

2 *Baltimore Sun*, February 9–17, 1904; *Baltimore American*, February 10–17, 1904.

3 James B. Crooks, *Politics and Progress: The Rise of Urban Progressivism in Baltimore, 1895 to 1911* (Baton Rouge, La., 1968), pp. 13–47, passim.

4 *Baltimore Sun*, February 9, 1904; February 11, 1904; February 13–14, 1904; *Baltimore American*, February 14, 1904.

5 *Baltimore Sun*, February 11, 1904. See also *Baltimore American*, February 14, 1904; February 16, 1904.

6 For problems with the streets in 1904 see "Report of Sub-Committee on Street Improvements," in Burnt District Commission, "Semi-Annual Report for Six Months Ending September 11, 1906," *BRCOD*, 1906, pp. 44–45 (hereafter all Burnt District Commission reports will be referred to as BDC,

"Report...date"). See also *Baltimore Sun*, March 5, 1904; March 27, 1904; *Baltimore American*, April 13, 1904. For a history of the street system, see "Mayor's Address" and City Commissioners, "Annual Report," and Commissioners for Opening Streets, "Annual Report," all in *BRCOD*, 1867–1903.

7   For a history of the city's activities in the Inner Harbor, see Harbor Board, "Annual Report," *BRCOD*, 1867–1904; see also "Mayor's Address," *BRCOD*, 1887, p. 78. The lack of space between the piers impeded dredging of the harbor as far back as 1873 ("Mayor's Message," *BRCOD*, 1873, pp. 36–37). For descriptions of conditions in 1904 see *Baltimore Sun*, March 4–5, 1904; May 5–15, 1904.

8   For a detailed history of the development and problems of the city's sewers, see City Commissioners, "Annual Report," and Board of Health, "Annual Report," and "Mayor's Address," all in *BRCOD*, 1867–1906. See also Sewerage Commissioners, "Annual Report," *BRCOD*, 1898–1906.

9   City Commissioners, "Annual Report," and Board of Health, "Annual Report," and "Mayor's Address," all in *BRCOD*, 1867–1906; Sewerage Commissioners, "Annual Report," *BRCOD*, 1898–1906. Quote from Board of Health, "Annual Report," *BRCOD*, 1883, p. 616.

10   *Baltimore Sun*, February 13, 1904; February 17, 1904; *Baltimore American*, February 11, 1904.

11   *Baltimore Sun*, February 9, 1904; *Baltimore World*, February 11, 1904; BDC, "Report...September 11, 1906," *BRCOD*, 1906, p. 33; Crooks, *Politics and Progress*, pp. 143–44.

12   BDC, "Report...September 11, 1906," *BRCOD*, 1906, p. 133.

13   "Report of Sub-Committee on Street Improvements," *BRCOD*, 1906, pp. 44–49.

14   Ibid.

15   *Baltimore American*, February 15, 1904; February 23, 1904; *Baltimore Sun*, February 25, 1904.

16   "Report of Sub-Committee on Street Improvements," *BRCOD*, 1906, pp. 44–45.

17   Ibid., pp. 47–48.

18   *Baltimore Sun*, February 20, 1904.

19   Ibid.

20   BDC, "Report...September 11, 1906," *BRCOD*, 1906, p. 33; *Baltimore American*, February 20, 1904; *Baltimore Sun*, February 20, 1904; February 22, 1904.

21   *Baltimore Sun*, February 14, 1904.

22   *Baltimore Sun*, February 18–19, 1904.

23   *Baltimore Sun*, February 18–20, 1904; *Baltimore American*, February 24, 1904.

24   *Baltimore Sun*, February 27, 1904.

25   *Baltimore Sun*, March 2, 1904; *Baltimore American*, February 20, 1904.

26   *Baltimore Sun*, February 17, 1904; BDC, "Report...September 11, 1906," *BRCOD*, 1906, pp. 40–41. The process of acquiring the land for the widening of Lexington (Douglas) Street had dragged on for nearly ten years.

27   *Baltimore Sun*, February 21, 1904.

28 *Baltimore American*, February 19, 1904; February 24, 1904; February 26, 1904; February 28, 1904; March 3, 1904; *Baltimore Sun*, February 19, 1904; March 2–3, 1904.

29 *Baltimore Sun*, February 23–March 2, 1904.

30 *Baltimore Sun*, February 27–28, 1904.

31 *Baltimore Sun*, February 20, 1904.

32 *Baltimore Sun*, February 18, 1904; February 20, 1904; March 5, 1904; *Baltimore American*, February 20, 1904.

33 *Baltimore Sun*, February 28, 1904; March 3, 1904.

34 *Baltimore Sun*, March 1, 1904.

35 *Baltimore Sun*, March 1–3, 1904.

36 *Baltimore American*, March 4, 1904; May 5, 1904.

37 *Baltimore American*, March 4, 1904; *Baltimore Sun*, March 5, 1904.

38 *Baltimore American*, March 5, 1904; *Laws of Maryland*, 1904, Chapters 87, 444.

39 *Baltimore American*, February 20, 1904; February 26, 1904; March 2, 1904; *Baltimore Sun*, February 28, 1904.

40 *Laws of Maryland*, 1904, Chapter 87.

41 Ibid.

42 *Baltimore Sun*, March 12, 1904.

43 For a discussion of structural reform, see Melvin G. Holli, *Reform in Detroit: Hazen S. Pingree and Urban Politics*, pp. 161–81; Samuel P. Hays, "Politics of Reform in Municipal Government in the Progressive Era," *Pacific Northwest Quarterly*, 55 (October 1964), pp. 157–69; Martin Schiesl, *The Politics of Efficiency: Municipal Administration and Reform in America: 1880–1920* (Berkeley, 1977).

44 *Baltimore Sun*, March 12, 1904; March 24, 1904.

45 *Baltimore Sun*, February 28, 1904.

46 *Laws of Maryland*, 1904, Chapter 87.

47 BDC, "Report . . . September 11, 1906," *BRCOD*, 1906, p. 34; *Baltimore American*, March 13, 1904; March 16, 1904; March 18, 1904. See also *Baltimore World*, March 11, 1904.

48 *Baltimore American*, March 18, 1904.

49 *Baltimore American*, March 20–25, 1904.

50 *Baltimore American*, March 23–24, 1904.

51 *Baltimore American*, March 13, 1904; March 18, 1904. But see also *Baltimore World*, February 27, 1904; March 1, 1904.

52 *Baltimore Sun*, March 24, 1904.

53 These sentiments were frequently expressed in newspaper editorials and articles. See, for example, *Baltimore American*, March 11, 1904; March 30, 1904; April 1, 1904; *Baltimore World*, March 1, 1904; March 22–25, 1904; *Baltimore Sun*, February 28, 1904.

54 *Baltimore Sun*, April 2, 1904.

55 *Baltimore Sun*, March 27, 1904; *Baltimore American*, March 27, 1904.

56 *Baltimore Sun*, March 25, 1904; *Baltimore American*, March 27, 1904. For the allocation of wharf space see *Baltimore Sun*, July 9, 1904; September 6–7, 1904. For business proposals relating to harbor improvements see

Manufacturers' Record, March 31, 1904, p. 229; *Baltimore American*, March 24, 1904.

57 *Baltimore Sun*, March 27, 1904; *Baltimore American*, March 27, 1904. This idea that all Baltimoreans ought to rally around the improvement plans, forgetting private interests that conflicted with the public interest, was a subject of considerable editorial preachment. See *Baltimore World*, March 23–24, 1904; *Baltimore Herald*, March 11, 1904; *Manufacturers' Record*, March 3, 1904. See also *Baltimore American*, March 13, 1904; March 30, 1904; April 1, 1904; April 7, 1904; April 17, 1904.

58 *Baltimore Sun*, March 27, 1904.

59 *Baltimore Sun*, March 25, 1904; *Baltimore American*, March 24, 1904.

60 *Baltimore Sun*, April 14, 1904.

61 *Baltimore World*, March 26, 1904.

62 *Baltimore American*, March 24, 1904.

63 *Baltimore American*, March 29, 1904; *Baltimore Sun*, March 29, 1904; *Baltimore Morning Herald*, March 29, 1904.

64 *Baltimore American*, March 29, 1904; *Baltimore Sun*, March 29, 1904; *Baltimore Morning Herald*, March 29, 1904.

65 *Baltimore American*, March 29, 1904; *Baltimore Sun*, March 29, 1904; *Baltimore Morning Herald*, March 29, 1904.

66 *Baltimore American*, March 29, 1904.

67 Ibid.

68 Ibid.; March 30, 1904; *Baltimore Sun*, March 30, 1904; *Baltimore World*, March 30, 1904; *Baltimore Morning Herald*, March 30, 1904.

69 *Baltimore American*, April 1, 1904; *Baltimore Sun*, April 1, 1904; *Baltimore World*, April 1, 1904; *Baltimore Morning Herald*, March 30, 1904.

70 *Baltimore American*, April 1, 1904; *Baltimore Sun*, April 1, 1904; *Baltimore World*, April 1, 1904; *Baltimore Morning Herald*, March 30, 1904.

71 *Baltimore American*, April 1, 1904; *Baltimore Sun*, April 1, 1904; *Baltimore World*, April 1, 1904; *Baltimore Morning Herald*, March 30, 1904.

72 *Baltimore American*, April 2, 1904.

73 Ibid.; April 3, 1904; *Baltimore Sun*, April 3, 1904.

74 *Baltimore American*, April 5–6, 1904.

75 *Baltimore American*, April 8, 1904; *Baltimore Sun*, April 8, 1904; April 10, 1904; *Baltimore Morning Herald*, April 9, 1904; *Baltimore World*, April 7, 1904.

76 *Baltimore American*, April 6, 1904; April 7, 1904.

77 *Baltimore American*, April 7, 1904; April 10, 1904; April 12, 1904.

78 *Baltimore American*, April 12–13, 1904.

79 *Baltimore American*, April 17, 1904; April 23, 1904; *Baltimore Sun*, April 17, 1904.

80 *Evening Herald*, April 18, 1904.

81 *Baltimore American*, April 19, 1904.

82 Ibid. Also *Baltimore World*, April 19, 1904.

83 *Baltimore Sun*, April 22–23, 1904.

84 *Baltimore Sun*, April 22–23, 1904; *Baltimore American*, April 21–27, 1904. See also *Baltimore World*, April 22, 1904.

85   *Baltimore Sun*, April 22, 1904; *Baltimore American*, April 22, 1904.

86   *Baltimore Sun*, April 22, 1904; *Baltimore American*, April 22, 1904. See also *Baltimore American*, April 23, 1904.

87   *Baltimore Sun*, April 22–23, 1904; *Baltimore American*, April 20–26, 1904.

88   *Baltimore Morning Herald*, April 26, 1904; *Baltimore World*, April 28, 1904.

89   *Baltimore American*, April 23–27, 1904; *Baltimore Morning Herald*, April 23–27, 1904; *Baltimore World*, April 21–27, 1904.

90   *Baltimore American*, April 23, 1904.

91   *Baltimore American*, April 22–23, 1904; *Baltimore Morning Herald*, April 23, 1904.

92   *Baltimore American*, April 22–23, 1904. See also *Baltimore Morni..g Herald*, April 23, 1904.

93   *Baltimore World*, April 21–27, 1904; *Baltimore Morning Herald*, April 23–27, 1904; *Baltimore Sun*, April 24, 1904. The *Evening News* also vigorously supported the widening of Baltimore Street. But unfortunately, no copies of this paper for this period are available for research, so it has been impossible to include its view in this analysis.

94   *Baltimore American*, April 23, 1904.

95   *Baltimore American*, April 27, 1904; *Baltimore Morning Herald*, April 26–27, 1904; *Baltimore World*, April 27, 1904.

96   *Baltimore World*, April 27–28, 1904; *Baltimore Morning Herald*, April 28, 1904.

97   *Baltimore Morning Herald*, April 27, 1904.

98   It even pitted progressive business leaders against each other. Progressive leaders who led the opposition to the widening of Baltimore Street included Charles Bonaparte and Mendes Cohen (Crooks, *Politics and Progress*, pp. 144, 224, 226).

99   *Baltimore American*, April 28, 1904.

100   *Baltimore American*, April 15, 1904; May 5, 1904; May 7, 1904; May 11, 1904.

101   *Baltimore American*, May 5, 1904.

102   *Baltimore American*, May 7, 1904; *Baltimore Sun*, May 7, 1904.

103   *Baltimore American*, May 7, 1904; *Baltimore Sun*, May 7, 1904.

104   *Baltimore American*, May 7, 1904; *Baltimore Sun*, May 7, 1904.

105   *Baltimore Sun*, May 12–13, 1904; *Baltimore American*, May 13, 1904.

106   *Baltimore American*, May 7–17, 1904; *Baltimore Sun*, May 7–16, 1904.

107   *Baltimore American*, May 14, 1904.

108   *Baltimore American*, May 17, 1904.

109   *Baltimore American*, May 18, 1904. Vote figures are from BDC, "Report… September 11, 1906," BRCOD, 1906, p. 34.

110   *Baltimore American*, May 18, 1904.

111   *Baltimore American*, April 28, 1904; May 19, 1904; *Baltimore Sun*, May 7, 1904; May 20, 1904.

112   *Baltimore American*, May 20–28, 1904; *Baltimore Sun*, May 21–28, 1904.

113   BDC, "Report…September 11, 1906," BRCOD, 1906, pp. 39–40.

114   Ibid.; also "Report…June 28, 1905," BRCOD, 1905, pp. 26–27, 42–43; *Baltimore Sun*, April 9, 1904; April 14–15, 1904; May 11, 1904; August 4, 1904; September 4, 1904.

115 BDC, "Report...September 11, 1906," *BRCOD*, 1906, p. 41.

116 BDC, "Report...June 28, 1905," *BRCOD*, 1905, pp. 35–43; *Baltimore Sun*, April 9, 1904; June 15, 1904; August 4, 1904; November 30, 1904.

117 BDC, "Report...June 28, 1905," *BRCOD*, 1905, pp. 41–42; "Report... September 11, 1906," *BRCOD*, 1906, p. 40; *Baltimore American*, June 2–3, 1904.

118 *Baltimore Sun*, April 26, 1904; August 17, 1904; August 24–25, 1904; *Baltimore American*, April 26, 1904; January 1, 1904.

119 *Baltimore Sun*, March 5, 1904.

120 Ironically, the *Manufacturers' Record* initially predicted that the Burnt District Commission would fail miserably, doing nothing aggressive to deal with the abutter problem (*Manufacturers' Record*, March 17, 1904, p. 176).

121 BDC, "Report...June 28, 1905," *BRCOD*, 1905, pp. 24–26; "Report... September 11, 1906," *BRCOD*, 1906, pp. 39–40.

122 *Baltimore Sun*, August 17, 1904; August 25, 1904; *Baltimore American*, December 22, 1904.

123 *Laws of Maryland*, 1904, Chapter 87; BDC, "Report...June 28, 1905," *BRCOD*, 1905, pp. 42–43.

124 BDC, "Report...June 28, 1905," *BRCOD*, 1905, pp. 42–43; *Baltimore Sun*, June 15, 1904; July 31, 1904; November 30, 1904.

125 *Baltimore Sun*, August 5, 1904; August 17, 1904; October 23, 1904; October 30, 1904.

126 *Baltimore American*, June 3, 1904.

127 BDC, "Report...September 11, 1906," *BRCOD*, 1906, pp. 28–29, 32–33. "Report...October 23, 1907," *BRCOD*, 1907, pp. 3–4.

128 For a history of problems with the overhead electric utility wires and poles, see "Mayor's Address," *BRCOD*, 1885, 1886, 1889, 1891, 1893, 1894, 1897, and Fire Department, "Annual Report," *BRCOD*, 1887, 1889, 1891, 1894, 1897, and Electrical Subway Commission, "Annual Report," *BRCOD*, 1894–1905.

129 "Mayor's Address," *BRCOD*, 1885, 1886, 1889, 1891, 1893, 1894, 1897, and Fire Department, "Annual Report," *BRCOD*, 1887, 1889, 1891, 1894, 1897, and Electrical Subway Commission, "Annual Report," *BRCOD*, 1894–1905. See also *Baltimore Sun*, January 6, 1905.

130 Electrical Subway Commission, "Annual Report," *BRCOD*, 1894, 1895, 1905.

131 *Baltimore Sun*, February 13, 1904; February 20, 1904.

132 *Baltimore Sun*, February 11, 1904.

133 *Baltimore American*, February 14, 1904. See also *Baltimore Sun*, February 11, 1904.

134 *Baltimore Sun*, October 8–9, 1904; October 18, 1904; October 21–22, 1904; October 26, 1904; October 28, 1904.

135 *Baltimore Sun*, October 26, 1904; October 28, 1904; January 6, 1905; Electrical Subway Commission, "Annual Report," *BRCOD*, 1905, pp. 7–8.

136 *Manufacturers' Record*, April 21, 1904, p. 300; June 16, 1904, p. 505; *Baltimore American*, June 13, 1904.

137 For a history of the conflict between the Fire Department and the Water Board,

see Fire Department, "Annual Report," *BRCOD*, 1872, 1875, 1880–1902, and Water Board, "Annual Report," *BRCOD*, 1872, 1876, 1882, 1896, 1897, 1902, 1903.

138   Fire Department, "Annual Report," *BRCOD*, 1872, p. 578; 1902, p. 22; *Manufacturers' Record*, April 21, 1904, p. 300; *Chicago Tribune*, July 18–August 27, 1874.

139   Fire Department, "Annual Report," *BRCOD*, 1904, pp. 27–28.

140   Ibid., p. 15; *Manufacturers' Record*, April 21, 1904, p. 300; June 16, 1904, p. 505; *Baltimore American*, June 13, 1904.

141   Fire Department, "Annual Report," *BRCOD*, 1905, p. 20; Water Board, "Annual Report," *BRCOD*, 1904, p. 18; 1905, p. 16.

142   *Baltimore Sun*, August 10, 1904; November 9, 1904; *Baltimore American*, March 23, 1904; May 13, 1904.

143   *Baltimore American*, February 19, 1904; February 22, 1904; February 24, 1904; February 26, 1904; *Baltimore Sun*, March 3, 1904.

144   *Baltimore American*, May 31–June 3, 1904; *Baltimore Sun*, May 31–June 3, 1904.

145   *Baltimore Sun*, November 24–25, 1904; November 27–29, 1904; December 6, 1904; January 13, 1904; February 16, 1904; *Baltimore American*, November 30–December 1, 1904; December 6–7, 1904; January 29, 1904.

146   *Baltimore Sun*, November 24–25, 1904; November 27–29, 1904; December 4, 1904; December 6, 1904; January 13, 1904; February 16, 1904; *Baltimore American*, November 28, 1904; November 30–December 1, 1904; December 6–7, 1904; January 29, 1904.

147   *Baltimore Sun*, November 25, 1904.

148   Clayton Colman Hall (ed.), *Baltimore: Its History and Its People* (New York, 1912), pp. 286–87. Notice that this analysis of the infrastructural improvement process in Baltimore in this period is completely different from that provided by Alan Anderson, *The Origin and Resolution of an Urban Crisis* (Baltimore, 1977). See *Baltimore Sun*, February 7, 1905; February 16, 1905.

149   For a vivid depiction of the conditions, see Sanborn Map Company, *Insurance Maps of Baltimore, Maryland* (New York, circa 1902) in Maryland Room of Enoch Pratt Library, Baltimore. See also *Baltimore Sun*, February 10, 1904; February 17, 1904; February 23, 1904; *Baltimore American*, February 28, 1904; *Baltimore City Directory* (Baltimore, 1904), p. 18.

150   *Baltimore Sun*, March 1, 1904; March 10, 1904; *Baltimore American*, March 8, 1904; March 11, 1904; March 19, 1904.

151   *Baltimore Sun*, March 1, 1904.

152   *Baltimore Sun*, May 19, 1904; *Baltimore American*, February 14, 1904; March 7, 1904; November 28, 1904; "Report on the Conflagration in Baltimore," *American Architect and Building News*, 84 (June 4, 1904), pp. 87–90; "Lessons of the Baltimore Fire," *American Architect and Building News*, 85 (July 9, 1904), pp. 11–13.

153   *Baltimore Sun*, May 10, 1904; May 17, 1904; May 27, 1904; *Baltimore American*, May 17–18, 1904; May 20, 1904; June 18, 1904.

154   *Baltimore American*, June 18, 1904.

155   *Baltimore Sun*, March 4, 1904; July 14, 1904; July 29, 1904.

156 The newspapers frequently reported on real estate market transactions. The market was extremely tight in the first four months after the fire. It loosened in June and thereafter, however, facilitating land assembly.

157 The papers discussed at length the B&O's plans and subterfuges and the rumors that they generated. See *Baltimore Sun*, April 9–10, 1904; September 9–29, 1904; *Baltimore American*, March 16, 1904; November 21, 1904.

158 Sanborn Map Company, *Insurance Maps of Baltimore* (New York, circa 1914). Compare with Sanborn Map Company, *Insurance Maps of Baltimore* (circa 1902), both in Maryland Room, Pratt Library, Baltimore.

159 Ibid. See also *Baltimore American*, February 7, 1905; BDC, "Report... September 11, 1906," *BRCOD*, 1906, p. 28.

160 *Baltimore City Directory*, 1905, p. 18.

161 BDC, "Report... September 11, 1906," *BRCOD*, 1906, p. 28; Sanborn Map Company, *Insurance Maps of Baltimore* (circa 1914).

162 BDC, "Report... September 11, 1906," *BRCOD*, 1906, pp. 28–29.

163 The maps are based on location data derived from the business sections of the *Baltimore City Directories* for 1903 and 1907 under the classifications "Jewelers – Retail"; "Drygoods Commission"; "Drygoods – Importers, Jobbers and Wholesale Dealers"; and "Banks" (which is in a separate appendix). Note that the 1903 classification of "Jewelers – Retail" excluded a hundred or so "fancy goods" dealers that were included in the 1907 classification. To make the listings comparable, only the jewelers that could be found in both years were included on the maps.

164 This description is based on an examination of material in the *Baltimore City Directories* for 1903 and 1907, the real estate and business news carried in the newspapers for 1904, 1905, and 1906, and Sanborn Map Company, *Insurance Maps of Baltimore*, for circa 1902 and circa 1914. The evidence as well as the description have been treated in an impressionistic rather than a quantitative manner for several reasons, including the large number of categories (and the recombinations of some) under which firms could list themselves in the *directory*; the fact that most categories showed firms located all over the city, with relatively few in the area of the burnt district; the high death rates of firms in small categories, which made tracing meaningless; the large number of firms (particularly in 1907) whose addresses were not street addresses but the names of buildings, the locations of which could not be determined; and the large number of firms in what appeared to be wholesale manufacturing or transportation companies whose addresses were large office buildings, a situation which implied (but did not prove) that the firms were better categorized (for purposes of this study) as office trades than as wholesale, manufacturing, or other nonoffice trades in the traditional sense of business land use. These problems seem to reflect the high degree of business specialization in this period, as well as the transition of Baltimore's central business district from a heterogeneous nineteenth century central business area into an increasingly homogeneous modern office–retail central business area.

165 Sanborn Map Company, *Insurance Maps of Baltimore*, circa 1902 and circa 1914.

166 *Baltimore American*, February 18, 1904.

167   Ibid; *Baltimore Sun*, February 27, 1904.

168   *Baltimore American*, February 18, 1904; *Baltimore Sun*, February 27, 1904.

169   *Baltimore American*, February 18, 1904; *Baltimore Sun*, February 27, 1904.

170   *Baltimore American*, February 18, 1904; *Baltimore Sun*, February 27, 1904. See also *Baltimore City Directory*, 1907.

171   *Baltimore American*, February 18, 1904; *Baltimore Sun*, February 26–27, 1904.

172   *Baltimore Sun*, February 26–27, 1904.

173   *Baltimore American*, February 21, 1904.

174   BDC, "Report...June 28, 1905," BRCOD, 1905, p. 30; *Baltimore Sun*, March 27, 1904; June 15, 1904; *Baltimore American*, March 27, 1904.

175   *Baltimore American*, November 21, 1904.

176   Comments on the benefits of structural and infrastructural redevelopment in the burnt district are scattered through the newspapers. See especially *Baltimore Sun*, October 28, 1904; February 7, 1905. See also *Merchants' and Manufacturers' Journal*, February 1906, p. 24; *Baltimore City Directory*, 1905, p. 18.

177   *Baltimore Sun*, February 7, 1905; City of Baltimore, *The Baltimore Book: A Resume of Commerce, Industrial and Financial Resources* (Baltimore, 1912), p. 7. See also *Baltimore American*, February 14, 1904; November 28, 1904.

178   Martin J. Schiesl, *The Politics of Efficiency: Municipal Administration and Reform in America, 1880–1920* (Berkeley, 1977), pp. 134–36, 174–76.

179   For an in-depth analysis of the many dimensions of administrative reform see Schiesl, *The Politics of Efficiency*. The critique of the administrative side of progressive reform was launched by Samuel P. Hays, "The Politics of Reform in Municipal Government in the Progressive Era," *Pacific Northwest Quarterly*, 55 (October 1964), pp. 157–69, and James Weinstein, "Organized Business and the City Commissioner and Management Movements," *Journal of Southern History*, 28 (May 1962), pp. 166–82 (basically the same as Chapter 4 of his *Corporate Ideal in the Liberal State* [Boston, 1968]).

180   For the most influential and well-known statements of the negative argument see sources cited in note 179. See also Melvin G. Holli, *Reform in Detroit: Hazen S. Pingree and Urban Politics* (New York, 1969), pp. 161–81. A critique of this interpretation of administrative (or "structural") reform is beginning to develop. See Schiesl, *The Politics of Efficiency*; Bradley Robert Rice, *Progressive Cities: The Commission Government Movement in America, 1901–1920* (Austin, 1977); Michael H. Frisch, "Urban Theorists, Urban Reform, and American Political Culture in the Progressive Period," *Political Science Quarterly*, 97 (Summer 1982), pp. 295–315. See also Kenneth Fox, *Better City Government: Innovation in American Urban Politics 1850–1937* (Philadelphia, 1977), which focuses heavily on the U.S. Census Bureau but is still relevant.

181   Baltimore Harbor Board, "Plan of Harbor Development" (typescript in Enoch Pratt Library, Baltimore, 1921); Maryland State Planning Commission, *Report on Wholesale Market Facilities for Greater Baltimore* (Annapolis, Md., 1948), pp. 6, 11, 25, 32, 35, 38; Robert G. Deupree, *The Wholesale Marketing of Fruits and Vegetables in Baltimore* (Baltimore, 1939), p. 39.

182   Alliance of Charitable and Social Agencies, *Poverty in Baltimore and Its Causes: Study of Social Statistics...* (Baltimore, 1918), pp. 29–30; James Ford, *Slums*

and Housing (Cambridge, Mass., 1936), p. 272; *Report of the Urban Renewal Study Board to Mayor Thomas D'Alesandro, Jr.* (Baltimore, 1956), pp. 19–21; *Appendices to the Report of the Urban Renewal Study Board to Mayor Thomas D'Alesandro, Jr.* (Baltimore, 1956), pp. 6–10.

Chapter 9. Power in the city

1 For reviews of the literature on this debate see, for example, David C. Hammack, "Problems in the Historical Study of Power in the Cities and Towns of the United States, 1800–1960," *American Historical Review*, 83 (April 1978), pp. 323–49; Nelson W. Polsby, *Community Power and Political Theory: A Further Look at Problems of Evidence and Inference* (New Haven, Conn., 1980); and Peter Bachrach, *The Theory of Democratic Elitism* (Boston, 1967).

2 See, for example, David C. Hammack, *Power and Society: Greater New York at the Turn of the Century* (New York, 1982), pp. 22–23 and passim; Peter Bachrach and Morton S. Baratz, *Power and Poverty: Theory and Practice* (New York, 1970), pp. 3–66; Carl J. Friedrich, *Man and His Government* (New York, 1963), pp. 499–515. See also Edward Pessen, "Social Structure and Politics in American History" and "Comments" by Robert H. Wiebe and Michael B. Katz, both in *American Historical Review*, 87 (December 1982), pp. 1290–1335, especially the comments by Katz. See also Michel Foucault, *The History of Sexuality, Volume I: An Introduction* (New York, 1980), especially pp. 81–114.

3 See, for example, Eugene Genovese, *Roll, Jordan, Roll: The World the Slaves Made* (New York, 1974); John W. Blassingame, *The Slave Community: Plantation Life in the Antebellum South* (New York, 1972).

4 See Hammack, *Power and Society*, for a more elaborate discussion of this subject. I believe I push the pluralist argument farther than he does, but his study is the best discussion of the distribution of power in a big city recently published by a historian.

5 For example, this seems to have been the case in Chicago after the great fire. As noted in Chapter 6, the Chicago Board of Public Works was very slow to extend water service to outlying working class areas, preferring to satisfy the demands of suburban real estate developers and middle and upper class homeowners first. Aldermen were soon hearing from their angry working class constituents, however. There was no organized working class protest movement, but the complaints were insistent enough to force the Aldermen to pressure the BPW into making amends. See *Chicago Tribune*, May 25, 1872; June 30, 1872; *Chicago Evening Post*, May 25, 1872. The BPW doubled the miles of water pipes it laid in fiscal 1873, then returned to its old habits in 1874. See BPW, *Annual Report* (years ending March 31, 1873; March 31, 1874; March 31, 1875).

6 This is not to say that in a general sense the poor residents of nineteenth and early twentieth century cities had as much power to obtain environmental improvement as the well-to-do. As noted earlier, the balance of power was skewed in favor of the middle and upper classes. The point is that it was hardly monopolized by elite groups. What is interesting is that the imbalance appears

to have been as much a *spatial* phenomenon as a matter of class difference. For a variety of reasons, suburban real estate developers and middle and upper class suburban homeowners were both more likely and better able to exert power to improve the built environment than either the inner city poor or inner city businessmen. Not that middle and upper class suburbanites were all-powerful either, however. Urban newspapers and city documents were full of the complaints of suburban homeowners who had not been able to obtain many kinds of environmental improvements in their neighborhoods. The point is that the balance of power was tipped in a way that favored certain groups at the expense of others, not only in a social sense, but also in a spatial sense that cut across class lines.

7   Bachrach and Baratz discuss power in similar terms in *Power and Poverty*, pp. 19–46.

8   Robert C. Ellickson and A. Dan Tarlock, *Land-Use Controls: Cases and Materials* (Boston, 1981), pp. 281–359; Chester Hartman, *Yerba Buena: Land Grab and Community Resistance in San Francisco* (San Francisco, 1974).

Sources of illustrations

Figure 6.3: Sanborn Insurance Company, *Map of Chicago: 1868-69* (map corrected to 1871, Chicago Historical Society).

Figure 6.4: [*Chicago Times*]. *New Chicago* (Chicago, 1872).

Figure 6.12: *Report of the Chicago Relief and Aid Society of the City of Chicago of Disbursement of Contributions for the Sufferers of the Chicago Fire*, p. 4.

Figure 6.13: Fales and Moses, "Thunen, Weber, and the Spatial Structure of the 19th Century City," p. 149.

Figure 6.14: Philpott, *The Slum and the Ghetto*, p. 19.

Figure 6.15: Sewers, Paved Streets, and Bridges, 1873. Hoyt, *One Hundred Years of Land Values*, p. 94.

Figure 7.2: *Boston Daily Advertiser*, January 29, 1873.

Figure 7.3: *Boston Daily Advertiser*, November 27, 1872.

Figure 7.4: Thomas Wood Davis, *Map of the Burnt District Showing Proposed Improvements in Streets.* November 12, 1872.

Figure 7.5: Boston Safe Deposit and Trust Company, *Plan of the Burnt District*, 1873.

Index

Abbott, Edith, 15
Accessibility needs (*see also* Transportation infrastructures), 16, 42–3, 73–6, 164, 166–7, 170
Administrative reforms in city government (*see also* Progressive reformers), 66–7, 308–19, 349n63
Agent-operated properties, 19–20
Agglomeration economies and spatial change, 69, 70, 71, 73, 79
  in Baltimore, 310–11
  in Boston, 73, 227, 234, 236, 239, 240
  in Chicago, 146, 153–6
Alexander Brown and Sons Building, Baltimore, 282–3
Allen, Frederick D., 224, 225
Allen, Freeman, 221
Apathy, 58, 200, 288, 330
Architectural plans, standard, 33
Architecture, 13–15, 26–33, 61, 82, 317
  in Baltimore, 303–6
  in Boston, 214–15, 225, 246, 247, 369n105
  in Chicago, 28, 119–20, 175
Arch Street, Boston, 184, 197, 217, 246
Atherton, Samuel, 219, 222
Atherton, William, 222
Atlantic Avenue, Boston, 192

Back Bay, Boston, 183, 185, 191, 344n14
Bacon, Jerome A., 223
Baltimore, 4–11 passim, 249–321, 331, 377n120, 379n163, n164
  infrastructures in, 4, 42, 43, 48, 53, 83, 253–302, 331, 345n28; *see also* Drainage systems; Electric utilities, Harbor, Baltimore; Parks; Sewerage systems; Streets; Water systems
  and spatial changes, 83, 84, 307–15
  structures in, 4, 17, 20, 25, 249, 251, 283, 287, 302–7, 314, 317, 379n156
Baltimore American, 43, 283–6, 293, 310, 313, 314

Baltimore & Ohio Railroad, 305
Baltimore City Directories, 379n163, n164
Baltimore Evening News, 376n93
Baltimore Morning Herald, 278, 281, 286–7
Baltimore Street, Baltimore, 253, 257, 280–7, 376n93
  City Council votes on, 277, 279–82, 286–7
  opposition to widening, 271, 275, 277, 279, 282–7, 332, 376n98
  retailers on, 308, 310–12
Baltimore Sun, 252, 254, 264, 272, 283, 301, 311, 316–17
Baltimore Water Company, 48
Baltimore World, 275, 281, 284, 286
Banks
  in Baltimore, 307–9, 312–13
  in Chicago, 141, 143–4, 148–51
Bates, Samuel W., 52
Beacon Hill, Boston, 76–7
Beacon Street, Boston, 200
Beebe Building, Boston, 369n105
Betterment assessments, 56–7
  in Baltimore, 259, 262
  in Boston, 184–5, 194, 195, 244
  in Chicago, 124, 125
Board of Aldermen
  Boston, 179, 196, 200, 201, 205, 207, 210
  Chicago, 3, 96–107 passim, 121–38 passim, 156, 165–6, 381n5
Board of Estimate, Baltimore, 263–8, 270, 279
Board of Health
  Baltimore, 255
  Chicago, 156
Board of Police, Chicago, 123
Board of Public Improvements, Baltimore, 263–8, 270, 279
Board of Public Works (BPW), Chicago, 95, 97, 121–7 passim, 171, 174, 357n78, 381n5

385

Slums (*cont.*)
 in Chicago, 112–14, 165
Smith, Arthur A., 222, 223
South Boston, 183, 185, 187, 191, 192, 351n14
South Division (South Side), Chicago
 infrastructures in, 133, 135, 136, 140
 and spatial changes, 141, 143, 145, 153, 162, 163, 168–71, 174, 363n187
 structures in, 107, 108, 113
South End, Boston, 181, 185, 227, 239, 240
South Side, Chicago, *see* South Division (South Side), Chicago
South Street, Baltimore, 309, 313
South Street, Boston, 228, 241
Spaciousness of buildings, 12–13, 26–7, 30, 118
Spatial change, 12, 68–85
 in Baltimore, 83, 84, 307–15
 Boston and, 73, 76–7, 81, 83, 216–18, 226–45, 334
 in Chicago, 78, 81–2, 109–13, 117, 140–74, 176, 243, 334, 360n126, 361n155, 363n187
Spatial phenomena (*see also* Displacement for infrastructures; Land use patterns), 382n6
Speculation, real estate, 31, 35, 99, 108, 114
Spillover effects (*see also* Externalities), 22–3
Sproesser, Albert M., 275
Staats Zeitung, Chicago, 101, 354n31
State-city interactions, 46
 Baltimore-Maryland, 46, 261–2, 268-9, 293, 294, 300
 Boston-Massachusetts, 207, 213–14
 Chicago-Illinois, 53–4, 124, 175
State Street, Boston, 182, 226, 236–7
State Street, Chicago, 112, 144, 152, 355n56
Steam utilities, 37
Steel frame structures, 14, 27–9, 82, 303, 304, 306, 317
Stetson, Caleb, 219, 222
Stocks for infrastructure improvements, 45
Stone and brick buildings, *see* Brick and stone buildings
Streetcars, 38, 53–4, 74, 76
Streets, 38, 41, 58, 83
 in Baltimore, 25, 45, 249–64 passim, 272–88, 291, 295, 307, 316, 319–20, 373n26; *see also* Baltimore Street, Baltimore
 in Boston, 4, 51, 53, 179, 182, 184–207, 218–22, 236–9, 244–8 passim, 316,

371n152; *see also* Congress Street, Boston; Devonshire Street, Boston
 in Chicago, 124–6, 128; *see also* Sidewalks in Chicago
 in New York City, 347n49
Strikes, 167
Strip problem in site assembly, 293, 294
Structures, 12–35, 80–85 passim, 89, 315, 333, 335
 in Baltimore, 4, 17, 20, 25, 249, 251, 283, 287, 302–7, 314, 317, 379n156
 in Boston, 4, 34, 179–84, 186, 212–26, 241–8 passim, 369n105
 in Chicago, 15, 28, 94–120, 145–7, 159–60, 175, 176, 216, 331, 353n24, 355n56; *see also* Fire limits ordinance, Chicago
Sub-Committee on Streets, Baltimore, 255–61, 263–5, 272, 273
Suburbs, 59, 60, 65, 71–2, 382n6
 of Boston, 209, 211
 of Chicago, 125, 127, 141, 163, 169–71, 174
Subways, 76
Summer Street, Boston, 181, 182, 185, 187, 197, 227, 237–40
Supply problems (*see also* Monopoly power)
 and infrastructure, 46–60, 200, 267
 spatial, 79–84, 148, 151, 158–9, 314; *see also* Leapfrogging; Neighborhood effects
 with structural redevelopment, 119
Supreme Court
 Illinois, 53–4, 124
 U.S., 133
Surrender clause for site assembly, 294–5
Swann, Sherlock, 269, 273, 278–9, 281
Synchronic analysis, *see* Theoretical (conceptual) approach

Taxes, 317
 and infrastructure redevelopment, 45–53 passim, 83, 124, 194, 244, 288, 295, 296, 301; *see also* Betterment assessments
 and spatial redevelopment, 83
 and structural improvements, 17
Technology
 infrastructural, 36, 41–2, 60–4, 67
 spatial adaptations affected by, 74
 structural, 13, 15, 26–32, 34, 35, 119–20, 214–17, 242, 303–4, 314, 315, 317; *see also* Architecture
Telephone networks, 76, 351n11
Tenements, 15, 17, 21–2, 31, 34, 35, 342n37